Mrs Alice M. Hart

Report on Agricultural Marketing Schemes

Mrs Alice M. Hart

Report on Agricultural Marketing Schemes

ISBN/EAN: 9783742802446

Manufactured in Europe, USA, Canada, Australia, Japa

Cover: Foto ©knipser5 / pixelio.de

Manufactured and distributed by brebook publishing software (www.brebook.com)

Mrs Alice M. Hart

Report on Agricultural Marketing Schemes

Ministry of Agriculture and Fisheries

Scottish Office

Report on Agricultural Marketing Schemes

Presented to Parliament by the Minister of Agriculture and Fisheries and the Secretary of State for Scotland by Command of His Majesty

May, 1935

LONDON

PRINTED AND PUBLISHED BY HIS MAJESTY'S STATIONERY OFFICE

To be purchased directly from H.M. STATIONERY OFFICE at the following addresses:
Adastral House, Kingsway, London, W.C.2; 120 George Street, Edinburgh 2;
York Street, Manchester 1; 1 St. Andrew's Crescent, Cardiff;
80 Chichester Street, Belfast;
or through any Bookseller

1935

Price 1*s.* 6*d.* Net

Cmd. 4913

AGRICULTURAL MARKETING ACTS, 1931 TO 1933

Report on Agricultural Marketing Schemes

The following report upon the operation of Agricultural Marketing Schemes in force in 1934 and upon schemes that have been submitted since the date of our last report but which are not yet in force, has been prepared in accordance with the requirements of Section 10 of the Agricultural Marketing Act, 1931.

WALTER E. ELLIOT,
Minister of Agriculture and Fisheries.

GODFREY P. COLLINS,
Secretary of State for Scotland.

CHARLES J. H. THOMAS,
Permanent Secretary, Ministry of Agriculture and Fisheries.

JOHN JEFFREY,
Permanent Under-Secretary of State for Scotland.

TABLE OF CONTENTS.

PART I.

PART II.

APPENDICES.

PART I.

SCHEMES IN OPERATION.

The following Agricultural Marketing Schemes were in operation in 1934:—

—	*Date of Approval Order.*	*Area of Scheme.*
Hops Marketing Scheme, 1932.	7th July, 1932.	England.*
Scottish Milk Marketing Scheme, 1933.	25th May, 1933.	Scotland, south of the Grampians.
Pigs Marketing Scheme, 1933.	5th July, 1933.	Great Britain.
Bacon Marketing Scheme, 1933.	5th July, 1933.	Great Britain.
Milk Marketing Scheme, 1933.	28th July, 1933.	England.*
Potato Marketing Scheme, 1933.	20th Dec., 1933.	Great Britain.
Aberdeen and District Milk Marketing Scheme. 1933.	28th March, 1934.	Counties of Aberdeen and Kincardine.
North of Scotland Milk Marketing Scheme, 1934.	6th July, 1934.	Counties of Inverness, Nairn, Ross and Cromarty, Sutherland and Caithness.

* "England" includes Wales.

THE HOPS MARKETING SCHEME, 1932.

The Hops Marketing Scheme, which applies to England, came into force on 7th July, 1932. Following an affirmative vote of registered producers, the provisions of the scheme came fully into operation on 6th September, 1932. A brief explanation of the scheme was given in the last report.

The Board consists of 14 members elected for local districts and four special members elected at the annual general meeting of registered producers. There was no change in the personnel of the Board during 1934. A contest was necessary in one district election only, when the sitting member was returned, and the four special members were re-elected at the annual general meeting.

The remuneration of the Board, voted by the registered producers at the annual general meeting in 1934, for the two years 1933-34 and 1934-35 was as follows:—

	Per annum.
	£
Chairman	800
Special Members	400 each.
District Members	200 each.

The number of producers registered with the Board on 1st September, 1934, was 1,043.

Amendment of the Scheme.

In June, 1933, the Board submitted draft amendments of the scheme, the principal feature of which was the provision of producers' selling quotas. After consideration of the objections made to the amendments and of the report of Mr. F. M. Russell Davies, K.C., who held the Public Inquiry, and after consultation with the Board of Trade, the Minister modified the draft amendments in certain particulars and laid them before Parliament in December, 1933. It was not found possible to take affirmative resolutions before the Christmas recess, and the draft was withdrawn and relaid in February, 1934. Developments which are referred to later resulted in further postponement, and affirmative resolutions were not passed until July. The amendments were brought into force on 14th July, 1934, by the Hops Marketing Scheme (Amendment) Order, 1934.*

Under the scheme, as amended, basic quotas have been allotted to all producers who were registered on 1st September, 1933, or who, in the opinion of the Board, were entitled to be registered at that date and were then occupying farms which were wholly or partly under hops in 1932. In general, the basic quota is the average annual quantity of hops picked on the farm of the registered producer during the five seasons 1928 to 1932, adjustments being made to ensure that an owner-occupier who centralized his production on one farm during the five-year period should not be penalized thereby, and also that in no case should the quota represent more than 20 cwt. nor less than 6 cwt. per acre on the 1932 acreage, nor less than 40 cwt. in all.

The Board are required by the scheme to estimate the total market demand for English hops of each season, except in the event of the quantity of English hops which the Board, or producers, may sell in that season being determined by or under any Act of Parliament. In the latter case, the quantity so determined shall be taken to be the total market demand.

A registered producer's selling quota for any season is the same fraction of the total market demand for English hops of that season as his basic quota is of the total of all basic quotas, e.g., if the total of the basic quotas is 100 and the market demand 90, a producer's seasonal quota will be nine-tenths of his basic quota. If a registered producer tenders to the Board hops in excess of his selling quota, the hops of highest value are to be selected for treatment as quota hops.

The Board's net receipts from the sale of all hops must be applied first to the payment of registered producers in proportion to the values of the quota hops of that season supplied by each producer, and then, if there is any balance, to payment in proportion to the values of non-quota hops.

---

* S.R. & O. 1934, No. 841.

When the estimated total market demand in any season exceeds 110 per cent. of the total of the basic quotas, the Board must allot further basic quotas.

If, in any season, the Board so determine, transfers of seasonal selling quotas between registered producers may be made. This arrangement is designed to give the scheme reasonable flexibility where, owing to climatic conditions, disease or other causes, the crops of some growers are heavy while other growers have short crops. Advantage was taken of this provision to transfer seasonal quotas for the 1934 season (the first to be dealt with under the amended scheme) to the extent of slightly less than five per cent. of the crop.

The quota provisions of the scheme are operative for a five-year period ending on 31st July, 1939.

The Joint Committee.

While the draft amendments were before Parliament, conversations were proceeding between the Hops Marketing Board and the Brewers' Society regarding the arrangements to be made, under the amended scheme, for the supply of hops to meet brewers' requirements. On 9th April, 1934, the Minister, after consultation with the Hops Marketing Board and the Brewers' Society, appointed a Provisional Committee consisting of four representatives each of the Board and of the Society, together with three impartial members, to consider, in principle, the following matters:—

(*a*) long-term planning in the production of hops;

(*b*) the fixation of the estimated total market demand for hops of each season;

(*c*) the determination of prices, with reference to (i) costs of production; (ii) the rate of profit to be fixed, having regard to the growers' willingness to accept a fixed rate provided the brewers agree to purchase not less than the quantity put forward as their firm requirements for the purpose of estimating the total market demand; (iii) the nature of the undertaking the Brewers' Society are able to give in this respect; and (iv) the marketability of the crop;

(*d*) the administration of any fund that might be established to purchase any unsold balance of the estimated total market demand; and

(*e*) any other relevant question which the Brewers' Society and the Hops Marketing Board may agree to refer to the Committee;

and, having done so, to make recommendations regarding the composition, functions and machinery of a Permanent Committee to deal with these questions.

The impartial members of the Committee were Lt.-Colonel Sir John R. Chancellor, G.C.M.G., G.C.V.O., D.S.O., who acted as Chairman, Mr. F. D'Arcy Cooper, and Capt. Oliver Lyttelton, D.S.O., M.C.

The report of the Committee,* which was presented on 21st June, 1934, was laid before Parliament together with a copy of an agreement between the Hops Marketing Board and the Brewers' Society, which the Committee were successful in negotiating.

The Committee recommended that there should be set up a Permanent Joint Committee, constituted in the same proportions as the Provisional Committee, whose main duties would be to estimate the total market demand for English hops; to advise as to the methods of determining costs of production; to adjust, should occasion arise, the agreed average price for hops; to administer the fund to be established under the agreement; to appoint arbitrators to settle any disputes which might arise as to the quality and marketability of hops offered for sale by the Board; to make recommendations in respect of the importation of hops and, generally, to supervise the administration of the agreement.

The main heads of the agreement, which will operate during the five-year period in which the quota provisions are in force, are :—

(i) the average price of English hops for each of the five crops commencing with the 1934 crop to be £9 per cwt., including factors' commission and the expenses of the Board;

(ii) brewers agree to make firm contracts in advance for at least two-thirds of the total market demand;

(iii) any unsold balance of the total market demand to be purchased out of a levy fund, the property in the hops so purchased to be vested in the Permanent Joint Committee;

(iv) in order to provide this fund, a levy of 10s. per cwt. to be added to the price of all hops sold by the Board; the fund to be controlled by the Permanent Joint Committee;

(v) the maximum liability of the levy fund to equal the actual value of one-third of the total market demand: when the fund reaches its maximum liability, the levy to be reduced or discontinued;

(vi) parties agree that the maximum level of importations of hops should be 15 per cent. of the total market demand, with safeguards for brewers who require special foreign hops, and that any application or representations to the Government to regulate imports should be made only through the Permanent Joint Committee.

Following publication of the report of the Provisional Committee, the Hops Marketing Board and the Brewers' Society set up a Permanent Joint Committee. The Minister nominated Sir John Chancellor, Mr. D'Arcy Cooper, and Capt. Lyttelton to be the impartial members, Sir John Chancellor to be the Chairman, and Mr. D'Arcy Cooper the Vice-Chairman, of the Committee.

---

* Cmd. 4623.

Trading Operations of the Board.

The acreage planted with hops in 1932, when the Board took office was 16,500. In 1933 it rose to 16,900, and in 1934 to 18,000. The quantity of hops tendered to the Board by the registered producers was 166,000 cwt. in 1932, 194,000 cwt. in 1933, and approximately 240,000 cwt. in 1934.

The aggregate sums received by the Board for the sale of hops in 1932 and 1933 were £1,471,700 and £2,928,000 respectively, the average prices realised per cwt. being £8 17s. 2d. and £15 1s. 8d. The total sums distributed to registered producers, after deducting selling commission, expenses of the Board and contributions to meet general expenses and reserves, amounted to £1,370,000 in 1932 and £2,785,000 in 1933, giving the growers net average prices of £8 5s. and £14 6s. 11d. per cwt. respectively.

As explained in the last report, the Board were able to sell the whole of the 1932 crop. The 1933 crop, which was of high quality, came on the market in very favourable circumstances. America had " gone wet "; at home, a penny had been taken off the beer duty; continental hops were selling at much more than the average of £15 per cwt. fixed by the Board for English hops. The whole of the crop was sold in a few days' trading.

In 1934, the Board had to deal with a crop larger in quantity and more varied in quality than the 1933 crop. On this account, the valuation of the hops tendered by individual producers proceeded more slowly, and trading in satisfaction of the contracts entered into by brewers did not commence until 17th December, 1934. Heavy buying was immediately experienced.

The Permanent Joint Committee notified the Hops Marketing Board that, for the purpose of the agreement, the estimated market demand for the 1934 crop should be 215,000 cwt. The Board, after taking this figure into account, prescribed the total market demand, including the demand for hops not under their jurisdiction, at 224,000 cwt., which allowed producers' selling quotas to be 97 per cent. of their basic quotas.

Firm contracts, entered into by or on behalf of brewers in respect of the 1934 crop, in accordance with the agreement, amounted to 90 per cent. of the market demand, as estimated by the Joint Committee, and to about 80 per cent. of the total quantity of hops tendered to the Board by registered producers.

A summary of the trading operations of the Board relating to the 1932 and 1933 crops and, as far as figures are available, to the 1934 crop, is given below.

Production and Marketing of Hops under the Hops Marketing Scheme.

—	1932.	1933.	1934.
Production.			
Acreage planted (including unpicked). ...	16,531 ac.	16,895 ac.	18,037 ac.
Average yield per acre ...	11·4 cwt.	12·8 cwt.	14·4 cwt.
Estimated total produce	188,000 cwt.	216,000 cwt.	259,000 cwt.
Marketing.			
Produce tendered to Board	165,908 cwt.	194,017 cwt.	245,496* cwt.
Aggregate price realised	£1,471,702	£2,927,610	£1,966,000*
Average price per cwt. (to merchants)	£8 17s. 2d.	£15 1s. 8d.	£8 1s. 6d.*†
Paid to registered producers	£1,370,417 (93·12%).	£2,785,068 (95·13%).	£1,822,480* (92·70%)
Average return per cwt.	£8 5s. 0d.	£14 6s. 11d.	£8 8s. 3d.*
Agents' commission per cwt.	7s. 2d. (4·06%).	9s. 9d. (3·24%).	7s. 3d. (3·99%)
Retained for Board's expenses, per cwt. ...	5s. 0d. (2·82%).	5s. 0d. (1·63%).	5s. 0d. (2·76%)

* Provisional † To which was added 10s. per cwt. for the Levy Fund.

Miscellaneous.

Accounts of the Board.—Copies of the Income and Expenditure Accounts and of the Board's Balance Sheets as at 31st March, 1932 and 1933 are printed in Appendix III.

Complaint regarding the Operation of the Scheme.—In December, 1933, the Minister directed the Committee of Investigation for England to consider and report upon a complaint made by the Brewers' Society as to the prices charged for 1933 English hops. After hearing evidence on behalf of the Society and the Hops Marketing Board, both of whom were represented by Counsel, the Committee reported to the Minister that the evidence and arguments placed before them disclosed no justification for the complaint.

SCOTTISH MILK MARKETING SCHEME, 1933.

This scheme for regulating the marketing of milk produced in the counties of Angus and Perth, the greater part of the county of Argyll and the whole of Scotland lying to the south of these counties came into full operation on 1st December, 1933. A brief outline of the provisions of the scheme was given in the report for 1933. These provisions are based on the principle of equalisation amongst the registered producers of the proceeds from the sales in the liquid milk and the manufacturing markets at prices and on terms regulated by the Board.

Producers who sell milk only in small quantities to their employees or to neighbours for their own consumption are exempt from registration under the scheme, the limits fixed by the Board as qualifying for this exemption being a maximum sale of three gallons daily and a maximum number of six customers. All other producers are required to register under the scheme and to sell their milk in accordance with its provisions. The milk must be sold only to or through the agency of the Board with the exception of direct sales made under prescribed conditions by producer-wholesalers, producer-retailers, and producers of Certified milk.

The total quantity of milk sold by the registered producers during the year ended 30th November, 1934, amounted to 106,379,073 gallons of which 87,694,544 gallons (82·43 per cent.) were sold to or through the agency of the Board and 18,684,529 gallons (17·57 per cent.) represented the total of the direct sales of the producers in the special categories. Of the total sales, 67,870,722 gallons (63·8 per cent.) were sold for liquid consumption and 38,508,351 gallons (36·2 per cent.) were sold or used for the manufacture of milk products. The statement on page 24 gives statistics of the gallonage of the sales in each month during the year.

The estimated total quantity of milk sold by the registered producers during December, 1934, was 7,370,000 gallons of which 76 per cent. was absorbed by the liquid market.

Election of the Board.

The first Board, consisting of the members named in the scheme and two members nominated by the Secretary of State for Scotland, remained in office until the first annual general meeting, which was held on 10th May, 1934, when they were replaced by a Board of eight members elected by the Selection Committee in accordance with the scheme.

In accordance with Section 14 of the Agricultural Marketing Act, 1933, the scheme was amended by the Scottish Milk Marketing Board (Co-opted Members) Order, 1934,* made by the Secretary of State on 15th June, and the Board, after consultation with the Market Supply Committee and with the approval of the Secretary of State, co-opted Mr. W. J. Harvey, 7, Cambridge Gardens, Leith, and Mr. John Dallas, Milton House, Cowcaddens, Glasgow, as members of the Board.

At the annual general meeting the retiring Board were voted a remuneration of £2,500 to be divided amongst the members of the Board as they might determine.

---

* S.R. & O. 1934, No. $\frac{645}{S. 37}$.

Different Types of Registered Producers.

The total number of producers registered as at 30th November, 1934, was 8,149. The producers who, during the month of November, sold milk as producer-wholesalers, producer-retailers and producers of Certified milk numbered 598, 2,849 and 89 respectively, many being included in more than one of the categories recognised under the scheme.

Producer-wholesalers, producer-retailers and producers of Certified milk are granted partial exemption from the provisions of the scheme. These producers make their own arrangements for the sale of their milk and for collecting payment of accounts, but they are required to observe the scale of prices fixed by the Board and to contribute to the cost of operating the scheme a sum per gallon equal in amount to nine-tenths of that payable by the other producers. They are entitled, however, to sell their surplus milk to or through the agency of the Board on the same terms and conditions as the ordinary producers.

A producer-wholesaler is a producer who is licensed by the Board to sell milk to a retail distributor who, because his daily purchases do not exceed a prescribed maximum gallonage,* is required to pay a wholesale price in excess of the Standard Price. A producer who is classed as a producer-wholesaler in respect of sales to certain distributors may be classed as an ordinary producer in respect of sales to other and larger distributors.

A producer-retailer is a producer who is licensed by the Board to sell milk of his own production to domestic consumers.

Owing to a disagreement as to the interpretation of the provisions of the scheme relating to the calculation of the amount of the contribution payable to the Board by producer-retailers, the Board agreed to bear the expense of a special case before the Court of Session. The decision was given on 20th July, 1934, in the Board's favour and the producers in the special categories were held liable for payment of monthly contributions on their sales representing nine-tenths of the full difference between the Standard Price (i.e., the price determined by the Board for untreated milk for liquid consumption delivered at the distributor's premises, railway station or pier) and the monthly average price payable to the ordinary producers.

The ordinary producer supplies milk either under contract to a distributor or, under the Board's directions, to one of the Board's depots or creameries. The Board receive payment from distributors according to returns rendered by producers and pay to the producer an average price per gallon determined monthly in the manner described below.

---

* December, 1933, 60 gallons; January-March, 1934, 50 gallons; April 1934, onwards, 20 gallons.

Payments to Producers.

The proceeds from the sale of milk to or through the agency of the Board, the contributions by producer-wholesalers, producer-retailers and producers of Certified milk and all other receipts of the Board, such as the profit in operating the Standard Haulage fund, are paid into the general " pool ". After allocation to producers of any sums realised on the sale of their milk in excess of the Standard Price and deduction of the amounts necessary to meet administrative expenses and to provide for reserves, the Board at the end of each month distribute the balance equally amongst the producers in proportion to the quantity of milk supplied by them during the month. A producer whose milk, by reason of its grade or quality or by reason of special services rendered by the producer to the buyer, realises a price higher than the Standard Price, is paid the excess in addition to the average price. The difference between the Standard Price and the average price represents the amount of the contribution per gallon by the producer towards the cost of operating the Scheme.

In the spring of 1934, the Board entered into agreements with 504 farm cheesemakers in terms of which each producer undertook for an agreed period to manufacture the whole of his production of milk into cheese on his farm. In respect that the prices realised by the producer on the sale of the cheese would be less than the return to him for the milk if sold through their agency, the Board agreed to pay to him an allowance representing the difference between the monthly average price (less the Standard Haulage Rate —see below) under the scheme and the value of the cheese calculated on the basis of the market prices for cheese in the month immediately preceding the month of manufacture. In addition, the Board paid to the producer, in respect of his services and the expenses of manufacture incurred by him, 1d. per lb. of cheese manufactured. For the purpose of the agreement, one lb. of cheese was regarded as being equivalent to one gallon of milk.

The undernoted quantities of milk were manufactured into cheese by farm cheesemakers under these agreements :—

1934.	*Gallons.*
February	16,204
March	581,007
April	1,164,104
May	1,981,987
June	1,461,626
July	1,863,367
August	1,495,799
September	1,145,270
October	549,631
November	68,508
	10,347,683

Haulage.

Producer-wholesalers and producer-retailers, selling milk as such, make their own arrangements for haulage and for payment of the cost.

The Board pay all charges for haulage of milk sold to them or through their agency. They are empowered by the scheme to fix the rates for haulage of milk by road, and producers who send milk by road transport must employ haulage contractors approved by the Board. These contractors include both distributors and producers.

The haulage rates fixed by the Board for the period 1st December, 1933, to 30th November, 1934, were as follows :—

	Per gallon.
	d.
Not exceeding 5 miles	½
Over 5 but not exceeding 10 miles	¾
Over 10 but not exceeding 20 miles	1
Over 20 but not exceeding 30 miles	1¼
Over 30 miles	1½

The rates for the period 1st December, 1934, to 30th November, 1935, are as follows :—

	Per gallon.
	d.
Not exceeding 5 miles	½
Over 5 but not exceeding 10 miles	¾
Over 10 but not exceeding 30 miles	1
Over 30 but not exceeding 40 miles	1¼
Over 40 miles	1½

The average price payable to the producers for milk sold to or through the agency of the Board was made subject to a deduction, termed " the Standard Haulage Rate ", representing the cost that would have been incurred in the haulage of the milk at the rates fixed by the Board from the producer's farm or premises to whichever of the following centres was nearest thereto, viz., Glasgow, Edinburgh or Dundee. The deduction calculated at that rate is made irrespective of the actual distance of the haulage of the producers' milk. As explained later, additional centres have been prescribed for the calculation of the Standard Haulage Rate payable by producers in the east of Scotland during the year 1935.

Contracts.

A Permanent Joint Committee has been set up consisting of representatives of the Board, the Scottish Milk Trade Federation, the Scottish Co-operative Milk Trade Association and various district associations of dairymen. The objects of the Committee are to negotiate (*a*) wholesale and retail prices of milk for liquid sale within the area of the scheme, (b) the price of milk for the various classes of manufacture, and (c) conditions of the sale of milk. The agreement constituting the Committee provides for calling a consultant into the negotiations in the event of failure to reach agreement. Contracts under the scheme were made for the following periods—(1) 1st December, 1933, to 31st March, 1934; (2) 1st April to 30th September, 1934; and (3) 1st October, 1934, to 30th September, 1935. The services of a consultant were utilised by the Committee when negotiations were proceeding in regard to the contracts for the first and third periods.

The parties to a contract are the seller (the producer), the buyer (the distributor) and the Board. One form of contract only is supplied by the Board; it prescribes the terms and conditions of sale and purchase of milk for liquid consumption and for manufacture. The ordinary basis of the contract is the sale of the whole of the producer's supply, the distributor accepting responsibility for any excess of supply over his requirements. The contract for the second period included provision for payment of a premium of 1d. per gallon by distributors who contracted to buy a level quantity of milk daily. In addition to that provision, the form of contract for the current period requires payment of a premium of 2d. per gallon in cases where the producer provides wholesale services.

The producers are required, in terms of the contract, to supply milk attaining a standard of butter fat content of not less than 3·4 per cent. during the months of February to July and 3·5 per cent. during the months of August to January.

Licences.

Licences in accordance with the provisions of the scheme were issued to producer-retailers at the beginning of November, 1933. These licences are granted subject to conditions prohibiting the sale of milk outwith the area of the scheme and stipulating a minimum standard of butter fat content as provided for in the contracts of ordinary producers.

Manufacturers' licences are issued by the Board subject to conditions providing for (1) proof of manufacture; (2) prohibition of the purchase of milk outwith the area of the scheme; (3) prohibition of the purchase of fresh cream outwith the area of the scheme without the consent of the Board; and (4) prohibition of the sale of fresh cream at a price less than that fixed by the Board.

Liquid Milk Prices.

During the first two contract periods the Standard Price, i.e., the price for the sale to distributors of untreated milk for liquid consumption, was determined by the Board at 1s. 2d. per gallon. In the current contract period, the Standard Price will average 1s. 2d. per gallon, the variations during different months of the year being as follows :—October, 1934—1s. 2d. per gallon; November, 1934, to February, 1935—1s. 3d. per gallon; March, 1935—1s. 2d. per gallon; April to July, 1935—1s. 1d. per gallon; August and September, 1935—1s. 2d. per gallon. The variation of the Standard Price in that manner is one of the adjustments made with a view to alleviating the effect of the scheme on level producers.

The prices for the sale of milk of the official grades are determined by the Board in relation to the Standard Price.

The prices per gallon payable by buyers such as hotels, restaurants, etc. (i.e., semi-retail prices) for the current contract period are as follows :—

	Bulk.	*Bottled.*
	s. d.	*s. d.*
Where the quantity delivered is :—		
(i) 2 gallons and under	2 0	2 0
(ii) Over 2 gallons and not exceeding 10 gallons	1 8	1 10
(iii) Over 10 gallons and not exceeding 50 gallons	1 6	1 8
(iv) Over 50 gallons	1 5	1 7

The price to institutions, whether rate-aided or charitable, during the current contract period has been fixed at not less than the Standard Price.

The Board have power to determine the retail price to be charged by producer-retailers, and distributors are under obligation in terms of their contract to charge the same retail price. The retail price as from 1st December, 1933, was fixed at 2s. per gallon, and this price was continued in the second and third contract periods. Broadly, the effect, in comparison with the retail prices charged before the scheme came into operation, was a decrease of 4d. per gallon in the winter months in certain parts of the east of Scotland, more particularly in Edinburgh, and an increase of 4d. per gallon in the summer months in western districts.

Manufacturing Milk Prices.

A Manufacturing Sub-Committee of the Permanent Joint Committee meets each month to determine the prices of milk for manufacture. These prices vary for the different milk products. The price of milk for the manufacture of cheese during the first contract period was a sum per gallon equal to the average price per lb. for the previous month of the finest New Zealand Cheese, less the sum of 1¾d. per gallon. For the second contract period the price was determined at a sum per gallon equal to the average price per lb. for the previous month of the finest New Zealand and Canadian Cheese, coloured and white, less the sum of 1¾d. per gallon, but in view of representations by manufacturers, the Board agreed to reduce the price in certain months. The determination of the price on the basis of that formula was continued by the Board during the current contract period pending a decision on a complaint by the manufacturers, which was referred to the Committee of Investigation for Scotland for consideration, and on the understanding that retrospective adjustments would be made, if necessary, in accordance with the decision.

During the period from 1st December, 1933, to 30th November, 1934, the price of milk for manufacture into fresh cream was fixed at 7½d. and the price of milk for the manufacture of margarine was 9d. per gallon. The average price obtained for milk for manufacture into butter was 5·30d. per gallon. Sales of milk for the manufacture of milk powder and condensed milk were made during the period as from 1st April at prices ranging respectively from 3¾d. to 4½d. and 4d. to 5d. per gallon; milk for manufacture into tinned cream was sold at 4½d. per gallon.

Manufacturing Operations of the Board.

The Board have purchased seventeen farmers' co-operative creameries at prices determined by arbitration, the total amounting to £180,055 18s. 3d. In consequence of an agreement entered into with the English Milk Marketing Board to reduce consignments of milk to England, these creameries were working during the summer of 1934 far beyond the capacity for which they were intended. With a view to making provision for all requirements next season, the Board have authorised expenditure amounting to £155,000 on additional buildings and equipment, including a new depot in Glasgow, a new condensery and two milk powder plants to make use of skim milk. They have also installed can-washing and sterilising machines at each creamery in order to eliminate risk of contamination from dirty containers.

The quantities of milk manufactured by the Board into various products at their creameries during the period 1st December, 1933, to 30th November, 1934, were as follows :—

Product.	*Gallons.*	*Percentage.*
Fresh Cream	6,350,632	40·99
Tinned Cream	1,255,362	8·09
Cheese	6,920,147	44·66
Butter	225,350	1·46
Condensed Milk	695,578	4·49
Other Products	48,278	0·31
Total ...	15,495,542	100·00

Monthly Average Prices paid to Producers.

The average price per gallon paid to the producers and the amount of the producers' contribution (i.e., the difference between the Standard Price and the average price per gallon) in respect of milk sold to or through the agency of the Board in each month from December, 1933, to December, 1934, were as follows :—

	Average Price.	*Producers' Contribution.*
	d.	*d.*
1933—December	12	2
1934—January ...	12	2
„ February ...	12	2
„ March ...	11	3
„ April ...	10	4
„ May ...	9	5
„ June ...	9	5
„ July ...	9¾	4¾
„ August ...	10½	3½
„ September	11	3
„ October ...	11½	2½
„ November	12¾	2¼
„ December ...	13	2

The Milk Act, 1934.

Repayable advances amounting to a total of £33,014 10s. 8d. were made to the Board under Section 1 of the Milk Act in respect of milk sold during the eight months April to November, 1934, for the manufacture of milk products. Particulars are given in the following statement :—

Product.	*Gallons.*	*Payments.*
		£
Butter	894,195	5,123
Cheese	4,157,676	25,475
Condensed Milk ...	225,314	858
Milk Powder	265,876	1,515
Tinned Cream ...	21,089	44
Total	5,563,650	£33,015

Advances amounting to £56,484 were also made to the Board under Section 3 of the Act in respect of 9,750,384 gallons of milk converted into cheese at farms during that period.

At the date of this report no advances had been made under Section 2 of the Act in respect of milk used by the Board for the manufacture of milk products.

Arrangements were made by the Board, with the approval of the Secretary of State under Section 11 of the Act, for the supply of milk at reduced prices in schools within the area of the scheme. All full-time schools or courses for children recognised for grant by the Scottish Education Department come within the scope of the arrangements, and also authorised courses of instruction for unemployed boys and girls established under the Unemployment Act, 1934, and recognised for grant by the Ministry of Labour. Teachers and local authorities are co-operating voluntarily in carrying out these arrangements, which came into force on 5th November, 1934. So far as possible, Grade A (T.T.) milk is being supplied and it is distributed in bottles containing one-third of a pint at a price of one halfpenny per bottle, i.e., at the rate of 1s. per gallon. Where Grade A (T.T.) milk is not available, the source and quality of the milk supplied are subject to the approval of the Medical Officer of Health.

There was a very satisfactory response to the offer of milk on these terms. The estimates supplied to the Board of the requirements of the schools showed that over 400,000 children will participate in the scheme during 1935.

Complaints regarding the Operation of the Scheme.

(1) *Consumers.*

The Consumers' Committee for Scotland reported on complaints received with respect to the following matters:—

(a) *Retail price of milk in the summer months.*—The Committee supported the complaints made regarding the Board's decision to continue during the summer months the retail price of 2s. per gallon. They stated that they saw no reason for the departure from the long established practice of discriminating between winter and summer prices and that they were not convinced that the Board's decision was justified.

The Committee's report was referred to the Committee of Investigation for Scotland who found that the Board's action was not unreasonable or against the public interest. They considered that the Board, in deciding to continue the retail price of 2s. during the summer months, had acted in a reasonable manner in a genuine endeavour to reconcile the conflicting interests of the producer, distributor and consumer.

Following upon suggestions in the reports of the two Committees on this subject, the Department of Agriculture for Scotland made arrangements for an enquiry into the cost of milk production to be carried out by the Advisory Officers in Agricultural Economics attached to the Agricultural Colleges, in collaboration with the Department's Advisory Officer in Farm Economics. The enquiry will extend over one year from 1st October, 1934, and the cost is being met by the undernoted contributions from the Milk Marketing Boards to the Colleges conducting the enquiry in their respective areas:—

£500 from the Scottish Milk Marketing Board to the Edinburgh and East of Scotland and the West of Scotland Colleges of Agriculture.

£150 and £100 from the Aberdeen and District and the North of Scotland Milk Marketing Boards respectively to the North of Scotland College of Agriculture.

(b) *Prices of milk to hotels and restaurants.*—The Consumers' Committee for Scotland did not consider that a case had been established for a reduction of these prices.

(c) *Price of bottled half-pints of milk.*—The Committee recommended that the price should be at the same rate per gallon as for pints and quarts. The Board agreed to reduce the price accordingly.

(d) *Prices of milk supplied to institutions administered by the Glasgow Corporation, to voluntary hospitals and under child welfare and maternity schemes.*—The Committee recommended that these prices should be reduced. Their report has been referred to the Committee of Investigation for Scotland for consideration.

The Board agreed, on representation by the Consumers' Committee, to reduce by 2d. per gallon the price of milk supplied under child welfare and maternity schemes.

(2) *Distributors.*

Complaints on the following subjects were referred to the Committee of Investigation for Scotland—

(a) *Price for milk supplied to small distributors.*—A complaint was made by the Dairymen's Association of Ayrshire and certain other associations of milk distributors regarding the price fixed by the Board during the first contract period for milk sold to distributors whose daily sales did not exceed 50 gallons. It emerged, on enquiry, that the Board were not enforcing payment by these distributors at the prescribed rate and proposed to amend the scale of prices for the next contract period in order to remove the grievance, and the Committee accordingly recommended that no action should be taken on the complaint. The adjustment in the scale of prices was duly made.

(b) *Supply of milk to retail co-operative societies.*—The Parliamentary Committee of the Co-operative Congress complained that the Scottish Co-operative Wholesale Society was being refused the right to supply milk to certain of its constituent retail societies. The Committee of Investigation, while finding that the Board's action regarding which particular complaint was made, was not unreasonable, recommended that the Board should permit the Wholesale Society to supply milk to retail societies where this could be economically done and suggested that, up to a limit of 25 miles, the cost of transport of the milk should be allowed to the Society by the Board so long as such cost was not appreciably greater than would be incurred by the Board in supplying the milk from one of the Board's creameries. This recommendation was made with respect to the supply of "accommodation" milk, i.e., milk required by the retail societies to meet special demands in supplement of their regular supplies from producers. The Board agreed to give effect to this recommendation.

(3) *Manufacturers.*

Price of milk for manufacture into cheese.—A complaint was received from the manufacturers on the Manufacturing Sub-Committee of the Permanent Joint Committee appointed under the scheme regarding the formula, contained in the Board's contracts, by which the price of milk for manufacture into cheese was determined. The complaint has been referred to the Committee of Investigation for Scotland.

(4) *Producers.*

(a) *Complaints by East of Scotland Milk Producers' Federation.*—Arising out of complaints made by the East of Scotland Milk Producers' Federation as to the effect of the operation of the scheme, the following questions were remitted to the Committee of Investigation for Scotland for consideration and report :—

(1) The position of level producers within the area of the scheme, and whether it is necessary or desirable to provide for payment to them of an additional price per gallon by way of level delivery premium, or otherwise.

(2) The necessity or advisability of amendment of the provisions of the scheme in regard to haulage charges.

(3) The desirability of the Board's contracting on the present basis of butter-fat content.

(4) Whether it is practicable, and, if so, whether it is advisable, that a system of regional prices should be instituted under the scheme.

(5) The extent and nature of the amendments which will be necessary to the scheme in order to give effect to the recommendations of the Committee in regard to the above matters.

The Committee issued an interim report on 23rd July. With regard to the first question they suggested that, for a specific limited period, some provision should be made by means of an additional payment per gallon or otherwise for alleviating the effects of the scheme on level producers generally, and accordingly proposed that the Board should discuss this suggestion with the producers affected with a view to agreement being reached as to the method to be adopted, the extent of the additional payment, and the time for which it should be made.

With regard to the third question, the Committee saw no objection in the public interest to a continuance of the system whereby the Board had contracted for a minimum butter-fat content in excess of the legal minimum of 3 per cent. ; while, as regards question (4), the Committee did not consider it practicable to institute a system of regional prices under the scheme.

The Committee deferred their conclusions on the remaining questions remitted to them pending further discussion between the Board and producers concerned.

Following on these discussions, certain proposals were formulated by the Board and submitted to the Committee, the principal proposals being as follows:—

(1) that a premium of 2d. a gallon should be given to level producers during the months of March to August, 1935, in respect of a certain basic quantity of milk or, alternatively, that the Standard Price should be varied so as to give higher returns for winter production;

(2) that six additional haulage centres should be provided in the eastern district;

(3) that powers should be given to the Board to enable them to discourage excessive production if necessary;

(4) that the contribution required from producer-retailers should be calculated on the basis of cow-stock instead of on that of milk sales.

The Committee made a final report in October after hearing further evidence from the parties. Their specific finding was that it was contrary to the interests of the complainants and not in the public interest that no effort should be made to mitigate the loss inflicted by the operation of the scheme upon level producers in general and, in particular, in the East of Scotland. Accordingly, so that some provision should be made for alleviating the effect of the scheme upon these producers, in order to enable them, if they so wish, to adjust their system of dairying to meet the changed conditions under the scheme, the Committee unanimously recommended the adoption of the second alternative in the Board's first proposal, and the adoption of the second and fourth proposals. As regards haulage centres, they proposed that the Board should be enabled to alter the centres prescribed from time to time should changed conditions make that advisable. As regards the third proposal, the Committee, with one dissentient, recommended that the Board should be given power to prescribe basic quantities that should qualify for the average price.

The Secretary of State, following upon conferences with representatives of the parties interested, intimated in a Parliamentary Statement on 10th December, 1934 (Official Report, Vol. 296, No. 15, Cols. 26-29) that he had decided to make adjustments in the scheme, for a period of one year, providing for:—

(*a*) a variation of the standard price of milk as recommended by the Committee of Investigation;

(*b*) twelve additional haulage centres to be prescribed in the East of Scotland area;

(*c*) a special premium of ½d. per gallon on milk sold by all ordinary level producers, i.e., producers who contract not to sell to or through the agency of the Board in any month during the year 1935 a quantity exceeding by more than 10 per cent. the quantity so sold in December, 1933;

(*d*) the levy on producer-retailers to be fixed on the basis of the number of cows in their possession; the levy to be at the rate of £5 per annum, provided that in the case of a producer-retailer who makes and observes a contract to handle all his own milk (that is, to sell no milk otherwise than by retail) the levy shall be at the rate of £4 per annum.

The Statement also referred to a proposal that the Board should review the financial arrangements with respect to the acquisition of creameries so as to effect a reduction in the contribution payable by producers for this purpose throughout the scheme area, and announced a decision reached in consultation with the Minister of Agriculture and Fisheries that a Milk Reorganisation Commission for Great Britain should be constituted which would undertake, in the course of the next twelve months, a comprehensive survey of the working of organised milk marketing in Great Britain and of the possibilities of further improvement, including the question of co-ordination or amalgamation of schemes.

With respect to the problem of the unpaid levies, which are owing by a considerable number of producer-retailers, against some of whom legal proceedings had been instituted by the Board, the Statement recorded that the Board had already undertaken that in cases of serious hardship they would not demand full payment of the unpaid levies immediately, and that it had been suggested to the Board that in such cases they should consider the possibility of devising a plan to provide for the payment of the amounts due by a system of instalments. It was pointed out, however, that the collection of the levy is a statutory duty of the Board and that the arrangements which were being made absolved neither the Board from that duty nor producers from their obligations under the scheme.

The necessary adjustments in the scheme for the year 1935 in accordance with these decisions were made on 29th December by the Scottish Milk Marketing Scheme (Amendment) Order, 1934,* and the Scottish Milk Marketing Scheme (Directions) Order, 1934.† In terms of the Orders, the haulage centres under the scheme for the year 1935 will be:—Alloa, Brechin, Crieff, Cupar, Dundee, Dunfermline, Dune, Edinburgh, Galashiels, Glasgow, Haddington, Kinross, Kirkcaldy, Perth and Stirling.

(b) *Complaint by the Association of Certified and Grade A (T.T.) Milk Producers.*—The Association complained that the scheme failed to encourage existing producers of Certified and Grade A (T.T.) milk to continue production of milk of these grades or to encourage other producers to undertake the production of milk of the higher grades. This complaint was referred to the Committee of Investigation on 6th December.

---

* S.R. & O. 1934, No. $\frac{1437}{S. 74}$. † S.R. & O. 1934, No. $\frac{1438}{S. 75}$.

Miscellaneous.

Finances of the Board.

A copy of the Profit and Loss Account of the Board for the period ended 31st January, 1934, and of the Balance Sheet as at that date will be found in Appendix III.

The loan of £1,500 made to the Board from the Agricultural Marketing (Scotland) Fund to provide for expenses in connection with the poll of the producers was repaid on 29th December, 1933.

The Secretary of State certified, in terms of Section 23 (2) of the Agricultural Marketing Act, 1933, that the expenses reasonably incurred by the persons who submitted the scheme in connection with the promotion, submission and bringing into operation of the scheme amounted to £375 17s. 5d.

Board's Journal.

Since April, 1934, the Board have published a monthly Journal giving particulars of their operations for the information of registered producers.

Imposition of Penalties on Registered Producers.

The Board have experienced considerable difficulty in obtaining returns in respect of sales by producer-retailers and producer-wholesalers, particularly in the Eastern Counties. In exercise of their powers under the scheme, the Board imposed penalties amounting to £880 10s. on eighty-three producers during the year to 30th November, 1934, mainly for failing to furnish information required by the Board. An appeal against the Board's action in imposing a penalty without giving the producer concerned an opportunity of being heard was referred to arbitration, and upheld by the arbiter. In accordance with that decision, the Board waived the penalties, amounting to £165, imposed on twenty-five of these producers prior to July.

Agreements with English Milk Marketing Board.

Before the scheme came into operation, the creameries in the South West of Scotland sent supplies of milk into England, the estimated quantity consigned during 1933 being 10,500,000 gallons. At the request of the English Board, the Scottish Board agreed to reduce the sales into England as far as possible, the English Board agreeing to make payment of suitable compensation in respect of the loss so sustained. With the exception of one contract entered into prior to the agreement with the English Board, the supply of milk into England from the area of the scheme has now ceased.

An agreement covering the period to 31st December, 1934, was also made between the Scottish and English Milk Marketing Boards, the Irish Free State Government and the manufacturers in Northern Ireland for the fixing of a minimum price for cream (see page 57).

[illegible]

[illegible]

Month.	Total Gallonage.	Sold to or through the agency of the Board.		Sold by Producer-Wholesalers and Producer Retailers, and Producers of Certified Milk.		Sold for liquid milk consumption.		Sold or used for manufacture of milk products.	
	Gallons.	Gallons.	Per cent.	Gallons.	Per cent.	Gallons.	Per cent.	Gallons.	Per cent.
December, [illegible]	[illegible]	[illegible]	[illegible]	[illegible]	[illegible]	[illegible]	[illegible]	[illegible]	[illegible]
January, [illegible]	[illegible]	[illegible]	[illegible]	[illegible]	[illegible]	[illegible]	[illegible]	[illegible]	[illegible]
February	[illegible]	[illegible]	[illegible]	[illegible]	[illegible]	[illegible]	[illegible]	[illegible]	[illegible]
March	[illegible]	[illegible]	[illegible]	[illegible]	[illegible]	[illegible]	[illegible]	[illegible]	[illegible]
April	[illegible]	[illegible]	[illegible]	[illegible]	[illegible]	[illegible]	[illegible]	[illegible]	[illegible]
May	[illegible]	[illegible]	[illegible]	[illegible]	[illegible]	[illegible]	[illegible]	[illegible]	[illegible]
June	[illegible]	[illegible]	[illegible]	[illegible]	[illegible]	[illegible]	[illegible]	[illegible]	[illegible]
July	[illegible]	[illegible]	[illegible]	[illegible]	[illegible]	[illegible]	[illegible]	[illegible]	[illegible]
August	[illegible]	[illegible]	[illegible]	[illegible]	[illegible]	[illegible]	[illegible]	[illegible]	[illegible]
September	[illegible]	[illegible]	[illegible]	[illegible]	[illegible]	[illegible]	[illegible]	[illegible]	[illegible]
October	[illegible]	[illegible]	[illegible]	[illegible]	[illegible]	[illegible]	[illegible]	[illegible]	[illegible]
November	[illegible]	[illegible]	[illegible]	[illegible]	[illegible]	[illegible]	[illegible]	[illegible]	[illegible]
TOTAL ([illegible] months).	[illegible]	[illegible]	[illegible]	[illegible]	[illegible]	[illegible]	[illegible]	[illegible]	[illegible]

PIGS AND BACON MARKETING SCHEMES, 1933.

The Pigs and Bacon Marketing Schemes, both of which apply to Great Britain, are component parts of a structure designed to secure an orderly and expanded market for the home bacon industry, and it will be convenient, therefore, to deal with the schemes together, as in the last report. Both schemes came into full operation on 9th September, 1933, after having been endorsed by large majorities of the registered producers voting on the initial polls.

The first Boards, consisting of members named in the schemes, with two members nominated by "the Minister" (the Minister of Agriculture and Fisheries and the Secretary of State for Scotland acting jointly), went out of office on 31st March, 1934. They were succeeded by elected Boards, consisting, in the case of the Pigs Marketing Board, of eight members elected by the registered producers voting in districts and three special members elected by the registered producers in general meeting; and in the case of the Bacon Marketing Board, of 14 members of whom 12 were elected by the registered producers in England and Wales, voting in classes, and two by registered producers in Scotland.

Elections of district members of the Pigs Marketing Board were held in each of the eight electoral districts on 3rd February, 1934, when seven of the eight sitting members were returned. The three special members were elected at the annual general meeting of registered producers held in London on 16th February. The meeting voted the sum of £4,990 as remuneration to members of the Board in respect of the period 7th July, 1933, to 31st March, 1934, divided as follows:—Chairman, £600; Vice-Chairman, £400; other members of the Executive Committee, £270 each; remaining members of the Board, £220 each.

At a general meeting of registered producers under the Bacon Marketing Scheme, held on 30th January, 1934, a resolution was passed, pursuant to paragraph 7 of the scheme, altering the limits determining the electoral classes of registered producers according to the quantities of bacon manufactured annually. The new limits fixed were 1,000 tons (instead of 800) and 2,000 tons (instead of 1,300) as the maximum annual bacon output for "small" and "medium" curers respectively. "Large" curers were those whose output exceeded 2,000 tons. The number of registered producers at 31st December, 1934, was 620. The elections of members of the Board were conducted at meetings held on 8th and 13th February, when 14 members were elected, of whom one was a newcomer. At the first annual general meeting of registered producers, held on 14th February, it was resolved that a sum of £2,800 should be paid as remuneration, exclusive of expenses, to members of the Board for the year beginning 1st April, 1934, the division between members to be left to the Board, and that remuneration at the same rate should be paid in respect of the period 6th July, 1933 (the date on which the scheme came into force), to 31st March, 1934.

After consultation with the Bacon Marketing Board, "the Minister" on 29th June, 1934, made the Bacon Marketing Scheme (Co-opted Members) Order, 1934,* amending the scheme so as to provide for the co-option by the elected members of the Board of two additional members. The two members co-opted by the Board, after consultation with the Market Supply Committee and with the approval of "the Minister," were the Hon. Jasper Ridley and Mr. W. Patrick Spens, K.C., M.P.

The origin, progress and main features of the schemes were described in the last report, which covered the operations of the Boards up to a date about midway through the first contract period. It also touched upon the difficulties which arose from the unexpectedly large volume of contracts in the initial period, and the means adopted for dealing with the situation, including the passing of the Agricultural Marketing (No. 2) Act, 1933.

One of the main objects of the schemes is to relieve the pig industry from the unsettling effects of cyclical price movements and at the same time to give the bacon-curing industry a more regular supply of raw material. The process by which it is sought to achieve these objects is a system of contracts for the supply of bacon pigs to registered curers, working in conjunction with a quantitative regulation of bacon imports. The Pigs Marketing Board have power to require that all sales of pigs by registered pig producers to registered bacon curers for conversion into bacon shall be made only in accordance with contracts prescribed by the Pigs Marketing Board after consultation with the Bacon Marketing Board; and under the Bacon Marketing Scheme a registered curer is prohibited, except in certain specified circumstances, from selling bacon not produced from pigs purchased in accordance with such contracts. The number of pigs contracted for in each year forms the basis of the regulation of imports of bacon in that year.

The form of contract first prescribed by the Pigs Marketing Board covered the four months November, 1933, to February, 1934, inclusive. This was followed by a contract covering the ten months March to December, 1934. The schemes are now in the third contract period, which runs for the full year, January to December, 1935.

---

* S.R. & O. 1934, No. 734.

First Contract Period.

November, 1933, to February, 1934.

Two forms of contract were prescribed by the Pigs Marketing Board, viz., a direct contract and a group contract, the latter being designed to meet the needs of small producers.

The direct contract was a contract made between a registered pig producer and a registered curer, and required the producer to undertake to deliver a stated number of pigs in stated months during the contract period, with a tolerance of 10 per cent. on monthly deliveries but of not more than 5 per cent. on total deliveries over the whole period. The producer was required to undertake to deliver his pigs in one or more of four weight-classes, as follows:—

Class 1.—Dead weight 7 score to 8 score 10 lb.
Class 2.—Dead weight 8 score 11 lb. to 9 score 10 lb.
Class 3.—Dead weight 9 score 11 lb. to 10 score 10 lb.
Class 4.—Dead weight over 10 score 10 lb.

A certain degree of tolerance was, however, permitted as regards the weights of pigs delivered. Wilful or negligent default in deliveries rendered the producer liable to pay to the Pigs Marketing Board by way of liquidated damages a sum of £1 for each pig which he failed to deliver, in addition to any damages for which he might become liable to the curer under the contract.

For the further protection of the curer, the Pigs Board undertook to make good deficiencies in delivery as far as was possible out of supplies of pigs under their control, and that, if no such supplies were available, they would use their best endeavours to purchase and re-sell to the curer pigs of the weights required, provided they were not liable to incur a greater loss than could be covered by a fund which the Board, by agreement with the Bacon Board, had earmarked for this purpose. If the Board had no pigs, or could not obtain them to replace the default, they were liable to pay to the curer, up to the extent of the fund so earmarked, any damages legally due to the curer from the producer, which the curer for any sufficient reason had been unable to recover from the producer. In accordance with this provision, the Pigs Marketing Board have earmarked for the purposes described 15 per cent. of the total levies received under paragraph 48 of the Pigs Marketing Scheme.

Pigs delivered in each weight class (except Class 4) were to be carcase-graded in five grades (A to E) according to measurements of shoulder fat and belly thickness taken at the factory. The contracts provided that weighing, classification and grading should be inspected by graders appointed by the Pigs Board.

The curer undertook to pay for all pigs delivered in pursuance of the contract according to a price scale which was drawn with regard to the weight-class and grade of every carcase, the standard being the Grade C pig in Class 1. The price was linked to the cost of production by being made to vary with the "feeding cost," i.e., the cost of an agreed ration of feeding stuffs compounded of barley meal (65 per cent.), English middlings (25 per cent.) and protein and mineral content—e.g., fish meal (10 per cent.).

With the feeding cost at 7s. 6d. per cwt. the price of the "basic" (Class 1 Grade C) pig was fixed at 12s. per score. The price of the "basic pig" varied 3d. per score upwards or downwards for every 3d. rise or fall in the feeding cost. Grade C pigs in Classes 2 and 3 and all pigs in Class 4 suffered deductions of 6d., 1s., and 1s. 6d. per score respectively, compared with the basic pig in Class 1. Pigs accepted in Class 4 but not specifically contracted for in that class suffered a further deduction of 6d. per score on the full weight of the pig for each 10 lb. or part of 10 lb. in weight over 11 score. A Grade A pig carried a premium of 1s. per score over a basic pig in the same Class. Grade B pigs received 6d. per score premium. Grade D pigs and Grade E pigs suffered deductions of 3d. and 6d. per score respectively, compared with the basic pigs in each Class. In all Classes a black or mainly black pig suffered a deduction of 6d. per score.

The expenses of delivery from producer's premises to bacon factory fell mainly on the curer, who had to bear all freight and feeding charges from the producer's railway station or road collecting station, or, in the case of the group contract, from the group collecting station, if the distance exceeded two miles. If the producer undertook delivery, the curer had to reimburse him. If, however, the curer collected the pigs at the producer's premises, he could recover an agreed sum up to 6d. per pig from the producer.

The contract provided that the curer should effect an insurance with the National Farmers' Union Mutual Insurance Society, Limited, of every pig delivered under the contract, except pigs contracted for in Class 4. The cost of insurance was 6d. per pig and by the terms of the contract, the curer deducted 3d. per pig from the purchase price as the producer's share. The curer was also required to deduct from the purchase price the levy of 1s. 2d. per pig due to the Pigs Board by the producer, and remit it to the Board, and he could be required to deduct and remit other sums which might be payable by the producer to the Board. The balance due to the producer had then to be paid over to him by the curer within 14 days from the date of grading.

The group contract followed generally the terms of the direct contract. For the purposes of this contract, producers formed a group under a "group agent", each producer in the group agreeing to sell a number of pigs to the Board, the group agent being a party to the contract. The group contractors, however, were not required to specify the class in which pigs were to be delivered and were not given the option of contracting to deliver pigs in Class 4. Moreover, the default clause in the group contract made the group agent liable to the Pigs Board in the sum of £1 for every pig not delivered, any damages so paid and costs incurred by him being made a debt due to him from the producer in default. Each producer in the group was required to deliver his pigs to such premises as might be designated by the Board, and the group agent was required to assist the producer with his deliveries. Where a producer failed to deliver his pigs, the group agent was responsible for endeavouring to obtain pigs from other members of his group or, with the Board's consent, by outside purchase, to replace the deficiency. Thus, although individual producers were ultimately liable for damages for their own defaults, membership of a group put them in a position, through the group agent, to call on the resources of the whole group to make god deficiencies.

Pigs sold to the Board on group contracts were re-sold to those curers who required pigs in addition to those bought on direct contracts, the Board charging the curer 1s. per pig in addition to the agreed contract price. From the price payable by the Board to the group contractors, the sum of 1s. per pig was deducted as the group agent's commission.

No contract ("direct" or "group") could take effect until it had been registered and confirmed by the Pigs Marketing Board, who could confirm a contract either unconditionally or subject to a reduction in the numbers of pigs agreed to be sold under it. Where such a reduction was made in a contract it remained binding on the parties in respect of the reduced numbers of pigs, except where the curer produced a certificate of the Bacon Marketing Board that the modification of the contract would involve him in loss. The object of this clause was to enable a limitation of supply to be effected in the event of pigs being contracted for in excess of the quantity which the Government was prepared to accept as the home quota of bacon. Finally, the contract could be voided if imports of bacon into the United Kingdom ceased to be regulated, or if the total quantity of bacon permitted to be sold in the United Kingdom rose above a certain limit.

The closing date for the registration of contracts for the delivery of pigs in the four months November, 1933, to February, 1934, was 12th October, 1933. The number of pigs contracted for, together with the relatively small number which it was calculated that registered curers would themselves produce, was 565,688, of which about 20 per cent. were on group contracts. Contracts were not evenly distributed between curers; while Wiltshire-cure factories in general had obtained all the pigs they needed, curers requiring the heavier classes of pig were short of their requirements. The Boards discussed ways and means of securing a more equitable distribution of pigs among curers, and it was eventually decided (a) to use group contracts to meet the needs of curers requiring fewer than 50 pigs per week, (b) to supply to all curers who had obtained contracts for more than 60 per cent. of their requirements a list of those whose contracts fell short of that figure, with the object of securing a voluntary assignment of contracts from the former to the latter, and (c) having obtained details of assignments of pigs of this kind, to level up supplies to curers as far as possible by means of the remaining pigs controlled by the Pigs Board under group contracts.

At the outset there was a glut of pigs, possibly due to October pigs being held back so as to effect delivery in the contract period. The difficulties were intensified by the unwillingness of some curers to take delivery of group contract pigs which, to a large extent, meant pigs from distant centres, involving heavy carriage charges. The Pigs Marketing Board at once took up this matter with the Railway Companies, and were successful in getting the rates from the far-western counties to the midlands substantially reduced. An undue proportion of low-grade and over-weight pigs also gave trouble in the early weeks, but with the assistance of County Pig Committees the Board were able to secure more attention on the part of producers to these important matters.

By the end of December the glut had not only been cleared but the position had become entirely reversed. Partly through miscalculation of the number of pigs that would be available and partly through the counter-attraction of the open market, where prices were relatively high, deliveries of pigs fell markedly below the contracted numbers in January and February, 1934, and the Pigs Board were obliged to take measures against defaulters to recover damages as provided in the contract.

The difficulties experienced by curers in taking delivery of pigs in November and December were aggravated by a fall in the bacon price which set in at the beginning of the contract period. This fall was due primarily to the fact that the large numbers of pigs contracted for, at the start of the scheme, involved a heavy reduction in imports which could only be effected by an Order under the Agricultural Marketing Act, 1933. In the interval required for the establishment of the necessary regulation machinery, imports were coming in at a high rate, depressing the market. Curers, however, had bound themselves for four months to buy pigs at a price which had been stabilised only with reference to costs of pig production, and regardless of fluctuations in the bacon market; and the situation became so serious that the Government had to provide special assistance to tide the schemes over the emergency.

This assistance took the form of a loan from the Agricultural Marketing Funds which, subject to further investigation and subject also to a recommendation of the Agricultural Marketing Facilities Committee for Great Britain, was to be made to the Bacon

Marketing Board and to be used by them to indemnify curers against an agreed part of their ascertained losses. The loan was to be repaid by means of special deductions to be made by curers from the prices returned to pig producers for pigs delivered in the ensuing contract periods.

Repayment of the loan was to be guaranteed by the Pigs Marketing Board under powers derived from the Agricultural Marketing (No. 2) Act, 1933. The method of assessing losses and the making of payments out of the fund created by the loan were to be under the supervision of the Wyndham Portal Committee, to which reference was made in the last report. The Bacon Marketing Scheme was to be amended so as to confer on the Bacon Board the necessary powers to enter into an agreement with the Pigs Board, and also to pay over the compensation money to individual curers. A further amendment enabled the Bacon Board to increase the amount of the levy on curers, provided that the curer was entitled, under the terms of the contract, to deduct the amount of the increased contribution from the price payable to the pig producer.

The statutory procedure which had to be followed in connection with the amendments took some time. However, the Bacon Marketing Scheme (Amendment) Order, 1934,* made by "the Minister" on 20th June, 1934, and the Agricultural Marketing (Guarantee No. 1) Order, 1934,† made on 25th June, enabled the arrangements to be completed.

Meanwhile, the Wyndham Portal Committee, after investigation of the accounts of representative groups of bacon factories of different types, came to the following conclusions, viz., that a loss had been occasioned to curers as a result of the operation of the Pigs and Bacon Marketing Schemes up to 31st December, 1933; that the data obtained as a result of the investigation should be used as a standard to be applied to all factories; that compensation should be paid at a flat rate of 7s. 5d. per pig, representing a part of the standard average loss; and that the compensation should be paid in respect of pigs bought from registered producers at the prescribed prices, and on which the Pigs Board levy was paid during the period 15th September to 31st December, 1933. With the concurrence of "the Minister," it was agreed that no account should be taken of profits or losses on pigs bought subsequent to 31st December, 1933.

The amount of the loan ultimately found to be required was £160,000, and after the making of the two Orders mentioned above and the completion of a Deed of Charge incorporating a guarantee of repayment by the Pigs Board, an advance of £144,000 was made from the English Agricultural Marketing Fund on 26th June, followed on 5th July by an advance of £16,000 from the Scottish

* S.R. & O. 1934, No. 679. † S.R. & O. 1934, No. 685.

Fund, secured by a separate Deed of Charge. The rate of interest charged was 3½ per cent. per annum.

The terms of the loan provided for repayment by six consecutive monthly instalments commencing on 31st July, 1934. The necessary funds for repayment were to be derived from contributions levied on pigs sold under contract and delivered between 1st March and 31st December, 1934, but since the collection of the levy on pigs delivered in December would not be completed before the end of that month, it was provided that any instalment might be paid within 30 days after the day appointed for payment. The levy was to be paid by bacon curers, who would recoup themselves from pig producers. The amount of the deduction from the pig purchase price to be made by curers in respect of the levy was to be determined monthly by the Pigs Marketing Board. The total sum repaid by the Bacon Board up to 31st December, 1934, was £141,873, comprising £140,142 in repayment of principal and £1,731 in interest.*

Deliveries in First Contract Period.—The contract system for the sale of pigs was a complete innovation in this country, and it was to be anticipated that many producers would meet with difficulty in accurately estimating their output several months in advance and, in consequence, in adhering to their contracts. This proved to be the case. The following table shows the number of pigs contracted for and delivered in each month of the first contract period. The deficiency, which was heavy—particularly in January and February, 1934—amounted to 15·6 per cent. of the total numbers contracted for over the whole period. Considerable numbers of pigs due in January and February were, however, delivered in subsequent months, by agreement with curers.

Numbers of Pigs Contracted for and Numbers Delivered (excluding Pigs Rejected) in the First Contract Period.

Month.	Direct Contracts.		Group Contracts.		Total.	
	Contracted.	Delivered.	Contracted.	Delivered	Contracted.	Delivered
1933.						
November ...	123,332	110,719	31,913	17,313	155,245	128,032
December ...	115,008	101,129	24,304	24,738	139,312	125,867
1934.						
January ...	110,691	93,121	23,298	18,570	133,989	111,691
February ...	122,571	76,819	25,211	16,925	147,782	93,744
	471,602	381,788	104,726	77,546	576,328	459,334

* The balance of principal and interest was paid off on 30th January, 1935.

The price of the standard feeding stuffs ration did not vary by so much as 3d. per cwt. in any month; consequently the basic contract price per pig remained at 12s. per score throughout the period.

Second Contract Period.

March to December, 1934.

As already indicated, it was decided that the second contract period should cover the ten months March to December, 1934, a step towards the objective of a yearly contract period which the Reorganisation Commission for Pigs and Pig Products had recommended as desirable.

Experience of the working of the contract system in the first period suggested the need for some modification of the contract terms, and on 1st January, 1934, the Boards invoked the aid of the Wyndham Portal Committee in drawing up the new contract.

As regards the first two months of the period, it was decided to adhere to the old method of fixing prices according to the price of an agreed feeding ration. In March and April the "basic" price per score was to be 12s. 6d. so long as the price of the agreed ration remained at 7s. 6d. per cwt. This was an advance of 6d. per score on the previous basic rate, but provision was also made for a deduction by the curer of 6d. per score towards repayment of the indemnity loan.

As from 1st May, a new method of price-fixing came into operation, the aim of which was to relate pig prices not only to feed prices but also to the prices realised by the bacon and offals obtained from the pig, thus relieving the curer of a part of the risk of loss in the event of feeding stuff prices moving upward while bacon and offal prices moved downward.

After prolonged negotiations, in which invaluable help was given by the independent members of the Wyndham Portal Committee, the two Boards agreed upon a scale of prices for this "co-partnership" form of contract. "Initial prices" of 11s. per score for the pig and 85s. per cwt. for bacon while the standard feeding stuff ration remained at 7s. 6d. were fixed as the basis of the relationship between pig and bacon prices. These prices were not intended to represent costs of production; they merely served to define a ratio which would obtain provided other factors did not vary. As regards these other "variables", it was agreed that for every 3d. per cwt. variation in the price of the standard ration above or below 7s. 6d. a corresponding variation of 3d. per score upwards or downwards should be made in the initial price of the pig, and of 1s. 9d. per cwt. in the initial price of bacon—on the broad principle that 7 score 2 lb. of pig equal 1 cwt. of bacon. Thus, with feed costs at 7s. 9d. the initial pig price was to be 11s. 3d. per score and the initial bacon price 86s. 9d. per cwt.

The initial bacon price, again, was based on the assumption that the offals from a 7 score 2 lb. pig would realise 10s. Any decrease or increase in the actual ascertained value of offals was to be added to or deducted from the initial bacon price.

For every 1s. 2d. variation in the ascertained price of English bacon above or below the initial price, as modified to allow for changes in feed prices or offal values, a corresponding variation was to be made in the pig price, by adding or deducting 1d. per score to or from the initial price. By this means the farmer received one-half of the profit or bore one-half of the loss on the actual price of bacon as compared with the initial price. It was provided, however, that in the months September to December, 1934, the producer would receive 75 per cent. instead of 50 per cent. of the surplus in respect of any excess over 18s. per cwt. in the margin between the actual and initial bacon prices.

The ascertained price, which was that of sizeable green Wiltshire whole sides delivered to the retailer, was arrived at each month from returns certified by an independent accountant from five Wiltshire curers selected jointly by the Boards, the value of offals being determined from similar data.

Apart from price conditions, the terms of the new contract did not differ materially from those of the previous contract. In one detail, namely the prescription with regard to insurance of pigs, the contract was modified in consequence of the findings of the Committee of Investigation for Great Britain upon complaints made by the Live Stock Offices' Association and the Parliamentary Committee of the Co-operative Congress. The complainants had been aggrieved by the action of the Pigs Board under the first contract in requiring all insurances to be effected with one company. The Committee of Investigation reported to " the Minister " that the complaints were justified and that compulsory insurance with an individual company to the exclusion of all other companies was neither necessary nor essential and was unfair to the other companies and to the insured, and was contrary to the public interest. The Pigs Marketing Board gave an undertaking to " the Minister " that the business of insuring pigs during the second contract period would not be withheld from any reputable company or society which was prepared to undertake the business on terms which the Board accepted from any other company or society. Accordingly, the new contract required the insurance to be effected " in an Insurance Company or Society to be approved by the Board ".

Another innovation was the prescription of two forms of direct contract, viz., a general contract and a Wiltshire contract. The latter was framed to meet the special needs of Wiltshire curers, and provided for the delivery of Class 1 pigs only, i.e., pigs within the weight range of 7 score to 9 score 10 lb. dead weight. Slight amendments were made in the grade measurements, with the object of making the grading a little more strict. Deductions in respect of pigs below Grade C were increased to 6d. per score for each grade instead of 3d. as before. On the other hand, the deductions in respect of Class 3 and Class 4 pigs as compared with Class 1 pigs were reduced from 1s. and 1s. 6d. per score to 9d. and 1s. 3d. respectively.

The new contract provided for the transport of all pigs for journeys of over five miles by the Railway Companies at a flat rate, irrespective of distance, in pursuance of an agreement reached between the Boards and the Railway Companies, which was subsequently sanctioned by the Railway Rates Tribunal. The rate fixed was 2s. per pig, less the railway freight rebate of 4d., i.e., 1s. 8d. net. A committee consisting of representatives of the Boards and of the Railway Companies was set up to consider cases where, owing to exceptional circumstances, freedom of action as regards transport was claimed by producers and curers in respect of pigs travelling distances of over five and up to 15 miles. Where reasonably required to do so, the Companies agreed to carry pigs by road from producer to curer for distances up to 15 miles, subject to a minimum load of 15 pigs.

The protracted nature of the negotiations did not leave much time to inform registered producers and curers of the full purport of the new contract, and the date for lodging contracts had to be extended from 21st February to 12th March, 1934. This meant that contracts could not be confirmed until well after the commencement of the contract period, and in the meantime arrangements were made to continue the rate of imports of bacon and hams at the existing level. Pig producers were invited to deliver, and curers to accept, pigs during the month of March as though the contracts had been confirmed, and with the co-operation of both sides of the industry, smooth working was secured. All contracts registered were confirmed unconditionally by 21st March.

Pig prices under the new method of price determination were on the whole slightly lower than in the first contract period and in September the basic price had fallen to 11s. 5d. per score. A rise in both bacon and feeding stuffs prices, however, improved the basic pig price very considerably in the last three months of the period.

The numbers of pigs contracted for and the numbers delivered in the second contract period are shown in the table on page 36. The table also gives the standard pig prices per score. As producers became more accustomed to the contract system, defaults in deliveries became less; during the second contract period deliveries were 7 per cent. below contracts compared with 15·6 per cent. in the first contract period.

PIGS AND BACON MARKETING SCHEMES, [illegible]

Numbers of pigs contracted for and numbers delivered (excluding pigs rejected) in the Second Contract Period.

Month.	Standard Pig Price (per score).	Bacon Contracts.		Group Contracts.		Total.	
		Contracted.	Delivered.	Contracted.	Delivered.	Contracted.	Delivered.
[illegible]	s. d.						
March	[illegible]	[illegible]	[illegible]	[illegible]	[illegible]	[illegible]	[illegible]
April	[illegible]	[illegible]	[illegible]	[illegible]	[illegible]	[illegible]	[illegible]
May	[illegible]	[illegible]	[illegible]	[illegible]	[illegible]	[illegible]	[illegible]
June	[illegible]	[illegible]	[illegible]	[illegible]	[illegible]	[illegible]	[illegible]
July	[illegible]	[illegible]	[illegible]	[illegible]	[illegible]	[illegible]	[illegible]
August	[illegible]	[illegible]	[illegible]	[illegible]	[illegible]	[illegible]	[illegible]
September	[illegible]	[illegible]	[illegible]	[illegible]	[illegible]	[illegible]	[illegible]
October	[illegible]	[illegible]	[illegible]	[illegible]	[illegible]	[illegible]	[illegible]
November	[illegible]	[illegible]	[illegible]	[illegible]	[illegible]	[illegible]	[illegible]
December	[illegible]	[illegible]	[illegible]	[illegible]	[illegible]	[illegible]	[illegible]
Month not specified		[illegible]		[illegible]		[illegible]	
Totals		[illegible]*	[illegible]	[illegible]	[illegible]	[illegible]	[illegible]

* The number contracted on "Wiltshire" Contracts was [illegible].

† [illegible]

Third Contract Period.

January to December, 1935.

It took even longer to settle contract terms for the third period than for either of the previous periods, and the terms of the contract for 1935 were not announced until 19th October, 1934.

The contracts run for the whole of the calendar year 1935 and retain the main features of previous contracts. The "co-partnership" basis of the formula for fixing pig prices has been varied in three main particulars:—

(*a*) The "initial" prices of pigs and bacon have been altered to 11s. 6d. per score and 96s. per cwt. respectively.

(*b*) The equality basis of sharing of bacon and feed price movements holds good only so long as the ascertained price of bacon does not fall below 90s. 3d. or rise above 96s. 3d. per cwt. Outside these limits the pig producer will carry a gradually increasing proportion of the "profits" or "losses," so that when the bacon price is below 86s. 9d. or above 101s. 9d. the basis of sharing will be 75 per cent. to the pig producer, and 25 per cent. to the bacon curer. When, however, the price of bacon is above 101s. 9d. and the feed price more than 9s. per cwt., or when the price of bacon is below 86s. 9d. and the feed price less than 6s. per cwt., feed price movements are again shared equally.

(*c*) The pig price is no longer varied to meet changes in the value of offals.

The price terms, moreover, incorporate a new feature in the shape of provisions included to secure adequate and regular deliveries throughout the year. Further, upon notification by the Bacon Board that a sufficient total number of pigs has not been secured on contracts in each of the twelve months to ensure to curers an economic throughput, the contract may become determinable at the instance of any of the parties thereto. The producer is required to undertake to supply during the months January to April at least 25 per cent., and during the months September to December not more than 45 per cent., of the total number of pigs for which he contracts. Pigs contracted for delivery and delivered and accepted in the first four months will rank for bonus, at rates varying according to the proportions of pigs so delivered, to be provided from a fund raised by a contribution of 2d. per score to be paid by curers on all pigs delivered and accepted for bacon throughout 1935.

Some adjustment has also been made in the price differences between classes, in the weight limits of Classes 2 and 6, and in the grade measurements of Grades B and D. The deduction in the case of pigs which are black or mainly black can in future only be made if the carcase shows this characteristic after dressing.

Transport and insurance arrangements have also been varied. The agreement with the Railway Companies to carry pigs at a flat rate has been extended to all pigs regardless of the distance involved, and the rate has been reduced from 1s. 8d. to 1s. 6d. net (station to station). The producer is responsible for putting the pigs on rail; if he does not do so there will be a deduction of 6d. per pig from the price paid to him. The Railway Companies also undertake to provide through road conveyance in all cases within 25 miles of the curer's factory, where loads of not less than 12 pigs can be made up with an average of not less than three pigs per collection. The rate for this service is 2s. 1d. per pig. Both the curer and the producer have the option of providing their own transport without limit as to distance; the flat rate per pig for road transport must, however, be paid in each case to the Railway Company and a rebate claimed on a fixed scale according to distance.

The obligation to insure all pigs sold under the contract has been abandoned. The curer, however, agrees to pay to the producer 1d. per score on pigs accepted towards the cost of any insurance which the producer may wish to effect. In the absence of compulsory insurance, the producer has to deliver sound, healthy pigs, and his liability extends up to the factory, notwithstanding that the curer takes delivery when the pigs are put on rail or road vehicle. The Pigs Board have negotiated with the Insurance Companies mainly interested in livestock insurance, a policy under which contract pigs can be insured by producers at rates of 1s. 6d. per pig for full cover and 1s. 2d. per pig for cover of the carcase including head but excluding offals. Arrangements have also been made to enable curers, by consent of the pig producers concerned, to carry the insurance risk for full cover at 1s. 2d. per pig.

A new clause of considerable importance has been inserted in the contract to provide against the contingency of a fall in bacon prices (or rise in feed prices) of such magnitude as to make the contract price uneconomic for curer or producer. Either Board may in such circumstances give three months notice to declare the contracts void. In that event, an appeal may be made to a referee as to whether the contracts shall remain in force or not, and if, after taking into account prices of pigs and bacon and all other relevant factors, the referee so decides, the contracts shall remain in force.

The original closing date for receipt of contracts by the Pigs Marketing Board was 14th November, 1934. As a result, however, of the short time allowed for signing contracts, the number of contracts received by that date was unsatisfactory. The agreement of "the Minister" was therefore obtained to a six-days extension of the contract period. The number of pigs covered by contracts received by the Pigs Board up to 20th November amounted to 1,688,000. This represented a small increase in the bacon pig output over 1934 but it was not regarded by the Boards as sufficient, having regard to the increase in the number of pigs on farms in Great Britain, as disclosed by the 1934 Agricultural Returns. The strict limitation of seasonal variations in the numbers of pigs contracted for had undoubtedly deterred a number of producers from contracting. Moreover, supplies were very unevenly distributed between factories. The agreement of "the Minister" to a further extension of the time for securing contracts was therefore obtained, with a view to providing sufficient pigs to give all curers an economic throughput, and a supplementary contract was issued which gave producers the opportunity of contracting with the Pigs Board, direct or through an agent, for an additional 450,000 pigs. The terms of this supplementary contract were, in most respects, the same as those of the direct contract, but there were no limitations as to the minimum and maximum percentage of pigs to be delivered in any period of the year and no provisions for the payment of level delivery bonuses. Curers were, however, required to pay to the Board 2d. per score on all pigs delivered and accepted for bacon under supplementary contracts, the proceeds to be added to the bonus fund.

The closing date for the receipt of supplementary contracts by the Pigs Board was 22nd December, 1934. By that date, however, contracts for only some 100,000 additional pigs out of the 450,000 required had been obtained, and it was decided subsequently to take steps to augment the supply of pigs to meet curers' requirements by the issue of a further supplementary contract.

Efficiency Measures.

The report of the Reorganization Commission, which was presented in October, 1932, contained, in addition to the draft marketing schemes for pigs and bacon and proposals with regard to the regulation of imports, a number of other important recommendations designed to increase the efficiency of the industry.

As regards pig production and marketing, the Commission's proposals included the standardization of quality and type of bacon pigs, the promotion of research into diseases of pigs, improved management, regularity of production, and organized assembly and transport of pigs.

On the bacon curing side, their main proposal was the establishment of a Development Board to carry out a programme of "rationalisation" of the curing industry. The Commission's proposals also covered the standardization of cure and grading of bacon, research into bacon production methods and the organization of marketing, including collective advertising.

Progress has been made in some of the directions indicated by the Commission. The negotiation of a flat rate for transport of all pigs and the steps taken in the 1935 contract to secure regular deliveries throughout the year have already been described. As regards the standardization of quality and type of bacon pigs, the grading of all pigs delivered on contracts and the payment of pigs by grade are probably the most effective means of securing progress as they appeal to the producer through his pocket. Complete data with regard to the results of grading are not yet available, but the percentage of pigs rejected by the curers fell from 7·2 in November, 1933, to 2·2 in December, 1934, while the numbers graded in the classes A, B and C increased from 47·8 per cent. to 58·8 per cent.

Progress on the curing side of the industry may be expected to result from the establishment of the Development Scheme for organising the production of bacon. A draft scheme, which was submitted by the two Boards under the Agricultural Marketing Act, 1933, is at present under consideration.

The question of the development of the tank curing method has attracted some attention. It is known that certain factories have increased their capacity for tank curing since the schemes came into operation, but more precise information is lacking. The Bacon Marketing Board are conducting enquiries with a view to obtaining this information.

The Bacon Marketing Board have co-operated in the circulation to curers of a leaflet on the technique of bacon curing, prepared by Dr. E. H. Callow, of the Cambridge Low Temperature Research Station, and issued by the Department of Scientific and Industrial Research.

Regulation of Bacon Supplies.

Quantitative regulation of bacon and ham imports dates from November, 1932, when, as a result of the low prices prevailing for bacon, agreement was reached with the eleven principal foreign countries exporting bacon to the United Kingdom, for a voluntary reduction of their supplies by some 15 per cent. compared with the three months November-January, 1931-32.

Further reductions in imports from these countries were made by voluntary agreement from time to time during 1933, the aim being to reduce foreign supplies, by the time the Pigs and Bacon Marketing Schemes came into operation, to a level which, combined with home and Dominion supplies, would give a total figure approximately equivalent to that at which the Reorganization Commission recommended the stabilisation of total market supplies, namely, 10,670,000 cwt. per annum.

In 1934, further reductions in imports from foreign countries were effected by Order* under the Agricultural Marketing Act, 1933. The gross supplies of bacon† from home, Dominion and foreign sources during 1934, compared with 1932, were as follows:—

—	*1932.*		*1934.*	
	000 cwt.	Per cent.	000 cwt.	Per cent.
United Kingdom‡	1,750§	12·6	2,307	21·7
Dominion‖	541	3·9	1,456	13·7
Foreign‖	11,651	83·5	6,871	64·6
Total ...	13,942	100·0	10,634	100·0

* The Bacon (Import Regulation) Order, 1933 (S.R. & O. 1933, No. 1050), since replaced by the Bacon (Import Regulation) Order, 1934 (S.R. & O. 1934, No. 844).

† Excluding tinned hams and salted pork and the output of unregistered curers in Great Britain.

‡ Includes imported pigs or pork cured in this country.

§ Based on 1930 Board of Trade Industrial Census—the latest official figure available.

‖ Gross imports. Exports and re-exports amounted to 262,000 cwt. in 1932 and 88,000 cwt. in 1934.

Miscellaneous.

Accounts of the Boards.—Copies of the Income and Expenditure Accounts and of the Boards' Balance Sheets as at 31st December, 1933 and 1934, are printed in Appendix III.

Expenses of Promoting the Schemes.—A certificate under Section 22 (2) of the Agricultural Marketing Act, 1933, was given by "the Minister" on 28th February, 1934, in respect of the expenses, amounting to £1,670 0s. 6d., incurred by the Food Manufacturers' Federation, Incorporated, in connection with the promotion, submission and bringing into operation of the Bacon Marketing Scheme. A similar certificate in connection with the Pigs Marketing Scheme was given on 12th June, 1934, in respect of expenses, amounting to £2,031 18s. 9d., incurred by the National Farmers' Unions of England and Scotland.

Imposition of Penalties on Registered Producers.—The schemes provide that the respective Boards shall impose upon and recover from registered producers who sell pigs or bacon, as the case may be, in contravention of the provisions of the schemes or of determinations of the Boards thereunder, monetary penalties. Failure to comply with a demand of the Board for returns or other information relating to the regulated product also renders a registered producer under either scheme liable to the imposition of a penalty by the Board. No penalties have hitherto been imposed by the Pigs Marketing Board. Penalties in respect of failure to render returns have been imposed by the Bacon Board on 13 registered curers, the total penalties amounting to £85.

Amendment of Schemes.—Amendments of the Bacon Marketing Scheme were submitted by the Bacon Board in March, 1934. These included three unopposed amendments which were approved in June by the Bacon Marketing Scheme (Amendment) Order, 1934,* and two other amendments designed to enable the Board to determine the quantity of bacon that may be sold in any year by any registered curer, and to secure that in any expansion of the market for home-produced bacon the extent to which any registered curer might participate with bacon produced from pigs of his own production should be regulated. Objections to the two latter amendments were lodged by the Parliamentary Committee of the Co-operative Congress, and a public inquiry into the objections was held by Mr. N. L. Macaskie, K.C., by direction of "the Minister." The objections and the report on the inquiry are under consideration.

The Pigs Marketing Board have recently submitted to "the Minister" a series of amendments to the Pigs Marketing Scheme. The period for lodging objections or representations with respect to the proposed amendments expired on 16th April, 1935.

Complaints regarding the Operation of the Schemes.

Reference has been made above (page 34) to the findings of the Committee of Investigation for Great Britain upon a complaint

* S.R. & O. 1934 No. 579.

which "the Minister" referred to them regarding a term of the first contract relative to the insurance of pigs.

The Committee have had under consideration complaints by the Parliamentary Committee of the Co-operative Congress as to (a) the omission in the third contract of any obligation to insure pigs and (b) the requirements in the third contract regarding the flat rate system for the transport of all live pigs purchased by curers; they have also had under consideration a complaint upon the latter point by the National Federation of Meat Traders' Associations.

Summary of Contracts.

—	*England.*	*Scotland.*	*Gt. Britain.*
Number of Contracts.			
First Period (November, 1933 to February, 1934)	16,952	1,880	18,832
Second Period (March to December 1934) ...	22,286	1,983	24,269
Third Period (January to December, 1935) ...	20,096	1,851	21,947*
No. of Pigs Contracted for.			
First Period:—			
Direct	446,855	24,747	471,602
Group	95,686	9,040	104,726
Total 1st Period ...	542,541	33,787	576,328
Second Period:—			
Direct.			
(a) General	776,483	8,784	785,267
(b) Wiltshire ...	227,569	62,658	290,227
Total Direct	1,004,052	71,442	1,075,494
Group	223,281	26,567	249,848
Total 2nd Period ...	1,227,333	98,009	1,325,342
Third Period:—			
Direct	1,416,756	121,949	1,538,705
Group	131,326	15,455	146,781
Supplementary ...	103,303	7,315	110,618 *
Total 3rd Period ...	1,651,385	144,719	1,799,687 *

* A further supplementary contract was issued on 15th March, 1935, for delivery of pigs in the months May to December, 1935. The closing date for receipt of these contracts by the Pigs Board was 15th April, 1935.

MILK MARKETING SCHEME, 1933.

The Milk Marketing Scheme, covering England and Wales, came into force on 28th July, 1933. At the initial poll of registered producers, 96 per cent. of those voting, counting numbers and productive capacity, were in favour of the scheme remaining in force, and accordingly it came fully into operation, at the end of the suspensory period, on 6th October, 1933.

The main features of the scheme were described in the last report. In each region (of which there are eleven) the registered producers receive a "pool" price, which is arrived at by distributing among the producers the total proceeds of the sale of all milk by wholesale in the region (after adjustments have been made in respect of inter-regional compensation payments and of the premiums earned by individual producers) in proportion to the quantities of milk sold wholesale by each.

The first Board administering the scheme consisted of the members named in the scheme and two members nominated by the Minister and held office until 30th June, 1934, when they were replaced by the elected board consisting of 12 regional members, 3 special members and 2 members co-opted by the Board after consultation with the Market Supply Committee.* Elections of the regional members were held on 2nd June, 1934; the special members were elected at the annual general meeting held on 8th June, 1934. Of the members of the first Board, 6 were re-elected as regional members and 2 as special members, so that the new Board included 6 regional members and 1 special member who had not previously held office. The members co-opted by the Board were Lord Cranworth and Mr. M. Hely-Hutchinson, the latter being one of the Minister's nominees on the first Board.

The remuneration of members of the first Board, voted by the registered producers at the annual general meeting, was:—Chairman £1,200, Vice-Chairman £700, other members £350 each.

Contact between the Board and the regions is maintained by regional committees elected by the registered producers in each region.

The number of producers registered under the scheme on 31st December, 1934, was 158,706.

The main work of the Board has been in connection with the regulation of sales of milk by registered producers and the administration of the pooling provisions of the scheme. Sales by wholesale by registered producers have been governed by the terms of contracts prescribed by the Board; producer-retailer sales have been controlled through the conditions attaching to the retail licences.

A statement showing the quantities of milk sold under the scheme during the period 6th October, 1933, to 31st December, 1934, is given on page 58.

Wholesale Contracts.

The scheme provides that the Board may, from time to time, after consultation with representatives of purchasers of milk by wholesale, prescribe the terms on which and the form in which

* During the period of 12 months from 30th June, 1934, the co-option of any person to the Board is subject to the approval of the Minister.

contracts for the sale of milk by registered producers (other than sales by retail) shall be made. The scheme also provided, however, that during the year following the end of the suspensory period, that is to say, from 6th October, 1933, to 5th October, 1934, the Board should not make any determination with regard to prices, or prescribe the terms of any contracts which affected prices, without first consulting representatives of the wholesale purchasers, together with three persons appointed by the Minister; and if, after such consultation, the Board and the purchasers' representatives failed to agree upon the price, the Appointed Persons should fix the price. The Minister appointed Mr. F. M. Russell Davies, K.C., Mr. A. E. Cutforth, C.B.E., F.C.A., and Mr. W. Fraser, C.B.E., to act in the circumstances referred to.

The Board have prescribed the terms and the form of the wholesale contracts for three periods :—

(i) 6th October, 1933, to 31st March, 1934.

(ii) 1st April to 30th September, 1934.

(iii) 1st October, 1934, to 30th September, 1935.

As regards the first and second contracts, the Board and the purchasers' representatives failed to agree upon prices, which were accordingly fixed by the Appointed Persons. In the case of the third contract, however, the Board and the purchasers' representatives were able to reach agreement.

The form of the three contracts was on similar lines. In each case the Board were a party to it and the purchase price was payable to them; the contract was conditional upon its registration with the Board, who were entitled to enforce any of the rights of the registered producer thereunder as well as their own. The main operative provisions of the contracts are compared in the following paragraphs.

Methods of Sale.—A registered producer may contract to sell either the whole output of his herd or of a stated number of cows, or he may contract to deliver a stated daily quantity of milk. In the latter case an additional premium, called the level delivery premium, is payable by the purchaser. The first contract provided for two rates of premium, 1d. per gallon for a variation of 5 per cent. either way from the level quantity, and ½d. per gallon for a variation of 10 per cent. In the second and third contracts, provision was made for one level delivery premium only, namely, ½d. per gallon for a variation of 10 per cent. During the first contract period, level delivery contracts comprised 26 per cent. of the total number of contracts; in the second period the percentage was 19.

Prices.—The following table shows the prices prescribed by the Board for liquid milk in the three contract periods. In the first and second periods the prices prescribed were those fixed by the Appointed Persons.

Liquid Milk.

Month.	First Contract. Period, Oct., 1933 to March, 1934.		Second Contract. Period, April to Sept., 1934.		Third Contract. Period, Oct., 1934 to Sept., 1935.
	South-Eastern Region.	All other Regions.	South-Eastern Region.	All other Regions.	All Regions.
	s. d.	s. d.	s. d.	s. d.	s. d.
October ...	1 4	1 3	—	—	1 4
November ...	1 4	1 4	—	—	1 4
December ...	1 5	1 4	—	—	1 5
January ...	1 5	1 4	—	—	1 5
February ...	1 4	1 4	—	—	1 6
March ...	1 9	1 2	—	—	1 4
April ...	—	—	1 1	1 0	1 4
May	—	—	1 0½*	1 0½*	1 0½*
June ...	—	—	1 0	1 0	1 0
July... ...	—	—	1 1	1 0	1 1
August ...	—	—	1 1	1 0	1 1
September ...	—	—	1 1	1 0	1 4

* The Board and the purchasers both agreed to contribute a levy of one-eighth of a penny per gallon on all milk sold through the Board in this month to provide funds for publicity.

The prices payable in respect of milk manufactured into milk products were as follows :—

Milk Utilised in Manufacture.

Milk manufactured into:—	Price per gallon.		
	Oct., 1933 to March, 1934.	April to Sept., 1934.	Oct., 1934 to Sept., 1935.
Butter ... ... Cheese* ... ... Condensed Milk for Export†	The average price per lb. for the previous month of Finest White Canadian Cheese and Finest White New Zealand Cheese less a sum of 1½d.		
	d.	d.	d.
Condensed Milk	6	6	6
Milk Powder	6	4½	4½
Fresh Cream	9‡	7½	7½
Tinned Cream	6‡	5	5
Chocolate	5	8	8
Sterilised Milk for Export	—	6	6
Soft Curd Cheese and Cream Cheese	—	—	7½
Ice Cream	—	—	7½
Other Milk Products ...	9	9	9

* As from 1st April, 1935, the Board may vary the formula for ascertaining the price of cheese in such manner as they think fit.

† During 1934-35, a minimum price of 4d. per gallon is operative in respect of milk manufactured into condensed milk for export.

‡ In March, 1934, the prices of fresh cream and tinned cream were reduced by the Appointed Persons to 7½d. and 5d. per gallon respectively.

Delivery.—Each contract provided that delivery could be made (1) direct to the purchaser's railway station or dairy, or (2) to a collecting depot approved by the Board, the producer paying in each case the costs of transport. Where milk was consigned to an approved depot, the purchaser was entitled to deduct from the purchase price an allowance for transit risks. Under the first contract, the allowance was ½d. per gallon; under the second contract it was ¾d. per gallon if the milk was subsequently delivered from the depot to any place in the South-Eastern region and 1d. per gallon if delivered elsewhere. The transit risk allowance in the third contract is ¾d. per gallon in all regions.

Conditions of Re-sale.

(a) *Re-sale by wholesale or semi-wholesale.*—In the first contract, the re-sale conditions applied only to re-sales by retail, but in the two subsequent contracts they were extended to cover minimum prices, according to quantity, at which the milk could be re-sold by wholesale or semi-wholesale. The second contract specified two quantity limits for this purpose: on re-sale up to and including 1,000 gallons per day it was required that the price should not be less than the wholesale buying price increased by 1d. per gallon, and on re-sale exceeding 1,000 gallons per day by ½d. per gallon. A more complete sub-division of the quantity basis was provided in the third contract.

(b) *Re-sale by retail.*—In the first contract period, the sale of milk by retail was governed by a clause inserted both in the wholesale contract and in the producer-retailers' licences that milk must not be sold at a price below the prevailing retail price in the district. The phrase "prevailing retail price" was not defined and neither prices nor districts were specified: instead, prices were left to be settled locally by retailers and producer-retailers. The system proved to be unsatisfactory in practice.

After reviewing the retail price position resulting from the operation of the first contract, the Consumers' Committee for England reported to the Minister that they were not prepared to accept as axiomatic the assumption that the fixing of wholesale prices necessitated the fixing of retail prices, though they appreciated that it might be difficult, under the scheme, to frame a satisfactory contract without some provision in regard to the minimum prices at which milk bought under the contract should be sold. But if it was necessary that the contract should contain such a provision, they suggested that it should be based, not on the prevailing retail price in the district, but on a minimum margin or margins above the wholesale price, and that the Board, in prescribing a minimum margin for any area, should base it upon a figure low enough to give no more than a reasonable return to the distributors in that area working under the most economical conditions or giving the least expensive services consistent with efficiency.

Accordingly, in the second contract the prevailing retail price clause was dropped and replaced by a clause providing that the purchaser would not sell by retail at less than a "minimum appropriate retail price," which was defined as a price exceeding the wholesale price by not less than specified minimum margins varying from 8d. per gallon in rural areas to 10d. per gallon in large cities.

In the third contract, minimum appropriate retail prices have been fixed for different areas as follows:—

	Urban districts with populations of less than 10,000 and all rural districts.	Urban districts, etc. with populations of 10,000 to 25,000.	Urban districts, etc. with populations exceeding 25,000.	
	All Regions.	All Regions.	South-Eastern Region.	All Regions except South-Eastern Region.
	s. d.	s. d.	s. d.	s. d.
Oct. 1934 ...	2 0	2 2	2 4	2 4
Nov. „ ...	2 0	2 2	2 4	2 4
Dec. „ ...	2 0	2 2	2 4	2 4
Jan. 1935 ...	2 0	2 2	2 4	2 4
Feb. „ ...	2 0	2 2	2 4	2 4
Mar. „ ...	2 0	2 2	2 4	2 4
Apl. „ ...	2 0	2 0	2 4	2 0
May „ ...	1 8	2 0	2 0	2 0
June „ ...	1 8	2 0	2 0	2 0
July „ ...	2 0	2 0	2 0	2 0
Aug. „ ...	2 0	2 0	2 0	2 0
Sept. „ ...	2 0	2 0	2 4	2 0

The retail price clauses of the second and third contracts contained an important proviso to the effect that the Board, if they thought fit, could reduce the minimum appropriate price in any area, if they received a resolution from the retailers in that area recommending a reduction. A resolution is deemed to have been duly passed if, in the opinion of the Board (whose decision is final), the persons voting in favour constituted a majority of the persons entitled to vote and represented the major part of the milk sold by retail in the area. In the third (the present) contract period, the Board have sanctioned reductions in some 276 districts, following the receipt of resolutions from local retailers.

The Consumers' Committee for England again considered the subject of retail prices as affected by the introduction of minimum margin arrangements and submitted a further report in which they expressed the view that the margins prescribed under the second contract were not low enough to make an allowance for the wide variations in the character and cost of the services rendered by different distributors.

In a subsequent letter to the Minister they added that the distributive margins secured under the minimum price arrangements of the third contract were, in general, even higher than those provided for in the second contract. An investigation into the costs and profits of milk distribution is now being undertaken by the Food Council.

Dividends and Discounts on Retail Sales.—Under the contracts, any registered Co-operative Society may return dividends on retail sales of milk where the dividend is payable not oftener than every three months. Other retailers may also allow their customers dividends or discounts on retail sales of milk payable not oftener than once in three months, and not exceeding the rate per £ actually paid on retail sales by any Co-operative Society operating in the district.

Sales of Contract Milk.—The numbers of wholesale contracts registered with the Board were 78,161 in the first contract period, 79,920 in the second contract period, and 63,264 in the third period. The total quantity of milk sold under the contracts during the year ended 30th September, 1934, was 716,248,568 gallons and of this quantity 523,630,238 gallons or 73 per cent. were sold for liquid consumption, and 192,618,330 gallons or 27 per cent. for manufacture.

The average prices received for the sale of milk for manufacture are shown in the following table :—

—	Gallonage.	Percentage of total quantity manufactured.	Realisation value per gallon (weighted Average).*
			pence.
Butter	41,100,607	21·44	3·61
Cheese	61,457,984	32·07	3·60
Condensed Milk	33,721,502	17·6	6·00
Condensed Milk for Export	5,844,207	3·03	3·62
Milk Powder	8,395,154	4·38	5·08
Fresh Cream	32,248,224	16·85	7·97
Tinned Cream	5,459,858	2·86	5·18
Other Products	4,390,794	1·77	9·00
Total or weighted Average	192,618,330	100·00	4·96

* Excluding repayable advances under the Milk Act, 1934. The average realisation value for the six months April to September, 1934, was, including the repayable advances, 5·56 pence per gallon.

The number of persons or firms purchasing milk under the wholesale contracts for the year ended 30th September, 1934, was 16,472 and the sum receivable by the Board under the terms of the contracts was £32,233,473.

Farm Cheesemakers.

The Milk Act, 1934, made provision for milk marketing boards to receive repayable advances in respect of milk manufactured into cheese on farms as well as in respect of milk manufactured into cheese in factories. The Board accordingly introduced, in the second contract period, a special farm cheesemakers' contract, and this arrangement has been continued, on terms more advantageous to the farm cheesemaker, in the third contract period.

In the second contract period, the net effect of the arrangement made between the Board and the farm cheesemakers was that the latter received in respect of their milk the advance accruing to the Board under the Milk Act, together with an additional allowance from the general funds of the Board of ½d. per lb. in the case of Caerphilly and soft cheese and 1d. per lb. in the case of other varieties of cheese. Under the present contract, the farm cheesemaker receives the advance accruing under the Milk Act, together with an allowance of 3d. per lb. in the first seven months and 2½d. per lb. in the last five months of the contract period, except in the case of Caerphilly or soft cheese where the allowance is at half these rates. He may also contract to make cheese over 12, 7 or 6 months, being free in the two latter cases to sell his milk in the other months.

The quantity of milk dealt with under the farm cheesemakers' contract during the six months April to September, 1934, was 18,846,042 gallons.

Producer-Retailers.

The scheme provides that no registered producer shall sell milk by retail except in accordance with the terms of a licence issued by the Board. The licence which was issued when the scheme came into operation was valid until 30th September, 1934. By a resolution of the Board, producer-retailers whose sales did not exceed one gallon a day were exempted from the licensing provisions. This resolution has since been rescinded with effect from the 1st October, 1934, and the position now is that every registered producer who sells milk by retail (except those who sell milk only to their employees for consumption in the employees' households) must be licensed by the Board. The new retail licence came into force in 1st October, 1934, and expires on 30th September, 1935. The main conditions of the producer-retailer's licence relate to (a) the contribution payable by the producer-retailer to the funds of the Board, and (b) the price at which the licensee may sell milk by retail.

As regards the latter, the first licence prohibited the producer-retailer from selling milk by retail at less than the prevailing retail price for his district. In the current licence, the producer-retailer is required to observe the same minimum appropriate retail prices as purchasers buying milk by wholesale.

The number of producer-retailers licensed by the Board on 31st December, 1934, was 69,100, and the average monthly gross contributions payable by them during the first year of the scheme were as under :—

Region.	*Average Contribution.* (pence per gallon.)
Northern	1·476
North-Western	1·648
Eastern	1·289
East-Midland	1·539
West-Midland	1·899
North Wales	1·711
South Wales	1·602
Southern	1·289
Mid-Western	1·742
Far-Western	1·886
South-Eastern	1·867
Average ...	1·582

If a producer-retailer sells no milk by wholesale, otherwise than on level delivery terms, he is entitled to the level delivery premium appropriate to his region in respect of his retail sales. The above averages do not take into account any level delivery premiums to which the producers may have been, and in most cases were, entitled.

The Finances of the Board—The Pooling Arrangements.

The moneys received by the Board under the scheme are dealt with each month in the following manner.

The Board are first required to debit each region with a general expenses levy, if any, in respect of each gallon of milk sold in the region. The purpose of this levy is to raise a fund to meet the expenses and liabilities of the Board, and to provide reserves. Next, the level delivery, special service and other premiums earned by registered producers are credited to the accounts of the producers concerned. Then, the inter-regional compensation levy, payable in respect of each gallon of milk sold for liquid milk consumption, is assessed and the appropriate amounts debited to each region. The object of this levy is to ensure that the pool prices do not vary unduly as between the regions by reason of the different quantities of milk sold for manufacturing purposes. The proceeds are distributed among the regions in such proportion as the Board think best, but they are under no obligation to secure that the pool prices shall be equalised in the various regions, and they may, in any month, defer the distribution of all, or part, of the proceeds of the levy until some later date.

The total amounts received by the Board for the sale of milk in each region, including any amounts due in respect of repayable advances under the Milk Act, 1934, are next credited to the regions concerned and, after making adjustments for any transport and freight charges which may be payable by individual producers, the net amounts then standing to the credit of the regional pools are distributed among the registered producers in the regions in proportion to the quantity of milk sold (other than by retail) by each registered producer, irrespective of the purpose for which the milk was, in fact, used.

General Expenses Levy.—During the first year of the scheme, the general expenses levy was at the rate of ½d. per gallon in ten out of the twelve months; in the other two months—May and June—no levy was charged but, as explained previously, producers and distributors each contributed ½d. per gallon in May to establish a fund for publicity purposes.

The actual cost of administering the scheme, including the expenses of its promotion and its administration at headquarters and in the regions, has worked out at one-twelfth of a penny per gallon. The remainder of the sum collected has been put to reserve.

Inter-Regional Compensation Levy.—The inter-regional compensation levy was fixed at the rate of 1d. per gallon in each month during the first year. In the early months, part of the proceeds were carried forward as a balance in the Inter-Regional Compensation Fund Account and used to supplement the apportionment in later months. The total amount collected and allocated during the year was approximately £2¼ million.

Repayable Advances under the Milk Act, 1934.—The amounts paid to the Board under the Milk Act in respect of repayable advances during the six months April to September, 1934, are shown below:—

Milk manufactured at factories (excluding the Board's factory).

	£
Butter	152,919
Cheese	238,815
Condensed milk for export ...	24,270
Milk powder	11,237
Total	£426,744
Milk used for farm cheese making ...	£70,467

The Regional Pool Prices.—A statement of the pool prices in each region for the year ended 30th September, 1934, together with those for October, November and December, 1934, is given on the following page.

Publicity Fund.—The sum realised for publicity through the May levies was £84,000. In accordance with the undertaking which is embodied in the terms of the wholesale contract, ten per cent. of this amount was reserved by the Board for research purposes and the balance, namely, £75,600, allocated for publicity through the National Milk Publicity Council.

Accounts of the Board.—Copies of the General Pool Account, the Inter-Regional Compensation Fund Account, the Income and Expenditure (General Expenses) Account and of the Board's Balance Sheet as at 31st March, 1934, are printed in Appendix III.

The Milk-in-Schools Movement.

This movement for increasing the sale of milk to schoolchildren represents an important development in the marketing of liquid milk. Its extension on a large scale has been made possible by the organisation of producers under milk marketing schemes and the facilities provided by Section 11 of the Milk Act, 1934, under which the Exchequer may contribute a sum not exceeding one-half the expenses incurred by a milk marketing board in carrying out any approved arrangements for increasing the demand for milk, subject to the total Exchequer expenditure on all approved schemes not exceeding £1,000,000, of which £860,000 has been allocated to England and Wales. The arrangements proposed by the Milk Marketing Board for England were formulated by an Advisory Committee under the Chairmanship of Lord Astor and, after approval by the Minister, came into operation on 1st October, 1934. Particulars of these arrangements, which were approved on 25th September, 1934, were laid before Parliament.* Briefly, they provide for the supply of milk to schoolchildren, for consumption on the school premises, at a reduced price of ½d. per one-third pint, the retailers agreeing to accept 6d. per gallon for their distributing services. Whenever possible, the milk is delivered in bottles and the source and quality of the supply is required to be approved by the appropriate Medical Officer. All full-time schools recognised for grant by the Board of Education are included in the scope of the scheme, as well as certain authorised courses of instruction for unemployed boys and girls under the Unemployment Act, 1934.

The returns so far available show that the scheme has been taken up with enthusiasm; it is estimated that nearly 6,000,000 gallons were consumed during the first three months, over 2½ million children receiving milk.

---

* No. 24–9999. H.M. Stationary Office.

[illegible]	[illegible]													[illegible]		
[illegible]	Oct.	Nov.	Dec.	Jan.	Feb.	Mar.	Apl.	May	June	July	Aug.	Sep.	[illegible]	Oct.	Nov.	Dec.
[illegible]	[illegible]	[illegible]	[illegible]	[illegible]	[illegible]	[illegible]	[illegible]	[illegible]	[illegible]	[illegible]	[illegible]	[illegible]	[illegible]	[illegible]	[illegible]	[illegible]
Average price for month	[illegible]	[illegible]	[illegible]	[illegible]	[illegible]	[illegible]	[illegible]	[illegible]	[illegible]	[illegible]	[illegible]	[illegible]	[illegible]	[illegible]	[illegible]	[illegible]

Accredited Producers Scheme.

The Board are required by the scheme to prepare, as soon as they think it practicable, a register of accredited producers who satisfy the Board that they are complying, and will continue to comply, with such conditions as may be prescribed for securing the purity and good quality of milk sold by them. To this end, the Board, in consultation with the County Councils' Association and the Association of Municipal Corporations, have formulated an Accredited Milk Scheme which will come into operation on 1st May, 1935. This scheme establishes a roll of accredited producers, and any registered producer who presents to the Board a Grade A Certificate given under the Milk (Special Designations) Order, 1928, will be entitled to have his name placed on the roll. A bonus, in addition to the pool price, will be paid monthly at the rate of 1d. per gallon to all accredited producers. The fund for payment of the bonus will be raised by a small levy on each gallon of milk sold by registered producers.

Producers of Grade A (T.T.) and Certified milk who sell their milk through the Board will be entitled to have their names entered on the roll.

Complaints regarding the Operation of the Scheme.

Consumers' Complaints.

Complaints by consumers related mainly to the retail price situation and were considered by the Consumers' Committee for England who, as stated previously, submitted two reports on this subject in 1934. They also reported upon a complaint of the Réunion des Gastronomes.

Other Complaints.

In 1934 the Minister directed the Committee of Investigation for England to consider and report to him upon two complaints as to the operation of the scheme and also upon the report of the Consumers' Committee relating to the complaint of the Réunion des Gastronomes.

The first of these complaints was made by the National Association of Creamery Proprietors. It related to the refusal of the Board to approve premises of certain members of the complainant Association as collecting depots for the purposes of the second contract (April to September, 1934). The Committee heard evidence from the Board and from the Association (both of whom were represented by Counsel and the main heads of their findings were :—

(i) The Board have a right to withhold their approval of collecting depots for good and sufficient reasons, and the general principles on which the Board proceeded were not unreasonable.

(ii) Having regard to the changes in trade, character and practice, the Board, in exercising this right, should have given the longest possible warning to enable buyers to effect any necessary re-adjustments. In deciding not to approve certain depots, the Board acted with somewhat undue haste and, in certain cases, acted arbitrarily.

(iii) The premises of three members of the Association should be placed on the approved list of depots for the second contract period, but the Board should be free to consider the approval of the premises of the reinstated cases for the ensuing contract period, provided due notice was given to the parties concerned. It should be open to any member of the Association whose premises were not on the approved list, and who was not heard by the Committee (and whose contracts had not been registered with the Board), to put forward evidence to the Milk Marketing Board in support of his claim to be placed on the same footing as the reinstated cases.

On being notified of the Committee's findings, the Board at once agreed to comply with (iii) above.

The second complaint was made by Amalgamated Master Dairymen, Ltd., and was to the effect that their members had been placed at a competitive disadvantage with large manufacturers of milk products by the action of the Board in restricting the allowance of manufacturing rebate to persons who buy at least 500 gallons per day and manufacture at least 300 gallons. The Association wished to have these restrictions entirely removed in regard to all milk manufactured into cream.

After hearing the parties, the Committee found that, to the extent that the restrictions imposed by the Milk Marketing Board prevented small manufacturers from claiming a rebate, the action of the Board might fairly be said to be contrary to the interests of Amalgamated Master Dairymen, Ltd. The Committee were, however, of the opinion that the action of the Board was justified, that it was in the interests of milk producers and milk manufacturers as a whole, and might, therefore, be said to have been in the public interest.

The Réunion des Gastronomes claimed that their members, who are concerned in the hotel and restaurant trade, should receive the manufacturing rebates in respect of milk used in their kitchens, notwithstanding the fact that the members were not in a position to comply with the requirements as to the purchase of 500 gallons per day and the manufacture of 300 gallons. The Consumers' Committee reported that, so far as the interests of consumers, as defined in Section 9 (6) of the Agricultural Marketing Act, 1931, were concerned, they saw no reason for recommending any departure from the arrangements made by the Board for the supply of milk to members of the Réunion. They added that the question whether there was a case for altering the arrangements in the interests of the hotel and restaurant trade did not appear to fall within their province.

The Report of the Consumers' Committee was referred to the Committee of Investigation for England who, on the evidence and arguments submitted to them on behalf of the parties, found that the action of the Milk Marketing Board of which complaint was made was reasonable, and that there was no justification for the complaint in the form in which it was referred to the Committee. On the broader issue, which was raised by the Réunion at the hearing, that their members are now having to pay higher prices for milk than in pre-scheme days, the Committee found (i) that it might be said that the provisions of the scheme in regard to prices and the action of the Board in putting these provisions into effect were contrary to the interests of members of the Réunion, but (ii) that the relevant provisions of the scheme and the action of the Board in putting them into force were in the interests of milk producers as a whole and might therefore, in the absence of counter-balancing considerations, be said to be in the public interest.

Miscellaneous.

Manufacturing operations of the Board.—Subject to certain exceptions and conditions, the Board are under an obligation to accept all milk for which a registered producer is unable to find a customer upon the terms of the contract prescribed by the Board. Owing to a concentration of unsold milk in the Cumberland district in the spring of 1934, the Board decided to purchase and equip a factory at Aspatria for the manufacture of Cheddar cheese. The factory commenced operations in April, and the quantity of milk manufactured during the six months ending on 30th September, 1934, was 805,000 gallons. The number of producers supplying the factory was 108.

Scottish Milk.—Before the scheme came into operation, considerable quantities of Scottish milk were available to English buyers at rates generally below those at which milk of English production could be bought. The cheaper supplies of Scottish milk continued to be sold in the English market after the English Milk Scheme came into operation, and, in consequence, an arrangement was made between the English and Scottish Milk Boards whereby the

English Board agreed to compensate the Scottish Board for milk withheld from the English market.

Fresh Cream.—Arrangements have also been made between the chief manufacturers of cream in England, Scotland, Northern Ireland and the Irish Free State with regard to the rates at which fresh cream shall be sold by wholesale. The agreement originally made took effect from 10th July, 1934. A second agreement operated from 29th October, 1934, and was superseded by a third on 5th January, 1935.

Contraventions of the Scheme.—In pursuance of the Agricultural Marketing Act, 1931, the scheme provides that the Board shall impose upon every registered producer who contravenes any provision of the scheme, such monetary penalties, not exceeding the maximum laid down, as the Board think just. The number of penalties imposed by the Board since the commencement of the scheme and up to the 30th November, 1934, was 418, amounting in the aggregate to £6,050.

Expenses of Promoting the Scheme.—A certificate under Section 22 (2) of the Agricultural Marketing Act, 1933, was given by the Minister on 6th March, 1934, in respect of expenditure amounting to £1,995 incurred by the National Farmers' Union in connection with the promotion, submission and bringing into operation of the scheme.

"*The Home Farmer*".—In order to keep registered producers fully acquainted with the progress of the scheme, the Board have circulated a journal monthly to their registered producers. The first issue of this journal, which is called "The Home Farmer", was made in May, 1934.

[illegible]

[illegible]

	[illegible]			[illegible]			Total Gallonage.	Per cent. Legal.	Per cent. [illegible]
	Under Wholesale Contracts.	By Licensed Persons Retailing.	Total.	Under Wholesale Contracts.	[illegible]	Total.			
[illegible]									
6th October to 31st October	[illegible]	[illegible]	[illegible]	[illegible]	—	[illegible]	[illegible]	[illegible]	[illegible]
November	[illegible]	[illegible]	[illegible]	[illegible]	—	[illegible]	[illegible]	[illegible]	[illegible]
December	[illegible]	[illegible]	[illegible]	[illegible]	—	[illegible]	[illegible]	[illegible]	[illegible]
[illegible]									
January	[illegible]	[illegible]	[illegible]	[illegible]	—	[illegible]	[illegible]	[illegible]	[illegible]
February	[illegible]	[illegible]	[illegible]	[illegible]	—	[illegible]	[illegible]	[illegible]	[illegible]
March	[illegible]	[illegible]	[illegible]	[illegible]	—	[illegible]	[illegible]	[illegible]	[illegible]
April	[illegible]	[illegible]	[illegible]	[illegible]	[illegible]	[illegible]	[illegible]	[illegible]	[illegible]
May	[illegible]	[illegible]	[illegible]	[illegible]	[illegible]	[illegible]	[illegible]	[illegible]	[illegible]
June	[illegible]	[illegible]	[illegible]	[illegible]	[illegible]	[illegible]	[illegible]	[illegible]	[illegible]
July	[illegible]	[illegible]	[illegible]	[illegible]	[illegible]	[illegible]	[illegible]	[illegible]	[illegible]
August	[illegible]	[illegible]	[illegible]	[illegible]	[illegible]	[illegible]	[illegible]	[illegible]	[illegible]
September	[illegible]	[illegible]	[illegible]	[illegible]	[illegible]	[illegible]	[illegible]	[illegible]	[illegible]
Total for [illegible]	[illegible]	[illegible]	[illegible]	[illegible]	[illegible]	[illegible]	[illegible]	[illegible]	[illegible]
[illegible]									
October	[illegible]	[illegible]	[illegible]	[illegible]	[illegible]	[illegible]	[illegible]	[illegible]	[illegible]
November	[illegible]	[illegible]	[illegible]	[illegible]	[illegible]	[illegible]	[illegible]	[illegible]	[illegible]
December	[illegible]	[illegible]	[illegible]	[illegible]	[illegible]	[illegible]	[illegible]	[illegible]	[illegible]

THE POTATO MARKETING SCHEME, 1933

The Potato Marketing Scheme, which applies to Great Britain, came into force on 21st December, 1933, following affirmative resolutions of the House of Lords on 12th December and the House of Commons on 20th December. The initial poll of registered producers was held in January, 1934, and of the registered producers voting 90·44 per cent., representing 90·6 per cent. of productive capacity, were in favour of the scheme, which accordingly came into full operation at the end of the suspensory period on 9th March, 1934. To provide funds for the conduct of the initial poll, the Minister of Agriculture and Fisheries and the Secretary of State for Scotland sanctioned a loan to the Potato Marketing Board of £8,300 from the Agricultural Marketing Funds. The loan was not taken up as the Board made other arrangements with their bankers.

The Potato Marketing Scheme is designed to improve and stabilise returns to potato growers and to promote marketing efficiency. Unlike its immediate predecessors, the Pigs, Bacon and Milk Schemes, it is not modelled upon the recommendations of a Reorganisation Commission but is the work of the producers' own representatives. The marketing powers with which the Board have been endowed are almost entirely regulatory in character.

The first Board held office until 31st October, 1934, and consisted of the members named in the scheme, together with two members nominated by the Minister and the Secretary of State, namely, Mr. W. Gavin, C.B.E., and Capt. the Hon. James Gray Stuart, M.V.O., M.C., M.P. In accordance with the scheme, the Board appointed an Executive Committee of seven of their members, an Advisory Committee for Scotland and a Retailers' Committee. The other Committees appointed by the Board were the Merchants' Authorization Committee and the Basic Acreage Committee. The Executive Committee have appointed a number of sub-committees to assist them in different phases of their work.

The first annual election of members of the Board was held in October, 1934. All the sitting district members of the Board in England and Wales were returned unopposed. In Scotland, there were ten candidates for six vacancies and, of the six elected, two were new members. At the subsequent general meeting of registered producers five members of the original Board were elected as special members; four of these were merchants. After consultation with the Market Supply Committee and with the approval of the Minister and the Secretary of State, the Board appointed Mr. Gavin and the Hon. J. G. Stuart to serve as co-opted members.

The remuneration of members of the Board voted by the registered producers at the annual general meeting was as under :—

	£
Chairman	1,500
Vice-Chairman	850
Members of the Executive Committee	600
Chairman of the Basic Acreage Committee ...	200
Other members of Basic Acreage Committee ...	150
Chairman of the Merchants' Authorization Committee	300
Other members of the Merchants' Authorization Committee	250
Other members of the Board	100

Registered Producers.—The numbers of producers registered with the Board as at 31st December, 1934, and their aggregate potato acreage were :—

	Number.	*Potato Acreage.*
England and Wales	52,708	427,300
Scotland	14,719	115,600
	67,427	542,900

Producers whose potato acreage is less than one acre are exempt from registration under the scheme.

The machinery of market regulation.

Since the powers of the Board are largely regulatory they can only be effective if based on accurate, full and up-to-date information and if backed by adequate "policing" powers. The Board have appointed a number of regional supervisors whose duties are to establish contact with and give guidance to producers and merchants, to verify producers' basic acreages, to visit markets and to keep the Board posted with detailed information. Market supervisors have also been appointed for several of the larger wholesale markets. The work of this marketing staff is co-ordinated at the Board's headquarters.

The Board depend largely upon the collaboration of wholesale merchants for the effective working of the scheme. Accordingly, they have introduced a system of authorizing merchants, as described later. The chief condition of authorization is that merchants shall co-operate with the Board in securing the observance of their determinations prescribing what potatoes may be sold and how they may be sold.

Regulation of the marketed supply.

This country is practically self-sufficient as regards the supply of maincrop potatoes. In the past, the chief cause of loss to potato growers has been the tendency, in years when the yield per acre has been above the average, for even a small surplus to be accompanied by a disproportionate fall in producers' prices.

The Board have powers under the scheme to regulate the marketed supply of potatoes in two ways—they may determine the description of potatoes that may be sold by registered producers, and by this power they can prohibit the sale for human consumption of potatoes capable of passing through a riddle of a prescribed gauge; or if, after estimating the total quantity of potatoes likely to be available for human consumption during any year beginning 1st September, they consider that there is likely to be a substantial excess over demand, they may determine the quantity of potatoes which registered producers may sell for human consumption. The scheme provides that, unless the Board otherwise determine, potatoes of the description "smalls", that is to say potatoes (other than new potatoes) which are capable of passing through a square mesh of 1½ inches, shall not be sold for human consumption during the period commencing on 1st September in any year and ending on 31st July next following.

The Board began operations in March, 1934, towards the end of a season of heavy production, when it was scarcely possible to do much to improve the situation. Nevertheless, a regulation prohibiting sales for human consumption of potatoes of less than 1⅝ inches or 1¾ inches in diameter, according to varieties, was issued on 10th April, 1934, and continued in force until 31st July. The introduction of this minimum size was followed by some strengthening of prices.

Preliminary estimates of the 1934 maincrop indicated that production was likely to be about the average for the preceding ten years. For some time after the crop came on the market the Board did not find it necessary to bring any special regulation into force, but the prohibition of the sale of "smalls" for human consumption operated from 1st September, 1934, as provided in the scheme. On 6th December, however, the Board made a determination prohibiting the sale for human consumption of potatoes capable of passing through meshes varying from 1⅝ inches to 1⅞ inches according to varieties and districts. The object of the regulation was to strengthen the market, check overloading of supplies and create a higher level of grading.

During the present season, the Board have begun to purchase in Scotland certain quantities of potatoes for future delivery, with a view to relieving the price situation in that country.

In connection with the regulation of the market supply, valuable data are provided by the census of stocks remaining on farms which is taken at intervals by the Board.

The quantitative regulation of home supplies has been accompanied by the regulation of imports. A system of control by voluntary arrangements with exporting countries was in operation when the Board took office, and continued until the end of October, 1934. Since 8th November, 1934, a system of regulation of imports by

Order* of the Board of Trade has been in force; no potatoes may now be imported from the Irish Free State or foreign countries except under licence. An association of potato importers has been formed to facilitate the granting of licences, but, if they so desire, non-members may apply for a licence direct to the Board of Trade. The quantities of imports permitted are fixed from time to time by the Board of Trade after consultation with the Market Supply Committee and the Departments concerned, and after consideration of actual and prospective market conditions.

The Potato Marketing Board have from the outset kept in close touch with Government Departments in connection with import regulation. They have also come to an arrangement with the Government of Northern Ireland and the principal potato exporting interests in that country, whereby, except in special circumstances, not more than 200,000 tons will be shipped annually to Great Britain. Finally, the Board have been in negotiation with the authorities and representatives of agriculture in Jersey, and with exporters in Spain, with a view to securing that exports from these countries shall end at an earlier date than has hitherto been customary.

The disposal of surplus.

The Board have power to buy and sell surplus potatoes, which are defined in the scheme as potatoes which registered producers are prohibited from selling for human consumption in Great Britain or potatoes which, in the opinion of the Board, are not required or are not likely to be required for human consumption. In connection with their general powers to encourage, promote or conduct agricultural education, research and co-operation with respect to potatoes and products derived therefrom, the Board may maintain laboratories, workshops and factories, and they may carry out experiments and employ skilled, professional and technical advisers.

As a first step towards the disposal of surplus, a sub-committee has been appointed to investigate the possibility of industrial utilisation of potatoes, and schemes for the manufacture of farina and for drying potatoes for stock feed have already been considered.

The Excess Acreage Levy.

If, in the opinion of the Board, their expenditure in the operation of the scheme is likely to be increased as a result of plantings by registered producers in excess of their "basic acreages", the Board may require the producers concerned to pay a special, non-recurring, levy not exceeding £5 per acre in respect of their excess acreage.

Generally, the basic acreage of a registered producer is the maximum number of acres in his occupation in 1934, which were under

* The Potato (Import Regulation) Order, 1934 (S.R. & O. 1934, No. 1160).

potatoes in 1933; but a producer has the option of selecting as an alternative, within a stated time after the date of his registration, either the average acreage he had under potatoes in the years 1931, 1932 and 1933, or the largest acreage (subject to a maximum of 7 acres) he had in any of those years. The acreage under potatoes in Great Britain in 1933 was 671,000 acres, the highest recorded since 1922.

In April, 1934, the Board announced that they would require each registered producer, who planted in excess of his basic acreage, to pay a levy of £5 per acre on his excess acreage. The excess plantings on which levy has been assessed amount to about 3,000 acres, or about one-half of one per cent. of the aggregate basic acreage of registered producers, which at 30th November, 1934, was:—

	Acres.
England and Wales	488,000
Scotland	138,000
Total	626,000

Market Intelligence Service.

Local and temporary maladjustments of supplies and demand frequently arise during the season as a result of growers' lack of confidence in market conditions due mainly to insufficient information. The Board have developed an extensive system of market intelligence based on weekly reports of their supervisors. With the aid of these, and of a periodic census of stocks remaining on farms, they are able to give valuable information and advice to growers and to the trade by means of direct communications, press notices, and weekly bulletins which are posted in a large number of markets. The information service given to the Press is particularly noteworthy. A full statement of prices in all areas of Great Britain accompanied by a survey of the current market conditions is issued weekly to the agricultural press and a number of other journals throughout Great Britain.

Measures to improve trading conditions and practices.

Prohibition of Sales on Commission.—The scheme provides that the Board may restrict or prohibit sales on commission, provided that an affirmative vote of registered producers is first obtained. The Board held a poll on 24th May, 1934, on the question whether sales on commission should be prohibited and the result was declared on 11th July. Of the votes admitted 78·90 per cent. were in favour of prohibition and 21·10 per cent. were against. (The productive capacities represented were 82·43 per cent. and 17·57 per cent. respectively.) The Board accordingly determined that commission sales should be prohibited from 1st September, 1934, except in certain cases, the most important being that of auctions approved by the Board.

Terms to be included in contracts for sale by registered producers.—Under their powers to determine the terms on which registered producers may sell potatoes, the Board prescribed, in August, 1934, certain conditions which registered producers must include in all contracts for the sale of potatoes (other than seed potatoes). In addition to the requirement that the contract shall state the net price payable by the purchaser, the principal conditions so prescribed were as follows:—

(i) that the contract shall be unenforceable in respect of potatoes of any description the sale of which by registered producers may be prohibited by the Board after the contract has been made and before it is performed;

(ii) that disputes between the registered producer and the purchaser shall be referred to arbitration;

(iii) that the purchaser shall not re-sell any description of potatoes which registered producers are prohibited from selling by or under the scheme;

(iv) that the Board shall be entitled to recover, through the purchaser, any debt owed to them by the registered producer.

Further conditions, prescribed in November, 1934, were:—

(v) that the purchaser shall not (subject to certain exemptions) arrange to re-sell the potatoes on commission;

(vi) that any contract for re-sale shall fix a net price.

Sales through Authorized Merchants.—By virtue of their powers to determine the persons to, or through the agency of whom, registered producers may sell potatoes, the Board adopted a resolution on 16th August, 1934, as a result of which registered producers have been prohibited, since 1st November, 1934, from selling potatoes except to merchants authorized by the Board, save in the case of the important classes of sales which are exempted by the scheme from determinations of this sort. These exemptions are:—

(*a*) sales of seed potatoes;

(*b*) sales of potatoes in lots of one hundredweight or less, when each sale is a separate transaction;

(*c*) sales of potatoes by the producer himself, or his whole-time employee, at statutory markets, or in other markets approved by the Board;

(*d*) sales of new potatoes;

(*e*) sales of potatoes for manufacture by the purchaser;

(*f*) sales of potatoes to Government Departments and local authorities, to hospitals, schools, etc., and to hotels, restaurants, etc.; and sales of potatoes to retailers.

A first list of authorized merchants was issued at the end of October, and will be supplemented from time to time by further lists. The number of mechants authorized as at 30th November, 1934, was 2,890.

The chief conditions to be observed by authorized merchants are that they shall not buy from producers whom they have grounds for believing to be neither registered nor exempted from registration under the scheme; that they shall afford facilities to the Board for inspecting consignments of potatoes, and collecting sums due to them from registered producers; and that they shall not buy from registered producers (except in certain exempted classes of sales) other than on the terms which the Board prescribe from time to time for the sale of potatoes by registered producers.

Retail Trade.—Contact with the retail section of the trade is maintained through the Retailers' Committee. The Board have no powers to determine retail prices, but they are, nevertheless, concerned to safeguard their registered producers against the effects of undercutting in the retail market.

Measures to stimulate consumption.

With the object of increasing the consumption of potatoes, the Board have conducted an energetic publicity campaign which has taken the following forms:—the issue of display posters to retailers; the publication of recipe books (the latest of these has had a wide sale, and has been placed on the L.C.C. approved list); press publicity in news items and editorial comment; displays at shows; and propaganda in the hotel and catering trade.

Miscellaneous.

The Finances of the Board.—Copies of the Income and Expenditure Account and of the Board's Balance Sheet as at 31st August, 1934, are printed in Appendix III. The Balance Sheet does not, however, give an accurate picture of the state of the Board's finances because at the time when it was drawn up the Board had made no levy on producers, their expenses being defrayed out of a loan from their bankers.

A levy at the rate of 5s. per acre planted with potatoes was made on all registered producers in September, 1934. A further levy of £5 per acre is payable by those registered producers who have planted in excess of their basic acreage.

The first year's income accruing from these levies will be called upon to pay for eighteen months' expenditure, including certain non-recurring items such as the expenses of promoting the scheme. The greater part of these levies has already been received by the Board, which now has a substantial credit balance.

Grant for Research.—The Board have agreed to make a grant not exceeding £200 for the purpose of assisting special research work in connection with greenfly and virus disease.

Penalties.—The Board have imposed penalties in six cases (five in England and one in Scotland) where registered producers had contravened the scheme. The total amount of the penalties was £60.

ABERDEEN AND DISTRICT MILK MARKETING SCHEME, 1933.

As stated in the Report for 1933, this scheme, applicable to the counties of Aberdeen and Kincardine, was submitted under the authority of Section 19 (3) of the Agricultural Marketing Act, 1931, by the Aberdeen and District Milk Agency.

The scheme, as modified after the public inquiry, received resolutions of approval from both Houses of Parliament, and an Approval Order* by the Secretary of State was made on 28th March, 1934, bringing the scheme into force on the following day.

Pending the declaration of the result of the initial poll, the Board was composed of the members of the Committee of Management of the Agency together with Mr. James A. Mackie, Marchmont, Rubislaw Den South, Aberdeen, and Mr. James G. Singer, 80, Guild Street, Aberdeen, who were appointed by the Secretary of State. A loan of £500 was made to the Board from the Agricultural Marketing (Scotland) Fund to meet expenses in connection with the poll. Of the producers voting at the poll, 70 per cent. (representing 67 per cent. of productive capacity) were in favour of the scheme. The result of the poll was announced on 28th June, 1934, and, as provided in the scheme, four additional members were thereafter elected to the Board as the representatives of producers who are not members of the Agency. On expiry of the suspensory period, the scheme became fully operative on 1st August, 1934.

The marketing provisions of the scheme are based on those of the Scottish Milk Marketing Scheme and the regulations governing the sale of milk under the co-operative marketing arrangements organized by the Aberdeen and District Milk Agency. Subject to the provision for exempting small producers from registration under the scheme, each producer, excluding producer-retailers and producers of Certified milk, is allotted a basic quantity of milk, to be determined by reference to his average production of milk for sale during the three winter months November to January, and receives payment monthly therefor at an average price per gallon, whether or not the milk has been sold for consumption in liquid form or sold or used by the Board for manufacturing purposes. The difference between the Standard Price (i.e. the prescribed price for the sale of untreated milk to distributors) and the average price represents the amount of the contribution payable by the producer to the Board in respect of his basic quantity. Payment for milk supplied in excess of a producer's basic quantity is made by the Board at a "surplus" price less a con-

* The Aberdeen and District Milk Marketing Scheme (Approval) Order, 1934. (S.R. & O. 1934, No. $\frac{309}{S. 21}$).

tribution per gallon assessed at the same rate as the contribution in respect of the producer's basic supply.

In the initial period of operation of the scheme, each producer who is a member of the Agency has been allotted the basic quantity assigned to him under the Agency's arrangements. The basic quantity for a producer who is not a member of the Agency has been determined at the full amount of his sales of milk for liquid consumption prior to the inception of the scheme.

Producer-retailers and producers of Certified milk are granted partial exemption from the provisions of the scheme requiring the sale of milk to or through the agency of the Board and are thus allowed to make their own arrangements for the sale of their milk. They are required to furnish monthly returns of their sales and to pay to the Board such contribution per cow as may be fixed from time to time by the Board. Milk produced by them in excess of the requirements of their customers is accepted by the Board and is paid for at the net " surplus " price.

As the contracts entered into by the Aberdeen and District Milk Agency prior to the commencement of the scheme for the period ended 31st October provided for payment by distributors of a Standard Price of 1s. 2d. per gallon, and, by agreement, for a retail price of 2s. per gallon, the Board prescribed these prices for the sale of milk under the provisions of the scheme during that period. On the failure of the Board and the representatives of the distributors to reach agreement with respect to the prices for the new contract period, the prices on the foregoing scale were continued until 31st December, 1934.

For the period 1st January to 31st October, 1935, the Board have determined the Standard Price at 1s. 3d. per gallon in each month excluding June, July and August when it will be reduced to 1s. 2d. per gallon. A special Standard Price of 1s. 4d. per gallon has been prescribed for the period in respect of sales to distributors in Peterhead where, it is stated, the distributive margin has always been less than in other parts of the area of the scheme. The retail price throughout the area during the year has been fixed at 2s. per gallon, but the Board have under consideration the reduction of that price in rural areas.

The total number of producers registered under the scheme as at 30th November was 878, of whom 479 were producers selling milk to or through the agency of the Board, 392 were producer-retailers and 7 were producers of Certified milk.

The following statement gives particulars (1) of the sales of milk by the registered producers in each month during the period ended 30th November, and (2) of the purposes for which the milk was sold.

——	August.	September.	October.	November.	Total.
Sales by the registered producers:	*Gallons.*	*Gallons.*	*Gallons.*	*Gallons.*	*Gallons.*
To or through the agency of the Board	503,613	483,150	506,403	493,144	1,986,310
Producer-retailers	128,710	121,559	102,785	129,109	482,163
Producers of Certified milk	10,485	10,699	10,707	10,925	42,816
TOTAL ...	642,808	615,408	619,895	633,178	2,511,289
Purposes for which the milk was sold:—					
Liquid milk consumption within area of scheme ...	503,763	477,646	474,040	484,486	1,939,935
Liquid milk consumption outwith area of scheme ...	112,724	120,240	127,094	127,982	487,990
Manufacture ...	26,321	17,522	18,761	20,760	83,364
TOTAL ...	642,808	615,408	619,895	633,178	2,511,289

The milk supplied to the Board in excess of the amount required by the liquid milk markets was diverted to the creamery of the Aberdeen and District Milk Agency for the manufacture, on the Board's behalf, of butter, cheese and cream. The milk so diverted included supplies by producers in excess of the basic quantities amounting to 8,504 gallons in August, 10,494 gallons in September, 13,902 gallons in October and 17,617 gallons in November.

The Board paid to the producers for each of the four months an average price of 1s. per gallon in respect of their basic quantities of milk and an average price of 6d. per gallon for milk supplied in excess of these quantities. These prices were net prices, the producer's contribution to the Board having been assessed for each of the four months at the rate of 2d. per gallon.

The contributions by producer-retailers and producers of Certified milk to the Board in respect of each of the four months were assessed at the rate of £2 per cow per annum calculated on the returns of their sales and taking the average production at two gallons per cow per day.

NORTH OF SCOTLAND MILK MARKETING SCHEME, 1934.

The submission of this scheme, which applies to the counties of Inverness, Nairn, Ross and Cromarty, Sutherland and Caithness, was referred to in the report for 1933.

In accordance with the conditions on which objections made to the scheme were withdrawn, modifications of its provisions in certain particulars were made by the Secretary of State. Resolutions approving the scheme were passed by both Houses of Parliament on 5th July, 1934, and, in terms of the Approval Order* of the Secretary of State, the scheme came into force on 7th July.

The Secretary of State appointed Mr. John Ross of Messrs. Macrae, Flett and Rennie, W.S., 57, Castle Street, Edinburgh, and Mr. W. D. Munro, Overskibo, Clashmore, Dornoch, as members of the first Board.

A loan of £500 was made to the Board from the Agricultural Marketing (Scotland) Fund to provide for expenses incurred in connection with the initial poll.

At the poll, 72·8 per cent. of the registered producers voting (representing 75·6 per cent. of productive capacity) were in favour of the scheme which was accordingly brought into full operation on 1st October, 1934.

After consideration of representations made on behalf of producers in the Western Islands of the counties of Inverness and Ross and Cromarty, the Board decided, by resolution, to exempt all producers in these islands from registration under the scheme.

The marketing provisions of the scheme are based largely on those of the Aberdeen and District Milk Marketing Scheme, but they extend the principle of allocation of basic quantities to all classes of producers except producers of Certified and Grade A (T.T.) milk. The producers of milk of these special grades receive payment at not less than the Standard Price (i.e. the price per gallon fixed by the Board for the sale of untreated milk to distributors) less the appropriate amount of the contribution payable by the "pooling" producers for all milk produced by them in excess of the requirements of their customers and sold to or through the agency of the Board. The contributions payable by producer-retailers and producers of Certified and Grade A (T.T.) milk, in respect of the sales made under their own arrangements are determined in the proportions of 7/10ths and 9/10ths respectively of the rate of contribution per gallon payable by the other producers. For the initial period of operation of the scheme, the producers' basic quantities were determined by the Board in accordance with returns supplied by the producers of the quantities of milk produced by them for sale during the period 1st September to 31st December, 1933.

The Board have general powers under the scheme, conferred in accordance with Section 10 of the Agricultural Marketing Act, 1933, to determine the quantity of milk or any description thereof, other than Certified or Grade A (T.T.) milk, that may be sold by any registered producer. It is understood, however, that these powers are not likely to be exercised under existing conditions.

* The North of Scotland Milk Marketing Scheme (Approval) Order, 1934. (S.R. & O. 1934, No. $\frac{708}{S.42}$).

The following prices were determined by the Board for the period ended 31st December, 1934 :—

Standard Price :—

1s. 2½d. per gallon.

Retail Prices :—

To domestic consumers—2s. per gallon.

To Institutions, etc., other than Charitable Institutions—1s. 6d. per gallon.

To Charitable Institutions not rate-aided (including haulage charges)—1s. 4d. per gallon.

The prices for Grade A (T.T.) milk and Certified milk were fixed by the Board at 2d. per gallon and 4d. per gallon respectively more than the price of ordinary milk.

The total number of producers registered under the scheme as at 31st December was 399 of whom 133 were producers selling milk to or through the agency of the Board, 256 were producer-retailers and 10 were producers of Certified and Grade A (T.T.) milk.

The following statement gives particulars (1) of the sales of milk by the registered producers during the period ended 31st December and (2) of the purposes for which the milk was sold.

	October.	*November.*	*December.*	*Total.*
Sales by the registered producers:—	*Gallons.*	*Gallons*	*Gallons.*	*Gallons.*
To or through the agency of the Board	66,294	59,881	61,982	188,157
Producer-retailers... ...	73,807	65,955	68,644	208,406
Producers of Certified and Grade A (T.T.) milk ...	10,321	12,053	11,229	33,603
Total	150,422	137,889	141,855	430,166
Purposes for which the milk was sold:—				
Liquid milk consumption	135,993	126,664	129,668	392,325
Manufacture	14,429	11,225	12,187	37,841
Total	150,422	137,889	141,855	430,166

The average "pooled" prices paid to producers in respect of their basic quantities of milk sold to or through the agency of the Board were 1s. 1½d. in the months of October and November and 1s. 1d. in the month of December, the producers' contribution to the Board having been assessed at the rate of 1d. per gallon for October and November and 1½d. per gallon for December.

The Secretary of State approved arrangements made by the Board under Section 11 of the Milk Act, 1934, for the supply of milk at reduced rates to schools, within the area of the scheme. These arrangements, which are similar to those made by the Scottish Milk Marketing Board, came into operation on 10th December.

PART II.

SCHEMES SUBMITTED BUT NOT YET IN OPERATION.

The following schemes which have been submitted since the date of the last report are not yet in force.

—	*Date of Notice of Submission.*	*Area of Scheme.*
Sugar Marketing Scheme.	9th February, 1934.	Great Britain.
Moray and Banff Milk Marketing Scheme.	1st May, 1934.	Counties of Moray and Banff.
Sugar Beet Marketing Scheme.	11th May, 1934.	Great Britain.
Argyll Milk Marketing Scheme.	6th July, 1934.	Parts of Argyll not included in Scottish Milk Marketing Scheme.
Scottish Raspberry Marketing Scheme.	11th December, 1934.	Scotland.

SUGAR AND SUGAR BEET DRAFT MARKETING SCHEMES.

In announcing, in July, 1933, the decision of the Government to continue as a temporary measure the subsidy on home grown sugar for one year after the expiry of the period covered by the British Sugar (Subsidy) Act, 1925, the Minister of Agriculture and Fisheries said that the decision was based on the understanding that the refiners and beet-sugar manufacturing interests would co-operate in submitting an agricultural marketing scheme, and that they would be prepared to co-operate with the growers of sugar beet in the promotion of a development scheme, under which the operations of sugar manufacture, refining and processing could be rationalized in the interests of greater productive efficiency. The General Committee of the United Kingdom Sugar Industry, which represented refining interests and beet-sugar manufacturers, submitted a Sugar Marketing Scheme in February, 1934. The National Farmers' Unions of England and Scotland submitted a Sugar Beet Marketing Scheme in May, 1934.

The principal provisions of the draft Sugar Marketing Scheme relate to the allocation of selling quotas for refined sugar produced in Great Britain. Notice of the submission of the scheme was published on 9th February, 1934, and a public inquiry into the objections received was held in London by Mr. Joshua Scholefield, K.C., from 1st to 9th May, 1934.

The draft Sugar Beet Marketing Scheme contains provisions (somewhat similar to the regulatory provisions of the Pigs Marketing Scheme) to regulate the marketing of sugar beet produced in Great Britain. Notice of submission was published on 11th May, 1934, and the public inquiry into objections was held on 30th and 31st July in London, by Mr. F. J. Wrottesley, K.C.

Further action with regard to the draft schemes has been suspended pending consideration of the report* of the Committee, under the Chairmanship of Mr. Wilfrid Greene, K.C., which was appointed by the Chancellor of the Exchequer and the Minister of Agriculture and Fisheries to inquire into the condition of the sugar industry in the United Kingdom.

MORAY AND BANFF MILK DRAFT MARKETING SCHEME.

This draft scheme, applicable to the counties of Moray and Banff, was submitted by a Committee appointed for the purpose by a general meeting of producers and acting with the written approval and concurrence of 76 producers. Its provisions are substantially similar to those of the original drafts of the Aberdeen and District and the North of Scotland Milk Marketing Schemes. The period for lodging objections and representations with respect to the scheme expired on 13th June, 1934. Such objections as were made with respect to the scheme were withdrawn after discussion between the Committee and the objectors, and it was therefore unnecessary to hold a public inquiry. The Committee explained, however, that in view partly of informal representations made on behalf of certain producers, they desired to have the opportunity of considering and proposing modifications in the scheme. Consideration of the draft scheme has, therefore, been deferred pending submission of these proposals.

ARGYLL MILK DRAFT MARKETING SCHEME.

This draft scheme was submitted on 8th June, 1934, for application to that part of the county of Argyll, including the Islands, situated outwith the area of the Scottish Milk Marketing Scheme. It was explained that the scheme had been prepared primarily with a view to securing for farm cheesemakers, numbering about 28, within that part of the county, the payments from the Exchequer under Section 3 of the Milk Act, 1934, in respect of milk converted into cheese at farms. The scheme provides for the exemption from registration of any producer who does not either manufacture milk into cheese at his farm or sell milk to a manufacturer of milk products.

The statutory notice of the submission of the scheme was published and no representations or objections with respect to it were received. At the request of the promoters, further consideration of the scheme has been deferred.

---

* Cmd. 4871.

SCOTTISH RASPBERRY DRAFT MARKETING SCHEME.

A draft scheme for regulating the marketing of raspberries grown in Scotland was submitted on 1st December, 1934. Apart from minor adjustments, its provisions are similar to those of the Scottish Raspberries Marketing Scheme, 1932, which, as explained in the report for the year 1933, was approved under Section 1 (8) of the Agricultural Marketing Act, 1931, but failed to receive the requisite support at the poll of the registered producers.

Evidence was furnished that 243 producers in various parts of the country whose total acreage under raspberries extends to 3,593 acres (representing as regards number and producing capacity more than two-thirds of the producers who voted at the poll on the previous scheme), associated themselves with the submission of the new draft scheme. The statutory notice of the submission was accordingly given. The period for the lodging of objections and representations with respect to the scheme expired on 23rd January, 1935.

APPENDIX

AGRICULTURAL MARKETING

STATEMENT SHOWING PRINCIPAL DATES

Regulated Product.	Area of Scheme.	Persons Sponsoring Submission of Scheme.	Date of Notice of Submission.	Date of Public Inquiry.
Raspberries	Scotland (mainland) ...	Representative Group of Producers.	22.2.32	4.10.32
Hops ...	England	N.F.U.	11.8.32	2.5.33 to 17.5.33
Milk ...	Scotland (South of Grampians).	Committee appointed by General Meeting of Producers.	10.6.32	21.11.32 to 28.11.32
Pigs ...	Great Britain	N.F.U. and N.F.U. of Scotland.	20.1.33	24.3.33 to 6.4.33
Bacon ...	Great Britain	Bacon Section of Food Manufacturers' Federation, Inc.	24.1.33	29.3.33 to 6.4.33
Milk ...	Scotland (Counties of Aberdeen and Kincardine).	Aberdeen and District Milk Agency.	17.2.33	12.6.33 to 14.6.33
Milk ...	England	N.F.U.	21.3.33	6.6.33 to 20.6.33
Potatoes ...	Great Britain	N.F.U. and N.F.U. of Scotland.	28.3.33	4.7.33 to 12.7.33
Milk ...	Scotland (Counties of Inverness, Nairn, Ross and Cromarty, Sutherland and Caithness).	J. C. Stewart, Esq. (Solicitor) on behalf of 204 Producers.	20.6.33	—
Sugar ...	Great Britain	General Committee of United Kingdom Sugar Industry.	9.2.34	1.5.34 to 9.5.34
Milk ...	Scotland (Counties of Moray and Banff).	Committee representing 78 Producers.	1.5.34	—
Sugar Beet	Great Britain	N.F.U. and N.F.U. of Scotland.	11.5.34	30.7.34 to 31.7.34
Milk ...	Scotland (the part of the County of Argyll not covered by the Scottish Milk Marketing Scheme).	Scottish Agricultural Organisation Society on behalf of 22 Producers.	6.7.34	—
Raspberries	Scotland	Committee appointed by General Meeting of Producers, and on behalf of 243 Producers.	11.12.34	—

I.

ACTS, 1931 to 1933.

IN THE PROGRESS OF MARKETING SCHEMES.

Date of Approval by Parliament.		Date of Approval Order and S.R. & O. Number.	Date Scheme came into force.	Date of Initial Poll.	Result of Poll (per cent. in favour).		Date on which Provisions of Scheme were brought fully into operation.
House of Commons.	House of Lords.				Votes.	Productive Capacity.	
21.3.33	29.3.33	24.3.33 (232/S.12)	27.3.33	11.7.33	Per cent. 48·4	Per cent. 39·9	Poll unfavourable.
5.7.32	6.7.32	7.7.32 (505)	8.7.32	6.8.32	94	92·8	6.9.32
11.5.33	24.5.33	25.5.33 (479/S.26)	26.5.33	13.9.33	77	78	1.12.33
28.6.33	4.7.33	5.7.33 (686)	6.7.33	5.8.33	99·5	99·2	9.9.33
28.6.33	4.7.33	5.7.33 (683)	6.7.33	5.8.33	89	92	9.9.33
27.3.34	15.3.34	28.3.34 (309/S.21)	29.3.34	18.6.34	79·4	87·4	1.8.34
27.7.33	27.7.33	28.7.33 (789)	29.7.33	2.9.33	98·4	98·6	6.10.33
20.12.33	12.12.33	20.12.33 (1180)	21.12.33	1.2.34	90·4	90·6	9.3.34
5.7.34	5.7.34	6.7.34 (703/S.43)	7.7.34	20.8.34	72·9	75·8	1.10.34
—	—	—	—	—	—	—	—
—	—	—	—	—	—	—	—
—	—	—	—	—	—	—	—
—	—	—	—	—	—	—	—
—	—	—	—	—	—	—	—

Amendments of Marketing Schemes.

In accordance with the First Schedule to the Agricultural Marketing Act, [illegible].

Scheme.		Result of Poll of Registered Producers (if demanded). (Per cent. in favour of submission.)		Date of Notice of Submission.	Date of Public Inquiry.	Date of Approval by Parliament.		Date of Approval Order, and S.R. & O. Number.
		Total.	Production Capacity.			House of Commons.	House of Lords.	
		Per cent.	Per cent.					
Hops ([illegible])	...	[illegible]	97·1	[illegible]	[illegible] to [illegible]	[illegible]	[illegible]	[illegible]
[illegible] ([illegible])	...	—	—	[illegible]	[illegible]	—	—	—
[illegible] ([illegible])	...	—	—	[illegible]	—	—	—	[illegible]

Amendments of Marketing Schemes.

By Order made by "The Minister" under Section [illegible] of the Agricultural Marketing Act, [illegible].

Scheme.	Title of Order.	Date of Order, and S.R. & O. Number.
Scottish Milk Marketing Scheme, [illegible] ...	Scottish Milk Marketing Board (Co-opted Members) Order, [illegible] ...	[illegible]
[illegible] Marketing Scheme, [illegible] ...	[illegible] Marketing Board (Co-opted Members) Order, [illegible] ...	[illegible]

Amendment of Marketing Schemes.

By Order made by "The Ministers" under Section 4 of the Agricultural Marketing (No. 2) Act, [illegible].

Scheme.	Title of Order.	Date of Order, and S.R. & O. Number.
Pigs Marketing Scheme, [illegible]	Agricultural Marketing (Commencement No. [illegible]) Order, [illegible]	[illegible]

Amendment of Marketing Schemes.

By Order made by "The Minister" under Section [illegible] of the Agricultural Marketing Act, [illegible].

Scheme.	Title of Order.	Date of Order, and S.R. & O. Number.
Scottish Milk Marketing Scheme, [illegible] ...	Scottish Milk Marketing Scheme (Amendment) Order, [illegible] ...	[illegible]

APPENDIX [illegible].

PARTICULARS OF LOANS TO MARKETING BOARDS FROM THE AGRICULTURAL MARKETING FUNDS.

Loans to Boards administering Schemes applicable to Great Britain.

Board.	Amount of Loan.	Date of Advance.		Purpose for which loan was made.	Due Date of Repayment.		Remarks.
		English Fund.	Scottish Fund.		English Fund.	Scottish Fund.	
	£						
Pigs Marketing Board	[illegible]	[illegible]	[illegible]	Initial Poll Expenses ...	[illegible]	[illegible]	In each case the loan was met from the English and Scottish Funds in the proportions of [illegible] and [illegible] respectively. The loans were repaid on [illegible].
Pigs Marketing Board	[illegible]	[illegible]	[illegible]	Initial Working Expenses	[illegible]	[illegible]	
Bacon Marketing Board	[illegible]	[illegible]	[illegible]	Payment of compensation to contracted producers under the Bacon Scheme for losses occasioned by [illegible] of that Scheme and the Pigs Scheme.	[illegible]	[illegible]	Subject to repayment of [illegible] of £[illegible] (together with interest due), date for final repayment could be extended to [illegible]. The loan was completely repaid by the latter date.

[illegible]

Hops Marketing Board	[illegible]	[illegible]	Initial Poll Expenses	[illegible]	The loan was repaid on [illegible]
Milk Marketing Board ...	[illegible]	[illegible]	Initial Poll Expenses	[illegible]	The loan was repaid on [illegible]
Milk Marketing Board ...	[illegible]	[illegible]	Initial Working Expenses	[illegible]	The loan was repaid on [illegible]

[illegible]

Scottish Raspberry Marketing Board.	(1) [illegible] (2) [illegible]	[illegible] [illegible]	Initial Poll Expenses Initial Poll Expenses	— —	[illegible]
Scottish Milk Marketing Board.	[illegible]	[illegible]	Initial Poll Expenses	[illegible]	Loan was repaid on [illegible] December, [illegible].
Aberdeen and District Milk Marketing Board.	[illegible]	[illegible]	Initial Poll Expenses	[illegible]	
North of Scotland Milk Marketing Board.	[illegible]	[illegible]	Initial Poll Expenses	[illegible]	

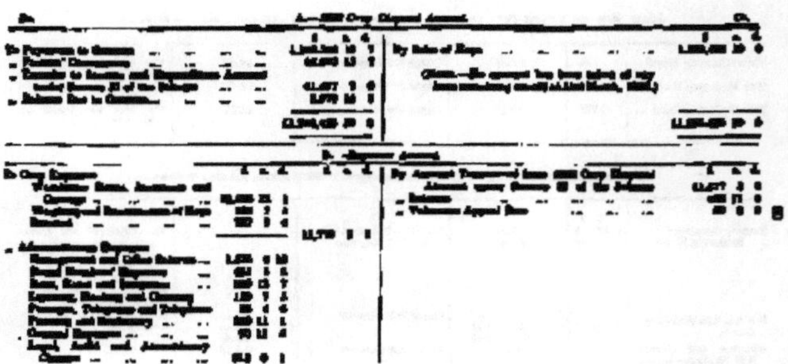

Balance Sheet as at 31st March, [illegible].

	£	s.	d.		£	s.	d.
To Creditors and Accrued Charges	[illegible]	[illegible]	[illegible]	By Furniture and Equipment at Cost—			
„ [illegible] Crop Disposal Account—				Less Depreciation	[illegible]	[illegible]	[illegible]
Balance due to Growers	[illegible]	[illegible]	[illegible]	„ Debtors and Payments in Advance	[illegible]	[illegible]	[illegible]
„ Reserve for Undistributed Expenses and disposal				„ Cash at Bank	[illegible]	[illegible]	[illegible]
of stock	14,000	0	0				
„ Income and Expenditure Account—							
Balance as per annexed account	[illegible]	[illegible]	[illegible]				
Note.—No account has been taken of any Hops remaining unsold at 31st March, [illegible].							
	[illegible]	[illegible]	[illegible]		[illegible]	[illegible]	[illegible]

W. [illegible],
[illegible],
[illegible] } Members of the Board.
[illegible], Secretary.

To the [illegible] registered under the Hops Marketing Scheme, [illegible].

I beg to report that I have audited the above Balance Sheet and annexed Income and Expenditure Account of The Hops Marketing Board and have obtained all the information and explanations I have required. In my opinion such Accounts are properly drawn up so as to exhibit a true and correct view of the state of the Board's affairs according to the best of my information and the explanations given to me and as shown by the books of the Board.

[illegible] House,
[illegible], London, E.C.2.
[illegible], [illegible].

[illegible],
Chartered Accountant.

THE [illegible] MARKETING BOARD.

[illegible] and Expenditure Account for the Year Ended [illegible] March, [illegible].

A.—[illegible] Crop Disposal Account.

Dr.	£ s. d.	Cr.	£ s. d.
To Payments to Producers	[illegible]	By Balance at 31st March, [illegible]	[illegible]
,, Agents' Commission	[illegible]	,, Sales of [illegible]	[illegible]
,, Transfer to Expenses Account	[illegible]		
	[illegible]		[illegible]

B.—[illegible] Crop Disposal Account.

	£ s. d.		£ s. d.
To Payments to Producers	[illegible]	By Sales	[illegible]
,, Agents' Commission	[illegible]		
,, Transfer to Income and Expenditure Account under Section [illegible] of the Scheme	[illegible]		

NOTE.—In making the final payment to Producers in respect of the [illegible] Crop a small quantity of [illegible] has been taken into account.

	[illegible] Camp 1st April to 31st July, [illegible].			[illegible] Camp 1st August, [illegible] to 31st March, [illegible].		
	£	s.	d.	£	s.	d.
To Camp Expenses—						
Warehouse Rent, Insurance and Cartage ...	[illegible]	[illegible]	[illegible]	[illegible]	[illegible]	[illegible]
Weighing and Examination of Bags	[illegible]	[illegible]	[illegible]	[illegible]	[illegible]	[illegible]
[illegible] Account ...				[illegible]	[illegible]	[illegible]
	[illegible]	[illegible]	[illegible]	[illegible]	[illegible]	[illegible]
" Administration Expenses—						
Management and Office Salaries ...	[illegible]	[illegible]	[illegible]	[illegible]	[illegible]	[illegible]
Board Members' Expenses ...	[illegible]	[illegible]	[illegible]	[illegible]	[illegible]	[illegible]
Rent, Rates and Insurance ...	[illegible]	[illegible]	[illegible]	[illegible]	[illegible]	[illegible]
Lighting, Heating and Cleaning ...	[illegible]	[illegible]	[illegible]	[illegible]	[illegible]	[illegible]
Postage, Telegrams and Telephone	[illegible]	[illegible]	[illegible]	[illegible]	[illegible]	[illegible]
Printing and Stationery ...	[illegible]	[illegible]	[illegible]	[illegible]	[illegible]	[illegible]
General Expenses ...	[illegible]	[illegible]	[illegible]	[illegible]	[illegible]	[illegible]
Legal, Audit and Accountancy Expenses ...	[illegible]	[illegible]	[illegible]	[illegible]	[illegible]	[illegible]
" Board Members' Fees— In accordance with a Resolution of the Annual General Meeting of [illegible] May, [illegible] ...	[illegible]	[illegible]	[illegible]			
" Refund to [illegible]— [illegible] Expenses ...	[illegible]	[illegible]	[illegible]			
" Election of Board Expenses ...				[illegible]	[illegible]	[illegible]
" Depreciation of Furniture and Equipment ...				[illegible]	[illegible]	[illegible]
" Reserves for Undetermined Expenses and Contingencies ...	[illegible]	[illegible]	[illegible]	[illegible]	[illegible]	[illegible]
" Balance Carried to Balance Sheet ...	[illegible]	[illegible]	[illegible]	[illegible]	[illegible]	[illegible]

	[illegible] Camp 1st April to 31st July, [illegible].			[illegible] Camp 1st August, [illegible] to 31st March, [illegible].		
	£	s.	d.	£	s.	d.
By Balances as at 31st March, [illegible]—						
Reserves for [illegible] expenses and disposal of [illegible] ...	[illegible]	[illegible]	[illegible]			
Balance of Income and Expenditure Account ...	[illegible]	[illegible]	[illegible]			
" Amount Transferred from [illegible] Camp Disposal Account under Section [illegible] of the [illegible] ...				[illegible]	[illegible]	[illegible]
" Interest on Investment (net) ...				[illegible]	[illegible]	[illegible]
" [illegible] Fees ...				[illegible]	[illegible]	[illegible]
" Amount Transferred from [illegible] Camp Disposal Account—Undistributed surplus ...	[illegible]	[illegible]	[illegible]			

BALANCE SHEET AS AT 31ST MARCH, [illegible].

	£ s. d.	£ s. d.		£ s. d.	£ s. d.
To Creditors and Accrued Charges ...		1,[illegible] [illegible] [illegible]	By Furniture and Equipment at Cost less Depreciation—		
" Reserves for Unascertained Expenses and Contingencies—			As at 31st March, [illegible] ...	[illegible]	
[illegible] Crop	[illegible] 0 0		Additions during year ...	[illegible]	
[illegible] Crop	[illegible] 0 0			[illegible]	
		[illegible] 0 0	Less: Depreciation at 10 per cent. per annum	[illegible] 14 6	
" Income and Expenditure Account— Balance as per annexed account					[illegible] 0
[illegible] Crop	[illegible] 14 9		" Investment at Cost—£[illegible] 3 per cent. Treasury Bonds [illegible] (Market Value £[illegible])		[illegible] 0 0
[illegible] Crop	[illegible] 0 0		" Debtors and Payments in Advance		[illegible] 14 3
		[illegible] 14 0	" Cash at Bank		[illegible] 13 11
		[illegible] 6 1			[illegible] 6 1

W. J. [illegible],
G. H. [illegible],
E. [illegible], } *Members of the Board.*
G. J. [illegible], *Secretary.*

To the Producers registered under the *Hops Marketing Scheme*, [illegible].

I have to report that I have audited the above Balance Sheet and Income and Expenditure Account of The Hops Marketing Board and have obtained all the information and explanations I have required. In my opinion such Accounts are properly drawn up so as to exhibit a true and correct view of the state of the Board's affairs according to the best of my information and the explanations given to me and as shown by the books of the Board.

Aldermary House,
[illegible], London, E.C.4.
[illegible]

[illegible],
[illegible] & Co.,
Chartered Accountants.

Digitised by the University of Southampton Library Digitisation Unit

THE SCOTTISH MILK MARKETING BOARD.

Profit and Loss Account,

For the period from [illegible] May, [illegible], to 31st January, [illegible]

(Period of Operation, 1st December, [illegible], to 31st January, [illegible]).

Dr.	£ s. d.	£ s. d.
Jan. 31, [illegible].		
To Advance Prices payable to Ordinary Producers		[illegible]
„ Salaries and [illegible] Head Office	[illegible]	
„ Salaries and Expenses: Regional Offices	[illegible]	
„ Stationery, Printing and Advertising	[illegible]	
„ Postages, Telephones and Telegrams	[illegible]	
„ Audit Fee and Expenses	[illegible]	
„ Legal Expenses	[illegible]	
„ Interest, Bank Charges and Stamp Duty on Cheques	[illegible]	
„ Rent, Rates and Insurance	[illegible]	
„ Travelling Expenses and Allowances	[illegible]	
„ [illegible] and Meetings [illegible] Expenses	[illegible]	
„ Miscellaneous Expenses	[illegible]	
		[illegible]
„ Formation and Preliminary Expenses written off	[illegible]	
„ Depreciation on Head Office Furniture and Equipment	[illegible]	[illegible]
„ Sums transferred to Reserve Fund for:—		
(a) [illegible] of [illegible] from [illegible]	[illegible]	
(b) Bad and Doubtful Debts, Income Tax, Advertising, [illegible] Expenses and all other Contingencies	[illegible]	[illegible]

Cr.	£ s. d.	£ s. d.
Jan. 31, [illegible].		
By Sales to Distributors, including supplies to Creameries operated by the Board		[illegible]
Less:—		
(a) Manufacturing Allowances	[illegible]	
(b) Freight and Handling Charges	[illegible]	[illegible]
		[illegible]
Note:— Pending the issue of the Arbiters' Award as to the price of [illegible], &c., to be taken over, the Creameries have been treated on the basis of Ordinary Distributors and no credit has been taken for any Profits of Creameries and likewise no provision has been made for any losses.		
„ Contributions assessed on Category Producers		[illegible]
„ Surplus [illegible]		[illegible]
„ [illegible] Stamps from Distributors payable to Producers	[illegible]	

Balance Sheet as at 31st January, [illegible]

Liabilities.	£	s.	d.	Assets.
1. Sundry Creditors and Credit Balances—				1. [illegible]
Sums due to Purchasers ...	[illegible]	[illegible]	[illegible]	[illegible] and Regional Offices—at cost
Drainage Charges (exclusive of estimated provision for unforeseen claims £[illegible]) ...	[illegible]	[illegible]	[illegible]	Less Depreciation written off ...
Sundry Creditors and Sundry Credit Balances ...	[illegible]	[illegible]	[illegible]	
Outstanding Cheques: Head Office ...	7,[illegible]	7	7	2. Stocks and Consumable Stores—
	[illegible]	[illegible]	[illegible]	At Cost [illegible] as certified by [illegible] Officer ...
2. Reserve Funds for—				Head Office: Stationery, &c. ...
(a) Instalments of Purchase Price of [illegible], Fees, Stamp Duties and Interest ...	[illegible]	[illegible]	[illegible]	3. Sundry Debtors, Charges Prepaid and Sundry Debit Balances—
(b) General Reserve for [illegible] Bad and Doubtful Debts, Income Tax, Advertising, Remuneration of Board, Arbitration Expenses and all other Contingencies ...	[illegible]	[illegible]	[illegible]	Due by [illegible] ...
				[illegible] Contributions
				[illegible] Debtors ...
				[illegible] and Sundry Debit Balances
				4. Cash at Bank and on Hand—
				Head Office—
				(a) At Bank ...
				(b) On Hand ...
				Regional Offices and [illegible] ...
				[illegible] in Transit ...
				5. [illegible] and [illegible] Deposits ...
				Less [illegible] off to date ...

Note:—

No provision other than a Reserve Fund as above has been made in respect of the purchase price of the [illegible] Property, Plant, Goodwill, Furniture and Fittings of the [illegible] taken over by the Board pending the issue of the Arbitors' Award as to the price payable, and no credit has been taken in respect of those items by the Assets per Contra.

Glasgow, [illegible] April, [illegible].

I have examined the Books and Accounts of The Scottish Milk Marketing Board for the period from [illegible] May, [illegible], to 31st January, [illegible], and have to report that—

(a) in my opinion, the foregoing Balance Sheet is properly drawn up so as to exhibit a true and correct view of the state of the Board's affairs and that the Profit and Loss Account exhibits a true and correct record of the Income and Expenditure of the Board according to the best of my information and the explanations given to me and as shown by the Books, and

(b) that the said Balance Sheet and Profit and Loss Account are sufficiently vouched,

all subject to the following observations:—

1. The Expenditure paid or provided for in the Accounts and incurred by those persons engaged in connection with the preparation, submission and bringing into operation of the Scheme which requires to be certified by the Secretary of State for Scotland in terms of Section [illegible] of the Agricultural Marketing Act, [illegible], has not yet been so certified, but the matter is presently before the Minister for certification.

2. The Register of Producers records a number of Producers whose production, if any, has not been dealt with in the Books of the Board and I am informed that this is due to the fact that the necessary information has not been supplied by these Producers or, alternatively, that such persons are properly exempt from the Provisions of the Scheme, but have not made application to have their names removed from the Register.

3. The Income and Expenditure on account of the Commission for the period under survey has not been incorporated in the Profit and Loss Account for the [illegible] ended on the last [illegible].

4. The Assessments on Category Producers have been shown at the amount as assessed by the Board.

Alexander [illegible], C.A., Public Auditor.

[illegible] MARKETING BOARD.

INCOME AND EXPENDITURE ACCOUNT FOR THE PERIOD ENDED [illegible] DECEMBER, [illegible].

Expenditure.	£ s. d.	*Income.*	£ s. d.
Office Expenses, including Salaries, Wages, Rent, Insurance, Printing, Stationery, Telegrams, Postage, etc.	[illegible]	Contract Fees	[illegible]
Marketing Expenses, including Graders' Wages and Expenses, Group Agents' Fees, etc.	[illegible]	Delivery and Grading Fees	[illegible]
Board's Travelling Expenses	[illegible]	Sundry Receipts	[illegible]
Legal Expenses and Audit Fee	[illegible]		
Loan Interest	[illegible]		
	[illegible]		
Depreciation	[illegible]		
Initial Poll and Working Expenses, Amount written off	[illegible]		
Reserve for Bad Debts	[illegible]		
Allocation to General Reserve	[illegible]		
	[illegible]		

Balance Sheet as at 31st December, [illegible].

Liabilities.	£	s.	d.	Assets.	£	s.	d.	£	s.	d.
[illegible] Certificates ...	[illegible]	[illegible]	[illegible]	Cash at Bank and in Hand ...				[illegible]	[illegible]	[illegible]
Loans for Initial [illegible] and Working Expenses ...	[illegible]	[illegible]	[illegible]	Sundry Debtors, less Reserve for Bad and Doubtful Debts ...				[illegible]	[illegible]	[illegible]
General Reserve ...	[illegible]	[illegible]	[illegible]	Furniture, Fittings, etc., at cost less Depreciation ...				[illegible]	[illegible]	[illegible]
Fund Account:				Initial [illegible] and Initial Working Expenses	[illegible]	[illegible]	[illegible]			
Surplus of Income over Expenditure ...	[illegible]	[illegible]	[illegible]	Less Amount Written off ...	[illegible]	[illegible]	[illegible]	[illegible]	[illegible]	[illegible]
	[illegible]	[illegible]	[illegible]					[illegible]	[illegible]	[illegible]

Notes.—

1. There are contingent liabilities in respect of—
   (i) Contracts for the purchase and sale of Pigs for [illegible] in January and February, [illegible].
   (ii) An arrangement with the [illegible] Board with regard to an indemnity to [illegible] up to a total sum of [illegible] against losses incurred by them.
   (iii) Remuneration of members of the Board.
2. There are other [illegible] due to [illegible] by the Board in respect of—
   (i) Deliveries of Pigs on [illegible] and [illegible] made prior to 31st December, but not notified to the Board before closing the Accounts.
   (ii) [illegible] and [illegible] not yet forwarded.

[illegible], Chairman.
[illegible], Vice-Chairman.
[illegible], General Manager and Secretary.

[illegible] MARKETING BOARD.

INCOME AND EXPENDITURE ACCOUNT FOR THE YEAR ENDED [illegible] DECEMBER, [illegible].

Expenditure.	£ s. d.	£ s. d.	Income.	£ s. d.
Office Expenses, including Salaries, Wages, Rent, [illegible], Printing, Stationery, Telephones, [illegible], Postage, etc. ...		[illegible]	[illegible] Fees ...	[illegible] 7 [illegible]
Marketing Expenses—			Delivery and Grading Fees ...	[illegible]
Graders' Wages and Expenses ...	[illegible]		Bank Interest ...	[illegible]
Group Agents' Commission ...	[illegible]		Sundry Revenue ...	[illegible]
[illegible] Expenses, [illegible] Expenses, etc. ...	[illegible] 7 11			
		[illegible] 7 [illegible]		
Board's Travelling Expenses ...		[illegible]		
Legal Expenses and Professional Charges ...		[illegible] 7		
Loan and other Interest ...		[illegible]		
		[illegible]		
[illegible] and Working Expenses [illegible]—				
[illegible] written off ...		[illegible]		
Depreciation ...		[illegible]		
Allocation to Reserve for [illegible], [illegible] per cent. on Income as per Section [illegible] of Scheme ...		[illegible]		
		[illegible]		
Surplus, carried down ...		[illegible]		
		£[illegible]		£[illegible]

[illegible] ACCOUNT.

Liabilities.	£	s.	d.	£	s.	d.
Sundry Creditors ...				[illegible]	[illegible]	[illegible]
Reserve for Claims on Companies						
Less Charges debited to date ...				[illegible]	[illegible]	[illegible]
General Reserve						
As per last Account ...	[illegible]	[illegible]	[illegible]			
Fund Account						
Balance as above ...	[illegible]	[illegible]	[illegible]			
				[illegible]	[illegible]	[illegible]

Notes.

(1) There are contingent liabilities in respect of

(a) [illegible] of Members of the Board.

(b) [illegible] for delivery of Pigs during [illegible], already contracted by the Board.

(2) There are sums [illegible] due to [illegible] by the Board in respect of

(a) Claims for [illegible] of Pigs under Contract, and

(b) Deliveries of Pigs on [illegible] made prior to [illegible] December, [illegible], but not notified to the Board before closing the Accounts.

[illegible], C.A., *Accountant*.

Assets.	£	s.	d.	£	s.	d.
Cash at Bank and in Hand ...						
Sundry Debtors and Payments in Advance						
Less Reserve for Bad and Doubtful Debts ...						
Furniture, Machinery and Fittings						
at Cost, less Sales and Depreciation ...						
[illegible]						
As per last Account ...	[illegible]	[illegible]	[illegible]			
Add [illegible] during year in respect of [illegible]	[illegible]	[illegible]	[illegible]			
	[illegible]	[illegible]	[illegible]			
Less [illegible] written off ...	[illegible]	[illegible]	[illegible]			

[illegible], *Chairman*.

[illegible], *Vice-Chairman*.

[illegible], *Secretary*.

BACON MARKETING BOARD.

Income and Expenditure Account for the period ended 31st December, 193[illegible].

Expenditure.	£	s.	d.	Income.	£	s.	d.
Salaries	[illegible]	[illegible]	[illegible]	Board Levy payable by Registered Producers for the period from [illegible] September to 31st December, 193[illegible]	[illegible]	[illegible]	[illegible]
Expenses of Members and Officials of Board	[illegible]	[illegible]	[illegible]	Sundry Receipts	[illegible]	[illegible]	[illegible]
Printing and Stationery	[illegible]	[illegible]	[illegible]				
Rent and Lighting	[illegible]	[illegible]	[illegible]				
Postages, Telegrams and Telephones ...	[illegible]	[illegible]	[illegible]				
Legal Expenses	[illegible]	[illegible]	[illegible]				
Office and General Expenses	[illegible]	[illegible]	[illegible]				
Reserve for Audit Fee	[illegible]	[illegible]	[illegible]				
Scottish Office Expenses	[illegible]	[illegible]	[illegible]				
Insurance and Bank Charges	[illegible]	[illegible]	[illegible]				
Depreciation	[illegible]	[illegible]	[illegible]				
	[illegible]	[illegible]	[illegible]				
Preliminary Expenses (of which £[illegible] [illegible]s. [illegible]d. is subject to the approval of the Minister of Agriculture and Fisheries)	[illegible]	[illegible]	[illegible]				
Balance, being excess of Income over Expenditure carried to Balance Sheet	[illegible]	[illegible]	[illegible]				
	£[illegible]	[illegible]	[illegible]		£[illegible]	[illegible]	[illegible]

Balance Sheet as at 31st December, [illegible].

Liabilities.	£ s. d.	Assets.	£ s. d.	£ s. d.
Sundry Creditors	[illegible]	Furniture, Fittings and Office Equipment, at cost	[illegible]	
Income and Expenditure Account:—		Less Depreciation at [illegible] per cent. per annum	[illegible]	
Balance at Credit as at 31st December, [illegible]	[illegible]			[illegible]
		Stock of Stationery as valued by Secretary		[illegible]
		Sundry Debtors:—		
		On [illegible] Levy Account	[illegible]	
		On open Account	[illegible]	
		Payments in Advance	[illegible]	
		Deposits	[illegible]	
				[illegible]
		Cash:—		
		At Bank	[illegible]	
		On Hand	[illegible]	
				[illegible]
	[illegible]			[illegible]

[illegible] } Members of the Board

[illegible], Assistant Secretary and Accountant.

Report of the Auditors pursuant to paragraph [illegible] of the [illegible] Scheme, [illegible].

[illegible]

London, E.C.[illegible]
[illegible]

[illegible] & Company,
Chartered Accountants.

BACON MARKETING BOARD.

INCOME AND EXPENDITURE ACCOUNT FOR THE YEAR ENDED 31ST DECEMBER, [illegible]

Expenditure.	£	s.	d.	Income.	£	s.	d.
Salaries	[illegible]	[illegible]	[illegible]	Gross Levy payable by Registered Producers ...	[illegible]	[illegible]	[illegible]
Expenses of Officials, Inspectors and Members of the Board	[illegible]	[illegible]	[illegible]	Sundry Receipts	[illegible]	[illegible]	[illegible]
Printing and Stationery	[illegible]	[illegible]	[illegible]	Interest	[illegible]	[illegible]	[illegible]
Rent and Lighting	[illegible]	[illegible]	[illegible]				
Postages, Telegrams and Telephones	[illegible]	[illegible]	[illegible]				
Legal and Professional Charges	[illegible]	[illegible]	[illegible]				
Accountants' Fees and Expenses	[illegible]	[illegible]	[illegible]				
Office and General Expenses	[illegible]	[illegible]	[illegible]				
Scottish Office Expenses	[illegible]	[illegible]	[illegible]				
Insurance and Bank Charges	[illegible]	[illegible]	[illegible]				
Agricultural and other Show Expenses	[illegible]	[illegible]	[illegible]				
Remuneration of Members of the Board (from [illegible] July [illegible], to [illegible])	[illegible]	[illegible]	[illegible]				
Depreciation	[illegible]	[illegible]	[illegible]				
	[illegible]	[illegible]	[illegible]				
Balance, being excess of Income over Expenditure carried to Balance Sheet	[illegible]	[illegible]	[illegible]				

Balance Sheet as at 31st December, 19[illegible]

Liabilities	£ s. d.	£ s. d.	£ s. d.
Bacon [illegible] Account (per contra)			
Advances from Ministry of Agriculture and Fisheries and the Department of Agriculture for Scotland, less repayments	[illegible]		
Provision for Interest to date of repayment	[illegible]		
		[illegible]	
Compensation payable to Registered Producers		[illegible]	
Bank Overdraft on Repayment Account		[illegible]	
			[illegible]
Sundry Creditors and Accrued Charges			[illegible]
Revenue and Expenditure Account			
Balance at Credit as at 31st December, 19[illegible]		[illegible]	
Add Excess of Income over Expenditure for year to date per account		[illegible]	
			[illegible]
			[illegible]

Assets	£ s. d.	£ s. d.
Furniture, Fittings and Other Equipment		
At cost, less Depreciation to 31st December, 19[illegible]	[illegible]	
Additional during [illegible]	[illegible]	
	[illegible]	
Less Depreciation at [illegible] per cent. for year to date	[illegible]	
		[illegible]
Stock of Stationery as valued by [illegible]		[illegible]
Bacon [illegible] Account (per contra)		
[illegible] Recoverable from Pig [illegible] Board	[illegible]	
Cash at Bank - Compensation Account	[illegible]	
		[illegible]
Sundry Debtors		
On Bacon Levy Account	[illegible]	
Deposits and [illegible]	[illegible]	
		[illegible]
Cash at Bank and in Hand		
At Bank		
On Current Account	[illegible]	
On Deposit Account	[illegible]	
Cash in Hand	[illegible]	
		[illegible]
		[illegible]

[illegible] } Members of the Board

J. A. D. [illegible], C.A.

MILK MARKETING BOARD.

Dr. — Account for the period [illegible] July, [illegible], to 31st March, [illegible]. — Cr.

(1) General Pool Account.

	£	s.	d.		£	s.	d.
To Amount Payable to Producers	[illegible]	[illegible]	[illegible]	By Charges to Purchasers for Milk Sales (see Reserves)	[illegible]	[illegible]	[illegible]
" Inter-Regional Compensation Levy	[illegible]	[illegible]	[illegible]	" Licensed Retailers' Commissions	[illegible]	[illegible]	[illegible]
" Expenses Levy	[illegible]	[illegible]	[illegible]	" Inter-Regional Compensation Fund Apportioned	[illegible]	[illegible]	[illegible]
" Pool Balance unallocated	[illegible]	[illegible]	[illegible]				
	£[illegible]	[illegible]	[illegible]		£[illegible]	[illegible]	[illegible]

Balance Sheet as at 31st March, [illegible].

Liabilities.	£ s. d.	£ s. d.	Assets.	£ s. d.
Sundry Creditors—			Office Furniture and Machinery—	
Payments to Registered Milk Sales (Marketing Sales for the month of March)	[illegible]		At cost less depreciation	[illegible]
Cartage [illegible] Accounts	[illegible]		Sundry Debtors less Reserves (including Purchasers in respect of Milk Supplies for the month of March)	[illegible]
Expenses due and accrued [illegible]	[illegible]		Cash at Bank on Operating Account and in Hand	[illegible]
Balance of Collecting and Deduction of proceeds of Milk sold in March, [illegible]	[illegible]	[illegible]		
Bank Overdraft		[illegible]		
Fund Account— Balance per account No. 1 above		[illegible]		
Inter-Regional Compensation Fund— Balance per account No. 2 above		[illegible]		
Income and Expenditure Account— Balance per account No. 3 above		[illegible]		
		[illegible]		[illegible]

Notes—(1) There are sums [illegible] due to and by the Board in respect of deliveries of milk prior to 31st March, [illegible], but not notified to the Board before closing the accounts.

(2) There is a contingent liability in respect of the remuneration of Members of the Board.

[illegible],
Chief Accountant.

[illegible], *Chairman.*
[illegible], *General Manager.*

	£ s. d.	£ s. d.
To General Administration Charges—		
Head Office—		
Salaries and Wages	[illegible]	
Rent, Lighting and Insurance	[illegible]	
Expenses and Allowances to [illegible]	[illegible]	
Telephones	[illegible]	
Postage	[illegible]	
Stationery and Office Equipment	[illegible]	
Publicity	[illegible]	
Travelling Expenses	[illegible]	
General Expenses including Hire of Machinery	[illegible]	
		[illegible]
Regional Offices—		
Salaries and Wages	[illegible]	
Car and Travelling Expenses	[illegible]	
Rent, Rates, Lighting and Insurance	[illegible]	
Expenses and Allowances to [illegible]	[illegible]	
Telephones	[illegible]	
Postage, Stationery and Advertising	[illegible]	
Publicity	[illegible]	
General Expenses	[illegible]	
		[illegible]
Legal and Professional Fees and Expenses		[illegible]
Expenses of Members of the Board		[illegible]
Bank Interest		[illegible]

	£ s. d.
By Levy on [illegible] [illegible]	[illegible]
„ Balance Carried Forward	[illegible]

	£ s. d.		£ s. d.	£ s. d.
Sundry Creditors and Accrued Charges	[illegible]	Premises and Furniture (at cost)—		
Amount due to [illegible]	[illegible]	Head Office	[illegible]	
		Regional Offices	[illegible]	
				[illegible]
		Office machinery (at cost)—		
		Head Office	[illegible]	
		Regional Offices	[illegible]	
				[illegible]
		Debtors and Deposits		[illegible]
		Cash in Hand		[illegible]
		Preliminary and Promotion Expenses		[illegible]
		Income and Expenditure Account—		
		Balance per Annexed Account		[illegible]
	[illegible]			[illegible]

Notes:—

1 [illegible]

2 [illegible]

3. No provision has been made for [illegible] of [illegible] of the Board.

4. No provision has been made for Depreciation in view of the short period during which the Board has been operating.

(Signed)

[illegible], Chairman.

[illegible], Vice-Chairman.

[illegible], Secretary.

[illegible] September, [illegible].

Ministry of Agriculture and Fisheries
Scottish Office

Report on Agricultural Marketing Schemes

FOR THE YEAR

1935

Presented to Parliament by the Minister of Agriculture and Fisheries and the Secretary of State for Scotland by Command of His Majesty
October, 1936

LONDON
PRINTED AND PUBLISHED BY HIS MAJESTY'S STATIONERY OFFICE
To be purchased directly from H.M. STATIONERY OFFICE at the following addresses:
Adastral House, Kingsway, London, W.C.2; 120 George Street, Edinburgh 2;
26 York Street, Manchester 1; 1 St. Andrew's Crescent, Cardiff;
80 Chichester Street, Belfast;
or through any bookseller
1936
Price 2s. 0d. net

Cmd. 5284

AGRICULTURAL MARKETING ACTS, 1931 TO 1933

Report on Agricultural Marketing Schemes

The following report upon the operation of Agricultural Marketing Schemes in force in 1935, and upon Schemes submitted since the date of our last report but not yet in force, has been prepared in accordance with the requirements of Section 10 of the Agricultural Marketing Act, 1931.

WALTER E. ELLIOT,
Minister of Agriculture and Fisheries.

GODFREY P. COLLINS,
Secretary of State for Scotland.

September, 1936.

TABLE OF CONTENTS

PART I.

SCHEMES IN OPERATION.

The following Agricultural Marketing Schemes were in operation in 1935 :—

Title of Scheme.	Date of Approval Order.	Area of Scheme.
Hops Marketing Scheme, 1932.	7th July, 1932.	England.*
Scottish Milk Marketing Scheme, 1933.	25th May, 1933.	Scotland, south of the Grampians.
Pigs Marketing Scheme, 1933.	5th July, 1933.	Great Britain.
Bacon Marketing Scheme, 1933.	5th July, 1933.	Great Britain.
Milk Marketing Scheme, 1933.	28th July, 1933.	England.*
Potato Marketing Scheme, 1933.	20th Dec., 1933.	Great Britain.
Aberdeen and District Milk Marketing Scheme, 1933.	28th March, 1934.	Counties of Aberdeen and Kincardine.
North of Scotland Milk Marketing Scheme, 1934.	6th July, 1934.	Counties of Inverness, Nairn, Ross and Cromarty, Sutherland and Caithness.

* "England" includes Wales.

A statement of the principal dates in the progress of the Schemes and a list of amendments are contained in Appendix I. Particulars of loans made to marketing boards from the Agricultural Marketing Funds are given in Appendix II.

HOPS MARKETING SCHEME.

The Hops Marketing Scheme, which applies to England, came into operation on the 6th September, 1932. It was amended in July, 1934*, to provide for producers' selling quotas during a period of five years ending in 1939. Under an agreement made between the Hops Marketing Board and the Brewers' Society, the average selling price of hops has been fixed at £9 per cwt. for each of the five seasons during which the quota provisions are operative. The administration of the agreement (a copy of which was laid before Parliament in June, 1934†) is supervised by a joint committee consisting of four representatives each of the Hops Marketing Board and the Brewers' Society together with three members appointed by the Minister, one of whom is Chairman and another the Vice-Chairman of the Committee‡.

The Board consists of 14 members elected annually for local districts and four special members elected at the annual general

* S.R. & O. 1934, No. 641.
† Cmd. 4623.
‡ See also report for 1934 (Cmd. 4918, page 7).

meeting of registered producers. There were two changes in the personnel of the Board during 1935; a vacancy caused by the death of a special member was filled by co-option, and a new member was elected for one of the districts.

The following remuneration of members of the Board was voted by registered producers at the annual general meeting on the 24th May, 1935: Chairman £800; Special Members £400; District Members £200.

The number of producers registered with the Board on the 31st December, 1935, was 1,008.

Trading operations of the Board.

1934 *crop.*—Provisional results of the Board's trading in 1934 hops were given in the last report*. The final total consignments to the Board of that crop amounted to 245,506 cwt. Total sales were 217,266 cwt. and exceeded the market demand, as estimated by the Joint Committee, by 2,266 cwt. There was no call, therefore, on the levy fund† in respect of 1934 hops.

The average selling price of the 1934 hops, exclusive of the levy of 10s. per cwt., was £9 1s. 5d. per cwt. and the aggregate sum realised was £1,971,296. After deducting selling expenses and contributions to meet the Board's expenses and to provide reserves, the sum available for payment to the registered producers was £1,840,142, giving an average return of £8 9s. 2d. per cwt.

The unsold surplus of 1934 hops amounted to 28,240 cwt. The Board retained this surplus until the volume of the 1935 crop was known; they then sold about 80 per cent. of it for purposes other than brewing, carrying forward about 6,000 cwt. as a reserve.

1935 *crop.*—The total of basic quotas for the 1935 crop was 231,681 cwt. Of this quantity, quotas in respect of 6,684 cwt. were held by producers who consigned their hops direct to brewers under contracts registered with the Board. Thus the total of the quotas of registered producers consigning hops to the Board was 224,997 cwt. The Permanent Joint Committee estimated the total market demand for 1935, exclusive of hops grown under registered contracts, to be 225,000, and the Board accordingly determined the annual quotas to be 100 per cent. of basic quotas, compared with 97 per cent. in 1934. There were a number of small transfers of annual quotas amounting in the aggregate to just over 5½ per cent. of the total crop, compared with just under 5 per cent. in 1934.

The quantity of hops tendered to the Board amounted to 232,340 cwt., of which 224,159 cwt. were quota hops and 6,181 cwt. were non-quota hops. The quality of the crop was above the average.

---

* Page 9.

† The agreement between the Board and the Brewers' Society provides that a levy of 10/- a cwt. shall be added to the selling price of all hops sold by the Board, and the proceeds of this levy are available for the purchase, by the Joint Committee, of any unsold balance of the market demand. The brewers agree to make firm contracts in advance for at least two-thirds of the market demand, and the maximum liability of the levy fund is one-third of the market demand.

The marketing of the 1935 crop was considerably delayed, due primarily to the late harvest and the subsequent dull weather which seriously interfered with the work of valuation. The Board are making arrangements to expedite the valuation of the crop in future.

The total valuation of the hops consigned to the Board was £2,084,848 of which £2,020,139 represented quota hops and £64,709 non-quota, giving average valuations for quota and non-quota hops of £9 0s. 8d. and £7 18s. 2d. per cwt. respectively and an average valuation of £8 19s. 8d. for all the hops tendered to the Board.

A summary of the trading operations of the Board from the commencement of the Scheme until the end of 1935 is given in the following table :—

Production and Marketing of Hops under the Hops Marketing Scheme.

	1932	1933	1934	1935
Production.				
Acreage planted (including unpicked)	16,631 ac.	16,838 ac.	18,037 ac.	18,251 ac.
Average yield per ac.	11·4 cwt.	12·8 cwt.	14·4 cwt.	13·6 cwt.
Estimated total production*	188,000 cwt.	216,000 cwt.	259,000 cwt.	248,800 cwt.
Marketing.				
Estimated market demand	—	—	215,000 cwt.	225,000 cwt.
Produce tendered to Board	165,908 cwt.	194,017 cwt.	245,506 cwt. Quota 217,368 cwt. Non-quota 28,138 cwt.	232,340 cwt. Quota 224,159 cwt. Non-quota 8,181 cwt.
Quantity disposed of	165,908 cwt.	194,017 cwt.	217,268 cwt.	
Aggregate sum realised ...	£1,471,709	£2,927,610	£1,971,296	
Average price per cwt. (to merchants)	£8.17.2	£15.1.8	£9.1.5†	
Paid to registered producers ...	£1,370,417 (93·12%)	£2,765,068 (95·13%)	£1,840,143 (93·35%)	
Average return per cwt.	£8.5.0	£14.6.11	£8.9.2‡	
Agents' commission per cwt.	7s. 2d. (4·06%)	9s. 8d. (3·24%)	7s. 8d. (3·99%)	
Retained for Board's expenses	5s. 0d. (2·83%)	5s. 0d. (1·63%)	5s. 0d. (2·76%)	

* Including hops sold under registered contracts and hops grown by brewers, not tendered to the Board.

† Excluding 10/- per cwt. for the Levy Fund.

‡ In respect of quota hops only.

Accounts of the Board.—Copies of the Income and Expenditure Account and of the Balance Sheet as at 31st March, 1935, are printed in Appendix III.

SCOTTISH MILK MARKETING SCHEME, 1933.

This Scheme, which came into full operation on 1st December, 1933, applies to the counties of Angus and Perth, part of the county of Argyll and the whole of Scotland lying to the south of these counties. A full description of the Scheme with detailed particulars of its working in the first year was given in the last report.*

The Scheme is administered by a Board consisting of eight elected members, two of whom retire annually, and two members co-opted by the elected members as provided in Section 14 of the Agricultural Marketing Act, 1933. The Selection Committee of fifty registered producers appointed in accordance with the provisions of the Scheme at the second annual general meeting held on 6th June, 1935, unanimously re-elected the two retiring members to the Board. After consultation with the Market Supply Committee, the elected members of the Board appointed Dr. J. D. Pollock, O.B.E., Manor House, Boswall Road, Edinburgh, and Mr. F. A. Rottenburg, Lochlane House, Crieff, to fill the vacancies caused by the death of Mr. W. J. Harvey, 7, Cambridge Gardens, Leith, and the resignation of Mr. J. D. Dallas, Milton House, Cowcaddens, Glasgow, the two members previously co-opted to the Board.

Lord Stair, the Chairman of the Board since its constitution, resigned from membership in July, 1935, owing to the demand on his time of other interests. The Board co-opted Mr. J. B. Douglas, Barstibly, Castle Douglas, to serve as a member and appointed Mr. T. G. Wilson, Carbeth, Balfron, to be Chairman.

The remuneration of the Board for the year 1934/5 voted by the registered producers at the annual general meeting was £2,500, a similar amount to that voted for the previous year, to be divided amongst the members of the Board as they might determine.

The total number of producers registered on 30th November, 1935, was 8,202 as compared with 8,149 at that date in the previous year.

The producers who during the month of November sold milk as producer-wholesalers†, producer-retailers and producers of Certified milk numbered 774, 2,427 and 104 respectively. The corresponding figures for November, 1934, were 596, 2,349 and 89. Many of the producers are included in more than one of the categories recognised under the Scheme. Producers who sell not more than three gallons daily to not more than six customers are exempt from registration.

Particulars are given in the statements on pages 22 and 23 of the gallonage of the sales of milk by the registered producers in each

* Pages 9–24.

† A producer-wholesaler, as defined in the Scheme and by resolution of the Board, is a producer who is licensed by the Board to sell milk to a retail distributor who, because his daily purchases do not exceed 20 gallons, is required to pay a wholesale price in excess of the Standard Price payable by distributors for untreated milk for liquid consumption.

month during the year ended November, 1935, in comparison with the corresponding statistics, as revised, for the previous year. The sales during the two years were as follows :—

	1933/34 *gallons.*	*1934/35* *gallons.*	*Increase* *gallons*	*per cent.*
Sold for liquid consumption.	68,496,384	71,145,018	2,648,631	3·87
Sold or used for manufacture.	39,099,978	44,326,335	5,226,357	13·37
Total	107,596,363	115,471,350	7,874,988	7·32

During the initial period of the operation of the Scheme, milk was being sold outwith the control of the Board under contracts made prior to the introduction of the Scheme. In the first three months of the Scheme, the quantity of milk sold under these contracts amounted to about 600,000 gallons per month.

The total quantity of milk sold by the registered producers during December 1985 was 7,797,141 gallons of which 5,838,008 gallons (74.87 per cent.) were absorbed by the liquid market.

Payments to Producers.

Sales to or through the agency of the Board.—The following table shows, in respect of each month in the year ended November, 1935, and in the previous year, the Standard Price paid by distributors for untreated milk for liquid consumption, the average price per gallon paid by the Board to the producers for milk sold to or through the agency of the Board, and the amount of the producers' contribution (i.e., the difference between the Standard Price and the average price).

	December, 1934 to November, 1935.			December, 1933 to November, 1934.		
	Standard Price per gallon.	Average Price per gallon.	Producers' Contribution per gallon.	Standard Price per gallon.	Average Price per gallon.	Producers' Contribution per gallon.
	d.	d.	d.	d.	d.	d.
December	15	13	2	14	12	2
January ...	15	13	2	14	12	2
February	15	12½	2½	14	12	2
March ...	14	11½	2½	14	11	3
April ...	13	9½	3½	14	10	4
May ...	13	8½	4½	14	9	5
June ..	13	8½	4½	14	9	5
July ...	13	8½	4½	14	9½	4½
August ...	14	10	4	14	10½	3½
September	14	11½	2½	14	11	3
October ...	14	12	2	14	11½	2½
November	15	12½	2½	15	12½	2½
Monthly Average	14	10·94	3·06	14·083	10·87	3·21

The weighted average price per gallon paid to the producers in respect of supplies during the year ended November, 1935, was 10·542d. compared with 10·570d. for the previous year.

The Standard Price for December, 1935, was 1s. 8d. per gallon and the average price paid to the producers for their sales in that month was 1s. 0¾d. per gallon.

Haulage Charges.—The average prices for sales to or through the agency of the Board are paid subject to deduction of haulage charges calculated at standard rates per gallon according to the distance of the producers' farms or premises from the nearest of the prescribed haulage centres. The standard rates of haulage in operation during the year ended November, 1935, were continued by the Board for a further year and are on the following scale.—Not exceeding 5 miles, ½d.; over 5 but not exceeding 10 miles, ¾d.; over 10 but not exceeding 30 miles, 1d.; over 30 but not exceeding 40 miles, 1¼d.; over 40 miles, 1½d. One of the adjustments made in the Scheme by Order* of the Secretary of State as from 1st January, 1935, provided for the addition to the list of haulage centres, originally restricted to Glasgow, Edinburgh and Dundee, of twelve centres in the East of Scotland area. This adjustment had the effect of reducing the haulage charges by amounts varying from ½d. to 1d. per gallon to 778 producers within that area.

Premiums.—The amendments made in the Scheme for the year 1935 also provided for payment of a bonus of ½d. per gallon to producers who, in accordance with undertakings given by them, did not in any month during the year sell to or through the Board a quantity of milk exceeding by more than 10 per cent. the quantity so sold by them in December, 1933. This bonus was earned by 329 producers in respect of sales amounting during the year to a total of 7,082,876 gallons.

Producers whose milk is sold at higher prices than the Standard Price are paid the excess in addition to the average price per gallon. In terms of contracts made with distributors for sales during the year ended September, 1935, 268 producers received a level delivery premium of 1d. per gallon and 201 producers earned a wholesale service premium of 2d. per gallon. The producers qualifying for payment of premiums at these rates under contracts for the year commencing October, 1935, numbered 296 and 288 respectively; additional contracts with similar provision may be made in respect of the supply of milk to buyers for seasonal trade.

The price of Grade A (T.T.) milk to distributors having been determined at 3d. per gallon more than the Standard Price, that sum per gallon was paid, in addition to the average price, in respect of milk of that grade sold as such in the ordinary market and also in respect of supplies provided at reduced rates for consumption in the

* S.R. & O. 1934, No. 1438/S.75.

schools. The total gallonage of Grade A (T.T.) milk sold as such to or through the Board during the year ended November, 1935, amounted to 2,568,750 gallons.

At the end of the year the number of registered producers with licensed tubercle-free herds was 875 as compared with 180 at the commencement of the operation of the Scheme in December, 1933.

Producer-wholesalers and producer-retailers.—The basis of assessment of the contributions payable by these producers was revised by the amendments made in the Scheme for the year 1935. As a result of the adjustments, 784 producers who gave undertakings to the Board that they would not sell any milk to or through the agency of the Board during the year, qualified for payment of contributions at the monthly rate of 6s. 8d. per cow (£4 per annum). The contributions of 829 producers, who did not give such undertakings and whose average daily sales of milk by "wholesale" or retail in November, 1934, exceeded eight gallons, were payable at the monthly rate of 8s. 4d. per cow (£5 per annum) and, in respect of their liability for payment of contributions at that rate, they were credited with the sum of 1½d. per gallon in the assessment of contributions on sales made by them to or through the agency of the Board. The contributions of other producers in these categories were payable in accordance with the original provisions of the Scheme, at a rate per gallon of their "wholesale" or retail sales equal to nine-tenths of the contributions payable in respect of sales or through the agency of the Board.

Producers of Certified Milk.—In accordance with the amending Order* made by the Secretary of State, after consideration of a report of the Committee of Investigation for Scotland (see page 19), the contribution payable in respect of Certified milk sold as such as from 1st August, 1935, was at the rate of ½d. per gallon. Under the powers conferred by the Order, the Board also paid a bonus to the producers of Certified milk of an amount equal to the excess over ½d. per gallon of the contribution paid or payable by them in respect of sales of Certified milk as such (784,020 gallons) during the period from 1st May, 1934, to 31st July, 1935.

Farm Cheesemakers.—404 producers entered into farm cheesemakers' agreements with the Board for the year 1935. The terms of these agreements were similar to those made in the previous year except for adjustments made for estimating the value of the milk to the producers at the market prices of home-farm cheese and not, as in the previous year, for a part of the season at the prices of imported cheese. The producers received payment from the Board of a sum per gallon representing the difference between the monthly average price for sales to or through the agency of the Board (less the standard haulage rates) and the estimated value of the milk for conversion into cheese. They were also paid a manufacturing allowance of 1d. per gallon.

---

* S.R. & O. 1935, No. 691/S.31.

The undernoted quantities of milk were converted into cheese by farm cheesemakers under the agreements :—

1935		Gallons
February	...	916
March	...	390,933
April	...	968,665½
May	...	1,620,930
June	...	1,767,742¼
July	...	1,745,547
August	...	1,359,718
September	...	836,609
October	...	189,210
November	...	2,728
	Total	8,868,188¾

In 1934, 472 farm cheesemakers completed agreements, and the total quantity of milk manufactured by them into cheese amounted to 10,316,576½ gallons.

Contracts.

Apart from a variation in the scale of liquid milk prices and certain minor adjustments, the terms and conditions prescribed in the form of contract supplied by the Board for use in respect of the sale and purchase of milk for liquid consumption and manufacture during the year 1st October, 1935, to 30th September, 1936, were similar to those laid down in the form of contract used for the previous year.

Distributors who purchase not more than 500 gallons daily are required to enter into direct contracts with producers to which the Board are a party. As it is frequently found necessary or desirable to make changes in the sources of supplies for large buyers, distributors who purchase more than 500 gallons daily and are in possession of manufacturers' licences from the Board are not required to complete individual contracts with producers, but, in terms of letters of agreement exchanged between them and the Board, all the milk supplied to them is held to have been sold and purchased in accordance with the conditions specified in the Board's official form of contract.

The producers are required, in terms of the contract, to supply milk attaining a standard of butter-fat content of not less than 3·5 per cent. during the months from August to January and not less than 3·4 per cent. during the months from February to July. Provision is also made that such additional standards of quality and cleanliness as may be determined by the Board shall be deemed to be incorporated in the contract and that the buyer shall be entitled to be relieved of supplies which are not of the required standards.

In cases where a distributor is relieved of an unsatisfactory supply, it is diverted to one of the Board's creameries to be kept under observation. All supplies of milk received at the Board's creameries are sampled and tasted daily, and inspectors of the Board visit the farms of producers whose milk does not attain the prescribed standards of quality to advise and assist them in rectifying the matter. Deductions are made from the prices payable to producers of milk of indifferent quality and, if a supply of unsatisfactory milk is maintained, the producer is given the alternative of accepting its return for the feeding of stock or of being paid the value of its use for that purpose.

During the summer of 1935 the Board arranged with the Agricultural Colleges and Local Authorities for the testing of about 3,000 supplies of milk with a view to obtaining data for considering the formulation of a policy for payment to producers for their milk according to its quality.

Liquid Milk Prices.

The Standard Price for the sale of untreated milk to the distributors for liquid consumption was determined by the Board for the year ending September, 1936, on the following scale—October, 1935, 1s. 2d. per gallon; November, 1935, to February, 1936, 1s. 3d. per gallon; March and April, 1936, 1s. 2d. per gallon; May and June, 1936, 1s. per gallon; July to September, 1936, 1s. 2d. per gallon. On that scale, the monthly average of the Standard Price is 1s. 2d. per gallon as in the previous contract periods.

The minimum retail price, previously determined at the level rate of 2s. per gallon, was again determined at that price for ten months of the year with a reduction to 1s. 8d. per gallon in the months of May and June, 1936. The reduction in these two months was decided upon as an experiment for the examination of the effect of the lower retail price on consumption. A complaint by the distributors that, with the continuance of the Standard Price at an average of 1s. 2d. per gallon over the year, the full cost of this reduction of the retail price would fall to be borne by them and would reduce the average distributive margin over the year from 10d. to 9·33d. per gallon was referred to the Committee of Investigation for Scotland for consideration and report (see page 20). In view of this complaint, the contracts and agreements entered into by the distributors for the year were made with a provision for amendment of the terms and conditions, including prices, by Order of the Secretary of State with right to the buyers to resile, on due notice, in the event of the amendments being unacceptable to them or of no amending Order being made.

For Grade A (T.T.) and Certified milk, the producers' prices were determined at 3d. and 10d. per gallon and the minimum retail prices at 4d. and 8d. per gallon more than the prices for ordinary milk.

Except for a reduction in the months of May and June, corresponding to that in the retail price, the minimum prices for supplies of ordinary milk to hotels, restaurants, etc., were determined on the same scale as previously, viz.,—over 2 but not exceeding 10 gallons—1s. 8d. per gallon; over 10 but not exceeding 50 gallons—1s. 6d. per gallon; over 50 gallons—1s. 5d. per gallon. An addition of 2d. per gallon to these prices was authorised for milk supplied in bottles. The semi-retail prices for graded milk were adjusted on similar scales.

The prices for supplies for institutions, rate-aided and voluntary, were continued at not less than the producers' prices, no control being exercised over the distributive margin.

Manufacturing Milk Prices.

Cheese.—Acting on the recommendation of the Committee of Investigation for Scotland (see page 18), the Board adjusted the prices of milk sold for manufacture into cheese in each month during the period from April, 1934, to January, 1935, by reference to the weighted average price in the preceding month of Canadian and New Zealand cheese. The monthly prices adjusted on that basis ranged from 2·81d. to 3·95d. per gallon. As from April, 1935, the prices for each month were regulated on a formula relating the value of the milk to the weighted average of the prices realised on the sale of cheese manufactured in the Board's creameries. Determined in that manner, the prices over the period ended December, 1935, ranged from 2.813d. to 4·560d. per gallon.

Butter.—Until March, 1935, the prices for milk for manufacture into butter were determined monthly by the Board after consultation with the Manufacturing Sub-Committee of the Permanent Joint Committee appointed under the Scheme. During the period from April, 1934, the prices for the bulk of the supplies ranged from 3·50d. to 4·28d. per gallon, higher prices being obtained from manufacturers with an outlet for the by-product. The prices for each month from April, 1935, were determined by reference to the realisation value of the Board's manufactures of butter, and over the period ended December, 1935, they varied from 3·068d. to 4·718d. per gallon for supplies exceeding 10,000 gallons per month; additional prices up to 2d. per gallon were payable for monthly purchases of less than that quantity.

Other Products.—The price of milk for manufacture of fresh cream was continued during the year 1935 at 7½d. per gallon except for a small quantity supplied in special circumstances in the month of March at 5½d. per gallon. Prices of 3¾d. and 4d. per gallon were obtained for milk for the manufacture of milk powder, while milk for manufacture into tinned cream and sweetened condensed milk, for which there was a very limited demand, realised 4d. and 4½d. per gallon and 4½d. to 5d. per gallon respectively. Milk was supplied during the later months of the year at 6d. per gallon for manufacture into unsweetened condensed milk.

Sale and Use of Milk for Manufacture.

The quantities of milk sold to manufacturers or used by the Board for manufacture into the various products during the year December, 1934, to November, 1935, and the realisation values per gallon were as shown in the following statement :—

Product.	Sold for Manufacture.		Used for Manufacture.		Total.		Realisation Value per gallon (weighted average)*
	Gallons.	Percentage	Gallons.	Percentage	Gallons.	Percentage	
							Pence.
Fresh Cream	5,892,071	32·46	6,273,994	36·28	12,166,065	34·32	6·806 (6·810)
Tinned Cream	32,997	·18	1,993,744	11·52	2,026,741	5·72	4·366 (4·603)
Cheese ...	6,018,991	33·16	6,072,015	35·09	12,091,006	34·10	2·780 (3·047)
Butter ...	4,300,916	23·70	1,378,469	7·96	5,679,385	16·02	4·000 (5·076)
Condensed Milk ...	1,430,901	7·88	1,570,608	9·09	3,001,509	8·46	5·227 (5·380)
Milk Powder	25,829	·14	—	—	25,829	·07	3·052 (5·234)
Other Products	440,508	2·43	13,836	0·08	463,344	1·31	0·279
Total ...	18,151,213	100·00	17,304,666	100·00	35,455,879	100·00	4·732

* The value of the milk used by the Board for manufacture is calculated at the prescribed prices for the sale of milk to private manufacturers. The figures in brackets show the average values after including the repayable advances under the Milk Act, 1934.

All the milk sold for manufacture into unsweetened condensed milk was supplied to a new large-scale condensery at Dumfries which commenced operations in June, 1935. Negotiations were in progress at the end of the year for the guarantee of a supply of milk to another large-scale condensery to be erected in Ayrshire. When this new factory is in full operation the Board, in pursuance of their policy of concentrating on the production of cheese and butter of high quality at their creameries, propose to discontinue the manufacture of condensed milk and tinned cream.

In June, 1935, the Board opened a new cheese-making factory at Abernethy, Perthshire, and they now own twenty creameries and depots in different parts of the area of the Scheme. Various improvements were carried out during the year in the accommodation and plant at the creameries. A new depot is in course of construction at Glasgow; it will be used for balancing the supplies of milk for the liquid markets in Glasgow and for the manufacture of butter and cream. Arrangements are also being made for the erection of another factory at Mauchline, Ayrshire.

Measures have been taken by the principal private manufacturers and by the Board to eliminate waste of the by-products of their main manufactures. In August, a new factory erected alongside the Board's creamery at Kirkcudbright commenced operations in the manufacture of milk powder with spray-process plant from separated milk supplied from the creamery. The factory is capable of dealing with 9,000 gallons daily, and the average price paid to the Board for the separated milk is ¾d. per gallon. Skim milk from several of the Board's creameries is sold for the manufacture of casein. The Board have made further arrangements to ensure that all surplus by-products at their creameries will be used for manufacture.

Repayable Advances under Sections 1, 2 and 3 of the Milk Act, 1934.

The repayable advances made to the Board in respect of milk sold or used for manufacture during the period from 1st April, 1934 to 31st December, 1935, amounted to a total of £259,426. Particulars of these payments are given in the following statement :—

Section 1—In respect of milk sold for manufacture :—

Product.	*Gallons.*	*Payments.* £
Butter ...	5,110,032	26,501
Cheese ...	10,252,986	58,742
Condensed Milk	614,270	2,449
Milk Powder	293,602	1,070
Tinned Cream	51,748	148
Fresh Cream ...	41,456	86
Total	16,364,096	£84,596

Section 2—In respect of milk used by the Board for manufacture :—

Product.	*Gallons.*	*Payments.* £
Butter	1,541,362	8,241
Cheese	12,510,708	67,744
Tinned Cream ...	541,415	2,256
Total	14,593,485	£78,241

Section 3—In respect of milk converted into cheese on farms :—

	Gallons.	*Payments.*
Farm Cheese	18,740,986	£96,589

Increasing the demand for milk.

Milk in Schools Scheme.—Contributions amounting to £48,420 were made to the Board towards the expenses incurred during the period from November, 1934, to December, 1935, in carrying out the arrangements approved by the Secretary of State for the supply of milk at reduced prices for consumption in the schools. After full development of the scheme, the average number of children receiving milk daily under these arrangements was about 350,000. The quantities of milk consumed in each month from November, 1934, are given in the following table:—

Month.				*Gallons consumed.*	*Estimated average number of school days.*
November, 1934		...	...	20,000	17
December,	,,	...	...	84,000	15
January,	1935	...	...	113,000	16
February,	,,	...	...	174,000	19
March,	,,	...	...	312,000	21
April,	,,	...	...	214,000	18
May,	,,	...	...	365,000	21
June,	,,	...	...	297,000	19
July,	,,	...	...	34,000	Holidays.
August,	,,	...	...	33,000	
September,	,,	...	...	288,000	18
October,	,,	...	...	311,000	23
November,	,,	...	...	264,000	18
December,	,,	...	...	201,000	14

Of the total quantity of milk consumed, 1,620,685 gallons were provided in Grade A (T.T.) milk and 1,088,659 gallons in ordinary milk approved as to source and quality by the appropriate Medical Officers.

Publicity and Propaganda.—As a supplement to the scheme for the supply of milk in schools, the Board made arrangements, with the approval of the Secretary of State, for a publicity and propaganda programme with a view to stimulating the consumption of milk by the community generally. In accordance with these arrangements, a campaign of press and poster advertisement was carried out by the Board, and propaganda work was undertaken amongst Women's Institutes, Clinics, Working Men's Clubs and similar organisations. Booklets, recipe books and other advertising matter designed to increase the sale of milk were supplied to retailers and other buyers of milk. Payments amounting to £7,742 were made from the Exchequer to meet one half of the Board's expenses in carrying out the approved programme.

In furtherance of this advertising campaign, the Board appointed a Propaganda Officer whose duties are to address meetings of Women's Guilds, Institutes and other organisations on the value of milk as a beverage and its uses for cooking and other domestic purposes.

Enquiry into the nutritional value of milk.—Reference is made on page 52 to the arrangements made by the English and Scottish Milk Marketing Boards, with the approval of the Minister of Agriculture and Fisheries and the Secretary of State, for an enquiry into the nutritional value of milk. In the area of the Scottish Scheme, the investigation is being made in connexion with the supply of milk to about 1,500 children attending schools in the county of Renfrew.

Agricultural Co-operation, Research and Education.

Arrangements were made for the continuance during the year 1935/36 of the enquiry into the cost of milk production which is being carried out by the Advisory Officers in Agricultural Economics attached to the Agricultural Colleges in collaboration with the Department's Advisory Officer in Farm Economics. The Board undertook to contribute £500, the same amount as in the previous year, towards the cost of the enquiry.

Other donations made by the Board during the year 1935 included the following:—£250 to the Institute of Animal Genetics in connexion with experimental work on inheritance in milk yield; £200 (as in the year 1934) to the Scottish Committee of Contagious Bovine Abortion; £100 to the Hannah Dairy Research Institute; and £200 to the Scottish Agricultural Organisation Society.

Complaints Regarding the Operation of the Scheme.

Consumers' Committee for Scotland.

Retail price of milk in the summer months.—A complaint was made to the Consumers' Committee for Scotland regarding the continuance of the retail price of 2s. per gallon in the scale of prices determined by the Board for the year October, 1934, to September, 1935. In their report on the complaint, the Committee maintained the view expressed by them in connexion with similar complaints made during the previous year, viz., that they saw no reason for the departure from the long-established practice of discriminating between winter and summer prices and that they were not convinced that the Board's decision was justified.*

Committee of Investigation for Scotland.

The complaints on the following subjects, referred to in the last report, were reported on by the Committee of Investigation for Scotland:—

(*a*) *Price of milk for manufacture into cheese.*—The Committee found that the interpretation by the Board of the formula used for the determination of the price for each month on the basis of the simple average of the prices per lb. in the preceding month of Canadian and New Zealand cheese was contrary to the interests of the manufacturers concerned and was not in the public interest. The Committee recommended that the words "average price" in

* For position in May and June, 1936, see page 18.

the formula should be construed as meaning a weighted average, and that retrospective adjustments should be made in the prices charged for the supply of milk for manufacture of cheese during the year 1934.

The Board agreed to give effect to these recommendations and arranged accordingly.

(b) *Complaint by the Association of Certified and Grade A (T.T.) Milk Producers.*—The Committee found that the provisions of the Scheme with regard to the rate of contribution payable by producers of Certified milk were contrary to the interests of such producers and were not in the public interest and recommended that the Minister should amend the Scheme to provide that, as from 1st May, 1934, the contribution payable by producers of Certified milk sold as such should be at the rate of one-halfpenny per gallon. They did not find that any provision of the Scheme was contrary to the interests of producers of Grade A (T.T.) milk.

Effect was given to the Committee's recommendation by the Scottish Milk Marketing Scheme (Amendment) Order, 1935* made by the Secretary of State on 16th July, 1935.

(c) *Prices of milk supplied to the Institutions administered by the Glasgow Corporation, to voluntary hospitals and under child welfare and maternity schemes.*—The Committee found that to the extent that Local Authorities and voluntary hospitals were required to pay substantially more for their supplies of milk than they paid prior to the inauguration of the Scheme, the price scale determined by the Board might be regarded as contrary to the interests of the Local Authorities and voluntary hospitals.

With regard to the question whether the determination of the Board in this matter was not in the public interest, the Committee were unable to give an unqualified answer. While recognising that the beneficent nature of the work carried out by the Local Authorities and by voluntary hospitals did not in itself justify a claim that they should obtain their supplies of milk under the Scheme at less than a reasonable price, the Committee pointed out that it would be unfortunate if the consumption of Grade A (T.T.) milk were abandoned to any extent in hospitals or in rate-supported institutions in favour of ordinary milk, and equally unfortunate if the consumption of milk of whatever grade were to be reduced. This consideration, coupled with the facts that the institutions are large consumers and do not purchase for trading purposes or for sale at a profit, and that there is little expense involved in handling or distribution, suggested to the Committee that there was a case for exceptional treatment of these institutions in certain directions; and in so far as these institutions had not received such treatment owing to the action of the Board, such action might be said to be not in the public interest.

---

* S.R. & O. 1935, No. 691/S.31.

The Secretary of State decided, after full review of the position, that as the question of granting preferential treatment to the Local Authorities and voluntary hospitals was not peculiar to Scotland and formed part of the wider question as to the considerations on which any general policy of fixing differential prices for different classes of consumers should be based, the matter was one to be kept in view in the formulation of a long-term policy for the milk industry and that it was not practicable in the meantime to require the Board, by amendment of the Scheme, to give effect to the Committee's suggestions.

The following complaints were referred to the Committee during the year:—

(d) *East Kilbride Dairy Farmers, Limited.*—The East Kilbride Dairy Farmers, Ltd., complained that they were not receiving fair treatment from the Board with respect to the cost of haulage to Glasgow of milk dealt with by or on behalf of their subsidiary Company, Kilmaurs Dairy Farmers, Ltd. The Committee found that the Board's action in refusing to accept liability for payment of the cost of haulage of milk after delivery to Kilmaurs Creamery was contrary to the complainants' interests, but they did not find that this action was not in the public interest.

(e) *East of Scotland Milk Producers' Federation.*—Representations by the East of Scotland Milk Producers' Federation that the adjustments made in the Scheme for the year 1935, in terms of the Scottish Milk Marketing Scheme (Amendment) and (Directions) Orders, 1934*, should be continued in operation pending the report of the Milk Reorganisation Commission for Great Britain and consequential action thereon were referred to the Committee for consideration and report. The Committee found that the provision in the Orders restricting the period of their operation to the year 1935 was contrary to the interests of the complainants and was not in the public interest.

The Scottish Milk Marketing Scheme (Amendment No. 2) Order, 1935†, made by the Secretary of State on 18th December, 1935, provided for the continuance of the adjustments in the Scheme subject to a minor modification granting to producer-retailers and producer-wholesalers who are eligible for assessment of their contributions to the Board at the rate of £5 per cow per annum, the option of being assessed, in accordance with the original provisions of the Scheme, on the basis of a contribution per gallon of their retail or wholesale sales equal to nine-tenths of that payable in respect of milk sold to or through the agency of the Board.

(f) *Milk Distributors on the Permanent Joint Committee.*—The milk distributors on the Permanent Joint Committee appointed

* S.R. & O. 1934, No. 1437/S.74 and No. 1438/S.75.
† S.R. & O. 1935, No. 1246/S.56.

under the Scheme submitted a complaint regarding the action of the Board, in the determination of the scale of prices for the year ending September, 1936, in (i) fixing the minimum retail price for the months of May and June at 1s. 8d. per gallon while maintaining the Standard Price payable by the distributors at a monthly average over the year of 1s. 2d. per gallon; (ii) refusing to adopt the recommendation of the consultant who was called into the negotiations that the cost of the reduction of the retail price in those two months should be borne equally by the producers and distributors; and (iii) failing the adoption of that recommendation, refusing to determine the prices for the year on the same scale as in the previous year.

The Committee had not reported on this complaint at the end of the year.*

Miscellaneous.

Finances of the Board.—Copies of the Profit and Loss Account of the Board for the year ended 31st January, 1935, and of the Balance Sheet as at that date are printed in Appendix III.

The Board were able to arrange for a loan of £200,000, repayable over a period of twenty years and bearing interest at the rate of 3 per cent., for the purpose of meeting the purchase price of the creameries taken over by the Board. Interest charges and repayment of capital in respect of the loan represent approximately ·036d. per gallon of the total sales by the registered producers during the first year which, calculated on the same gallonage of sales, will fall to ·0236d. per gallon in the twentieth year.

Board's Journal.—In the interests of economy, the Board discontinued publication of their monthly Journal after the issue for August, 1935, each registered producer now being furnished, instead, with a short News Letter giving details of the operations under the Scheme during the previous month.

Contraventions of the Scheme.—During the year to 30th November, 1935, the Board imposed penalties amounting to £704 on 67 producers, mainly for failing to furnish information required by the Board or for wilfully furnishing false information.

Agreement with the English Milk Marketing Board.—Under the agreement referred to in the last report,† payments amounting to about £180,000 were received by the Scottish Board from the English Board during the period ended December, 1935, as compensation for the reduction of the supply of milk into England as compared with the supply in the year 1933.

---

* The report has since been received and has been published.

† Page 23.

SCOTTISH MILK MARKETING SCHEME, [illegible].

Monthly Quantities of Milk sold to or through the Agency of the Board and Quantities sold by Producers of the Special Categories.

Month.	December, [illegible], to November, [illegible].					December, [illegible], to November, [illegible].				
	Total Sales.	Sold to or through the agency of the Board.		Sold by producer-wholesalers, producer-retailers and producers of Certified milk.		Total Sales.	Sold to or through the agency of the Board.		Sold by producer-wholesalers, producer-retailers and producers of Certified milk.	
	Gallons.	Gallons.	Per cent.	Gallons.	Per cent.	Gallons.	Gallons.	Per cent.	Gallons.	Per cent.
December ...	[illegible]	[illegible]	[illegible]	[illegible]	[illegible]	[illegible]	[illegible]	[illegible]	[illegible]	[illegible]
January ...	[illegible]	[illegible]	[illegible]	[illegible]	[illegible]	[illegible]	[illegible]	[illegible]	[illegible]	[illegible]
February ...	[illegible]	[illegible]	[illegible]	[illegible]	[illegible]	[illegible]	[illegible]	[illegible]	[illegible]	[illegible]
March ...	[illegible]	[illegible]	[illegible]	[illegible]	[illegible]	[illegible]	[illegible]	[illegible]	[illegible]	[illegible]
April ...	[illegible]	[illegible]	[illegible]	[illegible]	[illegible]	[illegible]	[illegible]	[illegible]	[illegible]	[illegible]
May ...	[illegible]	[illegible]	[illegible]	[illegible]	[illegible]	[illegible]	[illegible]	[illegible]	[illegible]	[illegible]
June ...	[illegible]	[illegible]	[illegible]	[illegible]	[illegible]	[illegible]	[illegible]	[illegible]	[illegible]	[illegible]
July ...	[illegible]	[illegible]	[illegible]	[illegible]	[illegible]	[illegible]	[illegible]	[illegible]	[illegible]	[illegible]
August ...	[illegible]	[illegible]	[illegible]	[illegible]	[illegible]	[illegible]	[illegible]	[illegible]	[illegible]	[illegible]
September ...	[illegible]	[illegible]	[illegible]	[illegible]	[illegible]	[illegible]	[illegible]	[illegible]	[illegible]	[illegible]
October ...	[illegible]	[illegible]	[illegible]	[illegible]	[illegible]	[illegible]	[illegible]	[illegible]	[illegible]	[illegible]
November ...	[illegible]	[illegible]	[illegible]	[illegible]	[illegible]	[illegible]	[illegible]	[illegible]	[illegible]	[illegible]
Total ...	[illegible]	[illegible]	[illegible]	[illegible]	[illegible]	[illegible]	[illegible]	[illegible]	[illegible]	[illegible]

SCOTTISH MILK MARKETING SCHEME, [illegible].

Monthly Quantities of Milk sold for Liquid Consumption and Quantities sold or used by the Board for Manufacture.

Month.	December, [illegible], to November, [illegible].					December, [illegible], to November, [illegible].				
	Total Sales.	Sold for liquid consumption.		Sold or used for manufacture.		Total Sales.	Sold for liquid consumption.		Sold or used for manufacture.	
	Gallons.	Gallons.	Per cent.	Gallons.	Per cent.	Gallons.	Gallons.	Per cent.	Gallons.	Per cent.
December ...	[illegible]	[illegible]	[illegible]	[illegible]	[illegible]	[illegible]	[illegible]	[illegible]	[illegible]	[illegible]
January ...	[illegible]	[illegible]	[illegible]	[illegible]	[illegible]	[illegible]	[illegible]	[illegible]	[illegible]	[illegible]
February ...	[illegible]	[illegible]	[illegible]	[illegible]	[illegible]	[illegible]	[illegible]	[illegible]	[illegible]	[illegible]
March ...	[illegible]	[illegible]	[illegible]	[illegible]	[illegible]	[illegible]	[illegible]	[illegible]	[illegible]	[illegible]
April ...	[illegible]	[illegible]	[illegible]	[illegible]	[illegible]	[illegible]	[illegible]	[illegible]	[illegible]	[illegible]
May ...	[illegible]	[illegible]	[illegible]	[illegible]	[illegible]	[illegible]	[illegible]	[illegible]	[illegible]	[illegible]
June ...	[illegible]	[illegible]	[illegible]	[illegible]	[illegible]	[illegible]	[illegible]	[illegible]	[illegible]	[illegible]
July ...	[illegible]	[illegible]	[illegible]	[illegible]	[illegible]	[illegible]	[illegible]	[illegible]	[illegible]	[illegible]
August ...	[illegible]	[illegible]	[illegible]	[illegible]	[illegible]	[illegible]	[illegible]	[illegible]	[illegible]	[illegible]
September ...	[illegible]	[illegible]	[illegible]	[illegible]	[illegible]	[illegible]	[illegible]	[illegible]	[illegible]	[illegible]
October ...	[illegible]	[illegible]	[illegible]	[illegible]	[illegible]	[illegible]	[illegible]	[illegible]	[illegible]	[illegible]
November ...	[illegible]	[illegible]	[illegible]	[illegible]	[illegible]	[illegible]	[illegible]	[illegible]	[illegible]	[illegible]
Total ...	[illegible]	[illegible]	[illegible]	[illegible]	[illegible]	[illegible]	[illegible]	[illegible]	[illegible]	[illegible]

PIGS AND BACON MARKETING SCHEMES, 1933.

The Pigs and Bacon Marketing Schemes, both of which apply to Great Britain, came into operation on 9th September, 1933.

In 1935 the Pigs Marketing Board was composed of 11 members, of whom 8 are elected by registered producers, voting in districts, and 3 are special members elected by registered producers in general meeting. Elections were held in four districts during 1935, the retiring member being returned in each case. At the annual general meeting held on 15th March, 1935, a new special member was elected in the place of the retiring member. The remuneration of members of the Board for the year ended 31st March, 1935, voted by registered producers at the meeting, was:—Chairman £1,000; vice-Chairman £750; other members £300 each.

The Bacon Marketing Board is composed of 16 members, of whom 12 are elected by registered producers in England and Wales voting by classes, 2 are elected by registered producers in Scotland and 2 are co-opted by the elected members after consultation with the Market Supply Committee. There was no change in the composition of the Board in the year under review. The annual general meeting of registered curers was held in London on the 28th February, 1936. It was resolved that a sum of £5,000 should be paid as remuneration to the Board for the year ended 31st March, 1936, this sum to be divided among the members in such manner as the Board might decide.

The number of registered pig producers in October, 1935, was approximately 144,000. Of these, 19,101 entered into contracts for the sale of bacon pigs under the Scheme in 1935. The number of registered curers on 31st December, 1935, was 628.

As stated in the last report,* a system of contracts for the sale of bacon pigs has been inaugurated under the Schemes in order to introduce stability into the industry. The Pigs Marketing Board have power to prescribe the form of contract, after consultation with the Bacon Marketing Board, and to require that sales of pigs by registered pig producers to registered curers shall be made in accordance with such contracts. Similarly, under the Bacon Marketing Scheme, a registered curer may not, except in special circumstances, sell bacon not produced from pigs purchased from registered pig producers under the prescribed contracts. The number of pigs contracted for in each year forms the basis on which imports of bacon are regulated.

Four contracts have so far been prescribed by the Pigs Marketing Board. The first of these ran from November, 1933, to February, 1934; the second from March, 1934, to December, 1934; the third from January, 1935, to December, 1935; and the fourth will

* Cmd. 4913, page 26.

run from January, 1936, to December, 1938. The first three contracts were fully described in the previous report* which also gave particulars of the results of the first two contract periods.

The Third Contract Period.

Number of pigs on contract.—The closing date for the receipt of contracts by the Pigs Marketing Board was 20th November, 1934. On this date, the contracts lodged with the Board were for 1,665,000 pigs, an increase of nearly 5 per cent. on the previous year. The bonus scheme, providing for the payment of premiums in respect of pigs contracted for delivery and delivered and accepted in the first four month of the year, was successful in securing a more even supply position. The distribution of contracts among individual curers was, however, irregular; some curers had only a small proportion of their estimated requirements, while others were well supplied. The number of pigs on group contracts and available for distribution among curers short of requirements showed a considerable reduction on the previous period and was inadequate to meet all needs. It was decided, therefore, to issue supplementary contracts.

The closing date fixed for the receipt of supplementary contracts was 22nd December. The contract (known as supplementary contract A) was between a registered producer and the Pigs Marketing Board, either direct or through an agent. The terms of the contract were the same as in the main contract except that there was no provision to secure regular deliveries throughout the year.

Contracts were received for an additional 111,000 pigs, making, with the direct contracts, approximately 1,800,000 pigs in all. This was a substantial increase in the actual contracting rate compared with the previous contract period, but the number of pigs on contract fell short of the number considered by the Bacon Marketing Board to be necessary to give an economic throughput to all registered curers.

Accordingly, the Pigs Marketing Board issued at the end of December, 1934, a further supplementary contract for the delivery of pigs during the period May to December, 1935. The terms of the contract (known as supplementary contract B) were identical with those of the first supplementary contract; and the closing date was 15th April, 1935. The contract was a direct contract between producer and curer but was to be valid only if the curer had not already obtained on previous contracts 70 per cent. of his stated requirements for the relevant period. The number of pigs contracted for on this contract was approximately 68,000.

As the number of pigs on contract still fell short of curers' requirements, the Pigs Marketing Board during May entered into direct

---

* Pages 27–39.

contracts with curers for approximately 165,000 pigs to be delivered between May and December. The Board decided, however, not to attempt to implement the contracts and agreed that curers should purchase pigs in the open market. The curers were required to make returns of these purchases to the Bacon Marketing Board.

The total number of pigs contracted for on direct, group and supplementary A and B contracts was 1,854,405 (see Table I, page 36). This was an increase of 248,096 pigs or 15 per cent. on 1934.

Distribution of Contracts and Pig Population.—Figures of contracting by district are not available for the whole of 1934, and a true comparison with that year is not possible. The following table shows, according to the districts defined in the Pigs Marketing Scheme, the number of pigs on contract in 1935 and in the last 10 months of 1934 :—

District.	Number of Pigs on Contract.		Per cent. of total.	
	Mar.-Dec. 1934. (10 months)	1935. (12 months)	1934.	1935.
South Western ...	277,084	365,140	20·9	19·7
South Eastern ...	203,881	291,093	15·8	15·7
Eastern	186,306	248,428	14·1	13·4
East Midland	165,865	216,573	12·4	11·7
West Midland... ...	221,793	297,501	16·7	16·0
Northern	133,266	234,431	10·0	12·6
Wales	35,454	52,153	2·7	2·8
Scotland ...	98,009	150,086	7·4	8·1
... ...	1,324,583	1,854,405	100·0	100·0

The total increase recorded in the June 4th returns in the number of pigs in Great Britain between 1934 and 1935 was 547,000 or 15 per cent. The number of sows in Great Britain increased by 51,000 in 1934, and again by 47,000 in 1935.

The following table shows the pig population in 1934 and 1935 as recorded in the June 4th returns according to the districts of the Pigs Marketing Scheme.

District.	1934.	1935.	Increase of 1935 on 1934.	Bacon Pigs on Contract in 1935 expressed as a percentage of the pig population.
			Per cent.	Per cent.
South Western ...	507,689	596,906	17·6	61·2
South Eastern ...	552,836	615,292	11·3	47·3
Eastern	502,476	560,856	11·6	44·3
East Midland	493,547	546,565	10·7	59·4
West Midland	495,329	567,898	14·7	52·4
Northern	527,852	645,024	22·3	36·8
Wales	240,599	280,742	16·7	18·6
Scotland	206,279	260,218	26·1	57·7
Total	3,526,457	4,076,586	15·6	45·6

It will be seen that the districts with the largest increase in pig populations are the Northern and Scotland, and that these districts also show the most striking increases in contracting under the Scheme. In the South-Western and West Midland districts, however, sales of bacon pigs on contract were already high in relation to pig population.

Number of Pigs Delivered.—Table II on page 67 shows, for each month, the number of pigs delivered against contracts during 1935. Total deliveries by pig producers during the year amounted to 1,806,937 pigs, of which 1,761,833 were delivered against 1935 contracts and the remainder were contracted for delivery in 1934, but delivered in 1935. On 1935 contracts alone, therefore, there was a deficiency of 73,072 pigs, or 3·94 per cent., but including all deliveries the deficiency was only 47,468 pigs or 2·56 per cent. The deficiency attributable to swine fever and other unavoidable causes was 1·72 per cent. of the pigs contracted for. This result was a great improvement on the two previous contract periods when the deficiencies were 20·8 per cent. and 7·05 per cent. respectively. The actual increase in the number of pigs delivered compared with the previous twelve months was 369,539 or 25·71 per cent.

Although the bonus scheme was largely successful in obtaining a more even supply distribution over the year, the position was not wholly satisfactory. With the exception of April, when producers were doing everything possible to deliver their pigs in time for the bonus, monthly deliveries in the first half of the year were substantially less than in the latter half. Heavy deliveries of pigs in October and November caused reactions in bacon prices, which in turn caused the pig price for December to fall.

The following table shows by means of index numbers how the monthly deliveries have varied in the two years of the Scheme :—

Monthly Deliveries of Pigs.
(Index Numbers.)

	1934.	1935.
January	93	76
February	78	72
March	58	87
April	62	119
May	61	88
June	67	84
July	93	101
August	114	101
September	127	117
October	151	129
November	135	127
December	126	99
Average	100	100

The limits of variation have been reduced from 151 : 58 to 129 : 72 —a very considerable reduction in the space of a year.

Contract Price.—The average monthly price in 1935 for the "basic" pig calculated in the manner described in the previous report* was 11s. 8½d. per score, including the premium of 2d. per score under the bonus scheme. In addition, curers paid to producers 1d. per score towards any insurance that the latter might desire to effect. The average price during 1934 was 11s. 11d. per score, which was reduced by the deductions for the repayment of the Government loan to 11s. 7½d. per score. The following table gives the standard price per score (excluding bonus payments) of the basic pig in each month in 1934 and 1935:—

Month.	*Price per Score of Basic Pig.* 1934. s.	d.	1935. s.	d.
January ...	12	0	11	8
February ...	12	0	11	5
March	12	6	11	11
April	12	6	11	0
May	11	11	10	11
June	11	8	11	5
July	11	7	11	9
August ...	11	6	11	4
September ...	11	5	11	0
October ...	12	2	10	2
November ...	12	0	11	4
December ...	12	1	10	2
Average	11	11	11	1½

* Page 37.

The low price of bacon during August and again during November accounted for the particularly low price of 10s. 6d. per score in October and December. The ascertained bacon price over the year was generally lower than for 1934 and foodstuffs prices were on the average higher.

The premiums distributed to producers who qualified under the bonus scheme by delivering certain percentages of pigs in the first four months of the year, were 2·9d., 5·8d. and 8·7d. per score respectively in the three classes specified under that scheme. The total sum distributed in bonus payments was £121,500.

Bacon put into Cure by Registered Curers.

There was a substantial increase in bacon production by registered curers in 1935 compared with 1934. The following are the details :—

Year.	Average number of curers making returns.	Home carcases and parts of carcases put into cure.	Imported pigs, carcases, and parts of carcases put into cure.	Total.
		000 cwt.	000 cwt.	000 cwt.
1934	616	1,491	251	1,742
1935	624	2,023	347	2,370
Increase per cent. over 1934 ...	—	35·7	38·2	36·1

Figures are not available for the output of curers exempted from registration under the Bacon Marketing Scheme.

Fourth Contract Period.

Prolonged discussions took place between the Pigs and Bacon Marketing Boards before the terms of the fourth contract were settled. The contract was issued in November, 1935.

Two forms of contract were prescribed, one for direct contracts between pig producers and curers and the other for direct contracts between pig producers and the Pigs Marketing Board. The latter contract, which took the place of the group contract, was designed to provide the Board with a "pool" of pigs which might be allotted to curers who had insufficient pigs on direct contract. The terms of the contracts are similar, but the "Board" contract allows the Board to expedite or postpone the delivery of pigs, and the producer receives an additional premium of 2s. 0d. per pig delivered under this contract. The closing date for the receipt of contracts by the Pigs Marketing Board was 26th November, 1935, but the period was extended, in the case of Board contracts, until 3rd December.

The terms of the 1936 contract are broadly the same as in the previous year. The main features of the contract are as follows:—

Basis of Contract.—The producer contracts to deliver a stated number of pigs in one or more of four weight classes* in stated months of the year with a tolerance of 10 per cent. in any month, subject to a maximum annual tolerance of 5 per cent. The number of pigs contracted for delivery in the first four months and the last four months of the year must not, respectively, be less than 25 per cent. or exceed 45 per cent. of the total number of pigs contracted to be sold during the year.

Delivery.—The pig producer is responsible for putting pigs on rail at his station; if he does not do so, the curer deducts 6d. from the price of the pig. The curer pays the transport charge, which is a flat rate of 1s. 6d. per pig from station to station, or 2s. 3d. per pig if the pigs are conveyed by road by the railway companies. A curer may arrange to transport the pigs in his own vehicles or arrange with the producer to carry them in the producer's vehicles, but the curer must in such cases pay the flat rate, and he may recover from the railway companies a rebate which varies according to the distance travelled. The flat rate charges are 2d. per pig higher than in 1935, but there have been increases in the scale of rebates.

Curer and producer may agree upon earlier or later deliveries than those specified in the contract. No pigs delivered after 28th February, 1937, will however be regarded as pigs delivered in pursuance of the contract.

Grading.—The five grades based on shoulder fat and belly measurements have been retained, with certain minor alterations.

Prices.—Pig prices continue to be fixed by reference to the ascertained price of bacon and the cost of the standard feeding stuffs ration on what is known as the "co-partnership" principle. A new formula has, however, been adopted, the starting point of which is that with bacon at 96s. and feeding stuffs at 7s. 6d. per cwt. the price of the "basic" pig (Class 1, Grade C) is 11s. 7d. per score. For each rise or fall of 1s. 2d. per cwt. in the bacon price above or below 96s., 1d. per score is added to or deducted from the pig price so long as the bacon price is not more than 98s. 4d. and not less than 90s. 2d. For every 10d. rise in bacon prices above 98s. 4d. a further penny per score is added to, and for every 10d. fall below 90s. 2d. a further penny per score will be deducted from, the pig price.

As long as bacon prices are over 90s. 2d. per cwt., an addition or deduction of 1½d. per score is made in the pig price for rises and falls of 3d. per cwt. in the price of feeding stuffs above or below

---

* Class I	Dead Weight	7 score to 8 score 10lb.
" II	" "	8 score 11lb. to 9 score 6lb.
" III	" "	9 score 6lb. to 10 score 10lb.
" IV	" "	Over 10 score 10lb.

the basic figures of 7s. 6d. If, however, bacon prices are 90s. 2d. or less, the addition or deduction in respect of variations of 3d. in the price of feeding stuffs is only 1d. per score. Over and above the prices so calculated, an addition of 1d. per score is made to the pig price when the bacon price is between 86s. 7d. and 97s. 1d. inclusive.

A return to one of the price features of the 1934 contract is made by an allowance for variations in the value of offals.

The "bacon price" referred to is the average price realised for sizeable green Wiltshire-style bacon (certified by an independent accountant) over a period of four or five weeks ending near the middle of the month prior to that to which it relates, adjustments being made to take into account any variations in the realised value of offals. The price is ascertained at six factories, three chosen by the Pigs Marketing Board and three by the Bacon Marketing Board. The cost of feeding stuffs is calculated over a period of sixteen weeks by reference to a ration containing barley meal, weatings and protein and mineral matter in agreed proportions.

The price difference of 3d. per score between Class I and Class II pigs remains unchanged, but Class III pigs are paid for at the same price as Class II. The basic price of Class IV pigs is 9d. per score, instead of 1s. per score, less than that of Class I.

These prices do not apply to deliveries of pigs which are not in the class contracted for. Such pigs, if accepted by the curer, are to be paid for at special prices. Where, however, a producer has contracted to supply Class I pigs, he may include one pig below seven score (but not below 6 score 15 lb.) in each delivery without penalty.

The bonus scheme.—The bonus scheme issued in connection with the contract provides for bonuses A and B and a special bonus. Bonus A, which will be three times as large as bonus B, will be earned by a producer who delivers 33⅓ per cent. of his pigs in the first four months of the year; bonus B by the delivery of not less than 25 per cent. of the year's total in the first four months. The special bonus, which was designed to secure regular deliveries in the bonus period, will be paid on the lowest monthly scorage of pigs delivered by a qualifying producer and accepted in any of these months. One-third of the total net bonus fund will be devoted to the payment of the special bonus.

The same contribution as in the previous contract, namely 2d. per score on all pigs delivered and accepted, is payable by curers into the bonus fund.

Insurance.—Curers deduct 6d. per pig from the price payable to the producer. In return the producer is paid the full price for any pig damaged in transit or which is found to be suffering from any disease which was not apparent when the pig left the farm. The curer may either insure against this risk or carry it himself.

Default by the producer.—A producer who defaults in the delivery of any pigs on direct contract (unless the default is due to unavoidable causes, such as accident or disease) is liable to pay 15s. per pig to the Pigs Marketing Board and 5s. per pig to the curer by way of liquidated damages. In the case of the "Board" contract, a defaulting producer pays £1 per pig to the Pigs Marketing Board.

If the producer is prevented from delivering pigs by accident, disease or any other cause outside his control, the Pigs Marketing Board undertake to do their best to make good the deficiency or, failing this, to pay the curer 8s. per pig, subject to a maximum liability on the part of the Board of £6,000 over the year.

Number of pigs contracted for; the supplementary contract.—The contracts received by the Pigs Marketing Board covered a total of slightly less than 2,000,000 pigs. Over 97 per cent. of these were on direct contracts with curers, and the number on "Board" contracts was insufficient to give all curers an economic throughput. A supplementary contract for supplying pigs to the Board was, therefore, issued. This contract was similar to the first "Board" contract for the same period, but the requirement to deliver at least 25 per cent. of contracted deliveries in the first four months was waived. The producer receives 1s. 6d. per pig above the contract price for pigs supplied on this contract. The closing date for the receipt of supplementary contracts was 14th January, 1936.

The number of pigs contracted for on these contracts was less than 60,000 so that the Pigs Marketing Board were still unable to fulfil curers' requirements. Accordingly, the Board, as in the previous year, agreed that curers should purchase pigs in the open market. Provision was made for the inclusion of 305,000 "open market" pigs in the "home quota", for the period March-December, 1936, on guarantees being obtained from individual curers that at least that number of pigs would be purchased. The Board also undertook to endeavour to secure that total purchases were not more than 450,000 pigs in the months March to December, 1936.

Regulation of Bacon Supplies.

The regulation of imports of bacon was continued by Order of the Board of Trade under the Agricultural Marketing Acts in the case of foreign supplies and by voluntary agreement in the case of Dominion supplies. The gross supplies of bacon, hams, salted pork and tinned hams from all sources (excluding the output of unregistered curers in Great Britain) in 1935 compared with 1932 and 1934 were as follows :—

	1932.		1934.		1935.	
	000 cwt.	Per cent.	000 cwt.	Per cent.	000 cwt.	Per cent.
United Kingdom*	1,750†	12·5	2,230	20·8	2,953	27·7
Dominion‡ ...	545	3·9	1,475	13·8	1,601	15·0
Foreign‡	11,732	83·6	6,987	65·4	6,107	57·3
Total	14,027	100·0	10,692	100·0	10,661	100·0

* Includes imported pigs and pork cured in this country.

† Based on 1930 Board of Trade Industrial Census, the latest official figures available.

‡ Gross Imports. Exports and re-exports amounted to 270,000 cwt., 97,000 cwt. and 128,000 cwt. in 1932, 1934 and 1935 respectively.

In reply to a question in the House of Commons on 7th June, 1935, the Minister of Agriculture announced that the Government had had the Pigs and Bacon Marketing Schemes under review and they considered that certain developments of the general plan for regulating bacon imports and assisting the home producer might be made to the advantage of all concerned. They proposed that the policy of maintaining a regulated market should be continued, but were prepared to contemplate an increase in the volume of imported supplies, subject to a limited charge on imports from foreign countries, the proceeds of which could be devoted to the assistance of the home industry as the situation might require.

In reply to a further question on 9th December, 1935, the Minister made it clear that, under the proposals previously announced, the subsidy payable from the proceeds of the levy on imports of foreign bacon was to compensate the home industry for any fall in price resulting from the contemplated increase in imports. The proposals did not provide for additional assistance while the present degree of import regulation is maintained.

Complaints regarding the Operation of the Scheme.

It was mentioned in the last report* that the Committee of Investigation for Great Britain had had under consideration complaints by (1) the Parliamentary Committee of the Co-operative Congress as to the omission in the third contract of any obligation to insure pigs, and (2) The Parliamentary Committee of the Co-operative Congress and the National Federation of Meat Traders' Associations as to the requirements in the third contract regarding the flat rate system for the transport of all live pigs purchased by curers.

The Committee heard oral evidence and Counsels' arguments in both cases. In the transport complaint, the substance of their finding was that the flat rate system of transport was necessary for the

* Page 42.

efficient operation of the Pigs and Bacon Marketing Schemes and that although some curers were, in consequence of the adoption of the flat rate system, undoubtedly paying more for transport than previously, the Pigs Marketing Board, in prescribing this system, had acted in the best interests of the pig industry as a whole.

In the insurance complaint, the Committee reported in favour of the compulsory insurance of pigs contracted for under the Pigs and Bacon Marketing Schemes. The Pigs Marketing Board were accordingly requested by " the Minister "* to prepare, in consultation with the Bacon Marketing Board, the insurance companies and any other interests concerned, an agreed scheme for insurance of all pigs consigned to registered bacon curers under contract after 31st December, 1935, and to submit the scheme to " the Minister."

The scheme mentioned on page 31 was thereupon prepared by the Boards, two firms of Lloyds' Underwriters having agreed to accept the risk for a premium of 1s. per pig. As the prescription of the 1936 contract was then a matter of urgency, " the Minister " did not ask the Pigs Marketing Board at that stage to prepare an alternative scheme for consideration, but he informed them that it was his intention to re-examine the matter at a later date in the light of the experience gained of the system proposed by the Board.

Amendments of the Schemes.

During 1934 the Pigs Marketing Board had under consideration a number of draft amendments to their Scheme. These were circulated to registered producers on 23rd November, 1934, and no request having been made for a poll, they were formally submitted to " the Minister " on 29th January, 1935.

In accordance with the provisions of the Marketing Acts, a period expiring on 16th April, 1935, was allowed for lodging objections or representations with respect to the proposed amendments. Objections to certain of the amendments were received from the Scottish Chamber of Agriculture, the Bacon Marketing Board, the National Federation of Meat Traders' Associations and the Parliamentary Committee of the Co-operative Congress, and, by direction of " the Minister ", a public inquiry was held into the objections by Mr. N. L. Macaskie, K.C.

After considering the objections and the Commissioner's report the Minister modified the amendments. The amendments as modified were accordingly laid before Parliament, and affirmative resolutions of both Houses were passed in December, 1935.

Apart from certain drafting amendments, the amendments fall into two groups. The first of these made certain alterations in the electoral procedure and in the provisions for the payment of remuneration to members of the Board and permits the removal from

* " The Minister " means, in relation to a Scheme applicable both in England and Scotland, the Minister of Agriculture and Fisheries and the Secretary of State for Scotland, acting in conjunction.

office of the Chairman or Vice-Chairman in certain circumstances. The second group concerns some of the marketing provisions of the Scheme; the Board were given wider powers to regulate the transport of pigs, and certain alterations were made in the procedure with regard to the registration and confirmation of contracts. The amendments were brought into force, with effect from 21st December, 1935, by the Pigs Marketing Scheme (Amendment) Order, 1935.*

Amendments to the Bacon Marketing Scheme were submitted in March, 1934, and of these, three which were unopposed were approved in June, 1934.† The other two amendments were designed to enable the Board to determine the quantity of bacon that may be sold in any year by a registered curer and to secure that, in any expansion of the market for home-produced bacon, the extent to which any registered curer might participate with pigs of his own production should be regulated. These amendments were objected to, and a public inquiry was held into the objections, as recorded in the last report.

After considering the report of the Commissioner appointed to hold the public inquiry (Mr. N. L. Macaskie, K.C.) "the Minister" made minor modifications, and the amendments were approved by Parliament on 1st August. The amendments were brought into force with effect from 3rd August, 1935, by the Bacon Marketing Scheme (Amendment) Order, 1935.‡

Miscellaneous.

Accounts of the Boards.—The accounts of the Boards for the year ended 31st December, 1935, are printed in Appendix III.

In the case of the Bacon Marketing Board, the levy of 6d. per cwt. on bacon sales realised about £56,500. The total expenditure of the Board (excluding provision for contingent liabilities) amounted to £33,000. The costs of operating the Scheme during the year were approximately 3d. per pig delivered.

The chief item of income of the Pigs Marketing Board, the delivery and grading fees, realised nearly £130,000. The costs of operating the Scheme were approximately one shilling per pig delivered.

The Pigs and Bacon Marketing Boards have paid to the Exchequer during the year the sums of £2,088 and £678 respectively, certified by "the Minister" to represent the expenses of the Reorganisation Commission for Pigs and Pig Products attributable to the preparation of the Pigs and Bacon Marketing Schemes.

---

* S.R. & O. 1935, No. 1808.
† S.R. & O. 1934, No. 679.
‡ S.R. & O. 1935, No. 791.

Publicity.—In December, 1935, the Pigs Marketing Board decided to circulate a monthly news bulletin to all contracting producers. The first number was issued in January, 1936. The two Boards have staged a joint educational exhibit dealing with the production of bacon pigs at a number of agricultural shows throughout the year.

TABLE I.

SUMMARY OF CONTRACTS.

	England.	Scotland.	Gt. Britain.
Number of Contracts			
First Period (November, 1933 to February, 1934)	16,952	1,880	18,832
Second Period (March to December, 1934)	22,286	1,983	24,269
Third Period (January to December, 1935)	21,644	2,001	23,645
Fourth Period (January to December, 1936)	16,871	1,663	18,534
Number of Pigs Contracted for			
First Period (4 months) :—			
Direct	446,855	24,747	471,602
Group	95,686	9,040	104,726
Total First Period ...	542,541	33,787	576,328
Second Period (10 months) :—			
Direct :—			
(a) General	775,679	8,784	784,463
(b) Wiltshire	227,569	62,658	290,227
Total Direct	1,003,248	71,442	1,074,690
Group	223,281	26,567	249,848
Total Second Period	1,226,529	98,009	1,324,538
Third Period (12 months) :—			
Direct and Livestock	1,416,702	121,949	1,538,651
Group	131,316	15,455	146,771
Supplementary	156,301	12,682	168,983
Total Third Period ...	1,704,319	150,086	1,854,405
Fourth Period (12 months) :—			
Direct	1,771,338	169,639	1,940,977
Board	45,822	6,478	52,300
Supplementary	42,885	3,914	46,799
Total Fourth Period	1,860,045	180,031	2,040,076

TABLE [illegible].

[illegible], January–December, [illegible].

Month [illegible].	Contracted for and delivered in [illegible].								Contracted in [illegible] Delivered in [illegible].		Open Market Purchases [illegible].		Total delivered and [illegible] pigs.	Number Reported on all Contracts.
	Direct Contracts.		Group Contracts.		Supplementary Contracts "A" and "B."		Total.							
	Con-tracted.	De-livered.	Con-tracted.	De-livered.	Con-tracted.	De-livered.	Con-tracted.	De-livered.	Direct.	Group.	Con-tracted.	De-livered.		
Jan. ...	[illegible]	[illegible]	[illegible]	[illegible]	[illegible]	[illegible]	[illegible]	[illegible]	[illegible]	4,777	—	—	[illegible]	[illegible]
Feb. ...	[illegible]	[illegible]	[illegible]	[illegible]	[illegible]	[illegible]	[illegible]	[illegible]	[illegible]	[illegible]	—	—	[illegible]	[illegible]
Mar. ...	[illegible]	[illegible]	[illegible]	[illegible]	[illegible]	[illegible]	[illegible]	[illegible]	[illegible]	[illegible]	—	—	[illegible]	[illegible]
April ...	[illegible]	[illegible]	[illegible]	[illegible]	[illegible]	[illegible]	[illegible]	[illegible]	[illegible]	[illegible]	—	—	[illegible]	[illegible]
May ...	[illegible]	[illegible]	[illegible]	[illegible]	[illegible]	[illegible]	[illegible]	[illegible]	[illegible]	[illegible]	[illegible]	[illegible]	[illegible]	[illegible]
June ...	[illegible]	[illegible]	[illegible]	[illegible]	[illegible]	[illegible]	[illegible]	[illegible]	[illegible]	[illegible]	[illegible]	[illegible]	[illegible]	[illegible]
July ...	[illegible]	[illegible]	[illegible]	[illegible]	[illegible]	[illegible]	[illegible]	[illegible]	[illegible]	[illegible]	[illegible]	[illegible]	[illegible]	[illegible]
Aug. ...	[illegible]	[illegible]	[illegible]	[illegible]	[illegible]	[illegible]	[illegible]	[illegible]	[illegible]	[illegible]	[illegible]	[illegible]	[illegible]	[illegible]
Sept. ...	[illegible]	[illegible]	[illegible]	[illegible]	[illegible]	[illegible]	[illegible]	[illegible]	[illegible]	[illegible]	[illegible]	[illegible]	[illegible]	[illegible]
Oct. ...	[illegible]	[illegible]	[illegible]	[illegible]	[illegible]	[illegible]	[illegible]	[illegible]	—	[illegible]	[illegible]	[illegible]	[illegible]	[illegible]
Nov. ...	[illegible]	[illegible]	[illegible]	[illegible]	[illegible]	[illegible]	[illegible]	[illegible]	...	77	[illegible]	[illegible]	[illegible]	[illegible]
Dec. ...	[illegible]	[illegible]	[illegible]	[illegible]	[illegible]	[illegible]	[illegible]	[illegible]	—	—	[illegible]	[illegible]	[illegible]	[illegible]
Total	[illegible]	[illegible]	[illegible]	[illegible]	[illegible]	[illegible]	[illegible]	[illegible]	[illegible]	[illegible]	[illegible]	[illegible]	[illegible]	[illegible]

MILK MARKETING SCHEME, 1933.

The Milk Marketing Scheme, which applies to England and Wales, came into operation on 6th October, 1933.

The total quantity of milk sold by registered producers under the Scheme from 6th October, 1933, to 30th September, 1934, was 845·3 million gallons; sales during the twelve months ended on 30th September, 1935, amounted to 981 million gallons, an increase of 135·7 million gallons or 16 per cent. The quantities sold under wholesale contracts and retail licences increased by 137·3 million gallons and 3·2 million gallons respectively, while farm production of cheese under the Scheme decreased by 4·8 million gallons.

The number of wholesale contracts in force rose from 76,407 in December, 1933, to 86,813 in September, 1935. Four regions, namely, the Far Western, Northern, South Wales and North Western, accounted for 80 per cent. of the additional contracts.

A detailed statement showing the quantities of milk sold under the Scheme since its inception until 31st December, 1935, is given in Table I on page 56.

The Board consists of 17 members; 12 are elected on a regional basis (one representative for each region except the North-Western, which has 2), 3 special members are elected by the registered producers in general meeting, and 2 members are co-opted by the elected members of the Board after consultation with the Market Supply Committee.

The elected personnel of the Board remained unchanged during 1935. Four of the regional members were due to retire in June; two were returned unopposed and the other two were re-elected. None of the special members was due to retire in 1935. Lord Cranworth, one of the co-opted members, resigned and was succeeded by Lord Eltisley.

The remuneration of the Board voted by the registered producers at the annual general meeting held on the 6th June, 1935, was :— Chairman £1,200, Vice-Chairman £700, other members £350 each.

The number of producers registered with the Board on 31st December, 1934, was 158,706. The number registered on 30th September, 1935, was 167,217. There were then 79,267 producers who held wholesale contracts, and 65,744 who held retail licences; and of these 19,927 sold both under a wholesale contract and by retail licence. On 31st December, 1935, the number on the register was 166,638, of whom approximately 86,641 did not hold either a wholesale contract or a producer-retailer's licence.

Wholesale Contracts.

The twelve months ended 30th September, 1935, constituted the third period for which contract terms have been prescribed by the Board for the sale of milk by wholesale. The two previous periods ran from 6th October, 1933, to 31st March, 1934, and from 1st April to 30th September, 1934. The terms of these contracts were fully described in the last report.*

* Cmd. 4913, pages 43–49.

The quantity of milk sold under the wholesale contracts during the year ended on 30th September, 1935, was 854 million gallons, and the receipts from the sale of this milk accruing to the Board were approximately £40·8 million. The corresponding quantity sold in the previous year was 716 million gallons, and the sum receivable was approximately £34·5 million. Particulars of regional sales are given in Table II on page 58.

The numbers of wholesale contracts in operation in September, 1935, compared with those for September, 1934, were as follows:—

Region.	*No. of contracts, September, 1934.*	*No. of contracts, September, 1935.*
Northern ...	6,610	7,585
North Western	19,643	21,090
Eastern ...	3,812	4,152
East Midland	6,755	6,849
West Midland	7,134	7,464
North Wales	1,751	1,907
South Wales	4,543	5,217
Southern ...	5,467	5,647
Mid Western	11,262	11,644
Far Western	6,326	8,727
South Eastern	6,617	6,531
Total	79,920	86,813

The numbers of contracts providing for level delivery and special service premiums in the two periods were:—

Region.	Level Delivery Contracts.		Other Special Services.		Total Premium Contracts.	
	1933–34.	1934–35.	1933–34.	1934–35.	1933–34.	1934–35.
1. Northern ...	1,387	1,074	624	156	2,011	1,230
2. North Western	4,157	3,988	1,209	905	5,366	4,893
3. Eastern ...	905	776	220	214	1,125	990
4. East Midland...	1,603	1,418	262	314	1,865	1,732
5. West Midland	1,104	999	202	210	1,306	1,209
6. North Wales ...	263	215	101	73	364	288
7. South Wales ...	703	656	288	323	991	979
8. Southern ...	1,204	1,023	363	338	1,567	1,361
9. Mid Western...	662	577	633	521	1,295	1,098
10. Far Western ...	1,469	1,409	196	207	1,665	1,616
11. South Eastern	1,663	1,519	638	668	2,301	2,187
Total	15,120	13,554	4,736	3,929	19,856	17,483

The number of wholesale buyers in the third contract period was 16,374 compared with 17,340 in the second period.

Sales by wholesale for liquid consumption.

The quantity of milk sold under the wholesale contracts for liquid consumption during the year ended September, 1935, was 552·8 million gallons compared with 523·8 million gallons in the previous year.

The monthly wholesale prices in the third contract period ranged between 1s. 5d. and 1s. 0d. a gallon, the weighted average price being 14·87d. per gallon over the year. About 60 per cent. of the milk was consigned on "direct contracts" that is to say, contracts for delivery direct to the purchaser's railway station or dairy, the remaining 40 per cent. being sold on "depot" contracts for delivery at approved collecting depots.

Sales for manufacturing purposes.

The following table shows the quantities of milk sold for manufacture into various commodities and the average prices realised during the years ended on 30th September, 1934 and 1935 respectively.

Product Manufactured.	1933/34.		1934/35.	
	Gallons of milk manufactured.	Average realisation price.*	Gallons of milk manufactured.	Average realisation price.*
		d. per gall.		d. per gall.
Butter	41,291,580	3·01 (4·50)	83,717,384	4·07 (5·36)
Cheese	61,686,709	3·60 (4·53)	91,390,191	3·60 (4·80)
Soft curd cheese and Cream Cheese.	—	—	1,240,375	7·50
Condensed Milk ...	34,045,256	6·00	49,808,506	6·00
Condensed Milk for export.	5,884,623	3·62 (4·62)	6,463,318	4·04 (5·26)
Milk Powder	8,357,747	3·03 (5·36)	12,967,136	4·50 (5·26)
Fresh Cream	32,530,318	7·96	41,347,704	7·50
Ice Cream	—	—	2,654,314	7·60
Tinned Cream ...	3,473,926	5·2	7,090,224	5·00 (5·36)
Chocolate	62,382	6·00	71,950	6·00
Sterilised milk for export.	—	6·00	4,267	6·00
Other Goods	3,332,068	9·00	2,933,747	9·00
Total	192,623,561	4·96 (5·49)	301,689,001	4·81 (5·64)

* The figures in brackets show the average prices after including the repayable advances under the Milk Act, 1934.

Price of Milk for Manufacture into Cheese.—The 1934/35 contract provided that the manufacturing price might be varied by agreement between the Board and the Central Milk Distributive Committee (representing the purchasers of milk by wholesale) or, failing agreement, on the certificate of a person brought into consultation pursuant to Section 18 of the Agricultural Marketing Act, 1933. An application was made to the Board by the Central Milk Distributive Committee for a revision in the price formula for milk for manufacture into cheese and butter, and the question was submitted to the late Mr. Edward Shortt, K.C., as the "consulted person". A compromise suggested by him that, during the months April-July, 1935, the price of milk for cheese should be based on the price of Finest White New Zealand cheese instead of on the average price of New Zealand and Canadian cheese, was accepted by both parties. In August and September the formula was to remain unchanged, but, as regards Canadian cheese, exceptional quotations and quotations for old cheese were to be excluded. The effect was that prices were rather more favourable to buyers, especially during the summer months. There was no change in the price formula of milk for butter.

Repayable advances under the Milk Act, 1934.—The amounts paid to the Board under the Milk Act by way of contingently repayable advances in respect of milk manufactured during the period October, 1934, to September, 1935, were as follows:—

	£	£
Milk products manufactured at factories other than Board's factories.		
Butter	447,677	
Cheese	483,608	
Condensed milk for export	43,283	
Milk powder	41,956	
Tinned cream	11,465	
		1,027,989
At Board's factories.		
Butter	286	
Cheese	10,966	
		11,252
Farmhouse Cheese		62,636
TOTAL		1,101,877

Pool Prices and Producers' Net Returns.

Producers selling milk by wholesale are credited with the appropriate regional pool price for each gallon of milk sold. Each regional pool price is based on the realisation value of the milk sold in that region, whether for manufacture or liquid consumption, but adjustments are made by means of the inter-regional compensation levy to ensure that the pool prices do not vary unduly as between the regions.

Regional pool prices for each region and each month from October, 1934, to December, 1935, are shown in Table III, on page 59.

The weighted average pool prices for the year ended 30th September, 1935, ranged from 11·39d. per gallon in the Far Western region to 12·78d. in the South Eastern region, the weighted average for the country as a whole being 11·99d. The corresponding weighted average for the previous year was 11·83d.

Theoretically, all milk delivered under the wholesale contracts is sold at the wholesale price, adjustments being made in the case of milk sold for manufacture by the allowance of rebates varying with the products manufactured. Before the pool prices are struck, deductions are also made to meet the expenses and liabilities of the Board, and to provide the sums necessary to pay the premium for accredited milk.

As stated previously, the weighted average wholesale price for milk sold for liquid consumption during the year ended 30th September, 1935, was 14·87d. per gallon. The rebates for manufacturing milk represented a deduction from the liquid price of 2·95d. per gallon; the lower price received for milk supplied to school children accounted for a further deduction of 0·22d.; the levy for the Board's expenses and for the provision of reserves amounted to 0·18d. and the amount required for the payment of the premium on accredited milk to 0·06d.; other deductions in respect of publicity, the rebates to farmhouse cheesemakers and the compensation paid to the Scottish Milk Marketing Board amounted to 0·1d. The credits received were: 0·24d. in respect of producer-retailers' contributions, 0·29d. in respect of the repayable advances under Sections 1 to 8 of the Milk Act, 1934, and 0·1d. in respect of payments received under Section 11. The net deduction from the average wholesale regional price was, therefore, 2·88d. per gallon, giving an average weighted pool price of 11·99d.

The pool price received by any individual producer is subject to deductions for transport charges and, in some cases, to charges for "transit risk" and collection in addition. On the other hand, he may qualify for the level delivery and accredited premiums, as well as for any additional premiums for special services that he may arrange with his buyer. The average effect of these adjustments, excluding the accredited premium, is shown in the following table for each region for the year 1934/35.

Region.	Average Pool Price.	Average Transport Deduction.	Average Premium Received (excluding the accredited premiums).	Average Net Return.
	d. per gall.	d. per gall.	d. per gall.	d. per gall.
Northern	12·10	2·03	0·11	10·18
North-Western ...	11·95	1·69	0·13	10·39
Eastern	12·45	1·88	0·13	10·70
East Midland ...	12·18	1·41	0·15	10·92
West Midland ...	11·47	1·98	0·08	9·57
North Wales ...	11·51	2·09	0·07	9·49
South Wales ...	12·05	2·58	0·07	9·54
Southern	12·50	1·49	0·16	11·17
Mid Western ...	11·59	2·29	0·06	9·36
Far Western ...	11·39	2·53	0·12	8·98
South Eastern ...	12·78	1·16	0·25	11·87
Weighted Average	11·99	1·83	0·12	10·28

Producer-Retailers.

Sales by producer-retailers during the year ended 30th September, 1935, amounted to 113·2 million gallons, compared with 110 million gallons in the preceding twelve months. The number of producer-retailers licensed by the Board was 65,744 in September, 1935, compared with 46,801 in September, 1934. Prior to 1st October, 1934, producer-retailers who sold less than one gallon of milk a day were not required to hold a producer-retailer's licence. From that date all producer-retailers were required to be licensed by the Board. There are about 20,000 licensed producer-retailers whose daily sales do not exceed one gallon, and the inclusion of these producers accounts for the increase in the number of licences in 1935.

Producer-retailers are required to contribute to the funds of the Board. The amount of the contribution in any region is equal to the sum of the inter-regional compensation levy, the accredited levy and three quarters of the difference between the wholesale liquid milk price (less the inter-regional and accredited levies) and the regional pool price. The producer-retailer is entitled to qualify for the level delivery premium and the accredited premium. A producer-retailer owning not more than 4 cows may elect to pay 10s. per cow per annum in lieu of the above contribution.

The average net contribution for the year, after making allowance for the level delivery premium, but not the accredited premium, was 1·99d. per gallon, compared with 0·69d. per gallon in the previous year. 88 per cent. of producer-retailers qualified for the level delivery premium in 1934/35. The following table shows the net contributions for each region :—

Region.	1933/34.	1934/35.
	d. per gallon.	d. per gallon.
1. Northern	0·80	2·01
2. North Western	0·95	2·00
3. Eastern...	0·65	1·78
4. East Midland	0·67	1·95
5. West Midland	1·24	2·40
6. North Wales	1·01	2·27
7. South Wales	0·89	1·92
8. Southern	0·65	1·79
9. Mid Western	1·16	2·44
10. Far Western	1·12	2·37
11. South Eastern...	0·79	1·58
Weighted Average	0·88	1·99

The gross monthly contributions of producer-retailers in each region in 1934/35 are given in Table IV on page 60.

Retail Prices.

Minimum appropriate retail prices were prescribed by the Board for the year ended 30th September, 1935, for (a) urban districts etc. with populations of less than 10,000 and all rural districts, (b) urban districts etc. with populations of 10,000 to 25,000, and (c) urban districts etc. with populations exceeding 25,000.

In the first of these categories, the minimum retail price was 2s. 0d. per gallon in all months except May and June, when it was 1s. 8d. per gallon; in the second category, the price was 2s. 2d. per gallon in the six winter months (October-March) and 2s. 0d. per gallon in the six summer months; in the third category, the price was 2s. 4d. per gallon in the winter months and 2s. 0d. per gallon in the summer months, except in London and in districts within the South Eastern region, where the winter price was continued during April and September.

The contract permitted the minimum retail price in any district to be reduced by the Board if they were requested to do so by a majority of the retailers operating in the district. Following the receipt of resolutions from local retailers, the Board sanctioned reductions in 354 towns and villages during the contract period.

In a report* published in February, 1935, the Consumers' Committee for England pointed out that the retail price of milk had risen since the Scheme came into operation, and that there was

* Report of the Consumers' Committee for England, dated 18th February, 1935; obtainable from the Ministry of Agriculture, 10, Whitehall Place, London, S.W.1.

a danger that higher wholesale prices might stimulate production and at the same time lead to a decrease in consumption. They suggested that the retail margin should be fixed low enough to give not more than a reasonable return to the distributor working under the most economical conditions, or giving the least expensive service consistent with efficiency, or that it should be fixed in relation to the different types of distributive services. This report raised questions which came within the scope of the enquiry being conducted by the Milk Reorganisation Commission for Great Britain, and was accordingly forwarded to the Commission for consideration in connection with any proposals they might formulate for improvements in the system of organised milk marketing.

Contract Terms for the Fourth Contract Period.

The Milk Marketing Board were unable to reach agreement with representatives of the wholesale purchasers of milk as to the prices and terms of the contract to be prescribed for the twelve months commencing on 1st October, 1935. The Board thereupon prescribed the contract, and the prescription was followed by complaints made to the Minister by the Central Milk Distributive Committee and the Parliamentary Committee of the Co-operative Congress regarding the prices and certain of the terms prescribed. The Minister directed the Committee of Investigation for England to consider and report upon the complaints. In the meantime, by agreement between the parties, an addendum was made to the contract to permit the Board by resolution to vary the prices and terms if so ordered or requested by the Minister after consideration of the report of the Committee of Investigation and to allow the contract to be voided by any party thereto on notice given within 14 days of the notification of the resolution or of a notification that no resolution was required.

After considering the written representations of the Board on the complaints, the Committee of Investigation were of the opinion that they could not make a full and proper report without hearing evidence. The Committee met to hear evidence on 7th October, but Counsel for the Central Milk Distributive Committee applied for an adjournment of five weeks in order that the evidence necessary to his clients' case could be prepared. The Committee decided, however, to hear the opening speeches of Counsel and of the Right Hon. A. V. Alexander, who appeared for the Parliamentary Committee of the Co-operative Congress. These speeches were delivered on 7th, 8th, 9th and 10th October. The Committee then adjourned until 11th November. Owing to the General Election intervening and to the death of the Chairman of the Committee, the Right Hon. Edward Shortt, K.C., the hearing was not resumed until 10th December. Mr. James Whitehead, K.C., succeeded Mr. Shortt as Chairman of the Committee.*

* The Committee reported in April, 1936, and their report has been published.

The main features of the contract are described in the following paragraphs.

Basis of Sale.— A producer has the option of contracting to sell either on a "cow basis" or on a "gallonage basis". On the "cow basis" he contracts to sell the whole output either from cows not exceeding a certain number or from a stated number of cows with an agreed maximum daily delivery. On the "gallonage basis", the producer contracts to sell a stated daily quantity with a maximum variation of 10 per cent., receiving an additional premium of ½d. per gallon, or an exact stated daily quantity, for which the premium is 1d. per gallon. Provision is also made for semi-wholesale and "accommodation" sales of varying daily quantities carrying a premium varying from 1½d. per gallon upwards according to the quantity purchased. Where, however, the purchaser is a Local Authority, a voluntary hospital, a public body or a registered dairyman, the premium is 1½d. per gallon for all quantities.

Prices.—The average price per gallon prescribed by the Board for milk for liquid consumption was 1s. 3½d. per gallon. The monthly prices are given in the following table, together with those in the previous contracts :—

	First and Second Contract Periods Oct. 1933 to Sept. 1934.		Third Contract Period Oct. 1934 to Sept. 1935.	Fourth Contract Period Oct. 1935 to Sept. 1936.
	South-Eastern Region.	All other Regions.	All Regions.	All Regions.
	s. d.	s. d.	s. d.	s. d.
October ...	1 4	1 3	1 4	1 5
November ...	1 4	1 4	1 4	1 5
December ...	1 5	1 4	1 5	1 5
January ...	1 5	1 4	1 5	1 5
February ...	1 4	1 4	1 5	1 5
March ...	1 2	1 2	1 4	1 5
April... ...	1 1	1 0	1 4	1 4
May	1 0½*	1 0½*	1 0½*	1 1½*
June... ...	1 0	1 0	1 0	1 1
July	1 1	1 0	1 1	1 1
August ...	1 1	1 0	1 1	1 1
September ...	1 1	1 0	1 4	1 4
Average ...	1 2¼	1 1½	1 3$\frac{1}{16}$	1 3½

* The 1d. in May represents the purchasers' share of the contribution for publicity. It has been excluded in the calculation of the average price.

The price per gallon of milk for manufacture into butter, cheese and condensed milk for export was, prior to 1st April, 1935, the average price per lb. for the previous month of Finest White Canadian Cheese and Finest White New Zealand Cheese, less 1½d. and subject to a minimum of 4d. per gallon in the case of condensed milk for export. By the award of the "consulted person," to which reference has already been made, the price formula for cheese was slightly varied in the months April-September, 1935, but remained unchanged for butter.

The contract prescribed for 1935/36 made still further alterations in the price of milk for manufacture into these three commodities. The price of milk for manufacture into butter was fixed at 8¾d. per gallon (4½d. in Cornwall). The price per gallon of milk for manufacture into cheese (other than soft curd cheese and cream cheese) was :—

October, 1935, to February, 1936, and September, 1936.—A sum equal to the average less a sum of 1½d. of (1) the average price per lb. for the previous month of Finest White New Zealand cheese and (2) the average of (a) the average price per lb. for the previous month of Finest White Canadian cheese (excluding old and exceptional quotations) and (b) the average price per lb. of Canadian Cheese New Season's make.

March to August, 1936.—The average price per lb. for the previous month of Finest White New Zealand Cheese less a sum of 1½d. per lb.

The same formula, subject to a minimum of 4d. per gallon, applied to condensed milk for export.

The prices of milk for manufacture into other commodities are given in the following table :—

Manufactured Product.	Oct. 1933 to March 1934.	April to Sept. 1934.	Oct. 1934 to Sept. 1935.	Oct. 1935 to Sept. 1936.
	d. per gall.	d. per gall.	d. per gall.	d. per gall.
Condensed Milk ...	6	6	6	6
Milk Powder ...	6	4½	4½	4½
Fresh Cream ...	9†	7½	7½	7½
Bottled Cream ...	*	*	*	7½
Tinned Cream ...	6‡	5	5	6
Chocolate	8	8	8	*
Sterilised Milk for Export	*	6	6	6
Soft Curd Cheese and Cream Cheese	*	*	7½	7½
Ice Cream	*	*	7½	7½
Other Products ...	9	9	9	9

* Not scheduled.

† Reduced to 7½d. in March 1934.

‡ Reduced to 5d. in March 1934.

In respect of milk manufactured in London, 1d. per gallon is charged in addition to the above prices.

Delivery.—As in previous contracts, delivery may be made direct to the purchaser's railway station or dairy or to a collecting depot approved by the Board, the producer paying the costs of carriage. The deduction allowed to the purchaser for "transit risk" on depot milk was prescribed at ¼d. per gallon compared with ½d. a gallon in the third contract.

Conditions of Re-sale.

(a) *Re-sale by Wholesale or Semi-Wholesale.*—The contract provides that in the case of re-sale by the purchaser either by wholesale or semi-wholesale, the re-sale price must be not less than the price for liquid milk plus a premium varying from ½d. to 1½d. per gallon according to the quantity sold in each consignment.

(b) *Resale by Retail.*—The minimum retail prices prescribed for 1935/36 were the same as those for the previous 12 months, quoted on page 44.

The contract, like the previous one, allows the minimum appropriate retail price in any area to be reduced by the Board if they are requested to do so by a majority of the retailers in that area. In an area of which the population exceeds 25,000, however, the Board are required to consult the Central Milk Distributive Committee before reducing the minimum price.

Sales at the Farmhouse Door.—A new provision enables milk to be sold by retail at 1d. per quart less than the appropriate minimum price "at the farmhouse door," that is, to customers who call for milk at the premises on which it is produced.

Co-operative Societies Dividends.—Dividends may be returned on retail milk sales by registered co-operative societies in certain circumstances; other retailers may also allow dividends or discounts at a rate not exceeding that paid by any co-operative society operating in the district.

Quality of Milk.—The purchaser may terminate the contract if the milk delivered by the vendor contains less than 3 per cent. of milk fat or less than 8·5 per cent. of non-fatty solids.

Farmhouse Cheesemakers.

As explained in the previous report,* the Milk Act, 1934, makes provision for the payment of repayable advances in respect of milk manufactured into cheese on farms. The Board have accordingly issued for each contract period since 1st April, 1934, special contracts for farm cheesemakers under which payment at the following rates per gallon has been made to the producer in respect of milk manufactured into cheese on the farm:—

* Page 49.

	Milk manufactured into Hard Cheese	Soft Cheese
1933/34 Contract		
1st April to 30th September, 1934	1d.	½d.
	plus Milk Act advance in each case.	
1934/35 Contract		
1st October, 1934—30th April, 1935	3d.	1½d.
	plus Milk Act advance, *plus*, if the advance is less than 1½d. one half the difference between the advance and 1½d.*	
1st May—30th, September, 1935	2½d.	1½d.
	plus Milk Act advance, *plus*, if the latter is less than 1½d., the difference between the advance and 1½d.	
1935/36 Contract		
1st October, 1935—30th April, 1936	5½d.	5d.
1st May—30th September, 1936	4½d.	4d.

* By agreement with the Board, farmhouse cheesemakers received the Milk Act advance plus the whole of the difference between that advance and 1½d. as from 1st April, 1935.

The Board deduct from these advances the levies for expenses and for the payment of the premium on accredited milk; but the farm cheesemaker is entitled to the accredited premium of 1d. per gallon if he qualifies.

The 1934/35 contract was available to producers owning 8 or more cows. Producers were required to manufacture all their milk into cheese during the six months April to September and could also do so in October or in all six winter months if they so desired.

The terms of the 1935/36 contract were made rather more favourable for producers. In addition to providing for substantially increased payments, the contract is available to producers owning 6 or more cows. Producers must undertake to manufacture all their milk into cheese in the five months May to September and in at least one other month.

The actual net advances per gallon (excluding the accredited premiums) paid to farm cheesemakers are shown in the following table :—

Month.	April—September, 1934.		October 1934—September 1935.	
	Hard Cheese.	Soft Cheese.	Hard Cheese.	Soft Cheese.
	d. per gall.	d. per gall.	d. per gall.	d. per gall.
October	—	—	5·28	3·78
November	—	—	4·96	3·48
December	—	—	4·80	3·00
January	—	—	4·82	3·32
February	—	—	4·52	3·02
March	—	—	4·56	3·06
April	2·58	2·08	4·25	2·75
May	2·60	2·10	3·875	2·625
June	2·52	2·02	4·00	2·75
July	2·25	1·75	3·871	2·331
August	2·17	1·67	3·869	2·319
September	2·14	1·64	3·844	2·294
Unweighted Average	2·38	1·88	4·287	2·899

The number of producers with farm cheesemakers' contracts and the gallonage of milk manufactured were as follows :—

Region.	April–September 1934.		October 1934–September 1935.			
	Contracts.	Gallonage.	Contracts.	Gallonage.		
				Oct.–Mar.	Apl.–Sept	Total.
Northern	103	247,556	105	87,735	235,153	322,888
North Western	625	9,131,899	310	1,418,761	4,387,585	5,806,846
West Midland	151	2,815,289	70	259,379	1,369,421	1,628,800
North Wales	97	1,513,330	44	116,750	721,779	837,529
Mid Western	320	4,912,609	274	542,872	4,673,002	5,215,874
Other Regions	28	224,367	17	48,876	145,047	193,923
Totals ...	1,324	18,846,042	820	2,478,373	11,531,987	14,005,860

Accredited Producers

The Board have prepared a register of accredited producers, and since 1st May, 1935, producers on the register have received a premium of 1d. per gallon on all milk sold by them. The conditions for enrolment prescribed by the Board are those required for the granting of a Grade A producer's licence under the Milk (Special Designations) Order, 1923. Any registered producer who presents a Grade A producer's licence to the Board is registered as an accredited producer. The usual fee for a Grade A licence (£1 1s. per year) is payable by the producer to his Local Authority. Producers of Grade A (T.T.) and Certified milk who sell their milk through the Board are also entitled to be placed on the register.

The conditions of the Grade A licence require the maintenance of an approved standard of cleanliness in the cow-shed and dairy, quarterly veterinary inspection of the dairy herd and periodic testing of milk samples. In some areas the quarterly veterinary inspections are provided free of charge, but in others it is the practice of the licensing authority to charge for clinical inspections.

The cost of the premium paid to accredited producers is met from the funds of the Board. The amount required to pay the premium in terms of a levy on all sales, the number of producers receiving the premium, and the quantities of milk sold by them are given in the following table for 1935 :—

Month.	Levy.	No. of producers participating	Gallonage.
1935.	d. per gall.		
May	—	2,885	6,057,556
June	—	5,711	10,593,941
July	·179	7,602	13,208,404
August	·181	9,003	13,554,853
September	·206	9,936	13,887,116
October	·228	11,228	16,206,502
November	·254	12,740	16,991,825
December	·273	13,655	18,037,430

Manufacturing Operations of the Board.

During the spring of 1934, the Board acquired a factory at Aspatria (Cumberland) for the manufacture of cheese. In April, 1935, the Board took occupation of two more factories, one at Wem (Shropshire) and the other at Frodsham (Cheshire), both of which were later transferred to the Board's ownership. In September a further factory at Treloquithack (Cornwall) began to be operated on the Board's account, and the Board subsequently also entered into possession of part of the manufacturing premises of Norfolk Dairy Farmers, Ltd., at Norwich.

Either butter or cheese has been manufactured at each factory except Norwich, where the majority of the milk has been separated, the skim milk being sold back to the farmers and the cream despatched to a butter factory. The total quantity of milk manufactured for the Board in the twelve months ended 30th September, 1935, was as follows :—

	Gallons.
Aspatria ...	1,409,592
Frodsham ...	489,987
Treloquithack ...	40,845
Wem	887,454

The Milk in Schools Scheme.

As was mentioned in the previous report,* Section 11 of the Milk Act, 1934, permits the Exchequer to contribute a sum not exceeding one-half of the expenses of a milk marketing board in carrying out any approved arrangements for increasing the total demand for milk, subject to a maximum contribution of £1,000,000. Under arrangements formulated by the Milk Marketing Board with the co-operation of distributors and approved by the Minister, milk is sold to school-children at ½d. for one-third of a pint; the retailer receives 6d. per gallon for distribution and the Board 6d. The Minister pays to the Board one-half the difference between the price received by them for school milk and the wholesale liquid price on the first 18 million gallons consumed in each year, and one-quarter of the difference on any excess.

Between 2½ and 2¾ million schoolchildren receive milk daily under the Board's arrangements as against some 900,000 formerly. The total quantity of milk consumed in the 1934/35 contract period was approximately 22¾ million gallons. The quantities of milk consumed in each month from October, 1934, are given in the following table :—

---

* Page 52.

	1934/35		1935/36	
	Gallons Consumed	Estimated Average School-days	Gallons Consumed	Estimated Average School-days
October	1,872,000	23	2,272,000	23
November	2,448,000	21	1,951,000	21
December	1,771,000	15	1,562,000	15
January	2,174,000	18		
February	2,347,000	20		
March	2,388,000	21		
April	1,548,000	15		
May	2,245,000	21		
June	1,586,000	17		
July	1,883,000	20		
August	450,000	Holidays		
September	1,984,000	21		

According to returns collected by the Board of Education, the number of children in England and Wales participating in the scheme at the end of September, 1935, was 2,528,000.

The Nutrition Survey.

In connection with the Milk in Schools Schemes, the Board and the Scottish Milk Marketing Board have undertaken an enquiry into the nutritional value of milk. The scheme has been prepared and supervised by an Expert Sub-Committee of the Board's Advisory Committee on Milk Publicity, of which Lord Astor is the Chairman, and received the approval of the Minister and the Secretary of State for Scotland on 28th March, 1935. The object of the enquiry is to ascertain the effect upon health of the consumption of milk in varying quantities, and to obtain such further evidence as may be possible as to the relative nutritional value of raw as compared with pasteurised milk. The cost of the enquiry (estimated at £10,000) is being borne by the Government (under the Milk Act, 1934) and the English and Scottish Milk Marketing Boards, in agreed proportions.

The principal tests are being carried out at elementary schools in five centres, Burton-on-Trent, Huddersfield, Luton, Renfrew and Wolverhampton. The children—about 8,000 in all—have been divided into four groups. Children in the first group (the control) receive a biscuit but no milk, those in the second, ⅓ pint of pasteurised milk, those in the third, ⅔ pint of pasteurised milk and those in the fourth, ⅔ pint of raw milk. Four full-time Medical Officers have been appointed to conduct this part of the investigation, which will extend over a period of twelve months.

Research and Publicity.

Under the terms of the 1934/35 contract, producers and purchasers each contributed a sum of ¼d. per gallon on all milk sold on wholesale contract in May, 1935, the resulting fund to be used as to one-tenth on research and the remainder on publicity. The National Milk Publicity Council agreed to the retention by the Board of £30,000 to meet half the cost of a publicity scheme which might rank for grant as to the other half under Section 11 of the Milk Act, 1934. A scheme was prepared by the Board and approved by the Advisory Committee on Milk Publicity for publicity by means of press advertising, a poster campaign and special forms of advertising covering particularly the period May to October, 1935, at an estimated cost of £60,000. The scheme was approved by the Minister and laid before Parliament; the total Exchequer grant paid was £29,125, being half the actual cost.

The Board have also encouraged the establishment of milk bars by operating a demonstration bar at various shows and exhibitions and providing advice on their establishment, but this activity did not qualify for Exchequer payments under the Milk Act.

The sum available for grants for research work was between £8,000 and £9,000. This sum has been apportioned between the Department of Scientific and Industrial Research, the Agricultural Research Council, the National Institute of Dairying at Reading, the London School of Hygiene and Tropical Medicine, and the Rowett Institute, in aid of various pieces of research work affecting the production and manufacture of milk and its nutritive value.

With the aid of funds provided by the Board an important investigation into production costs and the economics of milk production was commenced in November, 1934, under the auspices of the Conference of Advisory Agricultural Economists, and was continued in 1935. The Agricultural Economics Research Institute at Oxford and the Agricultural Advisory Departments of other Universities and Colleges in England and Wales participated in the scheme and financial and other economic data relating to milk production were collected from approximately 600 farms. An interim report of the investigation will probably be published when the analyses of the data have been completed.

The Reorganisation Commission.

As stated in the previous report*, the Secretary of State for Scotland announced in the House of Commons on 10th December, 1934, that he and the Minister of Agriculture were of opinion that

* Page 32.

sufficient experience had been gained of the working of organised milk marketing in Great Britain to enable an examination to be usefully made of the possibilities of further improvement, including the question of co-ordination or amalgamation of Schemes. The Minister and the Secretary of State proposed, therefore, to constitute a Milk Reorganisation Commission for Great Britain to undertake this comprehensive survey.

The Commission was appointed on 11th February, 1936, with Mr. A. E. Cutforth, C.B.E. as Chairman, the other members being Professor A. W. Ashby, M.A., Sir Iain Colquhoun, Bart., D.S.O., Sir John Orr, D.S.O., M.C., M.A., M.D., D.Sc., F.R.S., and Miss D. S. Tomkinson, O.B.E., M.A., J.P.

The Commission's terms of reference are :—

1. To consider the working of organised milk marketing in Great Britain under Milk Marketing Schemes and its incidence on production, distribution and consumption, and to make recommendations for further improvement

2. To consider and report on the extent to which and the manner in which organisation could be facilitated by closer co-operation between the Marketing Boards concerned, or by the amalgamation of some or all of the Schemes, including any schemes at present under consideration, or by other adjustments, and to prepare schemes for giving effect to any such adjustments.

3. To consider and report on the extent to which, and the manner in which, the organisation of milk marketing in Great Britain could be facilitated by closer co-operation between Milk Marketing Boards in Great Britain and the appropriate authorities in Northern Ireland.

Miscellaneous.

Poll on the Question of Revocation of the Scheme.—The Scheme provides that a poll on the question whether or not the Scheme shall be revoked may be demanded at any time by any five hundred registered producers. The Agricultural Marketing Act, 1931, however, provides that no such poll shall be taken within two years of the declaration of the result of the initial poll without the consent of the Board. The two-year period expired, in the case of the Milk Marketing Scheme, on 6th September, 1935.

The Board received a petition signed by 545 producers demanding a poll at the end of December, 1934. This demand was, as permitted by the provisions of the Act, refused. A further demand for a poll signed by 500 registered producers was received in July, 1935, and the Board consented to the poll being taken. The register was closed on 1st August, and polling day was 15th August.

A postal vote was taken, the vote being counted by an independent person, and the result was declared on 19th August as follows :—

In favour of revocation	...	18,747 producers (19 per cent.) owning 222,722 cows (13½ per cent).
Against revocation	...	79,711 producers (81 per cent.) owning 1,431,342 cows (86½ per cent.)

Accounts of the Board.—A copy of the Board's accounts as at 31st March, 1935, is printed in Appendix III.

During the year, the Board have paid to the Exchequer £6,143, certified by the Minister to represent the expenses of the original Reorganisation Commission for Milk attributable to the preparation of the Scheme.

Cream Prices.—Arrangements have again been made during the year between the chief manufacturers of cream in the United Kingdom regarding the prices at which fresh cream shall be sold by wholesale.

An agreement has also been concluded beween manufacturers in the United Kingdom, The Irish Free State and Denmark regarding the wholesale prices and conditions of sale of tinned cream.

Contraventions of the Scheme.—During 1935, penalties were imposed upon 316 registered producers for contravention of the Scheme. Sixty producers were penalised for selling milk by wholesale otherwise than under a contract prescribed by and registered with the Board ; 54 for selling milk by retail without holding a producer-retailer's licence ; 184 for failing to furnish information and returns : 3 for rendering false returns; and 15 for selling milk at less than the prescribed retail price. The aggregate amount of the penalties was £7,461.

TABLE [illegible].

[illegible]

Month.	Liquid Consumption.			[illegible]			Total Gallonage.	Per cent. Liquid.	Per cent. [illegible]
	Under [illegible] contracts.	By [illegible] [illegible].	Total.	Under [illegible] contracts.	[illegible]	Total.			
[illegible]	gallons.	gallons.	gallons.	gallons.	gallons.	gallons.	gallons.		
[illegible]*	[illegible]	[illegible]	[illegible]	[illegible]	—	[illegible]	[illegible]	[illegible]	[illegible]
[illegible]	[illegible]	[illegible]	[illegible]	[illegible]	—	[illegible]	[illegible]	[illegible]	[illegible]
[illegible]	[illegible]	[illegible]	[illegible]	[illegible]	—	[illegible]	[illegible]	[illegible]	[illegible]
[illegible]									
Jan.	[illegible]	[illegible]	[illegible]	[illegible]	[illegible]	[illegible]	[illegible]	[illegible]	[illegible]
Feb.	[illegible]	[illegible]	[illegible]	[illegible]	—	[illegible]	[illegible]	[illegible]	[illegible]
[illegible]	[illegible]	[illegible]	[illegible]	[illegible]	—	[illegible]	[illegible]	[illegible]	[illegible]
April	[illegible]	[illegible]	[illegible]	[illegible]	[illegible]	[illegible]	[illegible]	[illegible]	[illegible]
May	[illegible]	[illegible]	[illegible]	[illegible]	[illegible]	[illegible]	[illegible]	[illegible]	[illegible]
June	[illegible]	[illegible]	[illegible]	[illegible]	[illegible]	[illegible]	[illegible]	[illegible]	[illegible]
July	[illegible]	[illegible]	[illegible]	[illegible]	[illegible]	[illegible]	[illegible]	[illegible]	[illegible]
Aug.	[illegible]	[illegible]	[illegible]	[illegible]	[illegible]	[illegible]	[illegible]	[illegible]	[illegible]
Sept.	[illegible]	[illegible]	[illegible]	[illegible]	[illegible]	[illegible]	[illegible]	[illegible]	[illegible]
Total [illegible]	[illegible]	[illegible]	[illegible]	[illegible]	[illegible]	[illegible]	[illegible]	[illegible]	[illegible]

* [illegible] days only.

[illegible]—									
Oct.	[illegible]	[illegible]	[illegible]	[illegible]	[illegible]	[illegible]	[illegible]	[illegible]	[illegible]
Nov.	[illegible]	[illegible]	[illegible]	[illegible]	[illegible]	[illegible]	[illegible]	[illegible]	[illegible]
Dec.	[illegible]	[illegible]	[illegible]	[illegible]	[illegible]	[illegible]	[illegible]	[illegible]	[illegible]
1935—									
Jan.	[illegible]	[illegible]	[illegible]	[illegible]	[illegible]	[illegible]	[illegible]	[illegible]	[illegible]
Feb.	[illegible]	[illegible]	[illegible]	[illegible]	[illegible]	[illegible]	[illegible]	[illegible]	[illegible]
Mar.	[illegible]	[illegible]	[illegible]	[illegible]	[illegible]	[illegible]	[illegible]	[illegible]	[illegible]
April	[illegible]	[illegible]	[illegible]	[illegible]	[illegible]	[illegible]	[illegible]	[illegible]	[illegible]
May	[illegible]	[illegible]	[illegible]	[illegible]	[illegible]	[illegible]	[illegible]	[illegible]	[illegible]
June	[illegible]	[illegible]	[illegible]	[illegible]	[illegible]	[illegible]	[illegible]	[illegible]	[illegible]
July	[illegible]	[illegible]	[illegible]	[illegible]	[illegible]	[illegible]	[illegible]	[illegible]	[illegible]
Aug.	[illegible]	[illegible]	[illegible]	[illegible]	[illegible]	[illegible]	[illegible]	[illegible]	[illegible]
Sept.	[illegible]	[illegible]	[illegible]	[illegible]	[illegible]	[illegible]	[illegible]	[illegible]	[illegible]
Total [illegible]	[illegible]	[illegible]	[illegible]	[illegible]	[illegible]	[illegible]	[illegible]	[illegible]	[illegible]
1935—									
Oct.	[illegible]	—	—	[illegible]	[illegible]	[illegible]	—	—	—
Nov.	[illegible]	—	—	[illegible]	[illegible]	[illegible]	—	—	—
Dec.	[illegible]	—	—	[illegible]	[illegible]	[illegible]	—	—	—

TABLE [illegible]

[illegible]

Region.	[illegible]				[illegible]			
	Liquid.	Manufacturing.	Total.	Manufacturing as percentage of Total.	Liquid.	Manufacturing.	Total.	Manufacturing as percentage of Total.
	gallons.	gallons.	gallons.	Per cent.	gallons.	gallons.	gallons.	Per cent.
Northern ...	[illegible]	[illegible]	[illegible]	[illegible]	[illegible]	[illegible]	[illegible]	[illegible]
North Western ...	[illegible]	[illegible]	[illegible]	[illegible]	[illegible]	[illegible]	[illegible]	[illegible]
Eastern ...	[illegible]	[illegible]	[illegible]	[illegible]	[illegible]	[illegible]	[illegible]	[illegible]
East Midland ...	[illegible]	[illegible]	[illegible]	[illegible]	[illegible]	[illegible]	[illegible]	[illegible]
West Midland ...	[illegible]	[illegible]	[illegible]	[illegible]	[illegible]	[illegible]	[illegible]	[illegible]
North Wales ...	[illegible]	[illegible]	[illegible]	[illegible]	[illegible]	[illegible]	[illegible]	[illegible]
South Wales ...	[illegible]	[illegible]	[illegible]	[illegible]	[illegible]	[illegible]	[illegible]	[illegible]
Scotland ...	[illegible]	[illegible]	[illegible]	[illegible]	[illegible]	[illegible]	[illegible]	[illegible]
Mid Western ...	[illegible]	[illegible]	[illegible]	[illegible]	[illegible]	[illegible]	[illegible]	[illegible]
Far Western ...	[illegible]	[illegible]	[illegible]	[illegible]	[illegible]	[illegible]	[illegible]	[illegible]
South Eastern ...	[illegible]	[illegible]	[illegible]	[illegible]	[illegible]	[illegible]	[illegible]	[illegible]
Total ...	[illegible]	[illegible]	[illegible]	[illegible]	[illegible]	[illegible]	[illegible]	[illegible]

TABLE III

[illegible]

(pence per gallon)

Region	[illegible]													[illegible]		
	Oct.	Nov.	Dec.	Jan.	Feb.	Mar.	April	May	June	July	Aug.	Sept.	Weighted Average	Oct.	Nov.	Dec.
Northern	[illegible]	[illegible]	[illegible]	[illegible]	[illegible]	[illegible]	[illegible]	[illegible]	[illegible]	[illegible]	[illegible]	[illegible]	[illegible]	[illegible]	[illegible]	[illegible]
North Western	[illegible]	[illegible]	[illegible]	[illegible]	[illegible]	[illegible]	[illegible]	[illegible]	[illegible]	[illegible]	[illegible]	[illegible]	[illegible]	[illegible]	[illegible]	[illegible]
[illegible]	[illegible]	[illegible]	[illegible]	[illegible]	[illegible]	[illegible]	[illegible]	[illegible]	[illegible]	[illegible]	[illegible]	[illegible]	[illegible]	[illegible]	[illegible]	[illegible]
East Midland	[illegible]	[illegible]	[illegible]	[illegible]	[illegible]	[illegible]	[illegible]	[illegible]	[illegible]	[illegible]	[illegible]	[illegible]	[illegible]	[illegible]	[illegible]	[illegible]
West Midland	[illegible]	[illegible]	[illegible]	[illegible]	[illegible]	[illegible]	[illegible]	[illegible]	[illegible]	[illegible]	[illegible]	[illegible]	[illegible]	[illegible]	[illegible]	[illegible]
North Wales	[illegible]	[illegible]	[illegible]	[illegible]	[illegible]	[illegible]	[illegible]	[illegible]	[illegible]	[illegible]	[illegible]	[illegible]	[illegible]	[illegible]	[illegible]	[illegible]
South Wales	[illegible]	[illegible]	[illegible]	[illegible]	[illegible]	[illegible]	[illegible]	[illegible]	[illegible]	[illegible]	[illegible]	[illegible]	[illegible]	[illegible]	[illegible]	[illegible]
Scotland	[illegible]	[illegible]	[illegible]	[illegible]	[illegible]	[illegible]	[illegible]	[illegible]	[illegible]	[illegible]	[illegible]	[illegible]	[illegible]	[illegible]	[illegible]	[illegible]
[illegible]	[illegible]	[illegible]	[illegible]	[illegible]	[illegible]	[illegible]	[illegible]	[illegible]	[illegible]	[illegible]	[illegible]	[illegible]	[illegible]	[illegible]	[illegible]	[illegible]
[illegible]	[illegible]	[illegible]	[illegible]	[illegible]	[illegible]	[illegible]	[illegible]	[illegible]	[illegible]	[illegible]	[illegible]	[illegible]	[illegible]	[illegible]	[illegible]	[illegible]
South Eastern	[illegible]	[illegible]	[illegible]	[illegible]	[illegible]	[illegible]	[illegible]	[illegible]	[illegible]	[illegible]	[illegible]	[illegible]	[illegible]	[illegible]	[illegible]	[illegible]
Weighted Average price	[illegible]	[illegible]	[illegible]	[illegible]	[illegible]	[illegible]	[illegible]	[illegible]	[illegible]	[illegible]	[illegible]	[illegible]	[illegible]	[illegible]	[illegible]	[illegible]
Weighted Average price for [illegible]	[illegible]	[illegible]	[illegible]	[illegible]	[illegible]	[illegible]	[illegible]	[illegible]	[illegible]	[illegible]	[illegible]	[illegible]	[illegible]	—	—	—

[illegible]	May.	June	July.	Aug	Sep
[illegible]	[illegible]	[illegible]	[illegible]	[illegible]	[illegible]

POTATO MARKETING SCHEME, 1933.

The Potato Marketing Scheme, which applies to Great Britain, came into operation on 9th March, 1934.

The Board administering the Scheme is composed of 24 district members, 5 special members and 2 persons co-opted to the Board after consultation with the Market Supply Committee.* During the year, elections were held in five districts and resulted in two new members being elected to the Board. At the annual general meeting held on the 31st October, 1935, the two retiring special members were re-elected. The co-opted members were Mr. W. Gavin and Commander the Hon. A. D. Cochrane; the latter succeeded Capt. the Hon. J. G. Stuart who resigned from the Board on his appointment as a Lord Commissioner of the Treasury.

The remuneration of members of the Board voted at the annual general meeting was at the same rate as in the previous year, namely :—

	£
Chairman	1,500
Vice-Chairman	850
Members of the Executive Committee	600
Chairman of the Basic Acreage Committee ...	200
Other members of the Basic Acreage Committee	150
Chairman of the Merchants' Authorisation Committee	300
Other members of the Merchants' Authorisation Committee	250
Other members of the Board	100

The number of producers registered with the Board in December, 1935, and their aggregate potato acreage are given below, with comparable figures for December, 1934.

	Number.		Acreage.	
	1934.	1935.	1934.	1935.
England and Wales...	52,708	51,632	430,000	409,000
Scotland	14,719	13,771	116,000	109,000
	67,427	65,403	546,000	518,000

Producers whose potato acreage is less than one acre are exempt from registration under the Scheme. Producers in the Orkney and Shetland Islands have been exempted from all the provisions of the Scheme by a determination of the Board.

* Until 31st October, 1935, the co-option of persons to the Board was subject to the approval of the "Minister."

Potato Supplies and Prices.

Supplies.—The acreage under potatoes, the average yield per acre and the total production in Great Britain during the past six years are given in the following table :—

Year.	Area under potatoes.	Yield per acre.	Total Production.
	acres.	tons.	thousand tons.
1930/31	548,018	6·6	3,608
1931/32	574,874	5·5	3,154
1932/33	652,814	6·8	4,450
1933/34	671,447	6·8	4,555
1934/35	627,556	7·1	4,464
1935/36	594,392	6·3	3,705

Home supplies during the 1934/35 season varied little from the previous two years, though the proportion of sound ware potatoes was probably higher. The 1935 crop, however, was smaller than those of the previous three years, partly on account of a reduced acreage and partly on account of a lower yield per acre.

Information as to the supply position at different periods of the year has been obtained by the Board by means of periodical censuses of unsold stock remaining in the hands of registered producers and authorised merchants. The estimated stocks on the dates specified were :—

1934/35 crop.	*Unsold stock on farms* tons.	
10th–11th November, 1934.	2,334,000	(ware of marketable quality)
16th–17th February, 1935.	1,185,000	(marketable ware over specified riddles)
4th June, 1935.	78,000	(marketable ware)
1935/36 crop.		
9th–10th November, 1935.	1,884,000	(marketable ware over 1½″ riddle)

Prices in England.—The average of growers' prices for maincrop potatoes in 1934/35 was 75s. 6d. per ton, 16s. 6d. per ton above that of 1933/34 and 9s. 0d. per ton higher than in 1932/33. Prices were comparatively high in the early months of the season, due to a slow rate of marketing at that time before the size of the crop was accurately known. Prices also rose sharply at the end of the season, on account of a very severe frost which occurred in mid-May, causing damage to the new crop in many parts of the country and thereby increasing the demand for old potatoes.

Despite the smaller crop in 1935, growers' prices at the beginning of the season were much the same as in the previous year. In

December, however, the effects of the smaller crop began to be felt and prices rose to 115s. per ton, 46s. 6d. per ton higher than at the corresponding period in the previous year.

Wholesale and retail prices followed a very similar course to growers' prices throughout. Growers' and wholesale prices for the past four seasons to the end of 1935 are given in the following tables :—

Growers' Prices per ton.*

—	1932/33.	1933/34.	1934/35.	1935/36.
	s. d.	s. d.	s. d.	s. d.
September	68 6	53 6	91 0	67 6
October	66 0	57 6	86 0	88 6
November	70 0	58 6	81 0	91 0
December	70 0	59 0	68 6	115 0
January	69 6	59 0	67 6	
February	67 6	58 6	67 0	
March	59 0	57 6	65 0	
April	56 6	67 0	65 6	
May	71 6	62 0	89 0	
Average ...	65 6	59 0	75 6	

Wholesale Prices† per ton.

—	1932/33.	1933/34.	1934/35.	1935/36.
	s. d.	s. d.	s. d.	s. d.
September	84 0	78 6	117 0	108 6
October	86 6	79 6	109 0	109 6
November	87 0	82 0	103 6	118 6
December	85 6	80 0	95 0	132 6
January	88 0	79 6	92 6	
February	87 0	77 0	89 6	
March	83 0	76 0	85 0	
April	79 6	81 0	86 0	
May	87 0	80 6	101 6	
Average ...	85 6	79 0	97 6	

* Average to nearest 6d. of prices at Wisbech for King Edwards and white varieties.

† Average to nearest 6d. of prices of 1st and 2nd qualities Majestic and King Edward at 7 wholesale markets in England.

Prices in Scotland.—The average of growers' prices in Scotland in 1934/5 was 54s. 0d. per ton, 16s. 0d. per ton more than in 1933/34 and 24s. 0d. or 80 per cent. more than in 1932/33. The general trend of prices in the year under review was much the same as in England, but the fluctuations were relatively larger. Growers' and wholesale prices in Scotland for the past four seasons to the end of 1935 are given in the following tables :—

Growers' Prices per ton.*

—	1932/33.	1933/34.	1934/35.	1935/36.
	s. d.	s. d.	s. d.	s. d.
September	44 0	48 0	65 0	75 0
October	36 6	47 0	58 6	67 6
November	33 0	44 6	52 6	70 0
December	29 0	43 0	49 0	89 0
January	28 6	40 0	45 6	
February	26 6	38 0	44 0	
March	22 6	37 6	44 6	
April	17 0	30 6	52 0	
May	31 6	30 0	74 6	
Averages ...	30 0	38 0	54 0	

Wholesale Prices per ton.*

—	1932/33.	1933/34.	1934/35.	1935/36.
	s. d.	s. d.	s. d.	s. d.
September	60 0	54 6	87 6	100 0
October	53 0	63 6	77 6	88 0
November	47 0	62 6	72 0	91 0
December	46 6	60 6	70 0	112 0
January	46 6	60 0	67 6	
February	45 0	57 6	65 6	
March	41 6	46 6	67 0	
April	35 6	44 0	71 0	
May	46 6	45 0	91 6	
Averages ...	47 11	54 9	74 4	

* Averages to nearest 6d. of the prices at Aberdeen, Dundee, Edinburgh and Glasgow for Kerr's Pink, and other white varieties grown in grey soil.

Market Regulation.

Riddle Regulations.—The object of the riddle regulations is to regulate the quantity of home-grown potatoes coming on the market by prohibiting the sale for human consumption of small potatoes which pass through a square mesh of a prescribed size. The following are the riddle regulations which were in force during 1935 :—

Dates in force.	Size of riddle.	Varieties to which applicable.	Districts where applicable.
1934/35 Crop.			
6th December, 1934 to 29th January, 1935.*	1[illegible]"	King Edward, Red King and Golden Wonder.	Great Britain.
	1[illegible]"	Majestics ...	Scotland and North of England.
	1[illegible]"	Majestics ...	Wales and South of England.
	1[illegible]"	Other varieties ...	Great Britain.
29th January to 7th March.	1[illegible]"	King Edward and Red King (except limestone potatoes).	Scotland, Norfolk, Lincolnshire, Soke of Peterborough and Isle of Ely.
	1[illegible]"	White Varieties (except Kerr's Pink and Dunbar Red Soils).	Scotland.
	Riddles remained unchanged for other varieties		
7th March to 23rd May.	1[illegible]"	King Edward, Red King and Golden Wonder.	Great Britain.
	2"	Other Varieties.	Great Britain.
23rd May to end of Season.	1[illegible]"	King Edward, Red King and Golden Wonder.	Great Britain.
	1[illegible]"	Other Varieties.	Great Britain.
1935/36 Crop.			
1st August, 1935 to 23rd August.	1[illegible]"	All varieties.	Great Britain.
23rd August to 28th November.	1[illegible]"	All varieties.	Great Britain.
28th November onwards	1[illegible]"	All varieties.	Great Britain.

* On 3rd January, 1935, a slight alteration was made, certain parishes in Cambridge to which the 1[illegible]" riddle applied for Majestics being transferred to 1[illegible]" riddle.

The riddle regulation imposed in December, 1934, was designed to strengthen the market and check the overloading of supplies. Following the imposition of the riddle, the fall in potato prices, which had been practically continuous since the beginning of the season, was checked. Prices then remained fairly steady and the regulation was continued, apart from some minor changes in January, 1935, until the beginning of March when the results of the census of stocks of potatoes remaining unsold in February were known. This census showed, in the opinion of the Board, a surplus of 111,000 tons over the estimated requirements for the remainder of the season, and the riddle regulations were strengthened in order to keep part of this surplus off the market. Prices showed no material change until the severe frost in May increased the demand for old potatoes. The riddle regulations were then relaxed.

The low prices obtained for the 1935 crop at the beginning of the season led to a riddle of 1⅝ in. being imposed generally at the end of August, but when prices began to rise the riddle was again reduced to the basic riddle of 1½ in.

The sale of "seconds."—In order to assist individual registered producers who had an unusually high proportion of small potatoes in their crop, the Board introduced in September, 1935, a scheme for the sale, as "seconds," of potatoes rather smaller than the minimum permitted under the riddle regulations. "Seconds" were defined to be sound, marketable potatoes which have passed through a riddle of 1½ in. but stand on a riddle of 1¼ in. Producers had to satisfy the Board that they had a contract for the sale of such potatoes and they were required to use special bag labels issued by the Board. At first, permits for the sale of "seconds" were issued only to those registered producers who could show that at least one-fifth of their total crop consisted of "seconds," but this requirement was later waived and the definition of "seconds" was altered to apply to potatoes which passed through a riddle of 1⅝ in. but stood on a riddle of 1¼ in.

Purchase of Potatoes in Scotland.—At the beginning of the 1934/35 season, the Board were faced with a local glut of supplies in Scotland coupled with very low prices which, it was feared, might lead to a collapse of prices in the rest of the country. The Board, after consideration, decided to purchase potatoes in Scotland to relieve the situation. Buying was continued throughout the season, and 9,423 tons were purchased, all of which were sold during May, 1935.

Basic Acreage and the Excess Acreage Levy.—As explained in the previous report,* each registered producer has been allotted a "basic acreage", calculated in the manner prescribed in the Scheme. If, in the opinion of the Board, their expenditure in the operation of the Scheme is likely to be increased as a result of plantings by registered producers in excess of their basic acreages, the Board may require the producers concerned to pay a special non-recurring levy not exceeding £5 per acre in respect of their excess acreage. The basic acreage of any producer who has

---

* Page 62.

paid the excess acreage levy is increased in subsequent years by the number of acres on which the levy was paid.

The total basic acreage of registered producers in December, 1935, compared with November, 1934, was as follows :—

	1934.	1935.
England and Wales ...	491,000	515,000
Scotland	138,000	145,000
Total	629,000	660,000

The following table shows the proportion of registered producers and the proportion of the total basic acreage owned by producers in various acreage catagories :—

Basic Acreage.	*Per cent. producers in group.*	*Per cent. basic acreage in group.*
Under 5 acres	50·75	12·46
Between 5 and 10 acres	24·06	16·00
,, 10 ,, 20 ,,	14·23	18·97
,, 20 ,, 40 ,,	7·16	19·10
,, 40 ,, 100 ,,	3·01	17·48
,, 100 ,, 500 ,,	0·76	13·29
Over 500 acres	0·03	2·66

The table shows that half the registered producers have a basic acreage of less than 5 acres. On the other hand, the total amount of basic acreage is much more evenly distributed among the various groups.

Since April, 1934, the Board have required registered producers who have planted in excess of their basic acreage to pay a levy of £5 per acre. The amount of the excess acreage levies receivable in respect of the 1934 season was about £24,500, representing 4,900 acres. For the 1935 season, the excess acreage levy was assessed on 7,300 acres, but has been cancelled in respect of more than half of this area, either because the acreage in question was being used for growing seed potatoes, or for other reasons.

The Improvement of Trading Conditions.

Markets Plans.—One of the most important steps taken by the Board during the year was the initiation of "Markets Plans" to bring about some measure of price stability in the wholesale trade. These plans have developed out of an experiment introduced with the co-operation of distributors in the Glasgow area in July, 1934, for the voluntary regulation of distributive margins. In that area, price cutting by wholesalers had been prevalent, and it was feared that prices might be affected over a large part of the country with consequential repercussions on producers' prices as a whole. The experimental scheme proved successful in restoring stability, and the Board appointed a committee to consider the extension of the scheme on a national basis.

The generalised plan prepared by the committee suggested that "Markets Plan Committees" should be set up in defined areas to represent the authorised merchants established and trading in the areas. These Committees would recommend from time to time minimum prices below which specified kinds of potatoes should not be sold by wholesalers to retailers. The minimum prices should be arrived at by reference to growers' prices and should cover transport and distributive charges.

The Board have accordingly encouraged the formation of local associations of authorised merchants and the appointment of Markets Plan Committees. The Board assist the associations when formed and are able to give support to the Markets Plan Committees through the conditions of authorisation.

The Markets Plan Committee settles the merchant's margin for the district, subject to the approval of the Board, and also ascertains from time to time the average "arrived" price (i.e. the average cost to the merchant of potatoes delivered at his warehouse) for different varieties. The minimum price for sales by a wholesaler to a retailer is then determined by adding the approved margin to the arrived price, the minimum price being also subject to the approval of the Board. The merchant's margin varies from 10s. to 15s. per ton and is intended to cover the normal costs of wholesaling, including warehouse maintenance, delivery and a fair profit. In Scotland, where the margin is £1, it also includes bagging.

The growth of the Markets Plans Schemes has been rapid. At the end of 1935 plans were in operation in some 40 districts, covering all the important potato markets in Great Britain with the exception of London and Liverpool.

Authorisation of Merchants.—The main conditions of authorisation were described in the last report.* These have since been revised in certain respects, the most important new condition being the requirement to adhere to the appropriate Markets Plan. The Board also take power to examine an authorised merchant's books. The list of authorised merchants has been revised, "re-authorisation" being granted to those merchants who agreed to accept the new conditions.

A committee of the Board was set up to deal with applications for authorisation, which up to 31st August, 1935, amounted to 6,000. Of these, some 2,000 were applications clearly made under a misapprehension; for example, retailers and growers have applied. The number of merchants authorised by the Board was 3,700 at the date mentioned, and the revised list of authorised merchants issued at the beginning of January, 1936, contained 3,534 names.

---

* Page 65.

In dealing with the applications, the Merchants' Authorisation Committee has consulted, in appropriate cases, the National Federation of Fruit and Potato Trades, Ltd., and the Scottish Potato Trade Executive: many applications have also been remitted to the Potato Advisory Committee of the appropriate county branch of the National Farmers' Union and the National Farmers' Union of Scotland.

Authorisation of Auctioneers.—When sales on commission were prohibited following a poll under paragraph 70 (2) of the Scheme, the Board decided to exempt from the prohibition sales at auctions approved by them. The Board have since laid down the conditions that must be adhered to by authorised auctioneers. The most important of these are:—

(i) that the auctioneer shall not handle by auction in any year a greater quantity of potatoes than his average for the three years ended 31st December, 1934, and that his monthly sales shall not be substantially heavier than in the corresponding months of previous years;

(ii) that a reserve price, not less than the local wholesale price, shall be placed on each transaction; and

(iii) that returns of quantities sold and prices realised shall be made to the Board.

About 120 auctioneers have been authorised by the Board.

Market Intelligence.—The Board have continued and extended the arrangements described in the last report* for the provision of a market intelligence service. Notice boards are now maintained in 64 of the principal potato markets throughout Great Britain, and these are kept posted with the most up-to-date market information available.

The Disposal of Surplus Potatoes.

A committee of the Board has, during the year under review, been examining the possibilities of manufacturing various industrial products from potatoes. The only activity which has so far commended itself to the committee as offering reasonable prospects of success is the manufacture of feeding stuffs for stock. After a full examination of the project, the Board made an agreement with the Farmers' Marketing and Supply Company, Ltd., under which the Company were to erect a factory at Wisbech for the manufacture from surplus potatoes of a balanced meal for stock feeding, the Board guaranteeing supplies if the Company were unable to secure sufficient. The price to be paid by the Company for potatoes was to be subject to approval by the Board.

Contracts were entered into for the supply of potatoes to the factory in the latter part of 1935, the agreed price being £1 per ton

* Page 63.

delivered at the factory, and the factory was opened on 12th December. The maximum throughput of the factory is about 250 tons a week.

The "Bishop Auckland Experiment."

Another feature of 1935 was the experiment in the distribution of potatoes at especially low prices to unemployed persons in Bishop Auckland. The experiment attracted considerable attention, and a report* on it was issued by the Board.

The object of the experiment was to discover if there were potential new outlets for sales at differential prices; and if the differential prices could be justified economically on the basis of the difference in services rendered. The Board were anxious that the experiment should be carried through with the co-operation of distributors and without injuring their interests.

The experiment started in February, 1935, and was continued for 8 weeks. The procedure followed was for vouchers to be issued to the unemployed at the local Employment Exchange. These vouchers, after having been stamped by a retailer, enabled the holder to obtain a specified quantity of potatoes, depending on the size of his family, at 4d. a stone. (The prevailing retail price was 7d. a stone). The potatoes had to be fetched in the buyer's own bag from a central warehouse, open on two days a week, and were sold for cash. Retailers were compensated for their loss of trade by receiving from the Board 1d. per stone on the vouchers stamped by them.

The population of Bishop Auckland is 19,000 of whom 2,400 were then unemployed, representing, with their dependents, one third of the population. During the course of the experiment 21,000 vouchers were issued. Of these 19,400 were used, and 182 tons of potatoes were sold.

Retailers were asked to make returns of their sales before, during and after the experiment, so that the effect on retail sales could be estimated. The average weekly sales shown by these returns were as follows:—

			tons.	cwt.
Before experiment	... ...	... ...	16	12¼
During experiment	at shops ...	9 tons 18¼ cwt.		
	at warehouse ...	22 tons 15 cwt.		
			32	13¼
After experiment	... ...	... ...	18	14

Sales in retail shops fell to 60 per cent. of normal during this experiment; the quantity sold in the warehouse, however, even after making allowance for excess sales during the last week,

* "An experiment in the Distribution of Potatoes at Bishop Auckland (February to March, 1935)": Potato Marketing Board Miscellaneous Publications No. 2, price 1/– post free.

represented 131 per cent. of the normal. The Board estimated that if allowance is made for a decrease in sales by fish friers, the total increase in sales could hardly be less than 60 per cent.

The total cost of the experiment to the Board was £297, of which £111 was the cost of warehouse distribution and £121 represented the compensation to retailers; the balance is accounted for by loss in weight when bagging the potatoes and the loss in selling at 53s. 4d. per ton potatoes that had been bought at the current market price of 59s. 0d. per ton. The actual cost of distribution by the Board was 14s. per ton, or a fraction over a 1d. per stone.

At the end of their report, the Board set out some of the conclusions to be drawn from the experiment. They say that it definitely shows that, in a town with a high proportion of low level incomes and even at a time when prices are low, the consumption of potatoes can respond to price to a remarkable degree; also that it is possible to devise machinery for the distribution of cheap surplus supplies without endangering the existing price structure or destroying the retailers' contact with their customers, and that given the goodwill of retailers, the machinery works smoothly.

The Board recognise that there are a number of difficulties in the way of extending the principles of this experiment on a larger scale. They point out that, in this case, selling at reduced prices involved the Board—and therefore producers generally—in a loss, though in certain circumstances it might be of advantage to a producers' organisation to dispose of a surplus at reduced prices. The Board conclude that the experiment appears to show that a class of consumers is prepared to accept a smaller service from the retailer in return for lower prices; but such special sales should not be allowed to damage normal sales or upset the retail price structure which must remain the chief consideration.

Miscellaneous.

Standard of Dressing for Ware Potatoes.—The Board invited registered producers to adopt the following standard for ware potatoes :—

1. *General Conditions.*—Potatoes must be reasonably clean, free from soil, healthy and suitable for human consumption. Cracked or misshapen potatoes must be excluded.

2. *Size.*—The minimum size as determined by the Board's minimum riddle regulations for the time being in force.

3. *Tolerance.*—(a) *Size.*—The weight of potatoes per cwt. which may pass through a riddle having a square mesh, as specified by order of the Board, or as defined in paragraph 67 of the Scheme, or such riddle above the minimum riddle as may be prescribed in any contract between buyer and seller, shall be as follows :

Minimum riddle prescribed.	*Allowance.*	*No potatoes must pass through*
1½"	3 lb.	1¼" riddle
1⅝"	3 lb.	1⅜" „
1¾"	4 lb.	1½" „
1⅞"	5 lb.	1⅝" „
2" (or above)	6 lb.	1¾" „

(b) Waste.—The maximum allowance per cwt. for appreciably diseased, damaged, cut, cracked or greened potatoes is 6 lb.

(c) *Variety, etc.*—At least 95 per cent. by count of the potatoes must conform to specification as regards variety and type of soil.

The Board have power under Section 69 of the Scheme to prescribe the manner in which potatoes shall be graded by registered producers. Compulsory grades for potatoes may be introduced after experience of voluntary standards has been gained.

Finance.—A copy of the Board's accounts for the year ended 31st August, 1935, is printed in Appendix III. As in the previous year, a levy of 5s. per acre planted with potatoes was made on all registered producers during September. The amount of the annual acreage levy collectable in the year ended 31st August, 1935, was £135,000. The amount collectable in respect of the special levy of £5 per acre made on producers who planted in excess of their basic acreage was £13,500.

Publicity.—The Board have maintained producer and consumer publicity activities under the supervision of their Publicity Committee. Stands were taken at a number of agricultural shows during the year as well as at the Ideal Home Exhibition, and posters, recipe books, etc., have been distributed.

A series of mass meetings of registered producers has been held during the year at which members of the Board have explained the Scheme and the operations of the Board. The meetings were also valuable in providing members of the Board with first-hand impressions of the views of growers in various districts.

Penalties.—During 1935, penalties amounting in the aggregate to £1,013 were imposed on 296 registered producers. The majority of the penalties were imposed for failure to make the returns required by the Board.

Four successful prosecutions were also instigated by the Board against unregistered producers who were selling potatoes in contravention of the Scheme.

Varieties Grown by Registered Producers.—No. 3 of the Miscellaneous Publications of the Board, entitled " The Area under Potatoes in Great Britain ", contains information as to the varieties of potatoes grown by registered producers in 1934 and 1935, showing the acreage, by county, of each variety.

The following figures show the proportion of the total acreage planted by registered producers classified as First Earlies, Second Earlies and Maincrop in England and Wales, Scotland and Great Britain respectively in 1934 and 1935 :

	England and Wales.				Scotland.				Great Britain.			
	[illegible]		[illegible]		[illegible]		[illegible]		[illegible]		[illegible]	
	Acres.	Per cent.	Acres.	Per cent.	Acres.	Per cent.	Acres.	Per cent.	Acres.	Per cent.	Acres.	Per cent.
[illegible]	[illegible]	[illegible]	[illegible]	[illegible]	[illegible]	[illegible]	[illegible]	[illegible]	[illegible]	[illegible]	[illegible]	[illegible]
[illegible]	[illegible]	[illegible]	[illegible]	[illegible]	[illegible]	[illegible]	[illegible]	[illegible]	[illegible]	[illegible]	[illegible]	[illegible]
[illegible]	[illegible]	[illegible]	[illegible]	[illegible]	[illegible]	[illegible]	[illegible]	[illegible]	[illegible]	[illegible]	[illegible]	[illegible]
Portions not specified	[illegible]	—	4,570	[illegible]	[illegible]	—	[illegible]	[illegible]	[illegible]	—	[illegible]	[illegible]
Total	[illegible]	[illegible]	[illegible]	[illegible]	[illegible]	[illegible]	[illegible]	[illegible]	[illegible]	[illegible]	[illegible]	[illegible]

Of the maincrop varieties, King Edward VII and Majestic were by far the most popular, accounting for 38 per cent. and 35 per cent. respectively of the total maincrop acreage in 1935; these varieties with Kerr's Pink amounted to 85 per cent. of the total. Great Scot (71 per cent. of the acreage) was the most popular Second Early variety, and Eclipse, Epicure, Ninetyfold and Sharpe's Express (together 84 per cent. of the acreage) the most popular First Earlies.

ABERDEEN AND DISTRICT MILK MARKETING SCHEME, 1933.

This Scheme for the regulation of the marketing of milk produced in the counties of Aberdeen and Kincardine came into operation on 1st August, 1934.

As explained in the previous reports, the Board is composed of the members of the Committee of Management of the Aberdeen and District Milk Agency and four representatives elected annually by the registered producers who are not members of the Agency. At the first annual general meeting of the registered producers held on 26th March, 1935, the four members serving on the Board in the latter capacity were re-elected and thereafter Mr. J. A. Mackie, 69, Market Street, Aberdeen, and Mr. J. G. Singer, 60, Guild Street, Aberdeen, who were appointed by the Secretary of State to be members of the Board for the first year, were co-opted to membership for a further period in accordance with Section 14 of the Agricultural Marketing Act, 1933.

The registered producers at the general meeting voted the sum of £600 as remuneration to the members of the first Board, excluding the Chairman, to be divided amongst them as they might determine. The Chairman's remuneration is determined by the Board.

When the Scheme came into operation, the Board took over the working of the creamery of the Aberdeen and District Milk Agency at Kittybrewster, Aberdeen. The creamery is used as a depot for the collection, treatment and distribution of milk and for the manufacture of milk products. Negotiations were concluded in April, 1935, for the transfer of the creamery and other assets of the Agency to the Board as at 31st July, 1934, at a valuation of £9,500. After adjustments in respect of rent and other charges, the net amount payable was £9,240, of which a sum of £4,000 was left on loan to the Board. It was agreed in the negotiations that the Agency would remain in existence as a non-trading agricultural society registered under the Industrial and Provident Societies Acts, 1893 to 1928.

The total number of producers registered under the Scheme on 31st December, 1935, was 823, of whom 489 were ordinary producers (i.e., producers selling milk by wholesale to or through the agency of the Board), 326 were producer-retailers, and 8 were producers of Certified milk. Of the producers selling milk by wholesale, 95 also sold a proportion of their milk by retail. Provision is made in the Scheme for the exemption from registration of producers who sell milk only in small quantities to employees or to neighbours for their own consumption. In January, 1935, the Board decided that producers selling not more than two gallons daily to not more than

Printed image digitised by the University of Southampton Library Digitisation Unit

six customers should be granted exemption under that provision. After consideration of representations made by the Aberdeen and District Producer-Retailers' Association and further review of the position, the Board resolved in October, 1935, to reduce the qualifying limits for this exemption to a maximum sale of one gallon daily and a maximum number of four customers and to examine, with full regard to the circumstances in each case, any applications for exemption of producers whose sales exceed the modified limits.

The statement on page 80 gives particulars of the sales of milk under the Scheme in each month during the period ended December, 1935, and of the utilisation of the milk.

Payments to Producers.—The ordinary producers receive monthly payments from the Board for the basic quantities of their supplies at the Standard Price (i.e., the price for the sale of milk to distributors for liquid consumption) less the contribution per gallon required to cover the loss incurred in marketing milk which fails to realise that Price and to meet the administrative expenses. For supplies in excess of these quantities, they are paid a surplus price less a contribution per gallon at the same rate as that deducted in respect of the basic quantities. Apart from the allocation of interim and final basic quantities to new producers, no revision was made up to 31st December, 1935, in the basic quantities determined by the Board at the inception of the Scheme.

The following statement shows in respect of each month during the period December, 1934, to December, 1935, the gallonage of the sales by the producers within the limits of their basic quantities and in excess of these quantities, the net prices per gallon paid to the producers, and the amount of the producers' contributions :—

	Basic Quantities.		"Surplus" Supplies.		Producers' Contribution per gallon.
	Gallons.	Net price per gallon.	Gallons.	Net price per gallon.	
1934.		d.		d.	d.
December ...	498,768	12	29,858	5	2
1935.					
January ...	505,846	13	24,151	7	2
February ...	460,890	13½	19,881	7	1½
March	517,794	13	26,545	7	2
April	509,291	12	28,430	5	2
May	552,521	12	32,956	4	3
June	536,294	11	32,925	6	3
July	546,231	11	24,946	6	3
August ...	523,705	12	19,737	6	2
September ...	464,354	12½	9,366	4½	2½
October ...	507,549	13	15,114	5	2
November ...	495,278	13	26,902	5	2
December ...	515,421	13½	32,669	6	1½
Total gallonage for the year 1935	6,155,274 (95·63%)	—	281,119 (4·37%)	—	—
Monthly average prices ...	—	12·6	—	5·9	2·2

The weighted average of the prices per gallon paid to the producers for their sales of "basic quantity" and "surplus" milk over the year 1935 was 12·51d. and 5·11d. respectively.

The Board debit each producer's account with the amount actually paid at the standard rates in respect of the haulage of his milk for delivery at the distributor's premises or at the Board's creamery. The standard haulage rates prescribed by the Board are as follows:—

	Per gallon.
Not exceeding 5 miles	½d.
Over 5 but not exceeding 15 miles ...	¾d.
Over 15 but not exceeding 20 miles ...	1d.
Over 20 but not exceeding 30 miles ...	1¼d.
Over 30 miles	1½d.

Producer-retailers and producers of Certified milk make their own arrangements for the sale of their milk at the prices prescribed by the Board. The monthly contributions payable by these producers to the Board were assessed throughout the year 1935, as previously, at the rate of £2 per cow per annum calculated on the return of their sales and taking the average production at two gallons per cow per day. Milk produced by them in excess of the requirements of their customers may be sold to or through the agency of the Board and paid for at the net "surplus" price.

Liquid Milk Prices.—Particulars were given in the last report* of the prices determined by the Board for the period ended October, 1935. The prices prescribed for the year ending October, 1936, are on a similar scale, viz.:—

Standard Price for the sale of untreated milk to distributors.—1s. 3d. per gallon, with reduction to 1s. 2d. per gallon during May, June and July. 1s. 4d. per gallon throughout the year to distributors in Peterhead.

Retail Prices—

To domestic consumers—main area of Scheme—2s. per gallon.

In 30 specified rural districts—1s. 8d. per gallon.

In 9 specified rural districts—1s. 4d. per gallon.

To hotels, restaurants, etc. (in quantities of not less than 2 gallons)—1s. 6d. per gallon.

To institutions supported by voluntary contributions—Not less than the Standard Price.

To institutions under control of local authorities—Not less than 1d. per gallon over the Standard Price.

---

* Page 67.

Grade A (T.T.) Milk.—To distributors—in bulk 1s. 6d. per gallon, in bottles 1s. 10d. per gallon—minimum retail price —2s. 4d. per gallon.

Certified Milk.—To distributors—1s. 10d. per gallon—minimum retail price—2s. 4d. per gallon.

As shown in the statement on page 80, part of the milk surplus to the demand for liquid consumption within the area of the Scheme is sold for liquid consumption in other markets. This milk is supplied to English buyers at the prevailing regional liquid milk prices in England, the cost of treatment and transport of the milk being met by the Board.

Manufacturing Milk Prices.—In the early months of the operation of the Scheme when the agreements made by the Aberdeen and District Milk Agency were operative, no milk was sold specifically for manufacture, but all the distributors received 5 per cent. of their total purchases of milk at the modified price of 6d. per gallon. On the discontinuance of that arrangement as at 30th November, 1934, supplies of milk for manufacture were made available at the price of 9d. per gallon. As the Board were not satisfied that the whole of the milk purchased at that price was being used for manufacture, they suspended as from 1st March, 1935, the sale of milk at less than the Standard Price with the exception of supplies at 9½d. per gallon for the manufacture of ice-cream, and undertook to provide the distributors at wholesale rates with their requirements of cream, butter and cheese from the Board's manufactures of these products. This action of the Board, together with other matters, formed the subject of complaints which were referred to the Committee of Investigation for Scotland (see page 78).

In accordance with the assurance given to the Secretary of State, the Board arranged as from 1st September for the supply, on request, of milk at the price of 7½d. per gallon for the manufacture of cream. They also granted rebates for the reduction to 9d. per gallon of the price of milk supplied during the period from 1st March to 31st August on production of proof of its use for manufacture.

With these adjustments the total quantities of milk sold for the manufacture of milk products from December, 1934, to December, 1935, inclusive, were as follows:—

115,274	gallons at 9d. per gallon for use for any manufacturing purpose.
99,231	„ „ 7½d. „ „ „ „ „ manufacture of fresh cream.
34,551	„ „ 9½d. „ „ „ „ „ „ „ ice cream.
810	„ „ 4d. „ „ „ „ „ „ „ cheese.
250,056	gallons at an average price of 8·45d. per gallon.

Manufacturing Operations of the Board.—The total quantities of milk used by the Board for the manufacture of milk products from the commencement of the operation of the Scheme up to 31st December, 1935, were as follows :—

Product.	Gallons.	Percentage.
Fresh cream	318,807	43·34
Butter ...	295,864	40·22
Cheese ...	120,970	16·44
Total ...	735,641	100·00

The Milk Act, 1934.—The advances payable to the Board under Sections 1 and 2 of the Act in respect of milk used by the Board for the manufacture of butter and sold or used for the manufacture of cheese during the period ended 31st December, 1935, amounted to £2,103 17s. 8d.

In accordance with arrangements approved by the Secretary of State under Section 11 of the Act on 30th May, 1935, the Board, with a view to increasing the demand for milk, organised a publicity and propaganda campaign, which was carried out on similar lines to that undertaken by the Scottish Milk Marketing Board, at an estimated total cost of £1,600. In addition to the arrangements made under the approved scheme, the Board, for purposes of propaganda, installed and operated temporary milk bars at the Highland and Agricultural Society's Show and at a Trade Exhibition held in Aberdeen during the year.

The Board also co-operated in the arrangements made by the English and Scottish Milk Marketing Boards under Section 11 of the Act for an investigation of the nutritional value of milk (see pages 18 and 52) by supplying milk free of charge for a calf-rearing experiment undertaken at the Rowett Research Institute, Aberdeen, as a subsidiary to the main investigation.

Complaints regarding the operation of the Scheme : Consumers.—Complaints were made to the Consumers' Committee for Scotland on behalf of the consumers in rural districts in Aberdeenshire regarding the increase in the retail price of milk in these areas as a result of the operation of the Scheme. The Committee reported to the Secretary of State that, having regard to the proximity of rural consumers to the source of supply and in view of the simplicity and much smaller extent of the services given to such consumers as compared with the services rendered in processing and distribution of milk for urban consumers, they considered that the charging of the same retail price of 2s. per gallon to both classes was not justifiable.

The Board granted authority for the sale of milk by retail at minimum prices of 1s. 4d. and 1s. 8d. per gallon in certain specified rural districts.

Distributors.—Complaints were made by the Aberdeen and District Retail Dairymen's Association, the Northern Co-operative Society and a private manufacturer with respect to—

(*a*) the Standard price for milk determined by the Board for the period 1st January to 31st October, 1935, which allowed of an average distributive margin over the year of 9½d. per gallon.

(*b*) the termination by the Board as from 28th February, 1935, of the arrangements for the supply of milk for manufacturing purposes at manufacturing rates;

(*c*) the fixing of semi-retail prices by the Board, defined as applicable to all sales except retail sales and sales to institutions—i.e., prices for sales to hotels, restaurants, etc.;

(*d*) the haulage rates prescribed by the Board for the period 1st January to 31st October, 1935.

The Committee of Investigation for Scotland, to whom the complaints were referred for consideration and report, found that the Board's action under heads (*a*), (*b*) and (*d*) of the complaints was contrary to the interests of the complainants, but, except as regards the discontinuance of the supply of milk for manufacture at manufacturing prices, they did not find that it was not in the public interest. No finding was made in the case of (c), as it appeared at the hearing before the Committee that the question was one of dispute between the complainants and other distributors, producer-retailers and consumers who were not represented at the inquiry.

An assurance was given by the Board that they would make available on request supplies of milk for manufacture, from such surplus milk as remains after the liquid milk demand has been satisfied, at prices related to the price of the product manufactured, subject to the reservations that in allocating supplies the demand for milk at the highest rates should first be satisfied and timeous notice should be given by buyers of the quantities of milk required by them for manufacture. On the understanding that this assurance would be satisfactorily carried out, the Secretary of State considered it unnecessary to take further action on the Committee's findings.

Miscellaneous: Contraventions of the Scheme.—The number of penalties imposed by the Board on registered producers from the commencement of the Scheme up to 31st December, 1935, was forty-two, amounting in the aggregate to £210. These penalties were imposed mainly in respect of failure to supply information required by the Board.

Inquiry into the costs of milk production.—The Board undertook to provide a contribution of £150 for the year 1935/36, in supplement of the contribution of a similar amount for the previous year, towards the expenses of the inquiry into the cost of milk production which is being carried out by the Advisory Officers in Agricultural Economics attached to the three Agricultural Colleges in Scotland in collaboration with the Advisory Officer in Farm Economics of the Department of Agriculture for Scotland.

Accounts of the Board.—Copies of the Profit and Loss Accounts and of the Board's Balance Sheets as at 31st December, 1934, and 31st December, 1935, are printed in Appendix III.

[illegible]

[illegible]

Month.	Total Gallonage.	[illegible]		[illegible]		[illegible]		[illegible]		[illegible]	
[illegible]—	Gallons.	Gallons.	Per cent.	Gallons.	Per cent.	Gallons.	Per cent.	Gallons.	Per cent.	Gallons.	Per cent.
*August	[illegible]	[illegible]	[illegible]	[illegible]	[illegible]	[illegible]	[illegible]	[illegible]	[illegible]	[illegible]	[illegible]
*September	[illegible]	[illegible]	[illegible]	[illegible]	[illegible]	[illegible]	[illegible]	[illegible]	[illegible]	[illegible]	[illegible]
*October	[illegible]	[illegible]	[illegible]	[illegible]	[illegible]	[illegible]	[illegible]	[illegible]	[illegible]	[illegible]	[illegible]
*November	[illegible]	[illegible]	[illegible]	[illegible]	[illegible]	[illegible]	[illegible]	[illegible]	[illegible]	[illegible]	[illegible]
December	[illegible]	[illegible]	[illegible]	[illegible]	[illegible]	[illegible]	[illegible]	[illegible]	[illegible]	[illegible]	[illegible]
Total for [illegible]	[illegible]	[illegible]	[illegible]	[illegible]	[illegible]	[illegible]	[illegible]	[illegible]	[illegible]	[illegible]	[illegible]
[illegible]—											
January	[illegible]	[illegible]	[illegible]	[illegible]	[illegible]	[illegible]	[illegible]	[illegible]	[illegible]	[illegible]	[illegible]
February	[illegible]	[illegible]	[illegible]	[illegible]	[illegible]	[illegible]	[illegible]	[illegible]	[illegible]	[illegible]	[illegible]
March	[illegible]	[illegible]	[illegible]	[illegible]	[illegible]	[illegible]	[illegible]	[illegible]	[illegible]	[illegible]	[illegible]
April	[illegible]	[illegible]	[illegible]	[illegible]	[illegible]	[illegible]	[illegible]	[illegible]	[illegible]	[illegible]	[illegible]
May	[illegible]	[illegible]	[illegible]	[illegible]	[illegible]	[illegible]	[illegible]	[illegible]	[illegible]	[illegible]	[illegible]
June	[illegible]	[illegible]	[illegible]	[illegible]	[illegible]	[illegible]	[illegible]	[illegible]	[illegible]	[illegible]	[illegible]
July	[illegible]	[illegible]	[illegible]	[illegible]	[illegible]	[illegible]	[illegible]	[illegible]	[illegible]	[illegible]	[illegible]
August	[illegible]	[illegible]	[illegible]	[illegible]	[illegible]	[illegible]	[illegible]	[illegible]	[illegible]	[illegible]	[illegible]
September	[illegible]	[illegible]	[illegible]	[illegible]	[illegible]	[illegible]	[illegible]	[illegible]	[illegible]	[illegible]	[illegible]
October	[illegible]	[illegible]	[illegible]	[illegible]	[illegible]	[illegible]	[illegible]	[illegible]	[illegible]	[illegible]	[illegible]
November	[illegible]	[illegible]	[illegible]	[illegible]	[illegible]	[illegible]	[illegible]	[illegible]	[illegible]	[illegible]	[illegible]
December	[illegible]	[illegible]	[illegible]	[illegible]	[illegible]	[illegible]	[illegible]	[illegible]	[illegible]	[illegible]	[illegible]

NORTH OF SCOTLAND MILK MARKETING SCHEME, 1934.

This Scheme, which applies to the counties of Inverness, Nairn, Ross and Cromarty, Sutherland and Caithness, came into operation on 1st October, 1934.

The first Board consisting of the five members named in the Scheme and two members appointed by the Secretary of State held office until 5th July, 1935, and was then replaced by a Board of five members elected at the first annual general meeting of the registered producers. After consultation with the Market Supply Committee and with the approval of the Secretary of State, the members elected to the Board co-opted Mr. P. M. Pottie, Achareith, Nairn, and Mr. J. Ross, S.S.C., 57 Castle Street, Edinburgh, to be additional members.

The general meeting of the registered producers voted the sum of £450 as remuneration to the members of the first Board, excluding the Chairman, to be divided amongst them as they might determine. The Chairman's remuneration was fixed by the Board at £250.

The total number of producers registered under the Scheme on 31st December, 1935, was 379, of whom 128 were producers selling milk by wholesale to or through the agency of the Board, 241 were producer-retailers, and 10 were producers of Certified and Grade A (T.T.) milk. The majority of the producers selling milk by wholesale also sell a proportion of their production of milk by retail. Producers who sell milk only in small quantities to their employees or neighbours for their own consumption are exempt from registration under the Scheme, the limits fixed by the Board as qualifying for this exemption being a maximum sale of three gallons daily to not more than five customers. The sales of a very large number of the producers of milk in the area of the Scheme are within these limits.

The statement on page 85 shows the quantities of milk sold by the registered producers in each month during the period ended 31st December, 1935, and gives particulars of the utilisation of the milk.

Prices and sale of milk for liquid consumption.—The prices determined by the Board for the year 1935 were on the following scale :—

Standard Price for the sale of untreated milk to distributors.—1/8d. per gallon, with reduction to 1/2d. per gallon in April, May, June and July.

Retail Prices:—

Charitable institutions	1/4d. per gallon.
Domestic consumers	2/- per gallon.
Other institutions, hotels, restaurants, etc.—less than 10 but more than 2 gallons ...	1/8d. per gallon.
exceeding 10 gallons ...	1/6d. per gallon.

The prices for Grade A (T.T.) and Certified milk were 2d. and 4d. per gallon respectively more than the price for ordinary milk.

The Board determined the prices for the year 1936 on a similar scale except for the maintenance of the Standard Price at 1s. 3d. per gallon in each month throughout the year.

Of the total supply of milk under the Scheme during the year 1935 amounting to 1,913,625 gallons, 1,752,608 gallons (91·58 per cent.) were sold for liquid consumption within the area of the Scheme. In addition 57,583 gallons (3·0 per cent.) were sold to English buyers at the regional liquid milk prices prescribed by the English Milk Marketing Board.

Prices and use of milk for manufacture.—The total quantity of milk sold for manufacture during the year amounted to 87,236 gallons, of which 64,259 gallons were supplied at 10d. per gallon for use for any manufacturing purpose, 4,567 gallons at 7½d. and 8d. per gallon for the manufacture of fresh cream, and 18,410 gallons at prices varying from 3d. to 4d. per gallon for the manufacture of butter.

The Board found it necessary in certain months to arrange for the use of milk for manufacture on their behalf. The total quantity used for that purpose during the year amounted to 16,198 gallons, of which 13,862 gallons were manufactured into cheese and 2,336 gallons into butter.

Payments to producers.—As explained in the last report,* the Scheme, like the Aberdeen and District Milk Marketing Scheme, provides for the operation of a "basic-surplus" plan in accordance with which producers selling milk to or through the agency of the Board qualify for payment at the Standard Price for supplies within the limits of their basic quantities and at a surplus price for supplies in excess of these quantities. The payments are made subject to the deduction of a contribution per gallon of the amount required for the operation of the "pooling" provisions of the Scheme and for administrative expenses.

The producers' basic quantities as determined by the Board at the inception of the Scheme by reference to their production of milk for sale during the months of September to December, 1933, were continued without variation during the year 1935.

The following statement shows in respect of each month during the year 1935 the gallonage of the sales by the producers to or through the Board within the limits of their basic quantities and in

* Page 60.

excess of these quantities, the net prices per gallon paid to the producers, and the amount of the producers' contributions :—

	Basic Quantities.		"Surplus" Supplies.		Producers' Contribution per gallon.
	Gallons.	Net price per gallon.	Gallons.	Net price per gallon.	
		d.		d.	d.
January	60,009	13¼	1,501	4½	1½
February... ...	55,496	13¼	861	4½	1½
March	68,949	13¼	2,347	4½	1½
April	75,485	13¼	3,510	4½	1½
May	78,431	13¼	5,623	5½	1½
June	77,007	13¼	6,390	5¼	1½
July	81,048	13¼	5,536	5¼	1½
August	77,863	13¼	3,469	4½	1½
September ...	71,456	13½	1,805	4½	1½
October	69,947	13¼	1,524	4½	1½
November ...	66,584	13½	1,530	4½	1½
December ...	68,057	14	1,479	5	1
Total for the year 1935.	846,326 (95·96%)	—	35,565 (4·04%)	—	—
Monthly average prices.	—	13·20	—	4·79	1·46

The weighted average of the prices per gallon paid to the producers for their sale of "basic quantity" and "surplus" milk over the year 1935 was 13·17d. and 5·01d. respectively.

The Scheme empowers the Board to arrange for the payment of the costs of haulage of milk sold to them or through their agency, and to debit the accounts of producers with haulage charges calculated at standard rates according to the distance of each producer's farm or premises from the nearest of the three prescribed centres—viz. Inverness, Dingwall and Wick. Difficulties arose in putting these provisions of the Scheme into operation and, in the meantime, each producer has been responsible for meeting the actual cost of haulage of his milk.

The contributions payable by producer-retailers and producers of Grade A (T.T.) and Certified milk in respect of sales made by them under their own arrangements are at the rate of 7/10ths and 9/10ths respectively of that payable in respect of sales to or through the agency of the Board. Producer-retailers are allotted basic quantities for use in selling to or through the agency of the Board supplies of milk in excess of their customers' requirements, and all milk of the official grades tendered to the Board is paid for at the net price payable for the basic quantities of the ordinary producers.

Milk Act, 1934.—Advances amounting to £843 16s. 11d. were payable to the Board in respect of 38,214 gallons of milk sold or used by the Board for the manufacture of butter and 20,894 gallons used for the manufacture of cheese during the period from the commencement of the Scheme on 1st October, 1934, to 31st December, 1935.

Reference was made in the last report* to the approval under Section 11 of the Act of arrangements proposed to be made by the Board for the supply of milk at reduced prices for consumption in the schools. The conditions within the area of the Scheme are, however, such that it has not been found practicable to give effect to these arrangements except on a small scale. During the later months of the year, milk was being supplied to about 2,000 children attending schools in Inverness, Wick, Brora and Helmsdale. The total quantity of milk supplied up to 31st December, 1935, amounted to 7,869 gallons of which 4,528 gallons were of Grade A (T.T.) milk. The contribution payable from the Exchequer in respect of the supply of that quantity of milk at the reduced prices was £153 9s. 10d.

Miscellaneous.—A certificate under Section 22 (2) of the Agricultural Marketing Act, 1933, was given by the Secretary of State on 31st January, 1935, that the expenses incurred by the persons who submitted the Scheme in connection with the promotion, submission and bringing into operation of the Scheme amounted to £318 18s. 9d.

The loan of £500 made to the Board from the Agricultural Marketing (Scotland) Fund to provide for expenses in connection with the initial poll of the registered producers was repaid in full by three instalments in the months of October and November, 1935.

The Board agreed to provide for the year 1935/36 a contribution of £100, being the same amount as in the previous year, towards the expenses of the inquiry into the cost of milk production which is being carried out by the Advisory Officers in Agricultural Economics attached to the three Agricultural Colleges in Scotland in collaboration with the Advisory Officer in Farm Economics of the Department of Agriculture for Scotland.

Accounts of the Board.—Copies of the Profit and Loss Account and of the Balance Sheet of the Board as at 31st May, 1935, are printed in Appendix III.

---

* Page 70.

NORTH OF SCOTLAND MILK MARKETING SCHEME, [illegible]

Monthly Quantities of Milk sold by Registered Producers.

Month.	Total Gallonage.	Sold to or through the agency of the Board.		Sold by producer-retailers and producers of Certified milk.		Sold for liquid consumption.		Sold or used for manufacture of milk products.	
	Gallons.	Gallons.	Per Cent.	Gallons.	Per cent.	Gallons.	Per cent.	Gallons.	Per cent.
[illegible]—									
October	[illegible]	[illegible]	[illegible]	[illegible]	[illegible]	[illegible]	[illegible]	[illegible]	[illegible]
November ...	[illegible]	[illegible]	[illegible]	[illegible]	[illegible]	[illegible]	[illegible]	[illegible]	[illegible]
December ...	[illegible]	[illegible]	[illegible]	[illegible]	[illegible]	[illegible]	[illegible]	[illegible]	[illegible]
Total for [illegible]	[illegible]	[illegible]	[illegible]	[illegible]	[illegible]	[illegible]	[illegible]	[illegible]	[illegible]
[illegible]—									
January	[illegible]	[illegible]	[illegible]	[illegible]	[illegible]	[illegible]	[illegible]	[illegible]	[illegible]
February	[illegible]	[illegible]	[illegible]	[illegible]	[illegible]	[illegible]	[illegible]	[illegible]	[illegible]
March ...	[illegible]	[illegible]	[illegible]	[illegible]	[illegible]	[illegible]	[illegible]	[illegible]	[illegible]
April ...	[illegible]	[illegible]	[illegible]	[illegible]	[illegible]	[illegible]	[illegible]	[illegible]	[illegible]
May ...	[illegible]	[illegible]	[illegible]	[illegible]	[illegible]	[illegible]	[illegible]	[illegible]	[illegible]
June ...	[illegible]	[illegible]	[illegible]	[illegible]	[illegible]	[illegible]	[illegible]	[illegible]	[illegible]
July ...	[illegible]	[illegible]	[illegible]	[illegible]	[illegible]	[illegible]	[illegible]	[illegible]	[illegible]
August	[illegible]	[illegible]	[illegible]	[illegible]	[illegible]	[illegible]	[illegible]	[illegible]	[illegible]
September	[illegible]	[illegible]	[illegible]	[illegible]	[illegible]	[illegible]	[illegible]	[illegible]	[illegible]
October ...	[illegible]	[illegible]	[illegible]	[illegible]	[illegible]	[illegible]	[illegible]	[illegible]	[illegible]
November ...	[illegible]	[illegible]	[illegible]	[illegible]	[illegible]	[illegible]	[illegible]	[illegible]	[illegible]
December ...	[illegible]	[illegible]	[illegible]	[illegible]	[illegible]	[illegible]	[illegible]	[illegible]	[illegible]
Total for [illegible]	[illegible]	*[illegible]	[illegible]	[illegible]	[illegible]	[illegible]	[illegible]	[illegible]	[illegible]

* The Board paid the producers for supplies exceeding this total by [illegible] gallons, the quantity lost by shrinkage, etc., during the year after acceptance of the milk by the Board.

Printed image digitised by the University of Southampton Library Digitisation Unit

PART II.

SCHEMES SUBMITTED BUT NOT YET IN OPERATION.

No Schemes were submitted in 1935. The following draft Schemes were, however, still under consideration during the year :—

Scheme.	Date of Notice of Submission.	Area of Scheme.
	1934.	
Sugar Marketing Scheme.	9th February.	Great Britain.
Moray and Banff Milk Marketing Scheme.	1st May.	Counties of Moray and Banff.
Sugar Beet Marketing Scheme.	11th May.	Great Britain.
Argyll Milk Marketing Scheme.	6th July.	Parts of Argyll not included in Scottish Milk Marketing Scheme.
Scottish Raspberry Marketing Scheme.	17th December.	Part of Scotland.

Particulars of the progress of these Schemes are given in Appendix I.

Sugar and Sugar Beet Draft Marketing Schemes.

These Schemes were submitted in 1934 and the preliminary statutory steps, including the holding of public inquiries into objections, were taken in that year. Subsequently, as noted in the last report,* action on the Schemes was suspended pending consideration of the report of the inquiry into the Sugar Industry conducted by the Committee under the Chairmanship of Mr. Wilfred Greene, K.C. (now Lord Justice Greene).

On 30th July, 1935, the Government issued a White Paper in which they indicated their policy with regard to the future of the sugar industry. In view of the Government's proposals for the industry (which were subsequently embodied in the Sugar Industry (Reorganisation) Bill), the Sugar Marketing Scheme was not proceeded with.

As regards the Sugar Beet Marketing Scheme, the White Paper stated that it would be "for the promoters of the Scheme to re-examine it in the light of the new conditions and to decide whether they wish the Scheme to proceed, subject to such modifications as the Ministers concerned may propose." The promoters notified the Minister on 1st November, 1935, that they had decided to proceed with the Scheme. In view, however, of the alterations necessary to bring the Scheme into line with the new proposals, the promoters thought it desirable to withdraw the Scheme and re-submit it in amended form.

Moray and Banff Milk Draft Marketing Scheme.

As explained in the last report,* consideration of the draft of this Scheme, which was submitted in May, 1934, was suspended at the request of the promoters' Committee pending their proposals for modification of its provisions. Having decided to make several important amendments in the Scheme, the Committee submitted a revised draft on 12th October, 1935. After consultation with the

* Page 73.

Milk Reorganisation Commission for Great Britain, however, it was suggested to the Committee that further action should be deferred until the Report of the Commission is available.

Argyll Milk Draft Marketing Scheme.

Reference was made in the last report[*] to the submission of this Scheme in June, 1934, for application to that part of Argyllshire not included within the area of the Scottish Milk Marketing Scheme. The Scheme was designed to secure for some 26 farm cheesemakers the repayable advances from the Exchequer under Section 3 of the Milk Act, 1934, in respect of milk converted into cheese at farms, provision being made for exemption from registration of producers of milk not intended for sale or use for manufacture. In view of the difficulty of devising a workable scheme on that basis and of the appointment of the Milk Reorganisation Commission for Great Britain, the promoters agreed that the Scheme should be held in suspense pending the Commission's Report.

Scottish Raspberry Draft Marketing Scheme.

The submission of this draft Scheme in December, 1934, was referred to in the last report.[†] By the main provisions of the Scheme, the Board will be vested with regulatory and trading powers to act as a central marketing organisation for the regulation of the sale of raspberries for manufacture into jam or for canning. The proceeds from the sales of raspberries to or through the agency of the Board will be "pooled" with a view to payment to the growers for their supplies at average seasonal prices, subject to adjustments in respect of raspberries sold for canning or other purposes necessitating special expense in picking or packing and in respect of fruit of inferior quality. Sales of raspberries in packages not exceeding 24 lbs. in weight will be exempt from marketing regulation under the Scheme.

The period for lodging objections and representations with respect to the Scheme expired on 23rd January, 1935. There were seven objectors but, after discussions with the promoters' Committee, four of them withdrew their objections. Mr. Charles Mackintosh, Advocate, held a public inquiry into the outstanding objections in Edinburgh on 16th and 17th April.

It was strongly represented at the inquiry that provision should be made in the Scheme for the limitation of the quantity of raspberries which the Board would be bound to accept from the registered producers in seasons of heavy production when the supplies available are likely to exceed the requirements of the jam manufacturers and canners. As a result of this proposal, opposition to the Scheme developed amongst the producers in Lanarkshire where raspberries are grown mainly for the fresh fruit trade. Progress with the promotion of the Scheme was accordingly deferred to permit full discussion of the proposal amongst the representatives of the growers in different districts, but the producers in Lanarkshire maintained their opposition and expressed a desire to be excluded from the operation of the Scheme.

The question of the reduction of the area of the Scheme and other modifications to be made in its provisions prior to its submission to Parliament were under consideration at the close of the year.

---

[*] Page 72. [†] Page 73.

Printed image digitised by the University of Southampton Library Digitisation Unit

APPENDIX I.

Summary showing Principal Dates in the Progress of Marketing Schemes.

Regu-lated Product.	Area of Scheme.	Persons Sponsoring Submission of Scheme.	Date of Notice of Sub-mission.	Date of Public Inquiry.	Date of Approval by Parliament.		Date of Approved Order and S.R. & O. Number.	Date Scheme came into force.	Date of Initial Poll.	Result of Poll (per cent. of Growers).		Date on which Provisions of Scheme were brought fully into operation.
					House of Com-mons.	House of Lords.				Votes.	Produc-tive Capacity.	
										Per cent.	Per cent.	
[illegible]	Scotland (main-land)	Representative Group of Producers.	[illegible]	[illegible]	[illegible]	[illegible]	[illegible]	[illegible]	[illegible]	[illegible]	[illegible]	Poll un-favour-able.
Hops ...	England.	N.F.U.	[illegible]	[illegible]	[illegible]	[illegible]	[illegible]	[illegible]	[illegible]	[illegible]	[illegible]	[illegible]
Milk	Scotland (South of Grampians).	Committee appointed by General Meeting of Producers.	[illegible]	[illegible] to [illegible]	[illegible]	[illegible]	[illegible]	[illegible]	[illegible]	[illegible]	[illegible]	[illegible]
Pigs ...	[illegible]	N.F.U. and N.F.U. of Scotland.	[illegible]	[illegible] to [illegible]	[illegible]	[illegible]	[illegible]	[illegible]	[illegible]	[illegible]	[illegible]	[illegible]
Bacon	Great Britain.	Bacon Section of Food Manufac-turers' Federation, Inc.	[illegible]	[illegible] to [illegible]	[illegible]	[illegible]	[illegible]	[illegible]	[illegible]	[illegible]	[illegible]	[illegible]

Printed image digitised by the University of Southampton Library Digitisation Unit

[illegible] ...	Scotland (Counties of Aberdeen and Kincardine).	Aberdeen and District Milk Agency.	[illegible]	[illegible] to [illegible]	[illegible]	[illegible]	[illegible] ([illegible])	[illegible]	[illegible]	[illegible]	[illegible]	[illegible]
[illegible] ...	England.	[illegible]	[illegible]	[illegible] to [illegible]	[illegible]	[illegible]	[illegible] ([illegible])	[illegible]	[illegible]	[illegible]	[illegible]	[illegible]
[illegible]	Great Britain.	[illegible] and [illegible] of Scotland.	[illegible]	[illegible] to [illegible]	[illegible]	[illegible]	[illegible] ([illegible])	[illegible]	[illegible]	[illegible]	[illegible]	[illegible]
[illegible] ...	[illegible] (Counties of [illegible], [illegible], [illegible] and [illegible], [illegible] and [illegible]).	J. G. Stewart, Esq. (Solicitor) on behalf of [illegible] Producers.	[illegible]	—	[illegible]	[illegible]	[illegible] ([illegible])	[illegible]	[illegible]	[illegible]	[illegible]	[illegible]
[illegible]...	Great Britain.	General Committee of United Kingdom Sugar Industry.	[illegible]	[illegible] to [illegible]	Scheme not proceeded with.							
[illegible]	Scotland (Counties of [illegible] and [illegible]).	Committee representing [illegible] Producers.	[illegible]*	—	Consideration of Scheme suspended.							
Sugar Beet.	Great Britain.	[illegible] and [illegible] of [illegible].	[illegible]	[illegible] to [illegible]	Scheme withdrawn by promoters for amendment.							

* This draft Scheme was suspended and a revised draft submitted on [illegible].

Regulated Product.	Area of Scheme.	Persons Submitting Scheme	Date of Notice of Submission.	Date of Public Inquiry.	Date of Approval by Parliament		Date of Approved Order and S.R. & O. Number.	Date Scheme came into force.	Date of Initial Poll.	Result of Poll (if any such is held).		Date on which Provisions of Scheme were brought fully into operation.
					House of Commons.	House of Lords.				Votes.	Productive Capacity.	
Milk .	Scotland (the part of the County of Argyll not covered by the Scottish Milk Marketing Scheme).	Scottish Agricultural Organisation Society on behalf of [illegible] Producers	[illegible]	—	Consideration of Scheme suspended.							
Rasp-berries	Scotland.	Committee appointed by General Meeting of Producers, and on behalf of [illegible] Producers.	[illegible]	[illegible] and [illegible]								

AMENDMENTS OF MARKETING SCHEMES.

(a) In accordance with the First Schedule to the Agricultural Marketing Act, 1931.

Scheme.	Result of Poll of Registered Producers (if demanded). (Per cent in favour of amendment.)		Date of Receipt of Submission.	Date of Public Inquiry.	Date of Approval by Parliament.		Date of Approval Order, and S.R. & O. number.
	Votes.	Productive capacity.			House of Commons.	House of Lords.	
Hops Marketing Scheme, 1932	Per cent [illegible]	Per cent [illegible]	[illegible]	[illegible] to [illegible]	[illegible]	[illegible]	[illegible]
Bacon Marketing Scheme, 1933	—		[illegible]	[illegible]	[illegible]	[illegible]	[illegible]
Bacon Marketing Scheme, 1933	—	—	[illegible]	—	—	—	[illegible]
Pigs Marketing Scheme, 1933	—	—	[illegible]	[illegible] and [illegible]	[illegible]	[illegible]	[illegible]

(b) By Order made by "The Minister" under Section [illegible] of the Agricultural Marketing Act, 1933.

Scheme.	Title of Order.	Date of Order and S.R. & O. number.
Scottish Milk Marketing Scheme, 1933	Scottish Milk Marketing Board (Co-opted Members) Order, 1934.	[illegible]
Bacon Marketing Scheme, 1933	Bacon Marketing Board (Co-opted Members) Order, 1934.	[illegible]

(c) By Order made by "The Minister" under Section 4 of the Agricultural Marketing (No. 2) Act, 1933.

Scheme.	Title of Order.	Date of Order, and S.R. & O. number.
Pigs Marketing Scheme, 1933	Agricultural Marketing (Alteration No. 1) Order, 1934	[illegible]

(d) By Order made by "The Minister" under Section 9 (3) (a) of the Agricultural Marketing Act, 1931.

Scheme.	Title of Order.	Date of Order, and S.R. & O. number.
(Scottish) Milk Marketing Scheme, 1933	Scottish Milk Marketing Scheme (Amendment) Order, 1934	[illegible]
Do. do.	Scottish Milk Marketing Scheme (Amendment) Order, 1935	[illegible]
Do. do.	Scottish Milk Marketing Scheme (Amendment No. 2) Order, 1935	[illegible]

APPENDIX [illegible]

[illegible]

I.—[illegible]

Board.	Date of Advance.		Amount of Advance.		Date of Repayment.	Amount Repaid, including Interest.		Purpose of Loan.
	English Fund.	Scottish Fund.	English Fund.	Scottish Fund.		English Fund.	Scottish Fund.	
			£	£		£ s. d.	£ s. d.	
[illegible]	[illegible]	[illegible]	[illegible]	[illegible]	[illegible]	[illegible]	[illegible]	[illegible]
[illegible]	[illegible]	[illegible]	[illegible]	[illegible]	[illegible]	[illegible]	[illegible]	[illegible]
[illegible]	[illegible]	[illegible]	[illegible]	[illegible]	[illegible]	[illegible]	[illegible]	[illegible]

II.—[illegible]

Board.	Date of Advance.	Amount of Advance.	Date of Repayment.	Amount Repaid, including Interest.	Purpose of Loan.

III.—Loans from the Scottish Fund to Specific Marketing Schemes applicable to Scotland only.

Board.	Date of Advance.	Amount of Advance.	Date of Repayment.	Amount Repaid, including Interest.	Purpose of Loan.
		£		£ s. d.	
Scottish Raspberry Marketing Board...	[illegible] [illegible]	[illegible] [illegible]	— —	— —	Initial poll expenses. The loan has been written off as irrecoverable, the result of the initial poll having been unfavourable to the continuance in force of the Scheme.
Scottish Milk Marketing Board	[illegible] [illegible] [illegible]	[illegible] [illegible] [illegible]	[illegible]	[illegible]	Initial poll expenses.
Aberdeen and District Milk Marketing Board ...	[illegible]	[illegible]	—	—	Initial poll expenses. Loan due to be repaid on [illegible].
North of Scotland Milk Marketing Board ...	[illegible]	[illegible]	[illegible] [illegible] [illegible]	[illegible]	Initial poll expenses.

APPENDIX [illegible]

ACCOUNTS AND BALANCE SHEETS OF MARKETING BOARDS

THE HOPS MARKETING BOARD

Income and Expenditure Account for the Year ended [illegible] March, [illegible]

[illegible]

Dr.	£	s.	d.	Cr.	£	s.	d.
To Payments to Producers ...	[illegible]	[illegible]	[illegible]	By Sales of Hops ...	[illegible]	[illegible]	[illegible]
" [illegible] to Producers ...	[illegible]	[illegible]	[illegible]	Notes:—			
" [illegible] ...	[illegible]	[illegible]	[illegible]	1. The [illegible] Sales of Hops to [illegible] March, [illegible] to Producers [illegible] of the Valuations of [illegible] Hops, [illegible] any payment in respect of [illegible] Hops.			
" Transfer to [illegible] Account, under [illegible] of the Scheme ...	[illegible]	[illegible]	[illegible]	2. No [illegible] has been taken of any hops [illegible] at [illegible] March, [illegible].			
	[illegible]	[illegible]	[illegible]		[illegible]	[illegible]	[illegible]

[illegible] Account

	£	s.	d.		£	s.	d.
To [illegible] Expenses:—				By [illegible] under Section [illegible] of the [illegible]	[illegible]	[illegible]	[illegible]
Warehouse Rents, Insurance and Cartage	[illegible]	[illegible]	[illegible]	" Interest on Investments [illegible]	[illegible]	[illegible]	[illegible]
Weighing and Examination of Bags	[illegible]	[illegible]	[illegible]	" [illegible] Fees	[illegible]	0	0
Interest Account	[illegible]	[illegible]	[illegible]	" [illegible] Use of [illegible] made to [illegible] Deposit Account	[illegible]	11	[illegible]
	[illegible]	[illegible]	[illegible]				
" Administration Expenses:—							
Management and Office Salaries	[illegible]	[illegible]	[illegible]				
Board Members' Expenses	[illegible]	[illegible]	[illegible]				
Rent, Rates and Insurance	[illegible]	[illegible]	[illegible]				
Lighting, Heating and Cleaning	[illegible]	[illegible]	[illegible]				
Postages, Telegrams and Telephones	[illegible]	11	[illegible]				
Printing and Stationery	[illegible]	[illegible]	[illegible]				
General Expenses	[illegible]	[illegible]	[illegible]				
Legal, Audit and Accountancy Expenses	[illegible]	[illegible]	[illegible]				
" Board Members' Fees:—							
Year to [illegible] May, [illegible]:—							
In accordance with a Resolution of the Annual General Meeting of [illegible] May, [illegible]	[illegible]	[illegible]	[illegible]				
" Preliminary [illegible] Expenses	[illegible]	[illegible]	[illegible]				
" [illegible] Expenses	[illegible]	[illegible]	[illegible]				
" Depreciation of Furniture and Equipment	[illegible]	[illegible]	[illegible]				
" Reserve for [illegible] and Contingencies	[illegible]	[illegible]	[illegible]				
" Balance Carried to Balance Sheet	[illegible]	[illegible]	[illegible]				

Balance Sheet, 31st March, 19[illegible].

	£	s.	d.	£	s.	d.
To Creditors and Accrued Charges ...				[illegible]	[illegible]	11
" To Amount due to Purchasers [illegible] at [illegible] Cost ...				1,[illegible]	[illegible]	[illegible]
" Reserve for Unexpended Expenses and Contingencies:—						
As at 31st March, 19[illegible] ...	[illegible]	[illegible]	[illegible]			
Less Board Members Fees for the Year to 31st May, 19[illegible], in accordance with a Resolution of the Annual General Meeting of [illegible] May, 19[illegible] ...	4,[illegible]	[illegible]	[illegible]			
	[illegible]	[illegible]	[illegible]			
Add Amount transferred from Approved Account ...	[illegible]	[illegible]	[illegible]			
				[illegible]	[illegible]	[illegible]
" Income and Expenditure Account:—						
As at 31st March, 19[illegible] ...	[illegible]	[illegible]	[illegible]			
Add Balance as per annexed Statement ...	[illegible]	[illegible]	11			
				[illegible]	[illegible]	[illegible]

Note.—No account has been taken of any [illegible] [illegible] at 31st March, 19[illegible].

	£	s.	d.	£	s.	d.
By Furniture and Equipment at Cost Less Depreciation, as at 31st March, 19[illegible] ...	[illegible]	[illegible]	[illegible]			
Additions during year ...	[illegible]	[illegible]	[illegible]			
	[illegible]	[illegible]	[illegible]			
Less: Depreciation at [illegible]% per annum ...	[illegible]	[illegible]	7			
				[illegible]	[illegible]	[illegible]
" Investments at Cost:— £[illegible] [illegible]% Treasury Bonds, [illegible] (Market Value, £[illegible]) ...				[illegible]	[illegible]	[illegible]
" Deposits and Payments in Advance ...				[illegible]	[illegible]	[illegible]
" Cash at Bank ...				[illegible]	[illegible]	[illegible]

THE SCOTTISH MILK MARKETING BOARD

Profit and Loss Account for the Year ended 31st January, [illegible]

	£ s. d.	£ s. d.
To Average Price payable to Producers	[illegible]	
" Payments to Farm Cheesemakers	[illegible]	
" Level Delivery Bonus	[illegible]	
	[illegible]	
" Milk in Schools Allowance [illegible]		
Less Refunded by Exchequer [illegible]	[illegible]	
		[illegible]
" Salaries and National Insurance—Head Office	[illegible]	
" Salaries and Expenses—Regional Offices	[illegible]	
" Travelling Expenses and Allowances	[illegible]	
" Stationery, Printing and Advertising	[illegible]	

	Standard Commodities. £ s. d.	£ s. d.	Other Disposals. £ s. d.
By Sales	[illegible]		[illegible]
Less— (a) Manufacturing and Transport Allowances— [illegible]		[illegible]	
(b) Handling Charges— [illegible]		[illegible]	
(c) Freight— [illegible]	[illegible]	[illegible]	[illegible]
	[illegible]		[illegible]
			[illegible]
			[illegible]
" Commission earned on Category Producers			[illegible]
" Supplies from Haulage			[illegible]
" Estimated Compensation from Milk Marketing Board (England and Wales)			[illegible]

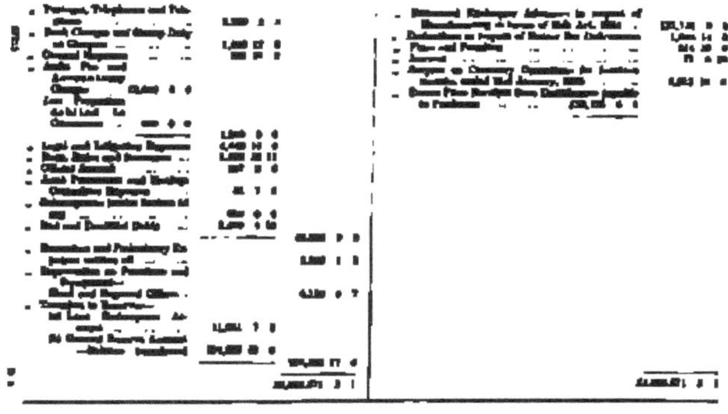

Balance Sheet as at 31st January, [illegible].

Liabilities.

	£ s. d.	£ s. d.
I. Loan	[illegible]	
Of which advanced to date		[illegible]
II. Sundry Creditors—		
(a) Ordinary Purchases	[illegible]	
(b) [illegible]	[illegible]	
(c) [illegible]	[illegible]	
(d) [illegible]—On Open Account	[illegible]	
(e) [illegible]	[illegible]	[illegible]
III. Reserve Accounts—		
(a) [illegible]	[illegible]	
(b) [illegible]	[illegible]	
(c) [illegible]	[illegible]	

Assets.

	£ s. d.	£ s. d.
I. Land—At Cost		[illegible]
II. Buildings—At Cost, Less Sold		[illegible]
III. Plant—At Cost, Less Sold		[illegible]
IV. Other Furniture and Equipment—		
(a) [illegible]	[illegible]	
(b) [illegible]	[illegible]	[illegible]
V. [illegible]		[illegible]
VI. [illegible]		[illegible]
VII. [illegible]		[illegible]
VIII. Goodwill—At Cost	[illegible]	
Less—Written off per Contra	[illegible]	
IX. Costs of Valuation and Purchase of Goodwill—		
(a) Expenses of Valuation	[illegible]	
(b) Expenses of Purchase and Stamp Duty	[illegible]	

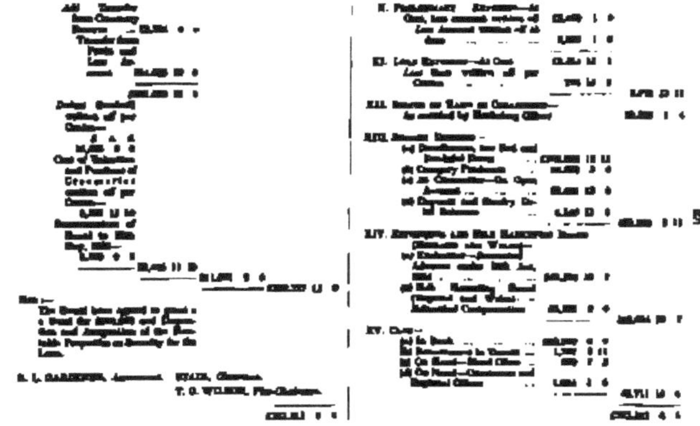

I have examined the Books and Accounts of The Scottish Milk Marketing Board for the year ended 31st January, 19[illegible], and have to report that:—

(a) In my opinion the foregoing Balance Sheet is properly drawn up so as to exhibit a true and correct view of the state of the Board's affairs and that the Profit and Loss Account exhibits a true and correct record of the Income and Expenditure of the Board according to the best of my information and the explanations given to me and as shown by the Books and

(b) That the said Balance Sheet and Profit and Loss Account are sufficiently vouched,

all subject to the following observations:—

1. The Register of Producers records a number of Producers whose productions, if any, have not been dealt with [illegible] the Board and I am informed that this is due to the fact that the necessary information has not been supplied by these Producers or, alternatively that such persons are properly exempt from the provisions of the Scheme, but have not made application to have their names removed from the Register.

2. The Assessments on Ordinary Producers have been shown at the amount assessed by the Board.

3. The Amounts included in the Accounts in respect of [illegible] in terms of Section 11 of the Milk Act, 19[illegible], and of Compensation from the Milk Marketing Board (England and Wales) are the amounts due, as estimated by the Board, pending the completion of negotiations which are at present in progress.

Glasgow,

[illegible] Feb. 19[illegible].

ALEXANDER [illegible], C.A.,

Public Auditor.

PIGS MARKETING BOARD.

Income and Expenditure Account for the Year ended 31st December, [illegible].

Expenditure.	£	s.	d.	Income.	£	s.	d.
Office Expenditure, including Salaries, Wages, Rent, Insurance, Printing, Stationery, Telephones, Telegrams, Postages, etc.	[illegible]	[illegible]	[illegible]	Contract Fees	[illegible]	[illegible]	[illegible]
Marketing Expenses:—				Delivery and Grading Fees	[illegible]	[illegible]	[illegible]
Graders' Wages and Expenses … £[illegible]				Bank Interest	[illegible]	[illegible]	[illegible]
Agents' Commissions … 11,437 [illegible]				Premiums for Defaults under Contracts, less expenses	[illegible]	[illegible]	[illegible]
Pig Movement Expenses, Agricultural Show Expenses, etc. … 1,759 [illegible]				Sundry Revenue	[illegible]	[illegible]	[illegible]
	[illegible]	[illegible]	[illegible]				
Board's Travelling Expenses	[illegible]	[illegible]	[illegible]				
Legal Expenses and Professional Charges	[illegible]	[illegible]	[illegible]				
Interest	[illegible]	[illegible]	[illegible]				
Reorganisation Commission's Expenses	[illegible]	[illegible]	[illegible]				
Development Fund Charges	[illegible]	[illegible]	[illegible]				
	[illegible]	[illegible]	[illegible]				
Depreciation	[illegible]	[illegible]	[illegible]				
Allocation to Reserve for Claims on Contracts, [illegible] per cent. [illegible] as per Section [illegible] of the Scheme	[illegible]	[illegible]	[illegible]				
Transfer to Reserve for Bad and Doubtful Debts	[illegible]	[illegible]	[illegible]				
	[illegible]	[illegible]	[illegible]				
Surplus carried down	[illegible]	[illegible]	[illegible]				
	£[illegible]	[illegible]	[illegible]		£[illegible]	[illegible]	[illegible]

[illegible]

	£	s.	d.		£	s.	d.
Transfer to General Reserve ...	[illegible]	[illegible]	[illegible]	Balance as at 31st December, [illegible] ...	[illegible]	[illegible]	[illegible]
Balance carried to Balance Sheet ...	[illegible]	[illegible]	[illegible]	*Less* transfer to General Reserve ... £[illegible] [illegible] [illegible]			
				[illegible] for year ended 31st March, [illegible] ... [illegible] [illegible] [illegible]			
					[illegible]	[illegible]	[illegible]
					[illegible]	[illegible]	[illegible]
				Surplus as above brought down ...	[illegible]	[illegible]	[illegible]
	£[illegible]	[illegible]	[illegible]		£[illegible]	[illegible]	[illegible]

Balance Sheet as at 31st December, [illegible].

Liabilities		£ s. d.	Assets	£ s. d.
Sundry Creditors		[illegible]	Cash at Bank and in Hand	[illegible]
Reserve for Claims and Contracts—			Sundry Debtors and Payments in Advance—	
Less Charges thereon to date		[illegible]	Less Reserve for Bad and Doubtful Debts	[illegible]
General Reserve—			Furniture, Machinery and Fittings—	
As per last Account	[illegible]		At Cost less Sales and Depreciation	[illegible]
Transfer from [illegible] Account	[illegible]	[illegible]		
[illegible] Account—				
Balance as above		[illegible]		
[illegible]		£[illegible]		£[illegible]

Notes—

(1) There are contingent liabilities in respect of—
(a) Remuneration of Members of the Board.
(b) Contracts for delivery of Pigs during [illegible] already confirmed by the Board.

(2) There are sums unascertained due to and by the Board in respect of—
(a) Charges for non-delivery of Pigs under Contract, and
(b) Deliveries of Pigs on Bacon and Pork Contracts made prior to 31st December, [illegible], but not notified to the Board before closing the Accounts.

[illegible], Accountant.

[illegible],
Chairman.
[illegible],
[illegible].
[illegible],
Secretary.

Report of the Auditors pursuant to Paragraph [illegible] of the Pigs Marketing Scheme, [illegible].

We have to report that we have audited the foregoing Income and Expenditure Account and Balance Sheet of the Pigs Marketing Board, made up to 31st December, [illegible], and have obtained all the information and explanations we have required. Subject to the notes thereon, we are of the opinion that such Balance Sheet is properly drawn up so as to exhibit a true and correct view of the state of the Board's affairs according to the best of our information and the explanations given to us and as shown by the Books of the Board.

[illegible] House,
[illegible], E.C.2.
[illegible] February, [illegible].

[illegible] & Co.,
Chartered Accountants,
Auditors.

[illegible] Pigs Delivery Bonus Fund Account.

Pigs Marketing Board Account.

	£ s. d.		£ s. d.
Amount due by Registered Curers to Pigs Marketing Board in respect of deliveries up to 31st December, [illegible]	[illegible]	Collected by Pigs Marketing Board up to 31st December, [illegible]— Paid into Joint Account [illegible]; Balance in hands of Pigs Marketing Board 70 0 0	[illegible]
		Outstanding for Collection by Pigs Marketing Board from Registered Curers at 31st December, [illegible]	[illegible]
	[illegible]		[illegible]

Pigs and Bacon Marketing Boards' Joint Account.

	£ s. d.		£ s. d.
Amounts paid in by Pigs Marketing Board ...	[illegible]	Bonus Distribution to Registered Pig Producers, [illegible], [illegible]	[illegible]
Interest up to 31st December, [illegible]	[illegible]	Class A Bonus at [illegible]d. per Score.	
Note.—In accordance with the terms of the [illegible] Bonus Scheme the Interest on the Joint Account is payable to the Pigs Marketing Board against their expenses of administering the Scheme.		Class B Bonus at [illegible]d. per Score.	
		Class C Bonus at [illegible]d. per Score.	
		Cash at Bank:— On Deposit Account [illegible]; On Current Account [illegible]	

BACON MARKETING BOARD.*

Income and Expenditure Account for the Year ended 31st December, [illegible]

Expenditure	£	s.	d.	Income	£	s.	d.
Salaries	[illegible]	[illegible]	[illegible]	Bacon Levy payable by Registered Producers	[illegible]	[illegible]	[illegible]
Expenses of Officials, Inspectors and Members of the Board	[illegible]	[illegible]	[illegible]	Fees and Penalties	[illegible]	[illegible]	[illegible]
Printing and Stationery	[illegible]	7	[illegible]	Sundry Receipts	[illegible]	[illegible]	[illegible]
Rent and Lighting	[illegible]	[illegible]	[illegible]	Interest	[illegible]	[illegible]	[illegible]
Postages, Telegrams and Telephones	[illegible]	[illegible]	[illegible]				
Legal and Professional Charges	[illegible]	[illegible]	11				
Advertisement Fees	[illegible]	[illegible]	[illegible]				
Office and General Expenses	[illegible]	[illegible]	[illegible]				
Branch Office Expenses	[illegible]	[illegible]	[illegible]				
Insurance and Bank Charges	[illegible]	[illegible]	[illegible]				
Agricultural and other Show Expenses	[illegible]	[illegible]	[illegible]				
Remuneration of Members of the Board	[illegible]	[illegible]	[illegible]				
Amount written off Furniture, Fittings and Office Equipment	[illegible]	[illegible]	[illegible]				
Contribution to Bacon Development Board	[illegible]	[illegible]	[illegible]				
Income Tax on Bank Interest	[illegible]	4	[illegible]				
Research and Special Expenses	[illegible]	[illegible]	[illegible]				
Preliminary Expenses (Proportion of Expenses of Reorganisation Commission chargeable to the Board)	677	11	11				
Provision for Contingent Liabilities	[illegible]	[illegible]	[illegible]				
	[illegible]	[illegible]	[illegible]				
Balance, being excess of Income over Expenditure carried to Balance Sheet	[illegible]	1	4				
	[illegible]	1	[illegible]		[illegible]	1	[illegible]

* The Bacon Fund Accounts are printed with the accounts of the Pigs Marketing Board, on opposite page.

BALANCE SHEET AS AT 31ST DECEMBER, 19[illegible]

LIABILITIES	£ s. d.	£ s. d.
SUNDRY CREDITORS AND ACCRUED CHARGES ...		[illegible]
SPECIAL RESERVES ...		
Estimated Balance of Contributions to ... in respect of 19[illegible]	4,[illegible] 0 0	
Provision for Contingent Liabilities ...	[illegible] 0 0	
		[illegible] 0 0
INCOME AND EXPENDITURE ACCOUNT		
Balance at Credit as at 31st December, 19[illegible]	[illegible] 13 7	
Add Excess of Income over Expenditure for year to date per account ...	[illegible] 1 4	
		[illegible]
		[illegible]

E. [illegible]

ASSETS	£ s. d.	£ s. d.
FURNITURE, FITTINGS AND OFFICE EQUIPMENT		
At cost, less Depreciation—		
As at 31st December, 19[illegible]	[illegible]	
Additions during 19[illegible] ...	[illegible]	
	[illegible]	
Less Amount written off for year to date ...	[illegible]	
		[illegible]
[illegible] Depreciation ...		[illegible]
STOCK OF STATIONERY ...		[illegible]
SUNDRY DEBTORS		
On [illegible] Levy Account ...	[illegible]	
[illegible] Account ...	117 1 1	
Deposit ...	5 0 0	
		[illegible]
CASH AT BANK AND ON HAND		
On Current Account ...	[illegible]	
On Deposit Account ...	[illegible]	
Cash on Hand ...	[illegible]	
		[illegible] 7 7
		[illegible]

J. A. D. GILLESPIE, C.A.

BACON INDEMNITY ACCOUNT.

Receipts and Payments Account

(i) Compensation Paid to Registered Producers in respect of Losses incurred during the period from [illegible] September, [illegible], to 31st December, [illegible].

Receipts.	£	s.	d.	Payments.	£	s.	d.
Advances from Ministry of Agriculture and Fisheries ...	[illegible]	0	0	Compensation paid to Registered Producers ...	[illegible]	[illegible]	[illegible]
Advances from Department of Agriculture for Scotland ...	[illegible]	0	0	Legal Expenses and Stamp Duty ...	[illegible]	[illegible]	[illegible]
				Balance (transferred to Repayments Account)	[illegible]	[illegible]	[illegible]
	£[illegible]	[illegible]	[illegible]		£[illegible]	[illegible]	[illegible]

(ii) Repayment of Advances from Ministry of Agriculture and Fisheries and Department of Agriculture for Scotland.

Receipts.	£	s.	d.	Payments.	£	s.	d.
Balance Transferred from above account ...	[illegible]	[illegible]	[illegible]	Repayments to Ministry of Agriculture and Fisheries and Dept. of Agriculture for Scotland ...	[illegible]	[illegible]	[illegible]
Amounts received from Pigs Marketing Board ...	[illegible]	11	[illegible]	Interest paid on advances ...	[illegible]	[illegible]	[illegible]
	£[illegible]	[illegible]	[illegible]		£[illegible]	[illegible]	[illegible]

MILK MARKETING BOARD.

Accounts for the Year ended 31st March, [illegible].

(1) General Fund Account.

	£ s. d.		£ s. d.
To amount payable to Producers ...	[illegible]	By Fund Balance brought forward, as at 1st April, [illegible] ...	[illegible]
" Amounts payable to Purchasers Commission, under the Milk ... Scheme and ... Manufacturing ...	[illegible]	" Balance of Inter-Regional Compensation Fund brought forward as at 1st April, [illegible] ...	[illegible]
" General Expenses Levy ...	[illegible]	" Charges to Purchasers for Milk Sales (see [illegible]) ...	[illegible]
" Publicity Levy ([illegible] and [illegible])—		" Licensed [illegible] Contributions (see [illegible])	[illegible]
Wholesale Producers ... [illegible]		" Advances recoverable under the Milk Act, [illegible]	[illegible]
Producers ... [illegible]			
Licensed [illegible] [illegible]			
	[illegible]		
" Fund Balance [illegible] ...	[illegible]		
	[illegible]		[illegible]

(2) Inter-Regional Compensation Fund Account

	£ s. d.		£ s. d.
To Apportionment of Levy to Regional Fund Accounts ...	[illegible]	By Balance brought forward as at 1st April, [illegible] ...	[illegible]
		" Levy charged to Regional Fund Accounts	[illegible]
	[illegible]		[illegible]

(3) [illegible] and Expenditure [illegible] Account

	£ s. d.	£ s. d.
To Head Office Expenses—		
Office Rent and [illegible]	[illegible]	
[illegible]	[illegible]	
Lighting and Power	[illegible]	
[illegible] and Equipment [illegible]	[illegible]	
Printing and Stationery	[illegible]	
Postage and Telephone	[illegible]	
Salaries and Wages	[illegible]	
Office Expenses	[illegible]	
		[illegible]
" Regional Expenses—		
Regional Committee Expenses and [illegible]	[illegible]	
Regional Offices	[illegible]	
		[illegible]
" General Publicity, [illegible] and Survey Work		[illegible]
" Bank Interest and Charges		[illegible]
" Expenses of Members of the Board		[illegible]
" Legal Expenses		[illegible]
" Audit Fee		[illegible]
" [illegible] of [illegible] General [illegible]		[illegible]
" Depreciation of Furniture and Equipment		[illegible]
" Reserve for Cost of Collection and Distribution of the proceeds of [illegible] sold in the month of [illegible]		[illegible]
" Balance carried to Balance Sheet		[illegible]

	£ s. d.
By General Expenses Levy—	
Amounts charged to General Fund Account	[illegible]
" [illegible] Fees, [illegible] of [illegible] and [illegible]	[illegible]
" [illegible]	[illegible]
" Reserve for Cost of Collection and Distribution of the proceeds of [illegible] sold in the month of March, 1954, brought forward	[illegible]

Balance Sheet as at 31st March, [illegible].

	£ s. d.	£ s. d.
To Sundry Creditors—		
Producers, in respect of Milk Sales (excluding Sales in the month of March, [illegible])	[illegible] 16 9	
Other Creditors, including liability to the Scottish Milk Marketing Board, expenses due and accrued due, etc.	[illegible] 17 [illegible]	
Publicity and Research Fund	[illegible] 17 4	
Government Grant Equalisation Fund, [illegible]	[illegible] 15 [illegible]	
		[illegible]
" Bank Overdraft		[illegible] 4
" Fund Accounts—		
Balance per Account No. 1 above		[illegible]
" Capital Reserve Account		[illegible] 14 [illegible]
" Reserve—		
Balance of Income and Expenditure Account at 1st April, [illegible]	[illegible]	
Less Remuneration of Members of the Board [illegible]		

	£ s. d.	£ s. d.
By Office Furniture and Equipment—		
At Head and Regional Offices	[illegible]	
" Motor Cars	[illegible] 7	
" Property—		
Freehold Land, Buildings and Plant	[illegible]	
At Cost less Depreciation		[illegible]
" Factory Stocks and Stores		[illegible]
" Sundry Debtors, less Reserves (including Purchasers in respect of Milk supplies for the month of March, [illegible])		[illegible]
" Cash at Bankers and in Hand		[illegible]

Notes.—1. There are [illegible] due to [illegible] by the Board in respect of [illegible] to 31st March, [illegible], but not [illegible] to the Board before closing the Accounts.

2. There are contingent liabilities in respect of—

(a) [illegible] of [illegible] of

POTATO MARKETING BOARD.

Dr. INCOME AND EXPENDITURE ACCOUNT FOR THE YEAR ENDED 31st AUGUST, [illegible]. Cr.

Dr.	£	s.	d.	£	s.	d.
To GENERAL ADMINISTRATIVE CHARGES :—						
Head Office :						
Salaries and Wages	[illegible]	14	[illegible]			
Rent, Lighting and Insurance	[illegible]	4	[illegible]			
Repairs and Alterations to Premises	[illegible]	[illegible]	[illegible]			
Telephone	[illegible]	[illegible]	[illegible]			
Postage	[illegible]	11	11			
Stationery and Office Equipment	[illegible]	[illegible]	[illegible]			
Travelling Expenses	[illegible]	[illegible]	[illegible]			
Hire of Machinery, [illegible] of Servers	[illegible]	[illegible]	[illegible]			
General Expenses	[illegible]	[illegible]	[illegible]			
	[illegible]	[illegible]	7			
Less : Amounts received from [illegible] in respect of [illegible]	[illegible]	[illegible]	[illegible]			
				[illegible]	[illegible]	7
Regional Offices :						
Salaries and Wages	[illegible]	[illegible]	4			
Car and Travelling Expenses	[illegible]	[illegible]	[illegible]			
Rents, Rates, Lighting and Insurance	[illegible]	[illegible]	[illegible]			
Repairs and Alterations to Premises	[illegible]	[illegible]	[illegible]			
Telephone	[illegible]	[illegible]	[illegible]			

Cr.	£	s.	d.	£	s.	d.
By ANNUAL ACREAGE LEVY RECEIVABLE				[illegible]	10	7
" EXCESS ACREAGE LEVY [illegible]	[illegible]	11	[illegible]			
Less : Amounts [illegible] to 31st August, [illegible], and [illegible] to Accounts to that date	[illegible]	[illegible]	[illegible]			
				[illegible]	11	[illegible]
" [illegible]				[illegible]	[illegible]	[illegible]
" [illegible]				[illegible]	[illegible]	[illegible]
" [illegible]				[illegible]	[illegible]	11

	£ s. d.	£ s. d.		£ s. d.
To Balance [illegible]	[illegible]		By Balance [illegible] ...	[illegible]
Add: [illegible] ...	[illegible]	[illegible]		
" [illegible] ...	[illegible]			
Less: [illegible] ...	[illegible]	[illegible]		
" [illegible] ...		[illegible]		
" [illegible] ...		[illegible]		
" Balance [illegible]		[illegible]		
		[illegible]		[illegible]

Balance Sheet, as at 31st August, [illegible].

Liabilities.	£ s. d.	£ s. d.	Assets.	£ s. d.	£ s. d.
[illegible]		[illegible]	[illegible]		
[illegible]			As at 31st August, [illegible]	[illegible]	
[illegible]	[illegible]		Additions	[illegible]	
Less paid to date	[illegible]			[illegible]	
		[illegible]	Less Amount written off	[illegible]	
[illegible]		[illegible]			[illegible]
[illegible]			[illegible]		
Balance per annexed Account		[illegible]	[illegible]		[illegible]
			[illegible]		[illegible]
Signed: [illegible], Chairman.					
[illegible]					
[illegible], Secretary.					
[illegible] October, [illegible].					
		[illegible]			[illegible]

[illegible]

We [illegible]

[illegible]

[illegible], London, [illegible]

[illegible] October, [illegible]

[illegible] & Co.,

Chartered Accountants,

Auditors.

THE ABERDEEN & DISTRICT MILK MARKETING BOARD.

PROFIT AND LOSS ACCOUNT FOR THE PERIOD FROM 1st AUGUST, [illegible], TO 31st DECEMBER, [illegible]

	£	s.	d.	£	s.	d.
To Salaries, Wages and National Insurance				[illegible]	[illegible]	[illegible]
" Travelling, General and Administrative Charges, etc.				671	7	7
" Rent, Rates and Insurance				[illegible]	[illegible]	[illegible]
" Repairs and Renewals				[illegible]	[illegible]	7
" Railway Carriage and Cartage				[illegible]	[illegible]	[illegible]
" Heating, Lighting, Power and Water				[illegible]	[illegible]	[illegible]
" Interest on Purchase Price of Agency				[illegible]	[illegible]	[illegible]
" Interest on Loan from Department of Agriculture				7	[illegible]	[illegible]
" Contribution to the North of Scotland College of Agriculture towards cost of the Inquiry into the cost of Milk Production				[illegible]	[illegible]	[illegible]
" Reserves—						
[illegible]	[illegible]	[illegible]	[illegible]			
Bad Debts	[illegible]	[illegible]	[illegible]			
				[illegible]	[illegible]	[illegible]
				[illegible]	[illegible]	[illegible]
" Profit for Period				[illegible]	[illegible]	[illegible]
				[illegible]	[illegible]	[illegible]

	£	s.	d.	£	s.	d.
By Ordinary Registered Producers' Contributions	[illegible]	[illegible]	[illegible]			
" Registered Producer-Retailers and Certified Milk Producers' Contributions	[illegible]	[illegible]	[illegible]			
	[illegible]	[illegible]	[illegible]			
Less—Losses on Handling Milk Surplus to the Area's Requirements	[illegible]	[illegible]	[illegible]			
				[illegible]	[illegible]	[illegible]
" Fines imposed on Registered Producers				[illegible]	[illegible]	[illegible]
" [illegible]				[illegible]	[illegible]	6
" Labels				[illegible]	[illegible]	[illegible]
				[illegible]	[illegible]	[illegible]

BALANCE SHEET AS AT 31ST DECEMBER, [illegible]

LIABILITIES.	£ s. d.	£ s. d.	ASSETS.	£ s. d.	£ s. d.
Loan from Department of Agriculture		[illegible]	Plant, Heritable Property, etc., taken over from the Aberdeen and District Milk Agency, Ltd.	[illegible]	
Bank		[illegible]	Plant Added Since	[illegible]	
Treasury Debentures		[illegible]			[illegible]
Aberdeen and District Milk Agency, Ltd.—Purchase Price		[illegible]	Expenses of Promotion of Scheme		[illegible]
Reserves:—			Sundry Debtors		[illegible]
Capital Expenditure	[illegible]		Stock in Hand		[illegible]
Bad Debts	[illegible]		Cash on Hand		[illegible]
		[illegible]			
Profit and Loss Account		[illegible]			
		[illegible]			[illegible]

Aberdeen, [illegible] March, [illegible].—I beg to report that having had access to all books, [illegible] and accounts of the Board, and having examined the Company's Profit and Loss Account and Balance Sheet, and verified the same with the books, [illegible], I [illegible] the same to be correct, duly [illegible] and in accordance with Law.

9, Golden Square, Aberdeen.

J. PATRICK JEFFREY, C.A., Auditor.

Profit and Loss Account for the Year ended 31st December, 19[illegible].

	£	s.	d.
To Salaries, Wages and National Insurance	[illegible]	[illegible]	[illegible]
" General, Administrative and Trading Charges, etc. ...	[illegible]	[illegible]	[illegible]
" Rent, Rates, Insurance, etc.	[illegible]	[illegible]	[illegible]
" Repairs and Renewals	[illegible]	[illegible]	[illegible]
" Railway Carriage and Haulage	[illegible]	[illegible]	[illegible]
" Heating, Lighting, Power and Water	[illegible]	[illegible]	[illegible]
" Advertising. Paid to Date	[illegible]	[illegible]	[illegible]
" Interest on Loans and Bank Overdraft	[illegible]	[illegible]	[illegible]
" Subscription to the Society of Scottish College of Agriculture towards cost of the Inquiry into the cost of Milk Production	[illegible]	[illegible]	[illegible]
" Transfers to Reserves— (£ s. d.) Capital Expenditure ... [illegible]; Bad Debts ... [illegible]	[illegible]	[illegible]	[illegible]
	[illegible]	[illegible]	[illegible]
" Balance—Profit for year	[illegible]	[illegible]	[illegible]
	[illegible]	[illegible]	[illegible]

	£	s.	d.	£	s.	d.
By Ordinary Registered Producers' Contributions	[illegible]	[illegible]	[illegible]			
" Registered Producers (Retailers' and Graded Milk Producers') Contributions	[illegible]	[illegible]	[illegible]			
	[illegible]	[illegible]	[illegible]			
Note.—The above contributions were raised for Capital purposes. *Less*—[illegible]	[illegible]	[illegible]	[illegible]			
				[illegible]	[illegible]	[illegible]
" Fees collected from Registered Producers ...				[illegible]	[illegible]	[illegible]
" Sundry Cans				[illegible]	[illegible]	[illegible]
" Labels				[illegible]	[illegible]	[illegible]
				[illegible]	[illegible]	[illegible]

Printed image digitised by the University of Southampton Library Digitisation Unit

Balance Sheet as at 31st December, [illegible].

Liabilities.	£	s.	d.	£	s.	d.
Loan from Department of Agriculture				[illegible]	[illegible]	[illegible]
Bank				[illegible]	[illegible]	[illegible]
[illegible] Agency Limited—Loan				[illegible]	[illegible]	[illegible]
Sundry Creditors				[illegible]	[illegible]	[illegible]
Reserves—						
Capital Expenditure—						
Balance at [illegible]	[illegible]	[illegible]	[illegible]			
Added during year	[illegible]	[illegible]	[illegible]			
	[illegible]	[illegible]	[illegible]			
Less—Written off per annum, Expenses of promotion of [illegible], Plant, etc.	[illegible]	[illegible]	[illegible]			
Bad Debts—						
Balance at [illegible]	[illegible]	[illegible]	[illegible]			
Added during year	[illegible]	[illegible]	[illegible]			
	[illegible]	[illegible]	[illegible]			
Less—Written off	[illegible]	[illegible]	[illegible]	[illegible]	[illegible]	[illegible]
Profit and Loss Account—						
Amount to Credit at [illegible]	[illegible]	[illegible]	[illegible]			
Add—Profit for year	[illegible]	[illegible]	[illegible]	[illegible]	[illegible]	[illegible]

Assets.	£	s.	d.	£	s.	d.
Plant and Movable Property—						
Value as at [illegible]	[illegible]	[illegible]	[illegible]			
Added during year at cost	[illegible]	[illegible]	[illegible]			
	[illegible]	[illegible]	[illegible]			
Less—Written off per annum	[illegible]	[illegible]	[illegible]	[illegible]	[illegible]	[illegible]
Expenses of Promotion of [illegible]—						
At [illegible]	[illegible]	[illegible]	[illegible]			
Less—Written off per annum	[illegible]	[illegible]	[illegible]			
Sundry Debtors				[illegible]	[illegible]	[illegible]
Stock in hand				[illegible]	[illegible]	[illegible]
Cash in hand				[illegible]	[illegible]	[illegible]

THE NORTH OF SCOTLAND MILK MARKETING BOARD

PROFIT AND LOSS ACCOUNT.

FOR THE PERIOD FROM [illegible] JULY, [illegible], TO 31ST MAY, [illegible].

(Period of Operations from 1st October, [illegible] to 31st May, [illegible].)

	£ s. d.	£ s. d.
To Amounts paid and payable to Ordinary Producers		[illegible]
" Salaries and National Insurance	[illegible]	
" Stationery, Printing and Advertising	[illegible]	
" Postages, Telephones, and Telegrams	[illegible]	
" Bank Charges and Stamp duty on Cheques	[illegible]	
" Travelling Expenses and Allowances	[illegible]	
" Secretary's Salary, allowance for General Assistance, Office Rent, Auditor's Fee, etc.	[illegible]	
" Interest on Loan from Department of Agriculture and Interest on Bank [illegible]	[illegible]	
" Chairman's Salary and provision for Board's Remuneration	[illegible]	[illegible]
" Preliminary Expenses written off	[illegible]	
" Expenses of Poll, Preliminary Expenditure and Expenses of a non-recurring nature written off	[illegible]	
" Depreciation on Office Furniture and Equipment	[illegible]	
" Amount written off cost of [illegible] —[illegible] Production	[illegible]	[illegible]
" Reserve for Redemption of Loan from Department of Agriculture	[illegible]	
" General Reserve Fund	[illegible]	
" Balance of Profit carried forward	[illegible]	[illegible]

	£ s. d.	£ s. d.
By Sales to Distributors (including [illegible] Cooling and Milk for Manufacture)		[illegible]
" Stocks on hand—		
[illegible]	[illegible]	
Cheese	[illegible]	[illegible]
" Contributions from Producers and Producer Retailers		[illegible]
" Government Subsidy on Manufactured Milk		[illegible]

BALANCE SHEET AS AT 31ST MAY, [illegible]

LIABILITIES.	£	s.	d.
Sundry Creditors and Credit Balances ..	[illegible]	[illegible]	[illegible]
Bank Overdraft ..	[illegible]	[illegible]	[illegible]
Department of Agriculture—			
Loan for 5 years at [illegible] per cent.	[illegible]	[illegible]	[illegible]
Loan Redemption Account ..	[illegible]	[illegible]	[illegible]
General Reserve Fund ..	[illegible]	[illegible]	[illegible]
Profit and Loss Account—			
Balance at Credit ..	[illegible]	[illegible]	[illegible]

ASSETS.	£	s.	d.	£	s.	d.
Office Furniture ..	[illegible]	[illegible]	[illegible]			
Less—Depreciation written off to date	[illegible]	[illegible]	[illegible]			
				[illegible]	[illegible]	[illegible]
Equipment ..	[illegible]	[illegible]	[illegible]			
Less—Depreciation written off to date ..	[illegible]	[illegible]	[illegible]			
				[illegible]	[illegible]	[illegible]
Stocks on hand—						
Milk ..	[illegible]	[illegible]	[illegible]			
Cheese ..	[illegible]	[illegible]	[illegible]			
				[illegible]	[illegible]	[illegible]
Sundry Debtors and Debit Balances ..				[illegible]	[illegible]	[illegible]
Formation Expenses ..	[illegible]	[illegible]	[illegible]			
Less—Written off to date ..	[illegible]	[illegible]	[illegible]			
				[illegible]	[illegible]	[illegible]
Expenses of Bill, Preliminary Expenses and Expenses of a non-recurring nature	[illegible]	[illegible]	[illegible]			
Less—Written off to date ..	[illegible]	[illegible]	[illegible]			
				[illegible]	[illegible]	[illegible]
Cost of Royalty on Production of Milk ..	[illegible]	[illegible]	[illegible]			
Less—Written off to date ..	[illegible]	[illegible]	[illegible]			
				[illegible]	[illegible]	[illegible]
Cash on hand ..				[illegible]	[illegible]	[illegible]

I have examined the Books of the North of Scotland Milk Marketing Board for the period from [illegible] July, [illegible], to [illegible], and have to report that :—

(a) In my opinion the foregoing Balance Sheet is properly drawn up so as to exhibit a true and correct view of the state of the Board's affairs and that the Profit and Loss Account exhibits a true and correct record of the Income and Expenditure of the Board according to the best of my information and the explanations given to me and as shown by the Books, and

(b) That the said Balance Sheet and Profit and Loss Account are sufficiently vouched,

subject to the following observations :—

The amounts credited in the Accounts in respect of Exchequer advances in terms of Section 11 of the Milk Act, 1934, are amounts due, as estimated by the Board, pending the completion of negotiations which are at present in progress.

Inverness,

[illegible] June, [illegible].

DONALD HEPBURN, C.A.,

Auditor.

MINISTRY OF AGRICULTURE AND FISHERIES
SCOTTISH OFFICE

REPORT ON AGRICULTURAL MARKETING SCHEMES

FOR THE YEAR 1936

Presented to Parliament by the Minister of Agriculture and Fisheries and the Secretary of State for Scotland by Command of His Majesty
May, 1938

LONDON
PRINTED AND PUBLISHED BY HIS MAJESTY'S STATIONERY OFFICE
To be purchased directly from H.M. STATIONERY OFFICE at the following addresses:
Adastral House, Kingsway, London, W.C.2; 120 George Street, Edinburgh 2;
26 York Street, Manchester 1; 1 St. Andrew's Crescent, Cardiff;
80 Chichester Street, Belfast;
or through any bookseller
1938
Price 2s. 0d. net

Cmd. 5734

AGRICULTURAL MARKETING ACTS, 1931 to 1933

REPORT ON AGRICULTURAL MARKETING SCHEMES

The following report upon the operation of Agricultural Marketing Schemes in force in 1936, and upon schemes that have been submitted since the date of our last report but which are not yet in force, has been prepared in accordance with the requirements of Section 10 of the Agricultural Marketing Act, 1931.

W. S. MORRISON,
Minister of Agriculture and Fisheries.

WALTER E. ELLIOT,
Secretary of State for Scotland.

April, 1938.

TABLE OF CONTENTS

PART I.

PART II.

APPENDICES.

MINISTRY OF AGRICULTURE AND FISHERIES

SCOTTISH OFFICE

REPORT ON AGRICULTURAL MARKETING SCHEMES

FOR THE YEAR

1937

Presented to Parliament by the Minister of Agriculture and Fisheries
and the Secretary of State for Scotland
by Command of His Majesty
May, 1939

LONDON

PRINTED AND PUBLISHED BY HIS MAJESTY'S STATIONERY OFFICE

To be purchased directly from H.M. STATIONERY OFFICE at the following addresses:
York House, Kingsway, London, W.C.2; 120 George Street, Edinburgh 2;
26 York Street, Manchester 1; 1 St. Andrew's Crescent, Cardiff;
80 Chichester Street, Belfast;
or through any bookseller

1939

Price 2s. 0d. net

Cmd. 6030

AGRICULTURAL MARKETING ACTS, 1931 to 1933

REPORT ON AGRICULTURAL MARKETING SCHEMES

The following report upon the operation of Agricultural Marketing Schemes in force in 1937, and upon Schemes that have been submitted but which are not yet in force, has been prepared in accordance with the requirements of Section 10 of the Agricultural Marketing Act, 1931.

R. H. Dorman-Smith,
Minister of Agriculture and Fisheries.

John Colville,
Secretary of State for Scotland.

May, 1939.

REPORT ON AGRICULTURAL MARKETING SCHEMES FOR THE YEAR 1937

PART I.

SCHEMES IN OPERATION.

The following Agricultural Marketing Schemes were in operation in 1937:—

Title of Scheme.	Date of Approval Order.	Area of Scheme.
Hops Marketing Scheme, 1932.	7th July, 1932.	England.*
Scottish Milk Marketing Scheme, 1933.	25th May, 1933.	Scotland, south of the Grampians.
Pigs Marketing Scheme, 1933.	5th July, 1933.	Great Britain.
Bacon Marketing Scheme, 1933.	5th July, 1933.	Great Britain.
Milk Marketing Scheme, 1933.	28th July, 1933.	England.*
Potato Marketing Scheme, 1933.	20th Dec., 1933.	Great Britain.
Aberdeen and District Milk Marketing Scheme, 1933.	28th March, 1934.	Counties of Aberdeen and Kincardine.
North of Scotland Milk Marketing Scheme, 1934.	6th July, 1934.	Counties of Inverness, Nairn, Ross and Cromarty, Sutherland and Caithness.

* "England" includes Wales.

HOPS MARKETING SCHEME, 1932.

The Hops Marketing Scheme applies to England. The Board is composed of 18 members, of whom 14 are elected annually for local districts and 4 are special members elected at the annual general meeting of registered producers. There was no change in the personnel of the Board during 1937.

The remuneration of members of the Board voted at the annual general meeting on the 7th May, 1937, was at the same rate as in the previous year, namely:—Chairman, £800; Special Members, £400 each; District Members, £200 each; Vice-Chairman of the Board, and the Chairman of each Standing Committee, an additional £100.

The number of producers registered with the Board on 31st December, 1937, was 980.

Acreage and Production.

The total acreage under hops in England in 1937 (including hops grown by producers who are exempt from the operation of the Scheme), was 18,093 acres, and the estimated total production 235,000 cwt., giving an estimated average yield of 13·0 cwt. per acre. In 1936 the corresponding figures were: acreage

18,317 acres; estimated total production 252,000 cwt.; estimated average yield 13·7 cwt. per acre. The lower yield in 1937 was attributable mainly to weather conditions, but the quality of the crop was very even and generally good.

Trading Operations of the Board.

In 1934 the Board made an Agreement* with the Brewers' Society under which the average price of hops sold by the Board was fixed at £9 per cwt. for the five seasons 1934-8 inclusive. The administration of the Agreement is supervised by a Permanent Joint Committee composed of four representatives each of the Hops Marketing Board and the Brewers' Society, together with three members, one of whom is Chairman of the Committee, nominated by the Minister. The Agreement also provides that a sum of 10s. per cwt. shall be added to the price of all hops sold by the Board, the proceeds being paid into a Levy Fund under the control of the Joint Committee. Any unsold balance of the "estimated market demand" for English hops, as determined by the Committee each year, is paid for from the Fund.

1936 *Crop*.—Provisional results of the Board's trading operations in 1936 hops were given in the last report†. The estimated market demand for that crop was 225,000 cwt. but total sales by the Board fell short of expectations and amounted to 216,647 cwt. The total amount realized from the sale of the hops was £1,954,916 (excluding the 10s. per cwt. levy), whereas the value of the estimated market demand of 225,000 cwt. at £9 per cwt. was £2,025,000. There was thus a difference of £70,084 between the actual and the anticipated receipts from the sale of hops, and this difference was made up by a call on the Levy Fund. After selling expenses and contributions payable to the Board had been deducted, producers received an average price of £8 8s. 5d. per cwt. for quota hops, representing the full amount of the valuation of those hops.

The unsold balance of the 1936 crop at 31st December, 1937, amounted to 10,567 cwt. No payment was made to producers in respect of the 4,946 cwt. of non-quota hops delivered to the Board in 1936.

1937 *Crop*.—The total of basic quotas for the 1937 crop was 231,891 cwt. Quotas in respect of 5,038 cwt. were held by producers who consigned their hops direct to brewers under contracts registered with the Board; and the quotas of registered producers consigning hops to the Board amounted therefore

* Particulars of this Agreement were given in a White Paper (Cmd. 4628), presented to Parliament in 1934.

† Cmd. 5734, page 3.

to 226,853 cwt. The Permanent Joint Committee estimated the total market demand for English hops, exclusive of hops grown by brewers for their own use and hops grown under registered contracts, to be 222,500 cwt., and the Board accordingly determined annual quotas to be 98 per cent. of basic quotas, compared with 97 per cent. in 1934 and 100 per cent. in 1935 and 1936. A number of transfers of annual quotas took place, enabling producers to adjust their consignments of quota hops more nearly to their production.

The total quantity of hops tendered to the Board was 208,608 cwt. of which 208,117 cwt. were quota hops and 491 cwt. non-quota hops. The gross valuation of the hops tendered was £1,879,100, of which £1,875,264 represented quota hops and £3,836 non-quota hops, giving an average valuation for quota hops and non-quota hops of £9 0s. 3d. and £7 16s. 3d. per cwt. respectively, and an average valuation of £9 0s. 2d. per cwt. for all hops tendered. The valuation of the 1937 crop was finished by the 28th November, 1937, and trading began on the following day, some five weeks earlier than in the previous season. During the first 28 days of trading hops are normally offered and sold only to merchants nominated by brewers who have entered into firm contracts with the Board, but owing to the crop being short, the Permanent Joint Committee granted 14 days' extension of the closed period of trading for the benefit of brewers who had contracted for less than the full amount of their estimated requirements.

As in previous years, two advance payments in respect of quota hops, amounting in all to not more than two-thirds of the valuation were made to producers before the end of the year. The Permanent Joint Committee decided that, as a substantial balance had accumulated in the Levy Fund, the levy on the 1937 crop should be reduced from 10s. per cwt. to 3s. per cwt.

Statistics relating to the production of hops and the trading operations of the Board for each year since the Scheme came into operation are given in the following table:—

Hops Marketing Scheme, 1932.

		[illegible]	[illegible]	[illegible]	[illegible]	[illegible]	[illegible]
Production (excluding hops grown by producers exempted from the operation of the Scheme).							
Average acreage (excluding exemptions) ...	acres	[illegible]	[illegible]	[illegible]	[illegible]	[illegible]	[illegible]
Average yield per acre	cwt.	[illegible]	[illegible]	[illegible]	[illegible]	[illegible]	[illegible]
Estimated total production	,,	[illegible]	[illegible]	[illegible]	[illegible]	[illegible]	[illegible]
Marketing.							
Estimated market demand	cwt.	—	—	[illegible]	[illegible]	[illegible]	[illegible]
Produce (tendered) to the Board ...	,,	[illegible]	[illegible]	[illegible]	[illegible]	[illegible]	[illegible]
	cwt.			Quota [illegible]	Quota [illegible]	Quota [illegible]	Quota [illegible]
	cwt.			Non-Quota [illegible]	Non-Quota [illegible]	Non-Quota [illegible]	Non-Quota [illegible]
Quantity disposed of	cwt.	[illegible]	[illegible]	[illegible]	[illegible]	[illegible]	
Receipts (gross value)	,,	[illegible]	[illegible]	[illegible]	[illegible]	[illegible]	
Paid to registered producers	—	[illegible]	[illegible]	[illegible]	[illegible]	[illegible]	
Average return per cwt.	,,	[illegible]	[illegible]	[illegible]	[illegible] for Quota hops, [illegible] for Non-Quota hops.	[illegible]	
Agents' commission (per cwt.)	..	[illegible]	[illegible]	[illegible]	[illegible]	[illegible]	
Retained for Board's expenses (per cwt.)	...	[illegible]	[illegible]	[illegible]	[illegible]	[illegible]	

Accounts of the Board.—Copies of the Income and Expenditure Account and of the Balance Sheet as at 31st March, 1937, are printed in Appendix III.

SCOTTISH MILK MARKETING SCHEME, 1933.

This Scheme applies to an area comprising the counties of Angus and Perth, part of Argyll and the whole of Scotland lying to the south of these counties.

The fourth annual general meeting of the registered producers was held on 1st June, 1937. The meeting voted £2,500, the same amount as in the previous year, to be divided amongst the members of the Board as remuneration for their services during the year 1936-7. The Board consists of 8 elected members, 2 of whom retire annually in rotation, and 2 co-opted members. There was no change during 1937 in the personnel of the Board. The Selection Committee which was appointed at the annual general meeting, as required by the Scheme, re-elected the 2 retiring members to the Board.

The total number of producers registered under the Scheme on 30th November, 1937, was 7,914, as compared with 7,929 on the same date in 1936. Of that number, 5,064 were producers selling milk only to or through the Board, and 2,850 were producer-retailers, producer-wholesalers* or producers of Certified milk.

Statements showing the quantities of milk sold by the registered producers in each month in the year ended November, 1937, in comparison with the corresponding statistics for the previous year, are given on pages 17 and 18. The total sales during the two years were as follows:—

	1935–36. Gallons.	*1936–37. Gallons.*	*Increase or Decrease. Gallons.*	*Per cent.*
Sold for liquid consumption ...	72,972,945	75,506,857	+ 2,533,912	+ 3·47
Sold or used for manufacture ...	50,005,787	44,169,151	− 5,836,636	−11·67
	122,978,732	119,676,008	− 3,302,724	− 2·69

The sales of milk by the registered producers during December, 1937, amounted to 7,542,206 gallons, of which 6,164,805 gallons (81·74 per cent.) were sold for liquid consumption.

* i.e., producers licensed to sell milk to distributors whose total daily purchases do not exceed 20 gallons.

Payments to Producers.

Sales to or through the agency of the Board.—The following table shows in respect of each month in the year ended November, 1937, and in the previous year, the Standard Price (i.e., the price paid by distributors for untreated milk for liquid consumption) and the average price per gallon paid by the Board to the producers for milk sold to or through the agency of the Board.

Month.	December, 1936 to November, 1937.		December, 1935 to November, 1936.	
	Standard Price per gallon.	Average Price per gallon.	Standard Price per gallon.	Average Price per gallon.
	d.	d.	d.	d.
December	15	12⅝	15	12⅝
January	15	13	15	12½
February	15	12½	15	12
March	14	11	14	11
April	14	10½	14	9⅝
May	13	9	12	8⅝
June	13	8¼	12	8⅝
July	14	9⅝	14	9⅝
August	14	10⅝	14	10
September ...	14	11⅜	14	10⅝
October	15	12⅝	14	11½
November	17	14⅝	15	12⅝
Monthly Average	14·42	11·35	14·00	10·77

The weighted average price per gallon paid to the producers in respect of supplies during the year ended November, 1937, was 10·942d. compared with 10·463d. for the previous year.

The Standard Price for December, 1937, was 1s. 5d. per gallon, and the average price paid to the producers for their sales in that month was 1s. 2½d. per gallon.

Haulage Charges.—The haulage charges, payable by the producers by deduction from the monthly average prices at standard rates per gallon according to the distance of their farms and premises from the nearest of the prescribed haulage centres, were on the same scale as in the previous years, viz., not exceeding five miles, ½d.; over five but not exceeding ten miles, ¾d.; over ten but not exceeding thirty miles, 1d.; over thirty but not exceeding forty miles, 1¼d.; over forty miles, 1½d. The average rate of the deduction in respect of the total sales during the year was 1·13d. per gallon.

Premiums.—The number of producers who qualified for payment of a bonus of ½d. per gallon by regulating their sales to or through the Board during the year 1937 at quantities not exceeding in any month more than 10 per cent. of the quantity so sold by them in December, 1933, was 448. The total supply of milk in respect of which this bonus was paid was 8,539,354 gallons.

The numbers of producers who, in accordance with the contracts with buyers of their milk during the year ended September, 1937, earned the level-delivery premium (1d. per gallon) and the wholesale service premium (2d. per gallon) were 376 and 297 respectively.

The total quantity of Tuberculin Tested milk sold as such to or through the Board during the period December, 1936, to August, 1937, was 2,181,802 gallons. A premium of 3d. per gallon, the amount by which the prescribed price for the sale of Tuberculin Tested milk to distributors exceeded the Standard Price, was paid to the producers concerned in respect of these sales. The payment of that premium to producers was thereafter discontinued except in respect of comparatively small supplies of Tuberculin Tested milk bottled on the farms and sold as milk of that grade through the Board, but, in accordance with adjustments made in the Scheme by Orders of the Secretary of State (see page 15), a bonus of 2d. per gallon was paid by the Board as from 1st September to the producers of all Tuberculin Tested milk sold in bulk to or through the Board whether or not a market was found for its sale as milk of that grade. The quantity of milk for which that bonus was paid for the period September to November, 1937, amounted to 2,167,224 gallons.

The number of registered producers with licensed tubercle-free herds at the end of the year was 701 as compared with 481 on 31st December, 1936.

Producer-Wholesalers and Producer-Retailers.—As stated in the last report,* the draft amendments submitted by the Board to deal with the situation arising from the judgment of the House of Lords in the "Ferrier" case provided for (*a*) the assessment of the contributions of producer-retailers and producer-wholesalers at 1⅛d. per gallon, and (*b*) the refundment of any sums paid by them in the past in excess of that rate on the gallonage basis of assessment. After considering the report of the public inquiry into the objections to the draft amendments, the Secretary of State decided to modify the proposals for compensation by increasing the amount payable in respect of the period prior to 1st January, 1935, by one-eighth of a penny per gallon. The Board's assent to this modification

* Cmd. 5734, pages 7 and 8.

having been obtained, the draft amendments, as modified, were laid before, and approved by, both Houses of Parliament. In terms of the Scottish Milk Marketing Scheme (Amendment) Order, 1937,* made by the Secretary of State, the amendments came into force on 1st August, 1937.

The compensation provided for by the amendments was payable to those producers who agreed to accept it in full settlement of all their claims. Of the producers entitled to the offer of compensation, 3,597 (93 per cent.) intimated to the Board within the prescribed period their acceptance of the offer.

The total amount of compensation payable amounted to £112,830. Except in the case of producers who had discontinued the sale of milk as producer-retailers or producer-wholesalers, the compensation was payable by suspension of the collection of the monthly contributions in respect of the producers' sales.

Producers of Certified Milk.—The contribution payable to the Board by producers in respect of Certified milk sold as such was at the rate of ½d. per gallon. These sales, during the year ended November, 1937, amounted to 776,186 gallons.

Farm Cheesemakers.—The number of producers who entered into agreements with the Board to make cheese on their farms during 1937 was 324 as compared with 390 in 1936. These agreements were made in the same terms as in the previous year except for adjustments in the manufacturing allowances. The producers retained the cheese made by them as part payment of the monthly average prices for their milk and received the balance of these prices from the Board in cash together with a manufacturing allowance of 1¾d. per gallon for March and April, 1½d. per gallon for May, and 1d. per gallon for the other months of the season.

The quantities of milk converted into cheese under the agreements during the year were as follows:—

	Gallons.
March	189,729
April	643,173
May	1,363,751
June	1,499,118
July	1,415,663
August	1,212,511
September ...	817,443
October	144,669
	7,286,057

* S.R. & O. 1937, No. 624/S. 36.

Contracts.

The terms and conditions in the form of contract supplied by the Board for use in respect of the sale and purchase of milk during the year ended September, 1938, were mainly the same as those applicable during the previous year. A provision was included to make it clear that the ownership of the milk does not pass from the seller to the buyer until delivery of the milk at the buyers' premises, railway station or pier. The minimum standards of butter fat content were fixed, as in the previous year, at not less than 3·5 per cent. for the months of August to January inclusive, and 3·4 per cent. for the months of February to July inclusive. Other standards of quality for all milk other than officially graded milk were also defined.

Liquid Milk Prices.

The Standard Price for the sale of untreated milk to the distributors for liquid consumption was determined by the Board for the year ended September, 1938, on the following scale:—October, 1937, 1s. 3d. per gallon; November, 1937, to January, 1938, 1s. 5d. per gallon; February, 1938, 1s. 3d. per gallon; March and April, 1938, 1s. 2d. per gallon; May and June, 1938, 1s. 1d. per gallon; July to September, 1938, 1s. 2d. per gallon. By this scale, provision was made for increased returns from producers' sales of milk in the winter months, the price for October being 1d. and the price for the three months November to January being 2d. higher than in the corresponding months of 1936-7. The prices for the other months were the same as in the previous year. The monthly average of the Standard Price over the year was 1s. 2¾d. per gallon, being $\frac{7}{12}$d. above the average for the year 1936-7.

The minimum retail prices for ordinary milk were determined at 2s. 4d. per gallon, being 4d. more than in the previous year, for the three months November, 1937, to January, 1938, and at 2s. per gallon, the same price as previously, for the other nine months. The distributors' margin over the year was thus increased by $\frac{5}{12}$d. to 10¼d. per gallon. "Semi-retail" prices for supplies to hotels, etc., were not determined by the Board for 1937-8, the distributors having agreed to observe the prices fixed by their own organisations. The prices for supplies to institutions and shipping companies were continued at not less than the Standard Price.

For Tuberculin Tested and Certified milk the producers' prices were determined, as in the previous year, at 3d. and 10d. per gallon more than the prices for ordinary milk. The minimum retail prices were fixed at 4d. and 8d. per gallon more than the prices for ordinary milk.

Manufacturing Milk Prices.

Cheese and Butter.—The prices for milk sold for the manufacture of cheese and butter were determined by the Board for each month of 1937, as in the previous year, in accordance with formulae based on the weighted average prices realised on the sale of cheese and butter manufactured by the Board. The price of milk for the manufacture of cheese ranged from 4·57d. to 7·056d. per gallon. The price of milk for the manufacture of butter varied from 3·839d. to 6·478d. per gallon; these prices were payable for monthly supplies exceeding 7,500 gallons, additional prices up to 2d. per gallon being charged for monthly purchases of less than that quantity.

Other Products.—Milk for the manufacture of fresh cream was supplied mainly at 7½d. per gallon until 30th September, and mainly at 8½d. per gallon thereafter. The prices of milk for manufacture of other products were as follows:—

	Until 30th September. per gallon.	*After 30th September per gallon.*
Tinned Cream	6½d.	7d.
Milk Powder	5½d.	7d.
Margarine	9d.	10d.
Condensed Milk	6d.	7½d.
,, ,, for export ...	Price of milk sold for cheese manufacture in England subject to a minimum of— 4d.	5d.

The prices shown above for the manufacture of condensed milk for the home markets and of milk powder were subject to an increase in each month by the same amount as the average price of milk sold in England for cheese manufacture in the three previous months exceeded 4½d. per gallon.

Sale and Use of Milk for Manufacture.—The quantities of milk sold for manufacture or used by the Board for manufacture into the various milk products during the year December, 1936, to November, 1937, and the realisation values per gallon, were as follows:—

Product.	Sold for manufacture.		Used by the Board for manufacture.		Total.		Realisation Value per gallon. (weighted average).*
	Gallons.	Per cent.	Gallons.	Per cent.	Gallons.	Per cent.	
							pence.
Fresh Cream	8,716,712	34·07	5,487,496	48·61	14,204,208	38·52	7·237 (7·158)
Tinned Cream and Condensed Milk	7,423,556	29·01	8,382	0·07	7,431,938	20·15	6·723 (6·637)
Cheese ...	3,578,826	13·99	2,451,334	21·71	6,030,160	16·35	6·041 (5·683)
Butter ...	5,167,512	20·19	3,341,972	29·60	8,509,484	23·08	4·492 (4·580)
Milk Powder	423,568	1·65	—	—	423,568	1·15	5·809 (5·770)
Other Products ...	277,550	1·09	369	0·01	277,919	0·75	9·588
	25,587,724	100·00	11,289,553	100·00	36,877,277	100·00	6·306 (6·252)

* The value of the milk used by the Board for manufacture is calculated at the prescribed prices for the sale of milk to private manufacturers. The figures in brackets show the average values after including the advances and deducting estimated repayments under the Milk Acts, 1934 to 1937.

The Board's manufacturing operations during the year were carried out at fifteen of their creameries. These included the Board's new factory at Bentfield, Mauchline, Ayrshire, which was completed and brought into use in April, 1937. The factory is equipped to deal with 12,000 gallons of milk per day for the manufacture of cream, butter or cheese. By-products from the Board's manufactures are transferred to an adjoining auxiliary factory, owned by a manufacturing company, for use in the making of powders by the spray-drying process.

Other creameries belonging to the Board have been equipped with machinery for the conversion of the by-products of the main manufactures into commodities such as casein, milk powders, whey powder and whey butter. A remunerative market is thus being found for by-products which went to waste before the Scheme came into operation. The net value of by-products now being salved is about £50,000 per annum.

The Milk Acts, 1934 to 1937.

The Milk (Amendment) Act, 1937, extended, with certain amendments, until 30th September, 1938, the provisions of the principal Act of 1934 relating to the payment to milk marketing boards of advances in respect of milk used for manufacture and of grants in aid of approved arrangements for increasing the demand for milk. While an extension was also made to September, 1940, of the period during which a contingent liability rests upon the boards to make repayments to the Exchequer in respect of milk used for manufacture, the Government announced that it was proposed to release the boards from any balance of this liability accruing after 30th September, 1937.*

Advances on Manufacturing Milk.—The quantities of milk sold or used for manufacture on which advances were made and the amounts advanced for the year 1937, compared with the corresponding figures for the year 1936, were as follows:—

Product.	1936. *Gallons.*	1936. *Payments.* £	1937. *Gallons.*	1937. *Payments.* £
Milk sold for manufacture :—				
Butter	4,999,823	14,163	1,524,824	4,663
Cheese	4,446,737	10,317	179,177	633
Milk Powder ...	378,919	954	—	—
Condensed Milk ...	190,786	231	62,302	241
Total ...	10,016,265	25,665	1,766,303	5,537
Milk used by the Board for manufacture :—				
Butter	3,173,268	6,626	931,043	2,751
Cheese	2,714,829	6,224	7,450	34
Total ...	5,888,097	12,850	938,493	2,785
Milk converted into cheese on farms :—				
Farm Cheese ...	6,033,237	9,801	189,729	870
Total	21,937,599	£48,316	2,894,525	£9,192

The estimated sums repayable by the Board, in accordance with Section 5 of the Milk Act, 1934, as amended by subsequent Acts, up to 30th September, 1937, amounted to £20,400.

Improvement of the Quality of the Milk Supply—Attested Herds Scheme.—Particulars of this Scheme were given in the report for 1936. The number of Attested Herds within the area of the Scottish Milk Marketing Scheme increased from 218 to 622 during the year. Bonuses paid in 1937 from the Exchequer

* Carried into effect by the Milk (Extension and Amendment) Act, 1938.

in respect of sales of milk from the Attested Herds amounted to £40,680 (equivalent to 9,763,000 gallons of milk) as compared with payments in the previous year of £11,409 (equivalent to 2,738,000 gallons of milk).

Arrangements for increasing the demand for Milk—Milk-in-Schools Scheme.—Under this Scheme milk is supplied for consumption by children in the schools at the reduced price of ½d. for one third of a pint. The Board undertakes to supply Tuberculin Tested milk so far as possible. The total quantity of milk consumed under the Milk-in-Schools Scheme during the calendar year 1937 amounted to 2,398,000 gallons of which 2,231,000 gallons (93 per cent.) were of Tuberculin Tested grade. The grant paid to the Board at the rate of 4½d. per gallon in respect of that supply amounted to £45,019.

The following table shows the quantities of milk consumed under the Milk-in-Schools Scheme in each month during the three years 1935 to 1937:—

Month.	1935.		1936.		1937.	
	Thousand gallons consumed.	Estimated average number of school days.	Thousand gallons consumed.	Estimated average number of school days.	Thousand gallons consumed.	Estimated average number of school days.
January ...	113	16	221	16	196	16
February	174	19	245	20	234	19
March ...	312	21	264	22	219	23
April ...	214	18	165	14	222	15
May ...	363	21	280	21	239	20
June ...	297	19	251	20	261	22
July ...	34	Holidays	23	Holidays	23	Holidays
August ...	83		26		23	
September	288	18	257	21	261	20
October ...	311	23	288	21	262	20
November	264	18	240	20	245	21
December	201	14	201	12	212	17
Total ...	2,634	—	2,461	—	2,398	—

The number of children taking milk under the Scheme on 1st November, 1937, was 319,400, representing 47·5 per cent. of the total number of children eligible to receive milk at the reduced price.

The Board asked the Education Authorities to consider whether school children could be assembled under suitable supervision to receive milk under the Scheme during the summer holidays. As a result, arrangements were made for supplying milk during the holidays in Edinburgh (29 centres), in Stirlingshire (15 schools) and at Cambuslang, Lanarkshire (1 school). The average daily number of children supplied under these arrangements was 6,458, the total quantity of milk consumed amounting to 9,479 gallons. The attendances at Cambuslang and Edinburgh represented respectively about 31 and 20 per cent. of the number of children taking milk in the schools on school days; a comparative figure for Stirlingshire is not available.

Part of the press and poster propaganda carried out by the Board during the year was designed to direct attention to the benefit to children of the regular consumption of milk in the schools. The Board's propaganda officers visited many of the schools to give short addresses to the children.

Nutrition Survey.—Certain schools in Renfrewshire were included in the investigation made of the effect on the health of children of the consumption of milk in varying quantities and the relative nutritional value of raw and pasteurised milk. A grant of £463 was paid to the Board to meet one-half of the cost, at 1s. per gallon, of providing milk free of charge to children at these schools during the period of twelve months covered by the investigation.

Reference is made on page 39 to the interim report on the results of the investigation.

Publicity and Propaganda.—A further campaign of publicity and propaganda, consisting largely of press and poster advertisement, was undertaken by the Board during 1937 at an estimated total cost of £28,000. Proposals for part of that campaign to be carried out during the nine months ending September, 1937, at an estimated cost of £15,000, were approved by the Secretary of State for payment of a grant-in-aid not exceeding £7,000.

The action taken by the Board, in addition to the arrangements assisted by grant under the Milk Acts, with a view to stimulating increased consumption of milk included the production of a milk propaganda film which was shown extensively in cinemas throughout the area of the Marketing Scheme. The film was also used at meetings addressed by the Board's propaganda officers.

The sales of milk under the Milk-in-Industry campaign were substantially increased. The milk is supplied at factories, offices and mines, etc. during working hours in one-third pint bottles at 1d. each. The number of employees taking milk daily under the scheme rose during the year from 23,000 to 50,000.

The Board continued to encourage the development of milk bars by demonstrations at exhibitions and shows and advice to persons contemplating the installation of bars. At the close of the year there were about 60 fully equipped milk bars throughout the area of the Marketing Scheme and equipment for the sale of milk drinks had also been installed at a large number of other premises.

Agricultural Co-operation, Research and Education.

The enquiry into the cost of milk production by the Advisory Economists at the Colleges of Agriculture in collaboration with the Department's Advisory Officer on Farm Economics was continued during the year. The Board made a further contribution of £295 towards the expenses of the enquiry.

Additional donations made by the Board included the following:—Hannah Dairy Research Institute, £395; Department of Scientific and Industrial Research, £250; West of Scotland Agricultural College, £250; Institute of Animal Genetics, £200; Animal Diseases Research, £200; Scottish Agricultural Organisation Society, £100; Ayrshire Agricultural Association, £10.

Complaints regarding the Operation of the Scheme.

Committee of Investigation for Scotland.

Complaint by the Association of Certified and Tuberculin Tested Milk Producers.—As stated in the last report* the Committee of Investigation for Scotland, in their report on a complaint by the Association of Certified and Tuberculin Tested Milk Producers, found that the provision in the Scheme, under which the producers of Tuberculin Tested milk sold through the agency of the Board qualified for payment of premium only if the milk was sold at a price exceeding the ordinary milk price, was contrary to the interest of these producers and was not in the public interest. After full consideration, the Secretary of State, in exercise of his powers under Section 9 of the Agricultural Marketing Act, 1931, made the Scottish Milk Marketing Scheme (Amendment No. 2) and (Directions) Orders, 1937†. The amendment of the Scheme authorises the Board to pay a bonus to registered producers for sales of milk of the grades defined in the Milk (Special Designations) Order (Scotland), 1936‡. The amendment further provides that, when arrangements have been made for paying a bonus for milk of an official grade sold to or through the agency of the Board, any sums received from the buyers in excess of the ordinary milk price are not to be allocated to the producers concerned unless the Board otherwise determines. The Directions Order required the Board to pay a bonus of 2d. per gallon to registered producers in respect of all milk of Tuberculin Tested grade sold by

* Cmd. 5734, page 16.
† S.R. & O. 1937, Nos. 818/S. 44 and 819/S. 45.
‡ S.R. & O. 1936, No. 687/S. 19.

them to or through the Board in containers of more than one quart capacity during the period from 1st September, 1937, to 30th September, 1938.

Consumers' Committee for Scotland.

Retail Price of milk.—The Consumers' Committee for Scotland, in a report dated 27th November, 1937* on complaints regarding the retail price of milk, commented adversely on the determination by the Scottish Milk Marketing Board of the retail prices for the year ended 30th September, 1938, at 2s. 4d. per gallon for the three months November to January, and at 2s. per gallon for the remaining months of the year, as compared with pre-Scheme prices in the year 1932-3. In its observations on the report the Board stated that, having regard to the increased costs of production and the danger of a shortage of milk in the winter months, it had no alternative but to make provision for higher returns for the producers' sales of milk in these months, and that the slight increase in the distributive margin over the year was made in view of the increase in the costs of distribution.

The Committee also renewed the recommendation made in previous reports that special consideration should be given to rate-aided and charitable institutions in the determination of prices for their milk supplies. While expressing sympathy with that recommendation, the Board pointed out that the prices determined by it for sales to institutions are the lowest prices at which milk is supplied to distributors and that, if these prices were reduced, the dairy farmers would be placed in the position of being compulsory contributors to the institutions.

Miscellaneous.

Finances of the Board.—Copies of the Profit and Loss Account of the Board for the year ended 31st January, 1937, and of the Balance Sheet as at that date, are printed in Appendix III.

Contraventions of the Scheme.— No monetary penalties were imposed by the Board on producers for contraventions of the Scheme during the year ended November, 1937.

Agreement with the English Milk Marketing Board.—The total quantity of milk consigned to England during the year 1937 was 3,073,187 gallons. The compensation payable to the Scottish Board by the English Board under the agreement referred to in the previous reports in respect of the limitation of the sales to that quantity during the year as compared with the sales in the year 1933, amounted to about £135,258.

* Copies of this report may be obtained from the Secretary to the Committee, 29, St. Andrew Square, Edinburgh.

Scottish Milk Marketing Scheme, 1933.

MONTHLY QUANTITIES OF MILK SOLD FOR LIQUID CONSUMPTION AND QUANTITIES SOLD OR USED BY THE BOARD FOR MANUFACTURE.

Month.	December, 1935, to November, 1936.					December, 1936, to November, 1937.				
	Total Sales	Sold for liquid consumption.		Sold or used for manufacture		Total Sales	Sold for liquid consumption.		Sold or used for manufacture	
	Gallons.	Gallons.	Per cent.	Gallons.	Per cent.	Gallons.	Gallons.	Per cent.	Gallons.	Per cent.
December ...	[illegible]	[illegible]	[illegible]	[illegible]	[illegible]	[illegible]	[illegible]	[illegible]	[illegible]	[illegible]
January ...	[illegible]	[illegible]	[illegible]	[illegible]	[illegible]	[illegible]	[illegible]	[illegible]	[illegible]	[illegible]
February ...	[illegible]	[illegible]	[illegible]	[illegible]	[illegible]	[illegible]	[illegible]	[illegible]	[illegible]	[illegible]
March ...	[illegible]	[illegible]	[illegible]	[illegible]	[illegible]	[illegible]	[illegible]	[illegible]	[illegible]	[illegible]
April ...	[illegible]	[illegible]	[illegible]	[illegible]	[illegible]	[illegible]	[illegible]	[illegible]	[illegible]	[illegible]
May ...	[illegible]	[illegible]	[illegible]	[illegible]	[illegible]	[illegible]	[illegible]	[illegible]	[illegible]	[illegible]
June ...	[illegible]	[illegible]	[illegible]	[illegible]	[illegible]	[illegible]	[illegible]	[illegible]	[illegible]	[illegible]
July ...	[illegible]	[illegible]	[illegible]	[illegible]	[illegible]	[illegible]	[illegible]	[illegible]	[illegible]	[illegible]
August ...	[illegible]	[illegible]	[illegible]	[illegible]	[illegible]	[illegible]	[illegible]	[illegible]	[illegible]	[illegible]
September	[illegible]	[illegible]	[illegible]	[illegible]	[illegible]	[illegible]	[illegible]	[illegible]	[illegible]	[illegible]
October ...	[illegible]	[illegible]	[illegible]	[illegible]	[illegible]	[illegible]	[illegible]	[illegible]	[illegible]	[illegible]
November ...	[illegible]	[illegible]	[illegible]	[illegible]	[illegible]	[illegible]	[illegible]	[illegible]	[illegible]	[illegible]
Total ...	[illegible]	[illegible]	[illegible]	[illegible]	[illegible]	[illegible]	[illegible]	[illegible]	[illegible]	[illegible]

Scottish Milk Marketing Scheme, 1933.

Monthly Quantities of Milk sold to or through the Agency of the Board and Quantities sold by Producers in the Special Categories

Month.	December, 1935, to November, 1936.					December, 1936, to November, 1937.				
	Total Sales	Sold to or through the agency of the Board		Sold by producer-wholesalers, producer-retailers and producers of Certified Milk		Total Sales	Sold to or through the agency of the Board		Sold by producer-wholesalers, producer-retailers and producers of Certified Milk	
	Gallons.	Gallons.	Per cent.	Gallons.	Per cent.	Gallons.	Gallons.	Per cent.	Gallons.	Per cent.
December ...	[illegible]	[illegible]	[illegible]	[illegible]	[illegible]	[illegible]	[illegible]	[illegible]	[illegible]	[illegible]
January ...	[illegible]	[illegible]	[illegible]	[illegible]	[illegible]	[illegible]	[illegible]	[illegible]	[illegible]	[illegible]
February ...	[illegible]	[illegible]	[illegible]	[illegible]	[illegible]	[illegible]	[illegible]	[illegible]	[illegible]	[illegible]
March ...	[illegible]	[illegible]	[illegible]	[illegible]	[illegible]	[illegible]	[illegible]	[illegible]	[illegible]	[illegible]
April ...	[illegible]	[illegible]	[illegible]	[illegible]	[illegible]	[illegible]	[illegible]	[illegible]	[illegible]	[illegible]
May ...	[illegible]	[illegible]	[illegible]	[illegible]	[illegible]	[illegible]	[illegible]	[illegible]	[illegible]	[illegible]
June ...	[illegible]	[illegible]	[illegible]	[illegible]	[illegible]	[illegible]	[illegible]	[illegible]	[illegible]	[illegible]
July ...	[illegible]	[illegible]	[illegible]	[illegible]	[illegible]	[illegible]	[illegible]	[illegible]	[illegible]	[illegible]
August ...	[illegible]	[illegible]	[illegible]	[illegible]	[illegible]	[illegible]	[illegible]	[illegible]	[illegible]	[illegible]
September	[illegible]	[illegible]	[illegible]	[illegible]	[illegible]	[illegible]	[illegible]	[illegible]	[illegible]	[illegible]
October ...	[illegible]	[illegible]	[illegible]	[illegible]	[illegible]	[illegible]	[illegible]	[illegible]	[illegible]	[illegible]
November...	[illegible]	[illegible]	[illegible]	[illegible]	[illegible]	[illegible]	[illegible]	[illegible]	[illegible]	[illegible]
Total ...	[illegible]	[illegible]	[illegible]	[illegible]	[illegible]	[illegible]	[illegible]	[illegible]	[illegible]	[illegible]

Printed image digitised by the University of Southampton Library Digitisation Unit

PIGS AND BACON MARKETING SCHEMES, 1933.

The Pigs and Bacon Marketing Schemes apply to Great Britain.

The Pigs Marketing Board consists of 13 members; 8 are district members elected on a regional basis, 3 are special members elected in general meeting, and 2 members are co-opted by the elected members after consultation with the Market Supply Committee: 4 district members and 1 special member retired in 1937. Of the 4 retiring district members, 2 were returned unopposed, 1 was re-elected, and 1 new district member was elected. The retiring special member was returned unopposed. The remuneration of members of the Board for the period ending 31st March, 1937, voted by the registered producers at the annual general meeting was £6,100 (£1,650 more than in the previous year) to be divided between the members in such proportions as the Board thought fit.

The number of registered pig producers on 31st December, 1937, was 146,615 of whom 15,060 offered to sell pigs under the 1937 contract which was subsequently declared void*. The number of contracts offered was 16,774, covering 1,895,600 pigs.

The Bacon Marketing Board is composed of 16 members; 12 are elected by registered curers in England and Wales voting by classes, 2 are elected by registered curers in Scotland, and 2 co-opted by the elected members, after consultation with the Market Supply Committee. There was no change in the personnel of the Board in 1937. The sum of £5,500 (the same as in the previous year) was voted by the registered curers at the annual general meeting as the remuneration of the members of the Board for the year ending 31st March, 1938, to be apportioned among the members as the Board thought fit.

The number of registered curers on 31st December, 1937, was 661.

Regulation of Sales of Pigs in 1937.

During January, the Pigs and Bacon Marketing Boards and the Bacon Development Board discussed the position created by the breakdown of the contract system. The outcome was a determination by the Pigs Marketing Board, under paragraph 37 of the Scheme, prescribing the terms and the conditions upon which registered producers were to sell pigs to registered curers. The determination, which came into operation on 15th February, 1937, applied to pigs weighing from 7 score to 10 score 10 lb. (inclusive) dead weight, and provided that sales of such pigs should be on the basis of the dead weight and grade of the pig, the price mutually agreed by the producer and curer being a basic pig price, subject to prescribed additions and

* See report for 1936 (Cmd. 5734), page 27.

deductions according to the weight and grade of the pig. The weight and grade specifications and the grade bonuses and deductions prescribed were the same as in the voided contract. The determination authorised the curer to deduct 6d. per pig as representing the producer's share of the cost of insurance against disease or damage in transit. The grading of pigs was undertaken by the curer but, as previously, an agent of the Pigs Marketing Board was empowered to check the grading, and for this service the Board prescribed a charge of 6d. per pig, under paragraph 38 of the Scheme. The main consideration in making the determination was the desire to maintain the practice of sale on a dead weight and grade basis.

Prices of Pigs and Feeding Stuffs.

The price of baconer pigs of first and second quality at representative markets in England and Wales (as published in the "Agricultural Market Report") averaged 12s. 10d. per score in January and thereafter declined gradually to an average of 11s. 6d. per score in June but from then to the end of the year prices rose steadily and averaged 13s. 7d. per score in December. There is no information about the actual prices paid for pigs sold under the determination.

Feeding stuff prices continued to rise during the first five months of 1937; for the remainder of the year, the ascertained monthly cost of a "standard ration" was more or less stable between 10s. 2½d. and 10s. 4½d. per cwt.; over the year as a whole the average cost was 10s. 1½d. per cwt.

Bacon Sales Quotas.

During 1937, sales by registered curers of bacon made from pigs produced in Great Britain were regulated in accordance with the Bacon Marketing Board's determination of 4th November, 1936.*

Bacon put into Cure by Registered Curers.

The quantity of bacon produced by registered curers in Great Britain declined in 1937 compared with 1936.

Year.	Average number of curers making returns.	Bacon from Home Carcases and parts of carcases.	Bacon from Imported Pigs and Carcases and parts of carcases.	Total.
		'000 cwt.	'000 cwt.	'000 cwt.
1934 ...	616	1,485	250	1,736
1935 ...	624	2,029	348	2,377
1936 ...	611	2,323	434	2,757
1937 ...	636	1,944	508	2,452

* See report for 1936 (Cmd. 5734), page 28.

Re-organization of the Industry.

A statement issued from the Ministry of Agriculture and Fisheries immediately after the 1937 contracts were declared void, indicated that the situation created by the breakdown of the contract system would require consideration of the future organization of the industry and that the Pigs and Bacon Marketing Schemes would be examined with the object of devising machinery by which the difficulties which had been experienced in the past and had led to the breakdown, might be avoided.

On the 29th July, 1937, the Minister of Agriculture and Fisheries made the following statement in the House of Commons:—

> " The Government have given careful consideration to the difficulties of the bacon industry which appear to be attributable, in part, to the increase of pig feeding costs and, in part, to the high cost of bacon manufacture in this country. They believe that if the industry were founded on a smaller number of efficient factories provided with adequate and regular supplies of pigs of good quality and conformation, sufficient economies could be secured in the cost of curing to enable the industry to be maintained during periods of high feeding costs.
>
> The Government accordingly would be willing to propose that some assistance should be accorded to the industry over a sufficient period to enable the contract system for the supply of bacon pigs to be re-established if they were assured that the re-organization of the bacon factories would so proceed as to hold promise of a reduction in curing costs which would enable both producers and curers to work at a profit. The Government desire to give further consideration, in consultation with the industry, to the nature of the changes that would be required and the form which they should take, with a view to laying detailed proposals before Parliament as early as possible.
>
> Meanwhile, the present arrangements for the regulation of imports will continue in force."

Discussions between representatives of the Pigs and Bacon Marketing Boards and the Agricultural Departments began early in September and continued during the remainder of the year.

Miscellaneous.

Regulation of Bacon Supplies.—The regulation of imports of bacon was continued by Order of the Board of Trade under the Agricultural Marketing Act, 1933, as regards foreign supplies and by voluntary agreement as regards Dominion supplies. The total supplies of bacon, hams, salted pork and tinned bacon and hams from all sources (excluding the output of unregistered curers in Great Britain) in 1937 compared with 1936 were as follows:—

	1936.		1937.	
	'000 cwt.	Per cent.	'000 cwt.	Per cent.
United Kingdom (a)	3,482	32·2	3,115	28·9
Dominion (b) ...	1,908	17·6	2,240	20·7
Foreign (b) ...	5,430	50·2	5,447	50·4
Total ...	10,820	100·0	10,802	100·0

(a) Includes bacon from imported pigs and carcases cured in this country.
(b) Gross imports; exports and re-exports amounted to 115,000 and 111,000 cwt. in 1936 and 1937, respectively.

The diagram on page 23 shows the net supply position during the four years the Marketing Schemes have been in operation. The proportions of the total supply of bacon produced in Great Britain increased from 16·5 per cent. in 1934 to 25·9 per cent. in 1936 (when the home output was at its peak), and was 23·1 per cent. in 1937; it is estimated that in the years immediately preceding the Schemes, the home producers' share of the market was between 10 and 12 per cent.

Retail Price of Bacon.—The retail price of bacon, as recorded by the Ministry of Labour, was on the average slightly higher in 1937 than in 1936. The index number of retail bacon prices for 1937 was 132 (July 1914 = 100) which was 7 points lower than the index number of retail food prices generally.

Accounts of the Boards.—The accounts of the Boards for the year ended 31st December, 1937, are printed in Appendix III.

ANNUAL TOTAL SUPPLIES OF BACON AND HAMS IN THE UNITED KINGDOM.

(SHOWING THE HOME PRODUCERS' SHARE OF THE HOME MARKET.)

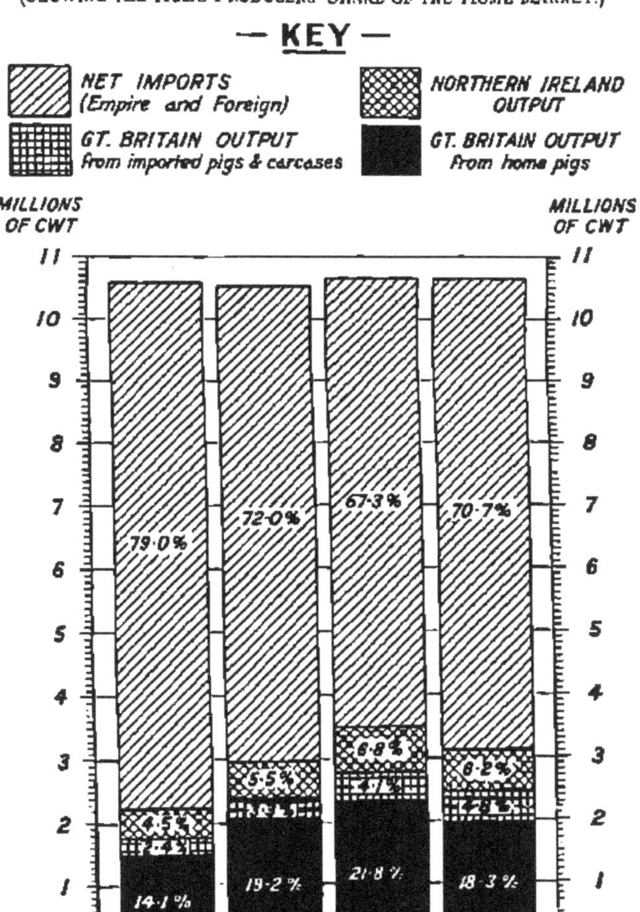

MILK MARKETING SCHEME, 1933.

The Milk Marketing Scheme applies to England and Wales, and is administered by a Board consisting of 17 members; 12 of these are elected on a regional basis, 3 are special members elected by producers in general meeting, and 2 are co-opted by the elected members after consulting the Market Supply Committee. There was no change in the personnel of the Board during 1937.

At the annual general meeting of registered producers, the remuneration voted to the Chairman of the Board was £1,500, to the Vice-Chairman £700, and to the other members £350 each.

At the end of December, 1937, there were 146,423 producers on the register, of whom 10,987 did not sell milk under the Scheme during the year.

Volume of Milk sold under the Scheme.

Total Sales.—The volume of milk sold under the Scheme in the four years of operation has been as follows:—

—	1933–34.* Million gallons.	1934–35. Million gallons.	1935–36.† Million gallons.	1936–37. Million gallons.
Sales under wholesale contracts—				
Liquid...	523·8	552·0	555·6	577·8
Manufacturing	192·6	301·7	342·4	289·2
Retail Sales of Producer-Retailers	110·0	113·2	108·2	103·3
Made into Cheese on farms...	18·8	14·0	17·7	19·6
Total	845·2	980·9	1,023·9	989·9
Sales for liquid consumption	633·8 (75 per cent.)	665·2 (68 per cent.)	663·8 (65 per cent.)	681·1 (69 per cent.)
Sales for manufacture	211·4 (25 per cent.)	315·7 (32 per cent.)	360·1 (35 per cent.)	308·8 (31 per cent.)

* The milk year 1933–34 did not begin until 6th October, 1933.

† The milk year 1935–36 contained an extra day owing to 1936 being a Leap Year.

A detailed statement showing the quantities sold during the year October, 1936, to September, 1937, is given in Table I on page 48.

Sales for Liquid Consumption.—Sales of milk for liquid consumption in 1936-7 totalled 681·1 million gallons, an increase of 2·6 per cent. over corresponding sales for the previous year. About 85 per cent. of the total was sold under wholesale contracts, and 15 per cent. by producer-retailers.

Sales for Manufacture.—The intake of milk manufactured in factories and depots declined in 1936-7 by 53·2 million gallons or 15·5 per cent. compared with the previous year, while the quantity of milk manufactured into cheese on farms increased by 1·9 million gallons or 10·7 per cent.

Particulars of the different milk products manufactured in 1936-7 are shown in Table II on page 49, with comparative figures for 1935-6. The outstanding feature was the decrease in the quantities of milk manufactured into cheese, butter, milk powder, condensed milk for export, and ice-cream, and the substantial increase in the manufacture of all other forms of cream.

Milk Prices.

Wholesale Liquid Milk Buying Prices.—The monthly wholesale prices per gallon of milk for liquid consumption in the contract year 1936-7 were the same as in the previous year, namely:—

1936	October ...	1s. 5d.	1937	April ...	1s. 4d.
	November ...	1s. 5d.		May ...	1s. 0d.*
	December ...	1s. 5d.		June ...	1s. 0d.*
1937	January ...	1s. 5d.		July ...	1s. 1d.
	February ...	1s. 5d.		August ...	1s. 1d.
	March ...	1s. 5d.		September ...	1s. 3d.

* In May, ½d. was added as the purchaser's share of the joint contribution for research and publicity.

The average monthly wholesale price of milk for liquid consumption was 15·25d. per gallon. The average price, weighted according to the volume sold each month, was 15·22d. per gallon.

Retail Prices.—The same minimum retail prices were prescribed for 1936-7 as for 1935-6. In 61 areas, covering 82 towns and villages, the Board reduced the appropriate minimum retail price at the request of a majority of the retailers responsible for the bulk of the sales in each of those areas.

Manufacturing Milk Prices.—The manufacturing milk prices were substantially the same as under the previous contract, except that the price for Stilton cheese was 1d. per gallon more than the formula price for hard cheese: the butter formula was revised so that the minimum price for milk produced in Cornwall was increased from 3⅛d. to 3⅜d., and that for milk produced outside Cornwall from 3d. to 3¼d.; the price of milk used for tinned cream was advanced from 6d. to 6⅜d. per gallon from January to September; the price of milk for milk powder was raised from a fixed price of 4⅜d. to a minimum of 5⅜d. per gallon, with a proviso that the price be increased in each month by the amount by which the average manufacturing price for cheese exceeded 4⅜d. per gallon, the price of milk for condensing being similarly constituted with a minimum of 6d.

The weighted average of the prices paid to the Board by purchasers for all manufacturing milk was 5·75d. per gallon as compared with 4·95d. per gallon in 1935-6, and 4·81d. per gallon in 1934-5. If repayable advances under the Milk Acts on certain classes of manufacturing milk are included, the weighted average return for manufacturing milk was 5·81d. per gallon compared with corresponding average returns of 5·45d. in 1935-6 and 5·64d. in 1934-5. A detailed statement of the returns received for the various categories of manufacturing milk (excluding and including Exchequer advances) in 1936-7, with corresponding figures for 1935-6, is contained in Table II on page 49.

Wholesale Contracts.

Numbers of Wholesale Contracts.—The numbers of contracts held in each region in September, 1936, and in September, 1937, were as follows:—

Region.	Number of Contracts.		Increase (+) or Decrease (—).	
	Sept., 1936.	Sept., 1937.	Number.	Per cent.
Northern	8,600	8,724	+ 124	+ 1·4
North Western ...	21,886	22,118	+ 232	+ 1·1
Eastern	4,366	4,717	+ 351	+ 8·0
East Midland ...	7,059	7,160	+ 101	+ 1·4
West Midland ...	7,987	8,212	+ 225	+ 2·8
North Wales ...	1,994	2,389	+ 395	+ 19·8
South Wales ...	5,970	7,142	+ 1,172	+ 19·6
Southern	5,576	5,594	+ 18	+ 0·3
Mid Western ...	11,889	11,709	— 180	— 1·5
Far Western ...	9,344	9,978	+ 634	+ 6·8
South Eastern ...	6,434	6,283	— 151	— 2·3
Total	91,105	94,026	+ 2,921	+ 3·2

Premium Contracts.—The decline noted in the previous report in the number of wholesale contracts carrying premiums for level delivery or special services continued in 1936-7, the number of premium contracts falling from 14,344 in 1935-6 to 13,412 in 1936-7:—

Region.	1935–36.			1936–37.		
	Level delivery.	Other special services.	Total premium contracts.	Level delivery.	Other special services.	Total premium contracts.
Northern... ...	839	250	1,089	767	197	964
North Western ...	3,285	791	4,076	3,139	717	3,856
Eastern	728	163	891	642	169	811
East Midland ...	1,206	197	1,403	1,087	185	1,272
West Midland ...	743	168	911	691	180	871
North Wales ...	149	73	222	129	136	265
South Wales ...	459	79	538	444	71	515
Southern ...	758	256	1,014	705	316	1,021
Mid Western ...	464	587	1,051	404	391	795
Far Western ...	1,227	138	1,365	1,158	144	1,302
South Eastern ...	1,266	518	1,784	1,176	564	1,740
Total ...	11,124	3,220	14,344	10,342	3,070	13,412

Sales of Milk under Wholesale Contracts.—There was a decline of 3·5 per cent. in the quantity of milk sold under wholesale contracts and receipts were £43·2 million as compared with £42·6 million in the previous year:—

Region.	Increase (+) or Decrease (−).	
	Gallons.	Per cent.
Northern	− 2,921,375	− 4·70
North Western	− 8,919,623	− 3·68
Eastern	+ 868,943	+ 1·99
East Midland	− 2,666,585	− 3·79
West Midland	− 2,771,567	− 3·50
North Wales	− 227,492	− 1·17
South Wales	+ 1,476,906	+ 4·06
Southern	− 2,886,417	− 4·25
Mid Western	− 8,566,868	− 5·82
Far Western	− 24,881	− 0·06
South Eastern	− 4,448,434	− 5·05
Total	−31,088,413	− 3·46

Particulars of regional contract sales are included in Table III on page 50.

Direct and Depot Milk.—About one-third of the wholesale contract milk sold for liquid consumption was consigned under depot contracts, the remaining two-thirds being delivered under direct contracts; these proportions have not varied greatly since the Scheme began. Of the milk used for manufacture, about 55 per cent. was dealt with under depot contracts and 45 per cent. under direct contracts.

Details of the volume of liquid milk and manufacturing milk sold under direct and depot contracts in 1935-6 and 1936-7 are given below:—

Year.	Type of Contract.	Liquid.		Manufacturing.		Total.	
		'000 Gallons.	Per cent.	'000 Gallons.	Per cent.	'000 Gallons.	Per cent.
1935–36	Direct	370,355	66·7	143,054	41·8	513,409	57·2
	Depot	185,219	33·3	199,391	58·2	384,610	42·8
	Total	555,574	100·0	342,445	100·0	898,019	100·0
1936–37	Direct	378,529	65·5	130,047	45·0	508,576	58·7
	Depot	199,223	34·5	159,138	55·0	358,361	41·3
	Total	577,752	100·0	289,185	100·0	866,937	100·0

Pool Prices.

The weighted average pool price paid for all contract milk in 1936-7 was 11·99d. per gallon, compared with 11·48d. in 1935-6. The following Table shows the average pool prices for each region during the two years in question.

Region.	*1935–36.*	*1936–37.*
	(Pence per gallon).	
Northern	11·40	11·94
North Western	11·43	11·99
Eastern	11·85	12·33
East Midland	11·62	12·14
West Midland	11·13	11·64
North Wales	11·09	11·57
South Wales	11·35	11·79
Southern	11·97	12·48
Mid Western	11·17	11·65
Far Western	11·01	11·47
South Eastern	12·25	12·71
All Regions	11·48	11·99

All contract milk, in theory, is sold at the wholesale price, and the following statement, showing, for the contract year as a whole, the weighted average additions to and deductions from this price, illustrates the manner in which the pool price is computed.

				Per gallon.
				d.
Weighted average price of all milk sold at wholesale price				15·04
Additions.	*Per gallon.*	*Deductions.*	*Per gallon.*	
	d.		d.	
Transport deductions on milk manufactured in depots and factories...	0·50	Rebates on manufacturing milk	2·97	
Contributions of Producer-Retailers ...	0·22	Levies for general expenses, liabilities and reserves of the Board...	0·14	
Exchequer payments under Sections 1–3 of the Milk Acts, 1934–37 ...	0·04	May publicity contributions	0·03	
Exchequer payments in respect of the Milk-in-Schools Scheme ...	0·11	Rebates on milk supplied under the Milk-in-Schools Scheme ...	0·25	
		Quality premiums to Accredited producers ...	0·38	
		Payments to farmhouse cheesemakers ...	0·09	
		Reserves for liability to make repayments under the Milk Acts ...	0·02	
		Compensation to the Scottish Milk Marketing Board	0·04	
	0·87		3·92	
Weighted average net deduction				3·05
Weighted average pool price				11·99

The pool price varies from region to region, according to the proportions of milk sold in each region for liquid consumption or for manufacture. As a result, however, of adjustments made through the inter-regional compensation levy on liquid sales, these differences in the regional pool prices are less than they would otherwise be. Since February, 1935, the monthly rate of this levy has been so calculated that there is never in any month a difference of more than 1d. between the highest and lowest pool prices. In 1936–7 the inter-regional compensation levy on liquid sales was at the following rates per gallon:—

2¼d. in October; 2d. in April; 1¾d. in November and March; 1½d. in December, January and February; 1¼d. in May and July; 1d. in June, August and September.

Table IV on page 51 shows the regional pool prices in each month from October, 1936, to December, 1937.

Wholesale Producers' Net Returns.—Transport charges, including "transit risk" and collection charges (where they are incurred), have to be deducted from, and any premium due for Accredited milk, level delivery and other services, have to be added to, the pool prices in order to ascertain the actual return to the producer.

An estimate of the effect of these adjustments on the wholesale producers' returns in 1936-7, region by region, is given in the following table:—

Region.	Average pool price.	Average transport charge.	Average premium for level delivery and special services.	Average premium for Accredited milk.	Average net return.
	(Pence per gallon).				
Northern ...	11·94	1·93	0·08	0·21	10·30
North Western...	11·99	1·53	0·10	0·47	11·03
Eastern ...	12·33	1·70	0·10	0·48	11·21
East Midland ...	12·14	1·36	0·11	0·31	11·20
West Midland ...	11·64	1·83	0·05	0·26	10·12
North Wales ...	11·57	1·92	0·06	0·52	10·23
South Wales ...	11·79	2·34	0·08	0·20	9·73
Southern ...	12·48	1·35	0·13	0·31	11·57
Mid Western ...	11·65	1·91	0·05	0·19	9·98
Far Western ...	11·47	2·23	0·12	0·14	9·50
South Eastern ...	12·71	1·06	0·22	0·30	12·37
All Regions ...	11·90	1·66	0·10	0·34	10·77

Producer-Retailers.

In December, 1937, 64,186 registered producers (of whom about 20,000 also sold milk by wholesale) held retail licences, as against 66,279 in September, 1936. The volume of milk sold under these licences decreased from 108·2 million gallons in 1935-6 to 103·3 million gallons in 1936-7 or by about 5 per cent. The following table shows, for each region, the volume of producer-retailer sales, and the proportion it represented of the liquid sales in the region.

Region.	Producer-retailer sales.	
	'000 Gallons.	As proportion of total liquid sales. (Per cent.)
Northern	8,106	17·6
North Western	34,476	18·0
Eastern	8,081	18·0
East Midland	7,918	13·4
West Midland	5,746	12·5
North Wales	2,242	18·8
South Wales	3,380	12·2
Southern	6,892	10·8
Mid Western	5,675	7·5
Far Western	4,707	25·4
South Eastern	16,089	16·8
All Regions	103,312	15·2

Producer-Retailers' Contributions.—The arrangements for producer-retailers' contributions to the Board's funds which operated in 1935-6* were continued until 30th September, 1937. The weighted average contributions of producer-retailers contributing on a gallonage basis during the year ending 30th September, 1937, compared with those of the previous twelve months are shown below.

	1935–36.	1936–37.
	(Pence per gallon).	
Average gross contribution	3·08	2·59
Average allowance for level delivery premium	0·87	0·85
Average allowance for accredited premium...	0·25	0·31
Average net contribution	1·96	1·43

As a result of an amendment of paragraph 65 of the Scheme which prescribes the formula for calculating the rate of this contribution, the producer-retailers' levy has, since 1st October, 1937, been fixed at the following rates per gallon:—

Category I (Tuberculin Tested milk), ¾d.
Category II (Accredited milk), 1d.
Category III (Other milk), 1¼d.

These rates are subject to a reduction of ¼d. if payment is made (together with all arrears) within fourteen days of the relevant accounting day. The contribution of a producer-retailer who

* See report for 1936 (Cmd. 5734), page 39.

sells any milk by wholesale (except on contracts carrying a level delivery premium) is increased by ¼d. per gallon on all his retail or semi-retail sales.

Tables V and VI on pages 52 and 53 give particulars of producer-retailers' contributions in each region for October, 1936, to September, 1937.

Farmhouse Cheesemakers.

The Farmhouse Cheesemaker's Agreement for 1936-7 was similar to that of the preceding year,* except that the gross payments in 1936-7 were at the rate of 4¼d. per gallon during the months October to April, and 3¼d. per gallon during May to September, for milk manufactured into hard cheese, and ¼d. per gallon less than these rates for milk manufactured into Caerphilly or soft cheese. In other words the rate per gallon was in all cases 1d. less than in 1935-6.

The following table shows the payments (excluding Accredited premiums) made by the Board in 1936-7 to producers of hard cheese and the extent to which these consisted of Exchequer payments received by the Board under the Milk Acts:—

Month.	Amount paid by Board to Farmhouse Cheesemakers.	Amount received by Board from Exchequer in respect of farm cheese milk.	Actual payment from Board's funds.
		Pence per gallon.	
October, 1936 ...	3·89	0·01	3·88
November	3·83	0·07	3·76
December	4·13	0·02	4·11
January, 1937 ...	3·31	0·59	2·72
February	2·91	0·99	1·92
March	3·05	1·10	1·95
April	4·15	Nil	4·15
May...	3·04	Nil	3·04
June	3·16	Nil	3·16
July	2·91	Nil	2·91
August	2·91	Nil	2·91
September	3·15	Nil	3·15

* See report for 1936 (Cmd. 5734), page 39.

The number of farmhouse cheesemakers' agreements and the gallonage of milk manufactured in 1935-6 and in 1936-7 were as follows:—

Region.	1935–36.		1936–37.	
	Agreements.	Gallons.	Agreements.	Gallons.
Northern	154	456,060	160	500,335
North Western ...	400	8,243,872	420	8,760,256
West Midland ...	102	2,508,377	112	2,762,643
North Wales ...	58	1,192,762	62	1,292,683
Mid Western ...	297	5,093,759	360	6,011,314
Other Regions ...	21	218,996	23	286,581
All Regions ...	1,032	17,716,026	1,137	19,623,069

The following are the estimated quantities of milk made into the various types of cheese under the agreements in 1935-6 and 1936-7:—

Types of Cheese.	1935–36.		1936–37.	
	Gallons.	Per cent.	Gallons.	Per cent.
Cheshire	9,066,416	51·18	10,347,023	52·73
Cheddar	5,283,435	29·82	6,034,741	30·75
Lancashire... ...	2,462,328	13·90	2,402,947	12·25
Wensleydale ...	559,289	3·16	440,005	2·24
Stilton	59,934	0·34	107,488	0·55
Leicester	136,689	0·77	120,279	0·61
Caerphilly	103,200	0·58	126,692	0·65
Gloucester	24,534	0·14	26,164	0·13
Other types ...	20,201	0·11	17,770	0·09
All types ...	17,716,026	100·00	19,623,069	100·00

Accredited Herds.

The Accredited Scheme which began in May, 1935, was continued throughout 1936-7 under the same arrangements as in 1935-6.*

There was a further increase of nearly 16 per cent. in the number of herds on the Accredited Roll which stood at 21,111 in September, 1937, compared with 18,251 in September, 1936. In December, 1937, there were 21,537 Accredited herds.

* See previous reports: Cmd. 5284, page 50 and Cmd. 5734, pages 41 and 42.

The numbers of Accredited herds by regions in September, 1936 and 1937, are shown below:—

Region.	Number of Accredited herds.		Increase (Per cent.)
	Sept., 1936.	Sept., 1937.	
Northern	906	1,152	27·2
North Western	6,471	7,282	12·5
Eastern	1,376	1,446	5·1
East Midland	1,394	1,649	18·3
West Midland	1,306	1,458	11·6
North Wales	772	864	11·9
South Wales	780	1,118	43·3
Southern	1,155	1,261	9·2
Mid Western	1,165	1,459	25·2
Far Western	605	865	43·0
South Eastern	2,321	2,557	10·2
All Regions	18,251	21,111	15·7

The increase in the volume of milk sold by Accredited producers in 1936-7 was 57 million gallons, or just over 20 per cent. more than in 1935-6. There was also an increase in the proportion of sales of Accredited milk to total sales by all registered producers, Accredited milk accounting for 34·01 per cent. in 1936-7 as against 27·34 per cent. in 1935-6.

The monthly quantities of milk in respect of which Accredited premiums have been paid from May, 1935, to December, 1937, are shown below:—

Month.	Volume of Accredited milk. ('000 Gallons.)		
	1935.	1936.	1937.
January	—	20,620	24,998
February	—	20,568	23,765
March	—	23,060	27,694
April	—	24,534	28,885
May	6,090	28,557	34,304
June	10,629	27,980	33,493
July	13,259	27,928	31,916
August	13,621	27,153	29,949
September	13,991	25,619	27,401
October	16,538	25,821	27,655
November	17,596	23,978	26,016
December	19,271	24,406	26,873
Total	110,995	300,824	342,949

Trading and Manufacturing Operations of the Board.

The Board operated 18 creameries and separating stations in 1937. Of these, one new creamery was opened at Camborne (Cornwall) in May, 1937, others being acquired at Land's End in May, 1937, and at Sturminster (Dorset), Gillingham (Dorset), Preston (Lancashire), and Pont Llanio (Cardiganshire) and Crudgington (Shropshire) in October, 1937. The Norwich Creamery has been rebuilt on a new and more extensive site on the outskirts of the town, the new premises also opening in October, 1937. The factory at Frodsham (Cheshire) was closed in October, 1937, though it is still available for emergency use. During the contract year 1936-7, the total intake of milk at the Board's creameries (excluding milk sub-sold for manufacture) was 14,564,805 gallons.

Publicity and Research.

As in previous years, wholesale producers and purchasers each contributed ½d. per gallon on sales during May, the funds thus raised being divided in the ratio 9:1 between publicity and research. The bulk of this expenditure by the Board on publicity is attributable to work undertaken by the National Milk Publicity Council and to the Board's share of the cost of the National Publicity Scheme under the Milk Acts.

The Board continued its efforts to encourage the development of milk bars on lines similar to those of the previous year, while the Board's advisory service included the provision of a demonstration staff for the benefit of those proposing to instal new bars. In December, 1937, there were 1,010 milk bars as compared with 587 in December, 1936. The greatest concentration was in the South Eastern and North Western regions, where there were respectively 321 and 285 milk bars in operation on 31st December, 1937. Of these, London accounted for 196. It is estimated that the quantity of milk used in milk bars was in the neighbourhood of 4 million gallons.

In 1937, 5,782,462 gallons of milk were distributed under the Milk-in-Industry campaign to 1,836,876 persons employed in 6,067 firms.

Research work financed by grants from the Milk Marketing Board was continued during the year into a variety of problems affecting the production and manufacture of milk. The total sum allocated by the Board in 1937 amounted to £15,382. This sum included further contributions to the Agricultural Research Council for research on contagious abortion (£2,000); to the Department of Bacteriology and Preventive Medicine in the University of Manchester for research on a rapid method of detecting tubercle bacilli in milk (£600); and to the National Institute of Research in Dairying, Reading, for work on the composition of milk, the feeding of dairy cows and the ripening of cheese (£2,232).

The Board again assisted, with a grant of £5,000, the investigation into the costs of milk production which has been undertaken since November, 1934, by advisory economists, in collaboration with the Agricultural Economics Research Institute at Oxford and 11 Agricultural Advisory Departments of the universities and colleges in England and Wales. Interim reports for the periods November, 1934, to September, 1935; October, 1935, to September, 1936; and October, 1936, to September, 1937, have been published.*

New grants were also approved as follows:—to the Agricultural Economics Research Institute, Oxford, for a survey of the domestic consumption of liquid milk (£5,000); to the Hannah Dairy Research Institute, Auchincruive, for research into problems connected with the condensing and drying of milk and the canning of cream (£300); and to the London School of Hygiene and Tropical Medicine for research on oxidation-reduction systems in cow's milk (£250).

The Milk Acts, 1934-7.

As indicated in previous reports, the Milk Marketing Board administers funds made available for the assistance of the milk industry in England and Wales under the Milk Acts, 1934-6, some of the provisions of which were extended for a further year by the Milk (Amendment) Act, 1937.

(a) *Exchequer payments on manufacturing milk.*—Prior to 1st August, 1937, the rate of payment in respect of milk used for manufacture was the difference between either the "cheese-milk price" or the net cost per gallon of the milk to the purchaser (whichever was the greater) and "standard prices" of 6d. per gallon in winter (October to March) and 5d. per gallon in summer (April to September).

As from 1st August, 1937, the Milk (Amendment) Act, 1937, altered the definition of "cheese-milk price" and provided that the calculation of the Exchequer payments on milk manufactured into butter should be determined in relation to a "butter-milk price" instead of the "cheese-milk price" as hitherto. Under this Act, "butter-milk price" and "cheese-milk price" mean sums certified by the Ministers to represent the price at which the greatest quantity of milk appears to them to have been sold during any month, for manufacture into butter and cheese respectively. In determining such sums, Ministers are required to take into account, but are not limited to the consideration of, the terms of any contracts relating to the sale of milk in that month for those purposes.

During each of the six months October, 1936, to March, 1937, the Board received Exchequer payments on milk manufactured into butter, cheese and condensed milk for export. From April

---

* **Milk Investigation Scheme.**

Cost of milk production in England and Wales.

Interim Reports issued by the Agricultural Economics Research Institute, Oxford, No. 1, price 2s. 6d. net and Nos. 2 and 3, each 1s. 6d. net.

to September, 1937, the cheese-milk price exceeded the standard price in every month, but under the new arrangements payments were made on milk manufactured into butter during August and September. The standard prices and the certified cheese-milk and butter-milk prices for each month from April, 1934, to the end of 1937 were as follows:—

Month.	Standard price.	Cheese-milk price.				Butter-milk price.
		1934.	1935.	1936.	1937.	1937.
		Pence per Gallon.				
January ...	6	*	3·93	4·46	5·41	†
February ...	6	*	4·23	4·57	5·01	†
March	6	*	4·19	4·50	4·90	†
April	5	3·42	4·18	4·33	5·36	†
May	5	3·40	4·26	4·43	5·92	†
June	5	3·48	4·04	4·71	6·26	†
July	5	3·75	4·00	4·97	6·46	†
August	5	3·83	3·79	5·10	6·06	4·31
September ...	5	3·86	3·93	5·89	5·77	4·83
October ...	6	3·72	4·30	5·99	6·40	5·55
November ...	6	4·04	4·83	5·93	6·59	6·23
December ...	6	4·25	4·36	5·95	6·76	6·17

* April, 1934, was the first month for which the cheese-milk price was certified.
† August, 1937, was the first month for which the butter-milk price was certified.

The following table shows for each product the quantity of milk manufactured on which payments were made and the amounts paid, during the contract years 1936-7 and 1935-6.

Products manufactured.	1935–36.		1936–37.	
	Quantity of Milk.	Amount of Exchequer payments.	Quantity of Milk.	Amount of Exchequer payments.
	Million gallons.	£	Million gallons.	£
At the Board's factories :—				
Butter	1·0	3,992	2·7	5,192
Cheese	3·8	15,245	0·8	878
At factories other than the Board's factories :—				
Butter	98·3	361,548	49·9	89,717
Cheese	69·5	251,661	19·4	31,665
Condensed Milk (export)...	10·1	36,425	3·0	5,001
Milk Powder	10·9	35,009	—	—
	188·8	684,843	72·3	126,383
Farm Cheese	12·7	36,775	4·3	5,151
Total	206·3	740,855	80·1	137,604

The Milk Acts require the Board to make payments to the Exchequer on manufacturing milk if in any of the 54 months beginning April, 1936, the cheese-milk price (or, in the case of butter after July, 1937, the butter-milk price) should exceed the standard price by more than 1d.; but the Government in a White Paper on Milk Policy (Cmd. 5533) issued in July, 1937, announced their intention of introducing legislation which would release the Board from any balance of its liability accruing after 30th September, 1937*.

(b) *Attested Herds Scheme.*—Particulars of the Attested Herds Scheme in England and Wales (which was described in the previous report†), since its initiation on 1st February, 1935, to the end of 1937 are given below:—

Year.	Number of Attested Herds at 31st December.	Attested bonuses for Calendar Years.	
		Total amount.	Milk equivalent.
		£	'000 Gallons.
1935 ...	55	770	185
1936 ...	192	3,200	768
1937 ...	813	14,875	3,570

(c) *Arrangements for increasing the demand for milk.*—The Milk (Amendment) Act, 1937, extended until the end of September, 1938, the period of Government assistance towards approved schemes for increasing the demand for liquid milk, and increased the maximum grant available for this purpose in Great Britain for the four-year period ended 30th September, 1938, by a further £500,000 to £2,000,000.

(i) *Milk-in-Schools Scheme.*—This Scheme, which began in October, 1934, and was revised in August, 1936‡, was continued under the revised arrangements in 1937. During the contract year 1936-7, Exchequer contributions amounting to £410,998 were paid to the Board under the Milk-in-Schools Scheme, or £13,621 more than the amount paid in the previous contract year.

There were 2,651,849 children receiving milk on 1st October, 1937, or about 223,000 more than on the same date in 1936. The total quantity of milk consumed in schools in 1936-7 was approximately 23·1 million gallons or 1·2 million gallons more

* Carried into effect by the Milk (Extension and Amendment) Act, 1938.

† Cmd. 5734, page 45.

‡ See report for 1936, Cmd. 5734, page 46.

than in 1935-6. The monthly quantities of milk consumed in the first three years of the Milk-in-Schools Scheme were as follows:—

Month.	1934–35.		1935–36.		1936–37.	
	Quantity consumed.	Estimated average number of school days.	Quantity consumed.	Estimated average number of school days.	Quantity consumed.	Estimated average number of school days.
	'000 Gallons.		'000 Gallons.		'000 Gallons	
October ...	1,972	23	2,273	21	2,237	22
November	2,449	21	1,952	18	2,200	21
December	1,772	15	1,563	15	1,798	17
January...	2,175	18	1,902	19	1,641	16
February	2,348	20	2,053	20	2,159	20
March ...	2,389	21	2,305	22	2,047	18
April ...	1,649	15	1,548	14	2,231	20
May ...	2,247	21	2,143	20	1,598	15
June ...	1,586	17	1,801	19	2,398	22
July ...	1,833	20	1,780	18	1,865	18
August ...	450	Holidays	474	Holidays	594	Holidays
September	1,984	21	2,126	22	2,346	22
Total	22,854	212	21,920	208	23,104	211

(ii) *Nutrition Survey.*—The inquiry referred to in the last two reports*, inaugurated by the Milk Marketing Board and the Scottish Milk Marketing Board, into the nutritional value of milk, was completed in 1937.

A report on the part of the inquiry dealing with laboratory experiments with rats was published in April, 1937. Interim reports on the other two parts of the inquiry, namely investigations on school children and on calves, were published in April and August, 1938, respectively.†

(iii) *Publicity and Propaganda.*—Proposals put forward by the Board for a third publicity campaign under the Milk Acts similar to the campaigns referred to in the last two reports were approved by the Minister on 24th December, 1936. The total amount budgeted for in these proposals was £60,000, of which £36,500 was allotted for press advertising during the period November, 1936, to September, 1937, and £11,000 for a

* Cmd. 5284, pages 52–53; Cmd. 5734, page 47.

† Milk and Nutrition: New Experiments Reported to the Milk Nutrition Committee.

Part I. The Effect of Commercial Pasteurisation on the Nutritive Value of Milk, as determined by Laboratory Experiment (2s. 6d. net, by post 3s.).

Part II. The Effects of Dietary Supplements of Pasteurised and Raw Milk on the Growth and Health of School Children (Interim Report) (1s. 9d. post free).

Part III. The Effect of Commercial Pasteurisation on the Nutritive Value of Milk as determined by Experiments on Calves (2s. post free).

These Reports are published by, and can be purchased direct from, the National Institute for Research in Dairying, Shinfield, Reading.

poster campaign in the nine months January to September, 1937, the remaining £12,500 being reserved for other forms of publicity to be undertaken as opportunity offered. Exchequer assistance to the third campaign amounted to approximately £29,527 compared with £29,857 in respect of the previous campaign.

(iv) *Other Cheap Milk Schemes.*—The Rhondda cheap milk scheme for nursing and expectant mothers, and children under five years of age, was continued during 1937 under the same arrangements as were described in the last report.* In addition, three similar schemes were introduced during the year, one at Jarrow which began on 1st January, another at Walker-on-Tyne, Newcastle, on 1st April, and the third at Whitehaven, Cumberland, on 1st October. The arrangements in each case were the same as in the Rhondda Scheme except that in addition to the milk supplied at the flat price of 2d. a pint under the other schemes, at Whitehaven milk was supplied to certain necessitous persons at a special price of 1½d. with the aid of a grant from the Whitehaven Council of Social Service and the Cumberland Friends' Unemployment Committee.

The total number of persons actually receiving milk during the month of December, 1937, under the four schemes was 9,578, of whom 1,123 were expectant mothers, 856 were nursing mothers, and 7,599 were children under five years of age.

The quantities of milk supplied each month under each of the schemes since their inception to the end of 1937, are shown in the following table:—

Month.	Cheap Milk Scheme.				
	Rhondda.		Jarrow.	Walker-on-Tyne.	Whitehaven.
	1936.	1937.	1937.	1937.	1937.
	Gallons.	Gallons.	Gallons.	Gallons.	Gallons.
January	—	14,270	391	—	—
February ...	—	14,158	2,687	—	—
March	—	16,945	4,131	—	—
April	—	17,437	4,074	1,051	—
May	—	18,534	4,105	4,080	—
June	—	18,464	4,000	4,070	—
July	344	18,773	4,089	4,850	—
August	4,492	18,385	3,926	4,698	—
September ...	6,881	18,148	4,014	4,639	—
October... ...	9,957	19,481	4,252	5,241	2,745
November ...	11,717	19,463	4,075	5,617	4,182
December ...	13,424	20,515	4,232	6,163	4,553
Total ...	46,815	214,573	43,986	41,309	11,480

* Cmd. 5734, page 47.

Amendments of the Scheme.

The public inquiry into the draft amendments of the Scheme submitted by the Board on 15th July, 1936, opened on 26th October, 1936.

As mentioned in the last report,* the Board had requested the Minister to permit it to rescind the resolution whereby sales of Tuberculin Tested milk were exempted from the marketing provisions of the Scheme. As this request was linked with the draft amendments, which contained provisions applicable to the sale of Tuberculin Tested milk, to some of which the Tuberculin Tested Milk Producers' Association had objected, it was arranged, by agreement with the parties concerned, that the public inquiry into the objections lodged against the draft amendments should be extended to cover the whole question of the exemption of Tuberculin Tested milk. The inquiry lasted twenty-nine days and was concluded on 11th January, 1937, nine days being taken up with the hearing of the special case of Tuberculin Tested milk.

After consideration of the objections and of the report of Mr. N. L. Macaskie, K.C., who held the public inquiry, the Minister modified a number of the amendments and consented to the withdrawal of the exemption of sales of Tuberculin Tested milk from Part VI of the Scheme. The main conditions attaching to the Minister's consent were (i) that producers of Tuberculin Tested milk selling by wholesale should receive a quality premium which was fixed for a period of two years at 1d. per gallon (in addition to any other premiums to which the producers were entitled) and thereafter the Tuberculin Tested premium would not be varied save on the certificate of an impartial consultant; (ii) that the rate of contributions payable in respect of Tuberculin Tested milk sold by retail should be ¾d. per gallon (with a rebate of ¼d. for prompt payment) for two years, with a similar safeguard against variation thereafter; (iii) that these same retail contributions and conditions should be applicable in respect of Tuberculin Tested milk sold by semi-retail (that is to say, in consignments not exceeding in the whole 10 gallons in a day to any one purchaser), and in respect of all sales of Tuberculin Tested milk bottled by the producer on his farm; and (iv) that the amount by which the prices prescribed for the sale by wholesale of Tuberculin Tested milk exceed the price for ordinary milk should be credited to the producer.

A draft of the amendments as modified by the Minister was laid before Parliament, and affirmative resolutions were passed by both Houses in July, 1937. On 3rd August, 1937, the Minister made an Order† under Section 1 of the Agricultural Marketing Act, 1931, approving these amendments together with certain others to which no objections had been received.

---

* Cmd. 5734, page 54.

† Milk Marketing Scheme (Amendment) (No. 2) Order, 1937 (S.R. & O. 1937, No. 744). A print of the Milk Marketing Scheme as amended to 3rd August, 1937, is obtainable from H.M. Stationery Office, price 1s. net.

In addition to the simplification of election procedure and the withdrawal, as from 1st October, 1937, of the exemption of sales of Tuberculin Tested milk from the operation of the Scheme, the amendments also provided for the withdrawal of the exemption from registration under the Scheme of wholesale producers possessing four cows or less; for the alteration of the system of assessing freight charges on "depot" milk, and manufacturing milk on "direct" contract; for the stabilisation of producers-retailers' contributions, as explained earlier*; and for certain other matters of a minor administrative nature.

Arrangements for the Sixth Contract Period October, 1937, to September, 1938.

In consequence of the inclusion of the sales of Tuberculin Tested milk within the scope of the Scheme the Board prescribed two classes of contracts for the sale of milk for the 12 months commencing on 1st October, 1937, one for milk not sold as Tuberculin Tested, and the other for milk sold as Tuberculin Tested.

1937-8 Contract Terms for the sale of Milk other than Tuberculin Tested.

The terms of this contract differed from those of the 1936-7 contract chiefly in the higher prices prescribed for liquid and manufacturing milk and in the arrangements for empowering the Board, during the currency of the contract, to divert supplies from the manufacturing market to the liquid market or from lower category manufacture to higher category manufacture.

Wholesale Liquid Milk Buying Prices.—The scale of wholesale prices was fixed at monthly rates averaging 15s. 11d. per dozen gallons, 8d. per dozen gallons more than the previous year's rate. The price for May, 1938, included the usual additional ⅛d. per gallon as the purchaser's share of the annual joint contribution of ¼d. per gallon towards expenditure on publicity and research.

Manufacturing Milk Prices.—The prices of milk for manufacture into soft curd and cream cheese, fresh cream, bottled cream, ice-cream, tinned cream and "other products" were all raised by 1d. per gallon, and for manufacture into sterilized milk for export by 1½d. per gallon, compared with the 1936-7 prices.

The prices of milk for manufacture into milk powder or condensed milk were determined, not, as in 1936-7, on a formula, but at 7d. and 7½d. per gallon respectively.

The price of milk for manufacture into Stilton cheese was again 1d. per gallon higher than the price of milk for hard cheese. A new feature in 1937-8 was that milk manufactured

* See page 31 of this report.

into blue vein cheese was the same as the price of milk for Stilton cheese.

Milk for manufacture into hard cheese or butter or condensed milk for export was priced according to the following formulae:—

Milk manufactured into.	1936–37. Price per gallon.	1937–38. Price per gallon.
Hard cheese made from milk delivered during the months, October to February inclusive, and in September.	The weighted average, less 1½d., of the following two prices, namely, (1) the average price per lb. for the previous month of Finest White New Zealand Cheese, and (2) the average of (a) the average price per lb. for the previous month of Finest White Canadian Cheese (excluding old and exceptional quotations), and (b) the average price per lb. for the previous month of Finest White Canadian Cheese New Season's Make.	The weighted average, less 1½d., of the following two prices, namely, (1) the average price per lb. for the previous month of Finest White New Zealand Cheese, and (2) the average of (a) the average price per lb. for the previous month of Finest White Canadian Cheese (excluding old and exceptional quotations), and (b) the average price per lb. for the previous month of Finest White Canadian Cheese New Season's Make, and to the resultant price there shall be added ½d.
Hard cheese made from milk delivered during the months, March to August, inclusive.	The average price per lb. for the previous month of Finest White New Zealand Cheese, less 1½d.	The average price per lb. for the previous month of Finest White New Zealand Cheese, less 1½d.
Butter made from milk:— (a) Produced elsewhere than in Cornwall.	The weighted average, less 16s., of the average prices per cwt. in the previous month, of New Zealand Finest, Australian Choicest and Danish butter (excluding exceptional quotations and quotations for unsalted butter), divided by 265 in the months October to February, inclusive, and in September, and by 285 in the months March to August inclusive, the resultant price to be increased by ⅟₁₀d., and the price thus determined to be subject to a minimum of 3½d. per gallon.	The weighted average, less 16s., of the average prices per cwt. in the previous month, of New Zealand Finest and Danish butter (excluding exceptional quotations and quotations for unsalted butter), divided by 265 in the months October to February, inclusive, and in September, and by 285 in the months March to August inclusive, the resultant price to be increased by ⅟₁₀d. (including an allowance of ½d. for the value of separated milk).

Milk manufactured into.	1936–37. price per gallon.	1937–38. price per gallon.
(*b*) Produced in Cornwall.	As above, except that the divisors were 225 and 245 respectively and the minimum price 3⅜d. per gallon.	As above except that the divisors were 225 and 245 respectively and the addition to the resultant price $\frac{1}{16}$d.
Condensed Milk for Export.	As for Hard Cheese above, subject to a minimum price of 4d. per gallon.	As for Hard Cheese above, subject to a minimum price of 5d. per gallon.

An extra 1d. per gallon was again payable in respect of milk brought into and manufactured in the City of London and the Metropolitan Police District. Similarly, an additional charge of ⅛d. or such smaller amount as would bring the price to be paid up to 8⅛d. per gallon (as compared with 7⅛d. in 1936-7) was payable in respect of milk brought into and manufactured in other towns with a population of 60,000 or more.

Retail Prices.—The minimum retail prices prescribed by the Board under the 1937-8 contract were higher for all areas than under the previous contract. The following figures, which represent the minimum retail price per dozen gallons over the year, show the comparative position under the two contracts:—

Local Government Areas having populations:		Minimum retail price per dozen gallons. 1936–37.	1937–38.
		s. d.	s. d.
Less than 10,000* ...	All regions	23 4	24 4
10,000 to 25,000 ...	All regions	25 0	26 0
Over 25,000	All except S.E. region	26 0	27 0
	S.E. region	26 8	27 8

* Also applicable to all Rural Districts.

Diversion of Supplies.—On 1st October, 1937, the new principle of diverting supplies was introduced. This was provided for by a clause in the contract empowering the Board to divert to the liquid milk market milk which would otherwise be used for manufacture, and to divert to higher category manufacture milk which would otherwise be used for lower category manufacture. "Lower category manufacture" was defined as the manufacture of milk into condensed milk which is exported, butter or cheese (other than soft curd, cream,

Stilton or blue vein cheese); and "higher category manufacture" as the manufacture of milk products other than lower category manufacture.

It was further provided that, where milk was diverted to the liquid market, the sub-purchaser should pay to the purchaser, in addition to the wholesale liquid price, a premium on a scale ranging from ½d. to 1½d. per gallon according to the size of the consignment; and that where milk was diverted to higher category manufacture the sub-purchaser should pay, in addition to the manufacturing price, a premium of ¾d. per gallon during the months October to March inclusive, and a premium of ½d. per gallon during the months April to September inclusive.

1937-8 Contract Terms for the Sale of Tuberculin Tested Milk.

At the Minister's request the Board appointed an advisory committee consisting of two representatives nominated by the Board, two representatives nominated by the Tuberculin Tested Milk Producers' Association, with an independent chairman, to advise the Board as to the minimum prices which should be fixed for Tuberculin Tested milk sold by wholesale and by retail. The recommendations of this advisory committee were incorporated in the terms of the contract for the sale of Tuberculin Tested milk during the year beginning 1st October, 1937.

Wholesale Buying Prices of Tuberculin Tested Milk.—These prices were fixed at 2d. per gallon higher in each month than the corresponding prices for liquid milk other than Tuberculin Tested, and accordingly the monthly rates for Tuberculin Tested milk averaged 17s. 11d. per dozen gallons. Provision similar to that made in the contract for ordinary milk, was made for the purchaser's May publicity contribution of ⅛d. per gallon.

Retail Prices of Tuberculin Tested Milk.—The minimum retail prices prescribed by the Board for Tuberculin Tested milk in the 1937-8 contract were fixed at rates from 2d. to 4d. per gallon higher than ordinary retail prices according to the season of the year and the locality in which the milk was sold. The following are the minimum retail prices per dozen gallons for the contract year 1937-8:—

Local Government Areas having populations:		Minimum retail price per dozen gallons. 1937–38.
		s. d.
Less than 10,000* ...	All regions	27 0
10,000 to 25,000 ...	All regions	29 0
Over 25,000	All except S.E. region ...	31 0
	S.E. region	31 8

* Also applicable to all Rural Districts.

The Producer-Retailer's Licence for 1937-8.

The chief differences in the terms of this licence were in the additional clauses governing the sale of Tuberculin Tested milk and in the conditions requiring all producer-retailers to keep books and records for inspection by the Board. The minimum retail prices set out in the producer-retailers' licence were the same as those laid down in the Board's contracts for the sale of Tuberculin Tested milk and of other milk.

The Farmhouse Cheesemaker's Agreement for 1937-8.

The terms of this agreement were the same as in the 1936-7 agreement. In addition to the sums payable by the Board in respect of milk manufactured into cheese on farms, producers who qualified received the Accredited bonus (but not the Tuberculin Tested bonus). On the other hand all producers were liable for the general expenses levy, the quality premium levy, and the May contribution for publicity and research.

Miscellaneous.

Consumers' Committee for England.—On 22nd December, 1937, the Consumers' Committee for England reported* to the Minister of Agriculture and Fisheries on the terms of the Milk Marketing Board's contract for the twelve months beginning 1st October, 1937.

The Committee recalled that prices for the 1935-6 contract year were fixed following a recommendation by the Committee of Investigation†, and that these prices were prescribed for 1936-7 also. As regards the wholesale prices fixed for 1937-8, the Consumers' Committee came to the conclusion that, in the absence of any estimate of costs of production as a whole or of the pool prices which might be expected, they were unable to express an opinion on the question whether, if the prices fixed in the two preceding years were accepted as a standard, the increase of $\frac{5}{8}$d. per gallon in the average wholesale price of liquid milk, provided by the 1937-8 contract could be regarded as reasonable.

Dealing with the increase of $\frac{1}{2}$d. per gallon in distributors' nominal minimum margins, the Committee remarked that for those distributors who perform full services and who had given effect, from 1st October, 1937, to the increases in wages proposed by the Milk Distributive Trade Board, the minimum distributive margins under the 1937-8 contract did not appear to be excessive under the conditions then existing. The Committee called

---

* Copies of the report may be obtained free of charge from the Secretary, Consumers' Committee for England, 10, Whitehall Place, London, S.W.1.

† See report for 1935 (Cmd. 5284), page 45.

attention to the observations made in the Food Council's report dated 24th September, 1937, on the costs and profits of retail milk distribution in Great Britain* as to the possibilities of effecting economies in distribution to the benefit of consumers.

Cream Prices.—The wholesale prices for fresh cream are governed by a schedule drawn up by agreement between the milk marketing boards concerned and representatives of the English, Scottish and Irish manufacturers, the latter including Eire and Northern Ireland.

The schedule of prices operating in 1936 was revised. As from 1st October, 1937, prices were increased by amounts varying between 1s. 6d. and 2s. 0d. per gallon, according to the size of the consignment.

Contraventions of the Scheme.—During the year 1937, penalties, totalling £11,382, were imposed upon 429 registered producers for contraventions of the Scheme. Of these producers, 82 were penalised for selling milk by wholesale otherwise than under a contract registered with the Board; 59 for selling milk by retail without holding a producer-retailer's licence; 155 for failing to make returns; 104 for rendering false returns; and 29 for retailing milk at less than the minimum retail price prescribed by the Board.

Accounts of the Board.—A copy of the Board's accounts and balance sheet made up to 31st March, 1937, is printed in Appendix III.

* Published by H.M. Stationery Office, price 9d. net.

Milk Marketing Scheme, 1933.

TABLE I.

QUANTITIES OF MILK SOLD UNDER THE MILK MARKETING SCHEME FROM OCTOBER, 1936, TO DECEMBER, 1937.

Month.	Liquid Consumption.			Manufacture.			Total Milk.	Per cent. Liquid.	Per cent. Manufactured.
	Under Wholesale Contracts.	By Producer-Retailers.	Total.	Under Wholesale Contracts.	Farm Cheese Milk.	Total.			
	Gallons.	Gallons.	Gallons.	Gallons.	Gallons.	Gallons.	Gallons.		
1936—									
October … …	[illegible]	[illegible]	[illegible]	[illegible]	[illegible]	[illegible]	[illegible]	[illegible]	[illegible]
November …	[illegible]	[illegible]	[illegible]	[illegible]	[illegible]	[illegible]	[illegible]	[illegible]	[illegible]
December …	[illegible]	[illegible]	[illegible]	[illegible]	[illegible]	[illegible]	[illegible]	[illegible]	[illegible]
1937—									
January …	[illegible]	[illegible]	[illegible]	[illegible]	[illegible]	[illegible]	[illegible]	[illegible]	[illegible]
February …	[illegible]	[illegible]	[illegible]	[illegible]	[illegible]	[illegible]	[illegible]	[illegible]	[illegible]
March …	[illegible]	[illegible]	[illegible]	[illegible]	[illegible]	[illegible]	[illegible]	[illegible]	[illegible]
April …	[illegible]	[illegible]	[illegible]	[illegible]	[illegible]	[illegible]	[illegible]	[illegible]	[illegible]
May …	[illegible]	[illegible]	[illegible]	[illegible]	[illegible]	[illegible]	[illegible]	[illegible]	[illegible]
June …	[illegible]	[illegible]	[illegible]	[illegible]	[illegible]	[illegible]	[illegible]	[illegible]	[illegible]
July …	[illegible]	[illegible]	[illegible]	[illegible]	[illegible]	[illegible]	[illegible]	[illegible]	[illegible]
August …	[illegible]	[illegible]	[illegible]	[illegible]	[illegible]	[illegible]	[illegible]	[illegible]	[illegible]
September …	[illegible]	[illegible]	[illegible]	[illegible]	[illegible]	[illegible]	[illegible]	[illegible]	[illegible]
Total 1936–37	[illegible]	[illegible]	[illegible]	[illegible]	[illegible]	[illegible]	[illegible]	[illegible]	[illegible]
October …	[illegible]	[illegible]	[illegible]	[illegible]	[illegible]	[illegible]	[illegible]	[illegible]	[illegible]
November …	[illegible]	[illegible]	[illegible]	[illegible]	[illegible]	[illegible]	[illegible]	[illegible]	[illegible]
December …	[illegible]	[illegible]	[illegible]	[illegible]	[illegible]	[illegible]	[illegible]	[illegible]	[illegible]

Milk Marketing Scheme, 1933.

TABLE II.

QUANTITIES AND WEIGHTED AVERAGE ANNUAL PRICES OF MILK SOLD FOR MANUFACTURE INTO VARIOUS PRODUCTS IN 1935–36 AND 1936–37.

Products.	1935–36. Gallons.	Per cent.	Price to Purchasers per gallon.	Realisation to Board including [illegible] per gallon.	1936–37. Gallons.	Per cent.	Price to Purchasers per gallon.	Realisation to Board including [illegible] per gallon.
			d.	d.			d.	d.
Butter	[illegible]	[illegible]	[illegible]	[illegible]	[illegible]	[illegible]	[illegible]	[illegible]
Cheese	[illegible]	[illegible]	[illegible]	[illegible]	[illegible]	[illegible]	[illegible]	[illegible]
Stilton Cheese ...	—	—	—	—	[illegible]	[illegible]	[illegible]	[illegible]
Soft Cheese ...	[illegible]	[illegible]	[illegible]	[illegible]	[illegible]	[illegible]	[illegible]	[illegible]
Condensed Milk ...	[illegible]	[illegible]	[illegible]	[illegible]	[illegible]	[illegible]	[illegible]	[illegible]
Condensed Milk for Export ...	[illegible]	[illegible]	[illegible]	[illegible]	[illegible]	[illegible]	[illegible]	[illegible]
Milk Powder ...	[illegible]	[illegible]	[illegible]	[illegible]	[illegible]	[illegible]	[illegible]	[illegible]
Fresh Cream ...	[illegible]	[illegible]	[illegible]	[illegible]	[illegible]	[illegible]	[illegible]	[illegible]
Ice Cream ...	[illegible]	[illegible]	[illegible]	[illegible]	[illegible]	[illegible]	[illegible]	[illegible]
Tinned Cream ...	[illegible]	[illegible]	[illegible]	[illegible]	[illegible]	[illegible]	[illegible]	[illegible]
Sterilized Cream ...	[illegible]	[illegible]	[illegible]	[illegible]	[illegible]	[illegible]	[illegible]	[illegible]
Sterilized Milk for Export ...	[illegible]	[illegible]	[illegible]	[illegible]	[illegible]	[illegible]	[illegible]	[illegible]
Other Goods ...	[illegible]	[illegible]	[illegible]	[illegible]	[illegible]	[illegible]	[illegible]	[illegible]

TABLE III.

Regional Sales of Milk on Wholesale Contracts.

Region.	1935–36.				1936–37.			
	Liquid Consumption.	Manufacture.	Total.	Per cent. Manufactured.	Liquid Consumption.	Manufacture.	Total.	Per cent. Manufactured.
	Gallons.	Gallons.	Gallons.		Gallons.	Gallons.	Gallons.	
1. Northern ...	[illegible]	[illegible]	[illegible]	[illegible]	[illegible]	[illegible]	[illegible]	[illegible]
2. North Western	[illegible]	[illegible]	[illegible]	[illegible]	[illegible]	[illegible]	[illegible]	[illegible]
3. Eastern ...	[illegible]	[illegible]	[illegible]	[illegible]	[illegible]	[illegible]	[illegible]	[illegible]
4. East Midland ..	[illegible]	[illegible]	[illegible]	[illegible]	[illegible]	[illegible]	[illegible]	[illegible]
5. West Midland ..	[illegible]	[illegible]	[illegible]	[illegible]	[illegible]	[illegible]	[illegible]	[illegible]
6. North Wales ...	[illegible]	[illegible]	[illegible]	[illegible]	[illegible]	[illegible]	[illegible]	[illegible]
7. South Wales ...	[illegible]	[illegible]	[illegible]	[illegible]	[illegible]	[illegible]	[illegible]	[illegible]
8. Southern	[illegible]	[illegible]	[illegible]	[illegible]	[illegible]	[illegible]	[illegible]	[illegible]
9. Mid Western ...	[illegible]	[illegible]	[illegible]	[illegible]	[illegible]	[illegible]	[illegible]	[illegible]
10. Far Western ...	[illegible]	[illegible]	[illegible]	[illegible]	[illegible]	[illegible]	[illegible]	[illegible]
11. South Eastern...	[illegible]	[illegible]	[illegible]	[illegible]	[illegible]	[illegible]	[illegible]	[illegible]
Total ...	[illegible]	[illegible]	[illegible]	[illegible]	[illegible]	[illegible]	[illegible]	[illegible]

Printed image digitised by the University of Southampton Library Digitisation Unit

Regional Pool Prices in Each Region, October, 1936—December, 1937.

(Pence per gallon.)

Region.	1936.			1937.									Weighted average, 1936–37.	1937.		
	Oct.	Nov.	Dec.	Jan.	Feb.	Mar.	Apr.	May.	June.	July.	Aug.	Sept.		Oct.	Nov.	Dec.
Northern ...	[illegible]	[illegible]	[illegible]	[illegible]	[illegible]	[illegible]	[illegible]	[illegible]	[illegible]	[illegible]	[illegible]	[illegible]	[illegible]	[illegible]	[illegible]	[illegible]
North Western	[illegible]	[illegible]	[illegible]	[illegible]	[illegible]	[illegible]	[illegible]	[illegible]	[illegible]	[illegible]	[illegible]	[illegible]	[illegible]	[illegible]	[illegible]	[illegible]
Eastern ...	[illegible]	[illegible]	[illegible]	[illegible]	[illegible]	[illegible]	[illegible]	[illegible]	[illegible]	[illegible]	[illegible]	[illegible]	[illegible]	[illegible]	[illegible]	[illegible]
East Midland	[illegible]	[illegible]	[illegible]	[illegible]	[illegible]	[illegible]	[illegible]	[illegible]	[illegible]	[illegible]	[illegible]	[illegible]	[illegible]	[illegible]	[illegible]	[illegible]
West Midland	[illegible]	[illegible]	[illegible]	[illegible]	[illegible]	[illegible]	[illegible]	[illegible]	[illegible]	[illegible]	[illegible]	[illegible]	[illegible]	[illegible]	[illegible]	[illegible]
North Wales	[illegible]	[illegible]	[illegible]	[illegible]	[illegible]	[illegible]	[illegible]	[illegible]	[illegible]	[illegible]	[illegible]	[illegible]	[illegible]	[illegible]	[illegible]	[illegible]
South Wales	[illegible]	[illegible]	[illegible]	[illegible]	[illegible]	[illegible]	[illegible]	[illegible]	[illegible]	[illegible]	[illegible]	[illegible]	[illegible]	[illegible]	[illegible]	[illegible]
Southern ...	[illegible]	[illegible]	[illegible]	[illegible]	[illegible]	[illegible]	[illegible]	[illegible]	[illegible]	[illegible]	[illegible]	[illegible]	[illegible]	[illegible]	[illegible]	[illegible]
Mid Western	[illegible]	[illegible]	[illegible]	[illegible]	[illegible]	[illegible]	[illegible]	[illegible]	[illegible]	[illegible]	[illegible]	[illegible]	[illegible]	[illegible]	[illegible]	[illegible]
Far Western	[illegible]	[illegible]	[illegible]	[illegible]	[illegible]	[illegible]	[illegible]	[illegible]	[illegible]	[illegible]	[illegible]	[illegible]	[illegible]	[illegible]	[illegible]	[illegible]
South Eastern	[illegible]	[illegible]	[illegible]	[illegible]	[illegible]	[illegible]	[illegible]	[illegible]	[illegible]	[illegible]	[illegible]	[illegible]	[illegible]	[illegible]	[illegible]	[illegible]
Weighted average price	[illegible]	[illegible]	[illegible]	[illegible]	[illegible]	[illegible]	[illegible]	[illegible]	[illegible]	[illegible]	[illegible]	[illegible]	[illegible]	[illegible]	[illegible]	[illegible]
Weighted average price, 1935–36 ...	[illegible]	[illegible]	[illegible]	[illegible]	[illegible]	[illegible]	[illegible]	[illegible]	[illegible]	[illegible]	[illegible]	[illegible]	[illegible]	[illegible]	[illegible]	[illegible]

Milk Marketing Scheme, 1933.

TABLE V.

Gross Contributions of Producer-Retailers in each Region Monthly from October, 1936, to September, 1937.

(Pence per gallon.)

Region.	1936–37.												
	Oct.	Nov.	Dec.	Jan.	Feb.	Mar.	Apr.	May	June.	July	Aug.	Sept.	Average contribution per gallon (weighted)
Northern	[illegible]	[illegible]	[illegible]	[illegible]	[illegible]	[illegible]	[illegible]	[illegible]	[illegible]	[illegible]	[illegible]	[illegible]	[illegible]
North Western	[illegible]	[illegible]	[illegible]	[illegible]	[illegible]	[illegible]	[illegible]	[illegible]	[illegible]	[illegible]	[illegible]	[illegible]	[illegible]
Eastern	[illegible]	[illegible]	[illegible]	[illegible]	[illegible]	[illegible]	[illegible]	[illegible]	[illegible]	[illegible]	[illegible]	[illegible]	[illegible]
East Midland	[illegible]	[illegible]	[illegible]	[illegible]	[illegible]	[illegible]	[illegible]	[illegible]	[illegible]	[illegible]	[illegible]	[illegible]	[illegible]
West Midland	[illegible]	[illegible]	[illegible]	[illegible]	[illegible]	[illegible]	[illegible]	[illegible]	[illegible]	[illegible]	[illegible]	[illegible]	[illegible]
North Wales	[illegible]	[illegible]	[illegible]	[illegible]	[illegible]	[illegible]	[illegible]	[illegible]	[illegible]	[illegible]	[illegible]	[illegible]	[illegible]
South Wales	[illegible]	[illegible]	[illegible]	[illegible]	[illegible]	[illegible]	[illegible]	[illegible]	[illegible]	[illegible]	[illegible]	[illegible]	[illegible]
Southern	[illegible]	[illegible]	[illegible]	[illegible]	[illegible]	[illegible]	[illegible]	[illegible]	[illegible]	[illegible]	[illegible]	[illegible]	[illegible]
Mid Western	[illegible]	[illegible]	[illegible]	[illegible]	[illegible]	[illegible]	[illegible]	[illegible]	[illegible]	[illegible]	[illegible]	[illegible]	[illegible]
Far Western	[illegible]	[illegible]	[illegible]	[illegible]	[illegible]	[illegible]	[illegible]	[illegible]	[illegible]	[illegible]	[illegible]	[illegible]	[illegible]
South Eastern	[illegible]	[illegible]	[illegible]	[illegible]	[illegible]	[illegible]	[illegible]	[illegible]	[illegible]	[illegible]	[illegible]	[illegible]	[illegible]
Average monthly contribution (weighted)	[illegible]	[illegible]	[illegible]	[illegible]	[illegible]	[illegible]	[illegible]	[illegible]	[illegible]	[illegible]	[illegible]	[illegible]	[illegible]
Average monthly contribution (weighted), 1935–36	[illegible]	[illegible]	[illegible]	[illegible]	[illegible]	[illegible]	[illegible]	[illegible]	[illegible]	[illegible]	[illegible]	[illegible]	[illegible]

Milk Marketing Scheme, 1933.

TABLE VI.

COMPARATIVE AVERAGE PRODUCER-RETAILERS' CONTRIBUTIONS IN EACH REGION IN 1935–36 AND 1936–37.

(Pence per gallon.)

Region.	1935–36.		1936–37.	
	Average gross contribution.	Average net contribution.*	Average gross contribution.	Average net contribution.*
Northern	3·21	2·13	2·70	1·56
North Western ...	3·20	2·11	2·68	1·55
Eastern	2·90	1·63	2·44	1·14
East Midland ...	3·07	1·93	2·59	1·39
West Midland ...	3·34	2·26	2·87	1·79
North Wales ...	3·29	2·11	2·85	1·65
South Wales ...	3·15	2·09	2·69	1·60
Southern	2·84	1·74	2·37	1·27
Mid Western ...	3·34	2·45	2·87	2·00
Far Western ...	3·39	2·31	2·91	1·60
South Eastern ...	2·64	1·36	2·18	0·59
All Regions ...	3·08	1·96	2·39	1·43

* These figures are adjusted to allow for level delivery and Accredited premiums.

POTATO MARKETING SCHEME, 1933.

The Potato Marketing Scheme applies to Great Britain. The Board consists of 24 district members, 5 special members and 2 persons co-opted to the Board after consultation with the Market Supply Committee. During 1937, elections were held in five districts, and 2 new district members were elected. The 2 retiring special members were re-elected at the annual general meeting of registered producers held on 28th October, 1937.

The remuneration of the Board voted at the annual general meeting was as follows:—

	£
Chairman	2,000
Vice-Chairman...	850
Members of the Executive Committee	600 each
Chairman of the Basic Acreage Committee ...	300
Other members of the Basic Acreage Committee ...	250 each
Chairman of the Merchants' Authorisation Committee	300
Other members of the Merchants' Authorisation Committee	250 each
Other members of the Board	100 each

The number of registered producers at the end of 1936 and 1937 respectively, and the acreage of potatoes planted by them, were as follows:—

	No. of Producers.		Acres Planted.	
	1936.	1937.	1936.*	1937.
England and Wales...	50,755	50,473	405,700	407,100
Scotland	13,447	13,327	108,800	111,080
Great Britain... ...	64,202	63,800	514,500	518,180

* Revised figures.

Supplies and Prices.

The Home Crop.—The following table shows the total acreage under potatoes, the estimated average yield per acre and the total production in Great Britain in each year since the Scheme came into operation:—

Crop Year.	Area under Potatoes. Acres.	Yield per Acre. Tons.	Total Production. '000 Tons.
1933–4	671,447	6·8	4,555
1934–5	627,556	7·1	4,464
1935–6	594,392	6·3	3,765
1936–7	589,626	6·5	3,804
1937–8	590,692	6·9	4,048

The acreage figures included in the above table are compiled from the Agricultural Returns and include plantings on all holdings of more than one acre, of which not less than ¼ acre is under potatoes. Producers with less than one acre under potatoes are exempted from registration under the Potato Marketing Scheme, and plantings by such producers are not included in the acreage figures relating to registered producers given in the earlier table.

The area under potatoes in 1937 was little larger than in the previous year, but a higher yield per acre resulted in production being increased by 244,000 tons. The quality of the crop was generally fair, and wastage proved to be about normal.

The Board continued to take a periodical census of the stocks of potatoes held by registered producers and authorised merchants. The estimated stocks on the dates specified were:—

Date.		Quantity of unsold stocks. (tons).	
1936 Crop.			
7/8th November, 1936	Registered producers	1,763,000	(marketable ware over 1½" riddle)
	Authorised merchants	66,000*	(marketable ware)
13/14th February, 1937	Registered producers	829,000	(marketable ware over 1½" riddle)
	Authorised merchants	71,000	(marketable ware)
4th June, 1937	Registered producers	47,000	(marketable ware)
	Authorised merchants	37,000	(marketable ware)
1937 Crop			
6/7th November, 1937	Registered producers	2,021,000	(marketable ware over 1½" riddle)
	Authorised merchants	62,000	(marketable ware)

* Revised figure

Prices in England and Wales.—Growers' prices at Wisbech for the 1936 main crop (September, 1936, to May, 1937), averaged 135s. per ton for King Edwards and white varieties, which was 22s. per ton higher than the average for the previous main crop season.

Growers' prices were moderate at the beginning of the season, rose steeply in October and November and remained fairly steady at the higher levels attained until April, when there was again a steep rise to 163s. 6d. per ton. Prices then fell very slightly in May to an average of 162s. 6d. per ton. During the first few weeks of the 1937-8 season, growers' prices were, on the average, 6s. 6d. per ton lower than in September, 1936, and were only slightly above the level of September, 1935. Prices remained at much the same level to the end of the year. The average price for December was 89s. per ton, being 26s. and 46s. 6d. per ton lower than in December, 1935 and 1936 respectively.

Wholesale prices followed the same general trend as growers' prices, but the margin between the two averaged 5s. per ton less than in the 1935-6 season. Growers' and wholesale prices in England and Wales for the past five seasons to the end of 1937 are given in the tables below:—

Growers Prices per Ton.*

	1933–4.		1934–5.		1935–6.		1936–7.		1937–8.	
	s.	d.	s.	d.	s.	d.	s.	d.	s.	d.
September	53	6	91	0	87	6	95	0	88	6
October	57	6	86	0	88	6	120	0	87	0
November	58	6	81	0	91	0	133	6	88	0
December	59	0	68	6	115	0	135	6	89	0
January	59	0	67	6	133	0	134	0	—	
February	58	6	67	0	123	0	132	0	—	
March	57	6	65	0	123	6	138	6	—	
April	67	0	65	0	128	0	163	6	—	
May	62	0	89	0	128	6	162	6	—	
Average	59	0	75	6	113	0	135	0	—	

* Averages to the nearest 6d. of prices at Wisbech for King Edwards and white varieties.

Wholesale Prices per Ton.*

	1933–4.		1934–5.		1935–6.		1936–7.		1937–8.	
	s.	d.	s.	d.	s.	d.	s.	d.	s.	d.
September	73	6	117	0	108	6	110	6	109	0
October	79	6	109	0	109	6	145	6	110	0
November	82	0	103	6	113	6	148	6	110	6
December	80	0	95	0	132	6	157	6	108	6
January	79	6	92	6	154	0	156	6	—	
February	77	0	89	6	154	0	155	0	—	
March	76	0	85	0	151	6	157	0	—	
April	81	0	86	0	149	6	173	6	—	
May	80	6	101	6	156	0	175	6	—	
Average	79	0	97	6	136	6	153	6	—	

* Averages to the nearest 6d. of prices of 1st and 2nd qualities Majestic and King Edward at wholesale markets in England.

Prices in Scotland.—Growers' prices in Scotland averaged 88s. per ton during 1936-7, a decrease of 6d. on the previous season, and an increase of 34s. per ton on the season 1934-5. During the early part of the season prices were poor, but they rose steadily throughout October and November and reached an average of 93s. 6d. per ton in December. Prices then remained fairly steady until April, when there was a sharp rise to 105s., and this level was maintained until the end of the season. At the beginning of the 1937-8 season prices were 7s. 6d. per ton above those for September, 1936, but this level was not maintained, and prices fell away slightly in subsequent months, in sharp contrast to the trend in the early months of the 1936 season. Wholesale prices, in general, moved in keeping with growers' prices, but the relationship was generally closer than in the previous year.

Growers' and wholesale prices in Scotland for the past five seasons to the end of 1937 are given in the following tables:—

Growers Prices per Ton.*

	1933–4.		1934–5.		1935–6.		1936–7.		1937–8.	
	s.	d.	s.	d.	s.	d.	s.	d.	s.	d.
September	43	0	65	0	75	0	65	6	73	0
October	47	0	58	6	67	6	70	0	70	6
November	44	6	52	6	70	0	80	6	70	6
December	43	0	49	0	89	0	93	6	68	6
January	40	0	45	6	99	6	90	0	—	
February	38	0	44	0	97	6	89	0	—	
March	27	6	44	6	99	0	92	6	—	
April	30	6	52	0	99	0	105	0	—	
May	30	0	74	6	99	6	105	6	—	
Average	38	0	54	0	88	6	88	0	—	

Wholesale Prices per Ton.*

	1933–4.		1934–5.		1935–6.		1936–7.		1937–8.	
	s.	d.	s.	d.	s.	d.	s.	d.	s.	d.
September	54	6	87	6	100	0	82	0	92	0
October	63	6	77	6	88	0	84	6	90	0
November	62	6	72	0	91	0	93	0	86	6
December	60	6	70	0	112	0	100	6	87	0
January	60	0	67	6	122	6	109	6	—	
February	57	6	65	6	120	0	108	6	—	
March	46	6	67	0	122	0	110	0	—	
April	44	0	71	0	122	6	121	6	—	
May	45	0	90	6	121	0	124	6	—	
Average	54	6	74	6	111	0	105	0	—	

* Averages to the nearest 6d. of prices at Aberdeen, Dundee, Edinburgh and Glasgow for Kerr's Pink and other white varieties grown in grey soil.

Retail Prices.—During the 1936-7 season the average retail price, as calculated by the Ministry of Labour for the cost of living index, was ¼d. per 7 lbs. below that of the previous season. Prices rose steadily throughout the season to a peak of 8½d. per 7 lbs. in May, 1937. At the beginning of the 1937-8 season, retail prices were ½d. per 7 lbs. higher than in September, 1936; but by December they were ¾d. per 7 lbs. lower than at the end of 1936.

*Retail Prices per 7 lbs.**

	1934–5.	1935–6.	1936–7.	1937–8.
	d.	d.	d.	d.
September	7¼	7	6¼	6¾
October	6¾	6¾	6¾	6¾
November	6	6¾	6½	6½
December	5¾	6¾	7	6¼
January ...	5¾	7	7½	—
February	5½	7½	7¾	—
March ...	5½	8	7¾	—
April ...	5¾	8	7¾	—
May ...	6¼	8	8½	—
Average ...	6	7¼	7	—

* Ministry of Labour.

Market Regulation.

Riddle Regulations.— From 20th November, 1936, onwards, no riddle regulations were in force in relation to the 1936 crop other than the basic riddle of 1½ inches laid down in the Scheme. At the beginning of the 1937-8 season larger riddles were imposed for certain varieties. These riddles remained in operation, subject to minor changes, until the 2nd December when they were superseded by slightly larger riddles of more general application. Details of the riddle regulations relating to the 1936 and 1937 crops are:—

Dates in force.	Size of riddle.	Varieties to which applicable.	Districts where applicable.
1936 Crop.			
27th August to 1st October, 1936.	1¾"	King Edward and Red King	Great Britain.
	1⅝"	All other varieties (except Kerr's Pink in Scotland).	" "
	2"	Kerr's Pink	Scotland.
1st October to 20th November, 1936.	1⅝"	King Edward, Red King and Golden Wonder.	Great Britain.
	1½"	All other varieties ...	" "
20th November, 1936, onwards.	1½"	All varieties	" "

Dates in force.	Size of riddle.	Varieties to which applicable.	Districts where applicable.
1937 Crop. 5th August to 6th September, 1937.	2"	Kerr's Pink and Red Skin	Scotland.
26th August to 7th October, 1937.	1½"	King Edward and Red King	Great Britain.
	1⅝"	All other varieties (including Kerr's Pink and Red Skin from 6th September).	" "
7th October to 2nd December, 1937.	1½"	King Edward, Red King and Golden Wonder.	"
	1⅝"	All other varieties ...	"
2nd December, 1937, to*	1⅝"	King Edward, Red King, Golden Wonder and Gladstone.	"
	1¾"	All other varieties ...	" "

* These riddles were still in force at the end of the calendar year to which this report relates.

Sale of " Seconds ".—During the 1936-7 season, 27,046 tons of " seconds ", representing 3,562 applications, were marketed at an average farm price of 70s. per ton. " Seconds " were defined as sound, marketable potatoes, capable of passing through a riddle of 1⅝ in. or less but standing on a riddle of 1¼ in. The plan for the sale of such potatoes, under control, was first introduced in September, 1935.

Northern Ireland.—At an earlier period, the Board had made informal arrangements with the Northern Ireland authorities for the regulation of the marketing of potatoes from Northern Ireland in Great Britain; and in February, 1937, these arrangements were given a more formal character in a covenant between the Board and the North of Ireland Potato Marketing Association, the body responsible for directing the marketing of Ulster-grown potatoes in Great Britain.

The covenant included the following provisions:—

(*a*) the Association undertook to limit shipments to Great Britain to a maximum of 200,000 tons in any year in which available supplies of United Kingdom potatoes appeared to exceed the normal consumptive demand;

(*b*) no steps were to be taken by the Association to limit shipments in any year in which there was reason to assume that total United Kingdom supplies were not in excess of requirements and in which imports of potatoes were permitted;

(*c*) sales of Northern Ireland potatoes in Great Britain were, with certain exceptions, to be made only to merchants authorised by the Board;

(*d*) the Association agreed to issue from time to time, after consultation with the Board, schedules indicating the minimum prices at which potatoes should be sold in Great Britain by Northern Ireland merchants; these prices to be on a fair competitive level with the prices prevailing in Great Britain.

Basic Acreage and the Excess Acreage Levy.

The Board continued in 1937 to require payment of the excess acreage levy of £5 an acre from producers planting in excess of their basic acreage. The amount of the excess acreage levies received and not refunded in respect of the 1936 crop was approximately £18,640, representing 3,728 acres. For the 1937 crop, the excess acreage levy was charged on approximately 4,700 acres.

The total basic acreage of registered producers in December in each of the years 1934 to 1937 was as follows:—

	1934.	*1935.*	*1936.*	*1937.**
	Acres.	Acres.	Acres.	Acres.
England and Wales	491,000	505,000	510,000	514,000
Scotland	138,000	135,000	136,000	137,000
	629,000	640,000	646,000	651,000

* November, 1937.

Plans for Improving Trading Conditions.

Markets Plans.—The Markets Plans Scheme which was initiated in 1935* continued throughout the 1936-7 season and was still in operation during the 1937-8 season. The number of Markets Plans was, however, considerably reduced. Plans were in operation in 40 districts, but at December, 1936, and December, 1937, the numbers were 22 and 17 respectively. The modification made in the Markets Plans Scheme during the 1936-7 season, namely the insistence by the Board that producers should be represented on the Markets Plans Committees, or, alternatively, that joint meetings of the Markets Plans Committees with producer representatives should be held at regular intervals, was continued during the 1937-8 season. The Board's present policy is to take no steps to encourage the formation of Markets Plans Committees, and not to lend its support and authority except where it is fully satisfied that adequate support will be forthcoming from the majority of merchants concerned.

Authorisation of Merchants.—As in previous years, the Board prescribed that, subject to certain exemptions provided for in the Scheme, registered producers should sell potatoes only to

* See report for 1935 (Cmd. 5284), pages 67 and 68.

merchants authorised by the Board. The conditions of authorisation remained unaltered. The number of authorised merchants on 1st January, 1938, was 3,462, as against 3,602 on 1st January, 1937.

Price Recommending Committees.—Price Recommending Committees were first established towards the end of 1935, and the numbers have since increased considerably. At the end of 1936 and 1937 there were respectively 12 and 29 Committees in widely different areas of the country. It is noteworthy that all the Committees operating during the 1936-7 season resumed their activities at the beginning of the 1937-8 season. The Committees consist of representatives of producers, and their purpose is to make recommendations regarding farm prices, for general guidance in the area concerned. These recommendations are brought to the notice of producers through the Board's market intelligence service and through the press.

In some areas the prices recommended are used by the Markets Plans Committees in the calculation of wholesaler-retailer prices.

Potato Exchanges.—Between November, 1935, and November, 1936, Potato Exchanges were established at Warrington, Chelford and Wigan. Growers meet at these Exchanges on certain days in each week and announce on notice-boards in the market, a scale of prices considered appropriate to current transactions. These three Exchanges continued in existence, and in October, 1937, a fourth was opened at Worksop.

Market Intelligence and Publicity.—The Board continued its market intelligence service for producers. It issues a weekly schedule of prices in a large number of growers' and wholesale markets, which is brought to the attention of producers through the medium of the press; the Board also maintains notice boards at about 85 of the principal markets throughout Great Britain for the posting of up-to-date market information and any important announcements that the Board may desire to make to registered producers and authorised merchants.

The Board again gave much attention to publicity, which was especially directed towards keeping the value of the potato prominently before consumers, and fostering improvements in the standards of potato cookery. During the summer the Board gave extensive publicity to home-grown early potatoes, window pelmets and posters being distributed to retailers and to fish friers and menu cards to catering establishments; while posters were exhibited on railway companies' vans and on the London Underground railway system. Recipe books were brought to the attention of Women's Institutes, schools and other organisations by means of a direct postal campaign. A campaign was instituted in October, 1937, with a view to encouraging improvements in cookery standards, and establishments reaching a prescribed standard were awarded a "Testimonial of Merit". The Board also co-operated with Messrs. Smith's Crisps, Ltd., in distributing free packets of potato crisps to school-children assembled in London on Coronation Day; and later in the year the Board prepared a tableau for inclusion in the Lord Mayor's Show.

Fish Friers and Long-Term Contracts.—As the outcome of discussions of matters of mutual interest between the National Federation of Fish Friers, Ltd., the National Federation of Fruit and Potato Trades, Ltd., and the Board, a tripartite committee consisting of four representatives of each organization was set up in September to explore proposals for long-term contracts between producers, authorised merchants and fish friers for the supply of potatoes at uniform prices. The Committee subsequently issued a report in which they expressed the view that long-term contracts between individuals for periods of two years or more were feasible, although they were of opinion that there was little prospect of any immediate general adoption of collective contracts amongst producers, merchants or fish friers for securing group responsibility for delivery or payment. The Committee felt that the creation of long-term contracts must depend upon individual initiative and negotiation, and they did not think scales of prices could be indicated for the benefit of those making such contracts; but they recommended that the several organisations should assist with their advice in the drawing up of contracts and encourage the scheme generally, and that specimen contracts should be made available.

The Committee further recorded their view that a tripartite committee appeared to be a satisfactory medium for reconciling the views of their respective organizations, and suggested that, if their recommendations were adopted, a permanent committee should be established (*a*) to watch the development of long-term contracts between producers, merchants and fish friers, and (*b*) to provide means for discussing trade problems affecting the three parties.

Research.

Industrial Uses for Potatoes.—Investigation into the manufacture of industrial products from potatoes continued, but operations on a commercial scale were again limited to the manufacture of cattle food from potatoes at the Wisbech factory of the Farmers' Marketing and Supply Company, Ltd. In this enterprise, the Board works in close co-operation with the Company. Of the 1936 crop, 4,350 tons were used for manufacture at the Wisbech factory. The potatoes were bought at 30s. per ton, compared with 20s. per ton in the previous season; but supplies were nevertheless short and the factory was unable to work to capacity. It was accordingly impossible to test fully the economic possibilities of this manufacturing process. Supplies of the 1937 crop were more readily available at between 20s. and 35s. per ton, and between September and December, 1937, 4,250 tons of raw potatoes in all were manufactured. During the 1936-7 season, experiments were conducted at the factory in the drying of carrots and parsnips, with a view to testing the practicability of keeping the plant in operation when potatoes are not available.

Experiments were also conducted into the canning of ware potatoes, and into the drying of potatoes for cattle food by grass driers which are idle during the winter months.

Blackening of Potatoes.—The co-operative investigation into the cause of blackening of potatoes on cooking, which was begun in July, 1936*, was continued with the aid of the grant of £300 per annum from the Potato Marketing Board to the Imperial College of Science and Technology.

Damage from Wireworm and Eelworm.—The Board made a grant of £120 per annum for five years from October, 1937, to assist an investigation into wireworm damage to crops, particularly potatoes, which is being conducted by the University of Manchester. It also agreed to contribute £200 per annum for three years for research work on the eelworm which is being conducted under the auspices of the West of Scotland Agricultural College, Glasgow.

Demonstration Plots.—The Board collaborated with the National Institute of Agricultural Botany in establishing demonstration plots for new varieties of early and maincrop potatoes. A Joint Committee was set up to make arrangements and to exercise a general supervision over the tests, and a substantial proportion of the cost involved is being borne by the Board. Demonstrations were first arranged in the 1936-7 season, and a new investigation covering sixteen counties was initiated at the beginning of the 1937-8 season.

Canning of Potatoes.—The Board co-operated with the Metal Box Company, Ltd., and the Fruit and Vegetable Preservation Research Station at Campden in a series of experiments into the economic and dietetic value of canned potatoes.

Miscellaneous.

Report of the Food Council.—In their Report for the year 1936,† presented to the President of the Board of Trade in March, 1937, the Food Council, who had reported as a Consumers' Committee in June 1936,‡ on the Potato Marketing

* See report for 1936 (Cmd. 5734), page 68.

† Report by the Food Council to the President of the Board of Trade for the year 1936. Obtainable from H.M. Stationery Office, price 6d. net.

‡ See report for 1936 (Cmd. 5734), page 68.

Scheme, stated that further inquiries had not altered their opinion that the Scheme had so far been worked with advantage to the producers and no very material disadvantage to the consumer.

The Council considered that the reduction in acreage in recent years suggested the advisability of suspending the levy of £5 per acre on plantings in excess of each registered producer's basic acreage. They suggested that the Board should take whatever steps might be practicable to improve the standard of dressing. On the other hand, they expressed pleasure that the conditions for the sale of "seconds" had been made less onerous, and that increased sales had been made; and that the assurances of the Potato Marketing Board and of persons engaged in the potato trade that prices would not rise materially at Christmas, 1936, and in the early part of 1937 had proved correct.

As regards the Markets Plans Scheme, the Council thought that, as long as the producer continued to be permitted to sell direct to the retailer, a safeguard was provided against any excessive margin to the wholesaler. They were of opinion, however, that producers would be wise to abandon all attempts to secure minimum margins either for wholesalers or retailers.

Varieties Grown by Registered Producers.—The Board published an analysis of the varieties of potatoes grown by registered producers in each county in Great Britain for the years 1935 to 1937.* This booklet, like its predecessor (which analysed the returns for the period 1934 to 1936), is illustrated by eight sketch maps showing the main producing areas and the predominating varieties in each of them. The following table shows the acreage in Great Britain planted with first and second earlies and maincrop varieties respectively, omitting acreages on which unspecified varieties were grown, in the three years 1935 to 1937:—

	1935.		1936.		1937.	
	Acres.†	Per cent.	Acres.†	Per cent.	Acres.	Per cent.
First Earlies ...	73,466	14·6	72,332	14·2	74,905	14·6
Second Earlies ...	39,899	7·9	33,959	6·7	29,777	5·8
Maincrop ...	391,065	77·5	402,911	79·1	408,479	79·6
Total ...	504,430	100·0	509,202	100·0	513,161	100·0

† Revised figures.

* "The Area under Potatoes in Great Britain." Potato Marketing Board Miscellaneous Publications No. 5. Price 6d. post free.

The chief feature of this statement is the decline in the second earlies, but no great significance should be attached to this as there is no clear distinction between the different varieties and potatoes grown as second earlies one year may well be grown as maincrop another year. As regards specific varieties, the Board's analysis shows a continuous decline in the production of King Edwards and a steady increase in plantings of Majestic potatoes. These two varieties represented some 70 per cent. of all maincrop potatoes in 1937—as in 1936. Majestic are now the most extensively grown variety of potato.

Standards of Dressing.—A Grading Committee was set up by the Board in 1936 to consider what further improvements could be effected in the preparation of potatoes for the market and to prepare a plan which would be acceptable to the general body of registered producers. The Committee continued its work and reported to the Board from time to time during 1937.

Penalties.—During 1937 penalties amounting to £1,556 were imposed upon 501 producers. As in the previous year, the great majority of the penalties were imposed for failure to furnish returns and other information.

Finance.—A copy of the Board's accounts for the year ended 31st August, 1937, is printed in Appendix III. As in previous years, a levy of 5s. per acre planted was made on all registered producers during September. The amount of annual acreage levy collectable in the year ended 31st August, 1937, was £131,322. The amount of the special levy of £5 per acre collectable from producers who planted in excess of their basic acreage was £19,547.

ABERDEEN AND DISTRICT MILK MARKETING SCHEME, 1933.

This Scheme regulates the marketing of milk produced in the counties of Aberdeen and Kincardine.

As explained in the previous reports, the Board consists of the members of the Committee of Management of the Aberdeen and District Milk Agency, 4 representatives elected annually by the registered producers who are not members of the Agency, and 2 co-opted members. The third annual general meeting of the registered producers, held on 25th March, 1937, voted £600, the same amount as in the previous year, for division amongst the members of the Board, excluding the Chairman, as remuneration for the year 1936; the Chairman's remuneration is determined by the Board. The 4 representatives of the producers who are not members of the Agency were re-elected to the Board and, after consulting the Market Supply Committee, the Board appointed Mr. James R. Rust, LL.D., 72,

Hamilton Place, Aberdeen, to fill the vacancy caused by the resignation of Mr. J. A. Mackie, one of the two co-opted members.

There was little variation during 1937 in the numbers of the registered producers and their classification. At the end of the year, the total number of registered producers was 825, of whom 509 were ordinary producers (i.e., producers selling milk by wholesale to or through the Board), 310 were producer-retailers, and 6 were producers of Certified milk. Of the producers selling milk by wholesale, 96 also sold a proportion of their milk by retail. Producers whose daily sales do not exceed one gallon and are made to not more than four customers are exempt from registration.

The total quantities of milk dealt with under the Scheme during 1937 in comparison with the corresponding figures for the previous year are shown in the following table:—

	1936.	*1937.*	*Increase or Decrease.*	
	Gallons.	*Gallons.*	*Gallons.*	*Per cent.*
Liquid consumption—				
Within the area of the Scheme	6,199,278	6,127,571	− 71,707	1·15
In markets in England	1,717,688	2,051,965	+ 334,277	19·46
Manufacture	1,028,710	899,650	− 129,060	12·55
Total	8,945,676	9,079,186	+ 133,510	1·49

The statement on page 70 gives particulars of the sales of milk under the Scheme in each month during the year and of the utilization of the milk.

Payments to producers.—The payments to ordinary producers for their sales of milk to or through the Board are regulated on the "basic quantity—surplus" plan provided for in the Scheme. In February the Board revised the basic quantities of 62 producers and allotted basic quantities to 22 new producers who, pending qualification for final determinations, had previously been operating on interim basic quantities.

As the total of the basic quantities exceeded considerably the requirements of the liquid market within the area of the Scheme and the supplies offered by the registered producers showed a tendency to increase, the Board temporarily reduced all the basic quantities by 25 per cent. during the period from May to August inclusive. The circumstances in which this adjustment was made were explained to the registered producers at a special general meeting held on 13th July, 1937.

The following table shows, in respect of each month during the year 1937, the sales by the producers to or through the Board within the limits of the basic quantities and in excess of these quantities, the net prices paid to the producers and the amounts of the producers' contributions:—

Month.	"Basic" Quantities.		"Surplus" Supplies.		Producers' contribution per gallon.*
	Gallons.	Net price per gallon.	Gallons.	Net price per gallon.	
		d.		d.	d.
January ...	541,707	12·5	55,945	5·5	2·5
February ...	522,055	11·75	9,466	5·0	3·25
March ...	596,469	11·75	12,824	5·0	3·25
April	588,867	11·5	17,380	4·0	3·5
May	487,406	10·5	164,846	4·0	3·5
June ...	471,346	11·0	144,608	4·5	3·0
July	483,094	11·0	90,247	4·5	3·0
August ...	471,104	12·0	63,789	4·5	3·0
September ...	504,545	12·0	3,013	4·5	3·0
October ...	544,297	12·5	5,453	5·0	2·5
November ...	549,780	12·75	20,013	5·75	2·25
December ...	574,613	12·75	30,658	6·75	2·25
Total	6,335,283 (91·11 per cent.)	—	618,242 (8·89 per cent.)	—	—
Monthly average (unweighted)	—	11·825	—	4·92	2·92

* Producers' contributions have been deducted before arriving at net prices.

The weighted average prices per gallon paid to the producers for their sales of "basic quantity" and "surplus" milk over the year were 11·86d. and 4·62d. respectively. The corresponding average prices for the year 1936 were 12·36d. and 4·86d.

The deductions per gallon made from the payments to the producers in respect of haulage charges were calculated on the same scale as in previous years, viz.:—not exceeding 5 miles, ¼d.; over 5 but not exceeding 15 miles, ½d.; over 15 but not exceeding 20 miles, 1d.; over 20 but not exceeding 30 miles, 1¼d.; over 30 miles, 1½d.

The quantity of milk sold by retail by the registered producers during the year amounted to 1,882,574 gallons and the sales made by producers of Certified milk under their own arrangements totalled 243,087 gallons. As in previous years, the monthly contributions payable to the Board in respect of these sales were assessed at the rate of £2 per cow per annum calculated on the producers' returns of the sales and taking the average production at two gallons per cow per day.

Liquid Milk Prices.—The minimum prices per gallon determined by the Board for the year ending October, 1938, were on the following scale:—

Ordinary milk.—

Standard Price for sales to distributors.—November, 1937, to April, 1938—1s. 3d.; May, June and July—1s. 2d.; August, September and October—1s. 5d. While the prices for the period November to July were on the same scale as in the previous year, the price of 1s. 5d. for the last three months represented an increase of 2d.

Retail.—This price was continued, as previously, at 2s. for the period November to July but was increased to 2s. 4d. for the three months August to October.

The Standard Price and retail price in Peterhead and Fraserburgh were determined at 1s. 4d. and 2s. respectively for the whole year. The Board gave authority for reductions in the retail price in certain specified rural districts.

Semi-retail (supplies to hotels, restaurants, etc., in quantities of not less than 2 gallons).—4d. more than the Standard Price during May, June and July, 1938, and 3d. more than the Standard Price for the remainder of the year.

Supplies to Institutions—supported by voluntary contributions—the Standard Price; under control of local authorities—1d. over the Standard Price.

Tuberculin Tested milk.—

To distributors—November to July—1s. 6d.; August to October 1s. 10d., with an additional charge of 4d. for supplies in bottles.

Retail.—4d. more than for ordinary milk.

To institutions (in quantities of not less than 10 gallons)—At the price of sales to distributors, no control over the charges for distribution being exercised by the Board.

Certified milk.—

To distributors—November to July—1s. 10d.; August to October—2s. 2d.

Retail.—4d. more than for ordinary milk.

To institutions—November to July—2s. 2d.; August to October—2s. 6d.

All the milk consigned by the Board to markets in England, amounting during the year to 2,051,965 gallons, was sold at the regional liquid milk prices prescribed by the English Milk Marketing Board. As from 1st January, 1937, the Board made a payment of 3d. per gallon to the English Milk Marketing Board in respect of milk consigned to England.

Sale and Use of Milk for Manufacture.—The milk surplus to the requirements of the liquid milk markets was sold or used by the Board for manufacture as follows:—

Product.	Sales.	Used by Board.	Total.	Per cent.
	Gallons.	Gallons.	Gallons.	
Fresh Cream ...	613,786	118,292	732,078	85·45
Butter	—	122,710	122,710	14·32
Cheese	—	1,980	1,980	0·23
	613,786	242,982	856,768	100·00

The milk for the manufacture of cream was sold from January to October at the price of 7½d. per gallon, and during November and December at 8¼d. per gallon.

The Milk Acts, 1934 *to* 1937.—Advances amounting to £55 were paid to the Board in respect of 17,558 gallons of milk used by the Board for the manufacture of butter during the year.

Contributions amounting to £2,098 were made to the Board towards the expenses incurred in supplying to schools during the year a total quantity of 115,223 gallons of milk, including 29,771 gallons of Tuberculin Tested grade, at the reduced price of ½d. for one-third of a pint. On 1st November, 1937, about 15,200 children were participating in the scheme, the number being approximately the same as at the close of the previous year.

The number of Attested Herds within the area of the Aberdeen and District Milk Marketing Scheme on 31st December, 1937, was eight showing an increase of five over the previous year. Bonuses amounting to £891 were paid from the Exchequer in respect of the sale of 214,000 gallons of milk from these herds during the year.

The Board carried out a further campaign of press advertising and other forms of publicity and propaganda on the same lines as in previous years. The total expenditure incurred by the Board amounted to about £1,500 towards which a grant of £500 was made from the Exchequer.

Supply of milk at a reduced price to necessitous persons.—Particulars were given in the last report* of the scheme organized by the Board for the sale of milk at a depot in Aberdeen at the reduced price of 2d. per pint to persons who are in receipt of outdoor poor relief. The scheme was continued throughout 1937 but the Board expressed disappointment that the persons for whose benefit it was intended did not take fuller advantage of the offer of milk at the reduced price. The average daily number of customers at the depot during the year was 64 and the average daily sales amounted to 14 gallons.

Contraventions of the Scheme.—During the year a penalty of £10 was imposed on a registered producer in respect of a contravention of the Scheme.

Accounts of the Board.—Copies of the Profit and Loss Account and of the Balance Sheet of the Board as at 31st December, 1937, are printed in Appendix III.

---

* Cmd. 5734, page 71.

Aberdeen and District Milk Marketing Scheme, 1932.

Quantities of Milk sold by Registered Producers.

Month	Total Milk.	Method of Sale.				Utilisation.					
		Sold to or through the agency of the Board.		Direct Sales by Producer-Retailers and Producers of Certified Milk.		Sold for Liquid Consumption within area of Scheme.		Sold for Liquid Consumption outside area of Scheme.		Sold or used for Manufacture of milk products.*	
1932	Gallons	Gallons	Per cent.	Gallons	Per cent.	Gallons	Per cent.	Gallons	Per cent.	Gallons	Per cent.
January ...	[illegible]	[illegible]	[illegible]	[illegible]	[illegible]	[illegible]	[illegible]	[illegible]	[illegible]	[illegible]	[illegible]
February ...	[illegible]	[illegible]	[illegible]	[illegible]	[illegible]	[illegible]	[illegible]	[illegible]	[illegible]	[illegible]	[illegible]
March ...	[illegible]	[illegible]	[illegible]	[illegible]	[illegible]	[illegible]	[illegible]	[illegible]	[illegible]	[illegible]	[illegible]
April ...	[illegible]	[illegible]	[illegible]	[illegible]	[illegible]	[illegible]	[illegible]	[illegible]	[illegible]	[illegible]	[illegible]
May ...	[illegible]	[illegible]	[illegible]	[illegible]	[illegible]	[illegible]	[illegible]	[illegible]	[illegible]	[illegible]	[illegible]
June ...	[illegible]	[illegible]	[illegible]	[illegible]	[illegible]	[illegible]	[illegible]	[illegible]	[illegible]	[illegible]	[illegible]
July ...	[illegible]	[illegible]	[illegible]	[illegible]	[illegible]	[illegible]	[illegible]	[illegible]	[illegible]	[illegible]	[illegible]
August ...	[illegible]	[illegible]	[illegible]	[illegible]	[illegible]	[illegible]	[illegible]	[illegible]	[illegible]	[illegible]	[illegible]
September ...	[illegible]	[illegible]	[illegible]	[illegible]	[illegible]	[illegible]	[illegible]	[illegible]	[illegible]	[illegible]	[illegible]
October ...	[illegible]	[illegible]	[illegible]	[illegible]	[illegible]	[illegible]	[illegible]	[illegible]	[illegible]	[illegible]	[illegible]
November ...	[illegible]	[illegible]	[illegible]	[illegible]	[illegible]	[illegible]	[illegible]	[illegible]	[illegible]	[illegible]	[illegible]
December ...	[illegible]	[illegible]	[illegible]	[illegible]	[illegible]	[illegible]	[illegible]	[illegible]	[illegible]	[illegible]	[illegible]
Total ...	[illegible]	[illegible]	[illegible]	[illegible]	[illegible]	[illegible]	[illegible]	[illegible]	[illegible]	[illegible]	[illegible]
Total for 1931	[illegible]	[illegible]	[illegible]	[illegible]	[illegible]	[illegible]	[illegible]	[illegible]	[illegible]	[illegible]	[illegible]

NORTH OF SCOTLAND MILK MARKETING SCHEME, 1934.

This Scheme came into operation on 1st October, 1934. It applies to the counties of Inverness, Nairn, Ross and Cromarty, Sutherland and Caithness, but by resolutions of the Board all producers in the Western Islands, and also those producers on the mainland, whose daily sales do not exceed three gallons and are made to not more than five customers, are exempt from registration.

The third annual general meeting of the registered producers was held on 15th October, 1937. Two of the five elected members of the Board were then due to retire; one was re-elected to the Board and the other, who did not seek re-election, was replaced by a new member. After consulting the Market Supply Committee the elected members co-opted Mr. P. M. Pottie, Achareidh, Nairn, and Mr. W. Michie, 62 Academy Street, Inverness, to membership of the Board for the year 1937-8.

The general meeting of registered producers voted £450, the same amount as in the previous year, to be divided amongst the members of the Board, excluding the Chairman, as remuneration for the year 1936-7. The Chairman's remuneration was determined by the Board at £450.

The total number of producers registered under the Scheme on 31st December, 1937, was 336, of whom 126 were ordinary producers (i.e. producers selling milk by wholesale to or through the Board), 195 were producer-retailers and 15 were producers of Certified and Tuberculin Tested milk. The total number of registered producers was 23 less than at the end of the previous year, the reduction having been made mainly by the deletion from the register of the names of producers entitled to exemption from registration.

The total quantity of milk dealt with under the Scheme during the year 1937 amounted to 2,029,783 gallons, of which 1,808,889 gallons (89·12 per cent.) were sold for liquid consumption within the area of the Scheme, 115,667 gallons (5·70 per cent.) were consigned to markets in England, and 105,227 gallons (5·18 per cent.) were sold or used for manufacture. Compared with the statistics for the year 1936, these figures show small increases of 19,634 gallons (0·98 per cent.) in the total supply of milk under the Scheme and of 9,477 gallons (0·53 per cent.) in the sales for liquid consumption within the area of the Scheme. The statement on page 75 gives particulars of the sales in each month during the year and of the utilization of the milk.

Prices and sales of milk for liquid consumption.—The prices for the year 1937 were determined by the Board on the same scale as in the previous year. The distributors accordingly paid a Standard Price of 1s. 3d. per gallon throughout the year for supplies to meet their estimated monthly requirements for the liquid milk trade. For any additional supplies of milk required by them, they paid the accommodation price of 1s. 6d. per gallon for quantities under 10 gallons and 1s. 4d. per gallon for 10 gallons or more.

The retail prices were:—

Domestic consumers ...	2s. per gallon—reduced to 1s. 8d. per gallon in Nairn until 15th November.
Hotels, restaurants etc.—	
2 gallons and under ...	2s.
Over 2 gallons but not exceeding 10 gallons ...	1s. 8d.
Larger quantities	As arranged with the Board but not less than 1s. 6d. per gallon.
Charitable institutions ...	1s. 4d. per gallon.

The prices for Tuberculin Tested and Certified milk were 2d. and 4d. per gallon respectively more than the prices for ordinary milk.

The prices paid by the buyers of milk consigned to England were the regional liquid milk prices prescribed by the English Milk Marketing Board.

The construction of the Board's depot in Inverness was completed in May, 1937. It is used for the processing and distribution of "accommodation" supplies of milk for distributors throughout the area of the Scheme, for the consignment of milk to England and the manufacture of milk products.

As explained in the last report* the Board took over the retail distribution of milk in Nairn and Dingwall as from 1st June and 1st August, 1936, respectively. The profit and loss accounts in respect of the operation of these retail services during the period ended 31st May, 1937, showed that a loss had been incurred at both centres amounting altogether to £1,702. The Board continued to retail milk from its depot at Nairn at the reduced price of 2½d. per pint until 15th November, 1937, but the sales were thereafter made at the retail price of 3d. per pint observed generally throughout the area of the Scheme.

Prices and use of milk for manufacture.—The quantity of milk sold for manufacture during the year amounted to 84,306 gallons. Of that quantity, 68,296 gallons were sold for the manufacture of cream at prices varying from 10d. to 1s. per gallon, the bulk of the sales being made at 10d. per gallon and the average price being 10·12d. per gallon. The remainder, 16,010 gallons, was sold for the manufacture of butter at prices varying from 2d. to 4½d. per gallon.

* Cmd. 5734, pages 76 and 77.

The Board also used 18,082 gallons for manufacture; 10,383 gallons were manufactured into cream, 5,507 gallons into butter and 2,192 gallons into cheese.

Payments to producers.—The basic quantities allocated to the registered producers were revised as from 1st April, 1937, in accordance with their sales during the winter months. As a result of this revision, an average reduction of about 5 per cent. was made in the basic quantities.

The following statement shows in respect of each month during the year 1937 the sales by the producers to or through the Board within the limits of their basic quantities and in excess of these quantities, the net price per gallon paid to the producers, and the amount of the producers' contributions.

Month.	"Basic" Quantities.		"Surplus" Supplies.		Producers' contribution per gallon.*
	Gallons.	Net price per gallon.	Gallons.	Net price per gallon.	
1937.		d.		d.	d.
January	83,799	13·5	1,045	3·5	1·5
February ...	76,795	13·5	[illegible]	3·5	1·5
March ...	90,569	13·5	3,132	3·5	1·5
April	87,974	13·5	6,155	4·5	1·5
May	93,457	13·5	10,159	4·5	1·5
June	90,773	13·5	8,957	4·5	1·5
July	91,991	13·5	4,862	4·5	1·5
August ...	87,780	13·5	2,409	4·5	1·5
September ...	82,496	13·5	1,723	4·5	1·5
October ...	80,931	13·5	1,199	4·5	1·5
November ...	75,781	13·5	1,043	4·5	1·5
December ...	76,980	13·5	1,646	4·5	1·5
Total	1,019,326 (95·90 per cent.)	—	43,355 (4·10 per cent.)	—	—
Monthly average (unweighted).	—	13·5	—	4·25	1·5

* Producers' contributions have been deducted before arriving at net prices.

The weighted average price per gallon paid to the producers for the total sales of milk to or through the Board during the year was 13·13d. per gallon compared with 13·35d. per gallon for the previous year. The producers pay the cost of haulage of milk sold by them to or through the Board.

The total sales of Certified and Tuberculin Tested milk during the year amounted to 162,783 gallons, of which 136,569 gallons were sold under the producers' own arrangements and 26,214 gallons were sold to or through the Board. For the latter sales, the producers are guaranteed payment at not less than the "basic quantity" price and, in respect of sales under their own arrangements, they pay monthly contributions to the Board at a rate per gallon equal to $\frac{8}{10}$ ths of the contributions payable on sales to or through the Board.*

The producers' retail sales of ordinary milk for the year amounted to 830,333 gallons, representing about 46 per cent. of the total sales for liquid consumption within the area of the Scheme. The contribution payable to the Board in respect of these sales is at a rate per gallon equal to $\frac{7}{10}$ ths of that payable in respect of wholesale sales.

The Milk Acts, 1934 *to* 1937.—Advances amounting to £15 were made to the Board in respect of 3,523 gallons of milk sold for the manufacture of butter during the year.

On 31st December, 1937, there were five attested herds within the area of this Milk Marketing Scheme. Bonuses from the Exchequer amounting to £174 were paid through the Board to the owners of these herds in respect of the sale of 42,000 gallons of milk from the herds during the year.

The contributions paid to the Board in respect of the operation of its scheme for the supply of milk at the reduced price of ½d. for one-third pint for consumption in the schools amounted to £421. The total quantity of milk supplied during the year was 21,258 gallons and included 14,224 gallons of Tuberculin Tested milk. About 3,250 children attending schools within the Board's area were receiving milk on 1st November, 1937.

Accounts.—Copies of the Profit and Loss Account and of the Balance Sheet of the Board as at 31st May, 1937, are printed in Appendix III.

---

* See Cmd. 5734, page 78.

North of Scotland Milk Marketing Scheme, 1935.

QUANTITIES OF MILK SOLD BY REGISTERED PRODUCERS.

Method of Sale.				Utilisation.					
Sold to or through the agency of the Board.		Direct Sales by Producer-Retailers and Producers of Certified and Tuberculin Tested Milk.		Sold for Liquid Consumption without aid of [illegible].		Sold for Liquid Consumption with aid of [illegible].		Sold or used for Manufacture of milk products.*	
Gallons.	Per cent.	Gallons.	Per cent.	Gallons.	Per cent.	Gallons.	Per cent.	Gallons.	Per cent.
[illegible]	[illegible]	[illegible]	[illegible]	[illegible]	[illegible]	[illegible]	[illegible]	[illegible]	[illegible]
[illegible]	[illegible]	[illegible]	[illegible]	[illegible]	[illegible]	[illegible]	[illegible]	[illegible]	[illegible]
[illegible]	[illegible]	[illegible]	[illegible]	[illegible]	[illegible]	[illegible]	[illegible]	[illegible]	[illegible]
[illegible]	[illegible]	[illegible]	[illegible]	[illegible]	[illegible]	[illegible]	[illegible]	[illegible]	[illegible]
[illegible]	[illegible]	[illegible]	[illegible]	[illegible]	[illegible]	[illegible]	[illegible]	[illegible]	[illegible]
[illegible]	[illegible]	[illegible]	[illegible]	[illegible]	[illegible]	[illegible]	[illegible]	[illegible]	[illegible]
[illegible]	[illegible]	[illegible]	[illegible]	[illegible]	[illegible]	[illegible]	[illegible]	[illegible]	[illegible]
[illegible]	[illegible]	[illegible]	[illegible]	[illegible]	[illegible]	[illegible]	[illegible]	[illegible]	[illegible]
[illegible]	[illegible]	[illegible]	[illegible]	[illegible]	[illegible]	[illegible]	[illegible]	[illegible]	[illegible]
[illegible]	[illegible]	[illegible]	[illegible]	[illegible]	[illegible]	[illegible]	[illegible]	[illegible]	[illegible]
[illegible]	[illegible]	[illegible]	[illegible]	[illegible]	[illegible]	[illegible]	[illegible]	[illegible]	[illegible]
[illegible]	[illegible]	[illegible]	[illegible]	[illegible]	[illegible]	[illegible]	[illegible]	[illegible]	[illegible]
[illegible]	[illegible]	[illegible]	[illegible]	[illegible]	[illegible]	[illegible]	[illegible]	[illegible]	[illegible]
[illegible]	[illegible]	[illegible]	[illegible]	[illegible]	[illegible]	[illegible]	[illegible]	[illegible]	[illegible]
[illegible]	[illegible]	[illegible]	[illegible]	[illegible]	[illegible]	[illegible]	[illegible]	[illegible]	[illegible]
[illegible]	[illegible]	[illegible]	[illegible]	[illegible]	[illegible]	[illegible]	[illegible]	[illegible]	[illegible]

* [illegible] gallons lost by [illegible], after acceptance of the milk by the Board.

PART II.

SCHEMES SUBMITTED BUT NOT YET IN OPERATION.

During 1937 no new schemes were submitted. Two schemes submitted during 1936 were under consideration during the year, as set out below:—

Scheme.	*Date of Notice of Submission.*		*Area of Scheme.*
Sugar Beet Marketing Scheme ...	12th June, 1936	...	Great Britain.
Milk Products Marketing Scheme	22nd July, 1936	...	" "

Particulars of the progress of these Schemes are included in Appendix I.

Moray and Banff Draft Milk Marketing Scheme.

The committee responsible for the submission of this draft Scheme, referred to in the last report,* intimated during the year that they did not wish to proceed further with the promotion of the Scheme.

Sugar Beet Draft Marketing Scheme.

As noted in the report for 1936,† an amended Sugar Beet Marketing Scheme was submitted during that year by the promoters (the English and Scottish National Farmers' Union), and a public inquiry into objections was held by Mr. F. J. Wrottesley, K.C. (now Mr. Justice Wrottesley) on the 8th and 9th October, 1936. After the report of the public inquiry had been considered, the persons nominated for the purpose were notified of the modifications proposed to be made by the Minister of Agriculture and Fisheries and the Secretary of State for Scotland. An extension of time was granted to enable these modifications to be fully considered, but subsequently the promoters decided not to proceed with the Scheme.

Milk Products Draft Marketing Scheme.

This Scheme was submitted by the National Association of Creamery Proprietors, and others, in July, 1936, for the regulation of the marketing of butter, cheese, condensed milk, dried milk, and cream in Great Britain. A public inquiry into the objections received was held in London and Edinburgh, the Commissioner being Mr. P. E. Sandlands, K.C. This inquiry commenced on 30th November, 1936, and concluded on 29th January, 1937.

Consideration of the report of the public inquiry was deferred, pending the introduction into Parliament of legislation to give effect to the Government's long-term milk policy, which was announced in July, 1937.

* Cmd. 5734, page 81. † Cmd. 5734, pages 82 and 83.

Southampton Library Digitisation Unit

Milk ...	Scotland (Counties of [illegible])	J. C. Stewart, Esq. [illegible] on behalf of [illegible] Producers.	[illegible]	—	[illegible]	[illegible]	[illegible]	[illegible]	[illegible]	[illegible]	[illegible]	[illegible]
Sugar ...	Great Britain.	[illegible] of United Kingdom Sugar Industry	[illegible]	[illegible] to [illegible]	[illegible]							
Milk ...	Scotland (Counties of Moray and Banff).	Committee representing [illegible] Producers.	[illegible]	—	[illegible]							
Sugar Beet.	Great Britain.	N.F.U. and N.F.U. of Scotland	[illegible]	[illegible] to [illegible]	[illegible]							
Milk ...	Scotland (the part of the County of Argyll not [illegible] by the Scottish Milk Marketing Scheme).	Scottish Agricultural Organisation Society on behalf of [illegible] Producers.	[illegible]	—	[illegible]							
[illegible]	Scotland *	[illegible] by General Meeting of Producers, and on behalf of all Producers.	[illegible]	[illegible] and [illegible]	[illegible]	[illegible]	[illegible]	[illegible]	[illegible]	[illegible]	[illegible]	[illegible]
[illegible]	Scotland (Counties of Moray and Banff).	Committee representing the Producers.	[illegible]	—	[illegible]							
Sugar Beet.	Great Britain.	N.F.U. and N.F.U. of Scotland.	[illegible]	[illegible] to [illegible]	[illegible]							
[illegible] Products	Great Britain	National Association of [illegible] Producers and others	[illegible]	[illegible] to [illegible]								

* The Scheme [illegible] for application to the whole of Scotland but, by [illegible] the [illegible], the area was [illegible] to that part of Scotland lying to the south of the Forth and Clyde Canal.

Amendments of Marketing Schemes

(a) In accordance with Section 1 of the Agricultural Marketing Act, 1933.

Scheme.	Result of Poll of Registered Producers (if amendment). (Per cent. in favour of amendment)		Date of Notice of Submission	Date of Public Inquiry.	Date of Approval by Parliament		Date of Approval Order and S.R. & O. number.
	Votes	Productive capacity.			House of Commons.	House of Lords.	
Hops Marketing Scheme, 1932 ...	[illegible]	[illegible]	[illegible]	[illegible]	[illegible]	[illegible]	[illegible]
[illegible] Marketing Scheme, 1933 ...	—	—	[illegible]	—	—	—	[illegible]
[illegible] Marketing Scheme, 1933 ...	—	—	[illegible]	[illegible]	[illegible]	[illegible]	[illegible]
Pigs Marketing Scheme, 1933 ...	—	—	[illegible]	[illegible]	[illegible]	[illegible]	[illegible]
Milk Marketing Scheme, 1933 ...	—	—	[illegible]	—	—	—	[illegible]
Milk Marketing Scheme, 1933 ...	[illegible]	[illegible]	[illegible]	[illegible]	—	—	[illegible]
Scottish Milk Marketing Scheme, 1933	—		[illegible]	[illegible]	[illegible]	[illegible]	[illegible]

Printed image digitised by the University of Southampton Library Digitisation Unit

(b) By Order made by "The Minister" under Section [illegible] of the Agricultural Marketing Act, 1933.

Scheme.	Title of Order.	Date of Order and S.R. & O. number.
Scottish Milk Marketing Scheme, 1933	Scottish Milk Marketing Scheme (Amendment) Order, [illegible]	[illegible]
Scottish Milk Marketing Scheme, 1933	Scottish Milk Marketing Scheme (Amendment) Order, [illegible]	[illegible]
[illegible] Milk Marketing Scheme, 1933	Scottish Milk Marketing Scheme (Amendment No. 2) Order, 1933	[illegible]
Milk Marketing Scheme, 1933	Milk Marketing Scheme (Amendment) Order, [illegible]	[illegible]
[illegible] Milk Marketing Scheme, 1933	[illegible] Milk Marketing Scheme (Amendment No. 2) Order, 1933	[illegible]

(c) By Order made by "The Minister" under Section [illegible] of the Agricultural Marketing Act, 1933.

Scheme.	Title of Order.	Date of Order and S.R. & O. number.
Scottish Milk Marketing Scheme, 1933	Scottish Milk Marketing [illegible] Order, [illegible]	[illegible]
Bacon Marketing Scheme, 1933	Bacon Marketing Board [illegible] Order, [illegible]	[illegible]
Pigs Marketing Scheme, 1933	Pigs Marketing Scheme [illegible] Order, [illegible]	[illegible]

(d) By Order made by "The Minister" under Section [illegible] of the Agricultural Marketing (No. 2) Act, 1933.

APPENDIX II.

PARTICULARS OF LOANS TO MARKETING BOARDS FROM THE AGRICULTURAL MARKETING FUNDS.

I.—Loans to Boards administering Schemes applicable to Great Britain.

Board.	Date of Advance.		Amount of Advance.		Date of Repayment.	Amount Repaid, including Interest.		Purpose of Loan.
	English Fund.	Scottish Fund.	English Fund.	Scottish Fund.		English Fund.	Scottish Fund.	
			£	£		£ s. d.	£ s. d.	
Pigs Marketing Board	[illegible]	[illegible]	[illegible]	[illegible]	[illegible]	[illegible]	[illegible]	Initial poll expenses.
Pigs Marketing Board	[illegible]	[illegible]	[illegible]	[illegible]	[illegible]	[illegible]	[illegible]	Initial working expenses.
Bacon Marketing Board	[illegible]	[illegible]	[illegible]	[illegible]	[illegible]	[illegible]	[illegible]	Payment of compensation to registered producers under the Bacon Marketing Scheme for losses occasioned by the working of that Scheme and the Pigs Marketing Scheme.

II.—Loans from the English Fund to Boards administering Schemes applicable to England only

Board.	Date of Advance.	Amount of Advance.	Date of Repayment.	Amount Repaid, including Interest.	Purpose of Loan.
		£		£ s. d.	
Hops Marketing Board	[illegible]	[illegible]	[illegible]	[illegible]	Initial poll expenses.
Milk Marketing Board	[illegible]	[illegible]	[illegible]	[illegible]	Initial poll expenses.
Milk Marketing Board	[illegible]	[illegible]	[illegible]	[illegible]	Initial working expenses.

Board.	Date of Advance.	Amount of Advance.	Date of Repayment.	Amount Repaid, including Interest.	Purpose of Loan.
		£		£ s. d.	
[illegible]	[illegible]	[illegible]		[illegible]	Initial poll expenses. [illegible]
[illegible]	[illegible]	[illegible]	[illegible]	[illegible]	Initial poll expenses.
[illegible]	[illegible]	[illegible]	[illegible]	[illegible]	Initial poll expenses.
[illegible]	[illegible]	[illegible]	[illegible]	[illegible]	Initial poll expenses.
[illegible]	[illegible]	[illegible]		–	Initial poll expenses. [illegible]

APPENDIX III.

THE HOPS MARKETING BOARD.

ACCOUNTS AND BALANCE SHEETS OF MARKETING BOARDS.

Income and Expenditure Account for the Year ended 31st March, 1937.

1935 Crop Disposal Account.

A.—Quota Hops only.

Dr.	£	s.	d.		£	s.	d. Cr.
To Payments to Producers	[illegible]	3	0	By Amount due to Producers, 31st March, 1936	[illegible]	2	11
" Auditors' Commission	[illegible]	3	0	" Sale of Hops and Amounts Recoverable from Levy Fund	[illegible]	1	1
" Transfer to Expenses Account under Section 36 of the Scheme, completing transfer due in respect of Quota Hops	[illegible]	[illegible]	8				
" Balance Carried to Non-Quota Hops Account	[illegible]	6	11				
	[illegible]	3	0		[illegible]	2	[illegible]

[illegible] Crop [illegible] Account—[illegible] Hops only

	£	s.	d.	
To Payments to Producers	[illegible]	[illegible]	[illegible]	By Sales of Hops [illegible]
" Agents' Commission	[illegible]	[illegible]	[illegible]	Notes:—
" Transfer to [illegible] Account under Section [illegible] of the Scheme	[illegible]	[illegible]	[illegible]	

Notes:—

1. The amount [illegible] from Sales of Hops of [illegible] Crop to 31st March, [illegible], being insufficient to pay to Producers [illegible] per cent. of the Valuations of Quota Hops, no sum was available to make any payment in respect of Non-Quota Hops.
2. No account has been taken of the [illegible] amount which will subsequently be recoverable from the Levy Fund in respect of the [illegible] Crop.
3. No account has been taken of the [illegible] of hops [illegible] at 31st March, [illegible].
4. The sum of approximately [illegible] is due to be transferred to [illegible] Account under Section [illegible] of the Scheme. This amount will be transferred out of the proceeds of [illegible] or out of the sum which will be recoverable from the Levy Fund in respect of the [illegible] Crop.

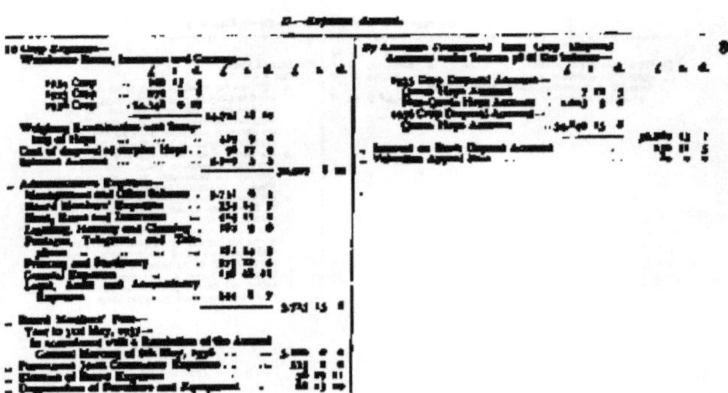

D.—Expenses Account.

	£	s.	d.	£	s.	d.	£	s.	d.
To Crop Expenses—									
Warehouse Rent, Insurance and Cartage—									
1934 Crop ..	[illegible]	[illegible]	[illegible]						
1935 Crop ..	[illegible]	[illegible]	[illegible]						
1936 Crop ..	[illegible]	[illegible]	[illegible]						
				[illegible]	[illegible]	[illegible]			
Weighing, Examination and Sampling of Hops				[illegible]	9	[illegible]			
Cost of disposal of surplus Hops ..				[illegible]	[illegible]	[illegible]			
[illegible] Account				[illegible]	[illegible]	[illegible]			
							[illegible]	[illegible]	[illegible]
" Administration Expenses—									
Management and Office Salaries .				[illegible]	[illegible]	[illegible]			
Board Members' Expenses ..				[illegible]	[illegible]	[illegible]			
Rent, Rates and Insurance ...				[illegible]	[illegible]	[illegible]			
Lighting, Heating and Cleaning .				[illegible]	9	[illegible]			
Postages, Telegrams and Telephones				[illegible]	[illegible]	[illegible]			
Printing and Stationery .				[illegible]	[illegible]	[illegible]			
General Expenses				[illegible]	[illegible]	[illegible]			
Legal, Audit and Accountancy Expenses . ..				[illegible]	[illegible]	7			
							[illegible]	15	[illegible]
" Board Members' Fees—									
Year to 31st May, 1937—									
In accordance with a Resolution of the Annual General Meeting of 8th May, 1936							[illegible]	[illegible]	[illegible]
" Permanent Joint Committee Expenses							[illegible]	[illegible]	[illegible]
" Election of Board Expenses .							[illegible]	[illegible]	[illegible]
" Depreciation of Furniture and Equipment .							[illegible]	[illegible]	[illegible]

	£	s.	d.	£	s.	d.
By Amounts Transferred from Crop Disposal Accounts under Section 38 of the Scheme—						
1935 Crop Disposal Account—						
Quota Hops Account .	7	[illegible]	[illegible]			
Non-Quota Hops Account .	[illegible]	[illegible]	[illegible]			
1936 Crop Disposal Account—						
Quota Hops Account ..	[illegible]	15	[illegible]			
				[illegible]	[illegible]	[illegible]
" Interest on Bank Deposit Account .				[illegible]	[illegible]	5
" Valuation Appeal Fees				[illegible]	[illegible]	[illegible]

	£	s.	d.	£	s.	d.
To Creditors and Accrued Charges ...				22,[illegible]	[illegible]	[illegible]
" [illegible] Crop Suspense Account ...				150	[illegible]	[illegible]
" To Amount Due to Producers in respect of 1935 Non-Quota Hops				[illegible]	[illegible]	[illegible]
" Reserve for Undetermined Expenses and Contingencies—						
As at 31st March, 1936 ...	[illegible]	[illegible]	[illegible]			
Add Amount transferred from Income and Expenditure Account	4,000	0	0			
				[illegible]	0	0
" Income and Expenditure Account—						
As at 31st March, 1936 ...	[illegible]	[illegible]	[illegible]			
Balance per annexed account ...	[illegible]	[illegible]	[illegible]			
	[illegible]	13	[illegible]			
Less Amount transferred to Reserve for undetermined Expenses and Contingencies ...	4,000	0	0			
				43,[illegible]	13	[illegible]
Note.—No account has been taken of any hops remaining unsold at 31st March, 1937.						
				£[illegible]	[illegible]	[illegible]

	£	s.	d.	£	s.	d.
By Furniture and Equipment at Cost Less Depreciation—						
As at 31st March, 1936 ...	[illegible]	[illegible]	[illegible]			
Additions during year ...	[illegible]	[illegible]	[illegible]			
	[illegible]	[illegible]	[illegible]			
Less Depreciation at [illegible] per cent. per annum ...	[illegible]	13	[illegible]			
				[illegible]	[illegible]	[illegible]
" Debtors and Payments in Advance ...				[illegible]	[illegible]	[illegible]
" Cash at Bank ...				[illegible]	9	[illegible]
				£[illegible]	[illegible]	[illegible]

W. J. [illegible],
[illegible] WEST,
J. W. [illegible]-HUTCHINSON, } Members of the Board.

[illegible] J. [illegible], Secretary.

To the Producers Registered under the Hops Marketing Scheme, 1932, as amended by the Hops Marketing Scheme (Amendment) Order, 1934.

I have to report that I have audited the above Balance Sheet and Income and Expenditure Account of The Hops Marketing Board and have obtained all the information and explanations I have required. In my opinion such Accounts are properly drawn up so as to exhibit a true and correct view of the state of the Board's affairs according to the best of my information and the explanations given to me and as shown by the books of the Board.

[illegible] House,
[illegible], London, E.C.2.
[illegible] April, 1937.

GERALD D. [illegible],
[illegible], [illegible] & Co.,
Chartered Accountants.

THE SCOTTISH MILK MARKETING BOARD.

PROFIT AND LOSS ACCOUNT FOR THE YEAR ENDED 31ST JANUARY, 1937.

	1937. £	£	1936. £
To Average Prices payable to Producers ...	[illegible]		[illegible]
" Bonus payable to Farm Cheesemakers	[illegible]		[illegible]
" Local Delivery Bonus	[illegible]		[illegible]
" Milk to Schools Allowance £[illegible]			
Less—Exchequer Refund ... [illegible]	[illegible]		[illegible]
" Producers' Claims and Allowances	[illegible]		[illegible]
		[illegible]	[illegible]
" Salaries and National Insurance—Head Office	[illegible]		[illegible]
" Travelling Expenses and Allowances	[illegible]		[illegible]
" Salaries and Expenses—Regional Offices	[illegible]		[illegible]
" Stationery, Printing and Advertising	[illegible]		[illegible]
" Postages, Telephones and Telegrams	[illegible]		[illegible]
" Bank Charges and Stamp Duty ...	[illegible]		[illegible]
" Heating, Lighting, Cleaning, Depreciation, Expenses and General Charges	[illegible]		[illegible]
" Fee and Expenses, Audit and Certification of Exchequer Advances and Compensation ...	[illegible]		[illegible]
" Legal and Litigation Expenses	[illegible]		[illegible]
" Rent, Rates and Insurance	[illegible]		[illegible]
" Bad and Doubtful Debts ...	[illegible]		[illegible]

	£	1937. £	1936. £
By Sales—			
Liquid		[illegible]	[illegible]
Manufacturing		[illegible]	[illegible]
		[illegible]	[illegible]
Deduct—			
Handling Charges ...	£[illegible]		
Freight	[illegible]		
		[illegible]	[illegible]
		[illegible]	[illegible]
" Contributions Levied on Category Producers		[illegible]	[illegible]
" Surplus from Haulage		[illegible]	[illegible]
" Compensatory [illegible] received from Milk Marketing Board (England and Wales)		[illegible]	[illegible]
" Repayment Exchequer Advances in respect of Manufacturing, in terms of Milk Acts 1934 and 1936		[illegible]	[illegible]
" Deductions in respect of Butter Fat Deficiencies, Penalties, etc.		[illegible]	[illegible]
" Interest		[illegible]	[illegible]
" Surplus from Experimental Creameries		—	[illegible]

„ Loan Interest (before Deduction of Income Tax)		[illegible]	[illegible]
„ Publicity and Propaganda ... [illegible]			
Less—Recoverable from Treasury [illegible]			
	[illegible]		[illegible]
„ Stores Ledger	[illegible]		[illegible]
„ Subscriptions (under Section [illegible]) ...	[illegible]		[illegible]
„ Milk (Agricultural) Investigation and Clean Milk Enquiry Expenses ... [illegible]			
Less—Refunded by Treasury ... [illegible]			
	[illegible]		[illegible]
		[illegible]	
„ Transfers to Reserve—			
(a) Loan Redemption	[illegible]		[illegible]
(b) Special Reserve	[illegible]		—
(c) Depreciation Reserve—[illegible] ...	—		[illegible]
(d) General Reserve .	[illegible]		[illegible]
		[illegible]	
		[illegible]	[illegible]

„ Excess Pool Returns from Distributors Payable to Producers ...	[illegible]	
„ Producers' [illegible] Payable to Producers	[illegible]	
	[illegible]	[illegible]

Balance Sheet as at 31st January, 1927.

Liabilities.

	1927. £	£	1926. £
I. Loan—			
As at 31st January, 1926	[illegible]		
Deduct—Repaid during year	[illegible]		
		[illegible]	[illegible]
II. Sundry Creditors—			
(a) [illegible] Producers ...	[illegible]		[illegible]
(b) [illegible] ...	[illegible]		[illegible]
(c) [illegible]	[illegible]		[illegible]
(d) At Creameries on Open Account	[illegible]		[illegible]
(e) Charges Accrued and Sundry Credit Balances	[illegible]		[illegible]
		[illegible]	
III. Reserve Accounts—			
(a) Loan Redemption Account—			
As at 31st January, 1926 ... [illegible]			
Add — Transferred from Profit and Loss Account [illegible]			
£[illegible]			
Deduct — Written off per contra ... ... [illegible]	[illegible]		[illegible]
(b) [illegible] Reserve—			
[illegible] during year to 31st January, 1927 ... [illegible]			
Deduct — [illegible]			

Assets.

	1927. £	1926. £
I. Land—At Cost, less Sales	[illegible]	[illegible]
II. Buildings—At Cost, less Sales and Depreciation	[illegible]	[illegible]
III. Plant—At Cost, less Sales and Depreciation ...	[illegible]	[illegible]
IV. Office Furniture and Equipment—		
(a) At Head and Regional Offices— At Cost, less Depreciation ... £[illegible]		[illegible]
(b) At Creameries— At Cost, less Sales and Depreciation ... ... [illegible]	[illegible]	[illegible]
V. Churns, Utensils and Fittings— As per Valuation Certified by Marketing Officer ...	[illegible]	[illegible]
VI. [illegible]— At Cost, less Sales and Depreciation ..	[illegible]	[illegible]

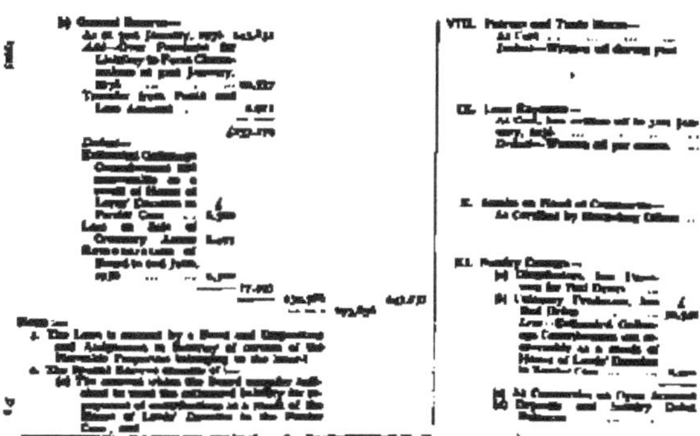

Balance Sheet as at [illegible] January, [illegible]—continued.

Liabilities.

(c) The [illegible] monthly [illegible] which [illegible] from [illegible] 1st August, [illegible] to [illegible] January, [illegible] the [illegible] Compensation [illegible] Amendments [illegible] the [illegible]

3. The [illegible] Balance [illegible] on Capital [illegible] January, [illegible]

T. G. [illegible], Chairman.
F. A. [illegible], Vice-Chairman.
ANDREW MARTIN, C.A.,
Auditors.

Assets.

XII. [illegible] and Milk [illegible] Board (England and Wales)—

(a) [illegible] under Milk Acts, [illegible]

(b) Milk Marketing Board (England and Wales) Compensation [illegible] ... ...

XIII. Cash—

(a) In Bank ... ...

(b) [illegible] ... ...

(c) On Hand—Head Office ... ...

(d) On Hand—[illegible] and [illegible] Offices ... ...

PIGS MARKETING BOARD.

INCOME AND EXPENDITURE ACCOUNT FOR THE YEAR ENDED 31ST DECEMBER, 1937.

EXPENDITURE.	£ s. d.	£ s. d.	INCOME.	£ s. d.
Office Expenses, including Salaries, Wages, Rent, Insurance, Printing, Stationery, Postages, Telephones, Telegrams, Interest on Loans, etc. ...		[illegible]	Delivery and Grading Fees ...	[illegible]
			Bank Interest ...	[illegible]
			[illegible] ...	[illegible]
			Penalties, and Damages for Breaches under Contracts	[illegible]
			Sundry Receipts ...	[illegible]
Recording Expenses—				[illegible]
Graders' wages and Expenses	[illegible]		Deficit Carried Down ...	[illegible]
Sundry Expenses ...	[illegible]			
		[illegible]		
Board's Travelling and Subsistence Allowances ...		[illegible]		
Legal Expenses and Professional Charges ...		[illegible]		
Bad Debts ...		[illegible]		
		[illegible]		
Depreciation		[illegible]		
		[illegible]		[illegible]

FUND ACCOUNT FOR THE YEAR ENDED 31ST DECEMBER, 1937.

	£ s. d.		£ s. d.
Deficit as above brought down ...	[illegible]	Balance as at 31st December, 1936 ...	[illegible]
Balance carried to Balance Sheet ...	[illegible]	Less Board's Fees for year ended 31st March, 1937	[illegible]

Balance Sheet as at 31st December, 1937.

Liabilities	£	s.	d.	Assets	£	s.	d.	£	s.	d.
Sundry Creditors	[illegible]	[illegible]	[illegible]	Cash at Bank and in Hand	[illegible]	13	10			
Reserve for Claims on Contracts—				Investments—						
Less Charges thereon to date	14,3[illegible]	[illegible]	[illegible]	3½ per cent. War Stock at par ...	[illegible]	13	[illegible]	[illegible]	[illegible]	[illegible]
Fund Account—				Market Value—31st December, 1937 £[illegible]						
Balance as above	[illegible]	[illegible]	[illegible]							
				Sundry Debtors—						
				Less Reserve for Bad and Doubtful Debts ...				[illegible]	[illegible]	[illegible]
				Furniture, Stationery and Fittings—						
				At cost, less sales and depreciation	[illegible]	[illegible]	[illegible]			
				Weighing Machinery—						
				At cost, less sales	[illegible]	[illegible]	[illegible]			
								[illegible]	[illegible]	[illegible]
	£[illegible]	9	5					£[illegible]	9	5

Notes :—

(1) There is a contingent liability in respect of indemnification of Members of the Board.

(2) There are sums unascertained due to and by the Board in respect of :—

(a) Claims for non-delivery of Pigs under Contract ;

(b) Deliveries of Pigs made prior to 31st December, 1937, but not notified to the Board before closing the accounts.

R. R. KER, *Accountant.*

JOHN A. POLL, *Chairman.*
EDWARD T. MORRIS, *Vice-Chairman.*
J. HENRY, *Secretary.*

Report of the Auditors pursuant to Paragraph [illegible] of the Pigs Marketing Scheme, 1933.

We have to report that we have audited the foregoing Income and Expenditure Account and Balance Sheet of the Pigs Marketing Board, made up to 31st December, 1937, and have obtained all the information and explanations we have required. Subject to the above notes, we are of the opinion that such Balance Sheet is properly drawn up so as to exhibit a true and correct view of the state of the Board's affairs according to the best of our information and the explanations given to us and as shown by the Books of the Board.

[illegible], [illegible] & Co.,
Chartered Accountants,
Auditors.

[illegible] House,
[illegible], London, E.C.[illegible]

Image digitised by the University of Southampton Library Digitisation Unit

1936 Bonus Scheme.

Final Statement of 1936 Bonus Fund Account as at 31st December, 1937.

	£ s. d.		£ s. d.	£ s. d.
To amounts Due by Registered Curers to The Pigs Marketing Board, in respect of deliveries of 1936 contracted Pigs made on or before 31st December, 1936, and utilised in the Fund up to and including 31st December, 1937, less amounts written off as irrecoverable	117,369 [illegible] 9	By Bonus Distributions made to Registered Pig Producers—		
" Interest on Bank Deposit Account up to 31st December, 1937	776 3 0	Class A Bonus at the rate of [illegible]d. per score, on [illegible] score 10 lbs.	[illegible]	
		Class B Bonus at the rate of [illegible]d. per score, on [illegible] score 17 lbs.	[illegible]	
			[illegible]	
		Special Bonus at the rate of [illegible]d. per score, on [illegible] score 10 lbs.	[illegible]	[illegible]
		" Administration Expenses of the Scheme, being amounts due to the Pigs Marketing Board—		
		Interest earned on Administered Fund, per contra, in accordance with Conditions of the Scheme ...	776 3 0	
		Further contribution as agreed by the Pigs and Bacon Marketing Boards pursuant to Condition "B" of the Scheme	1,[illegible]	

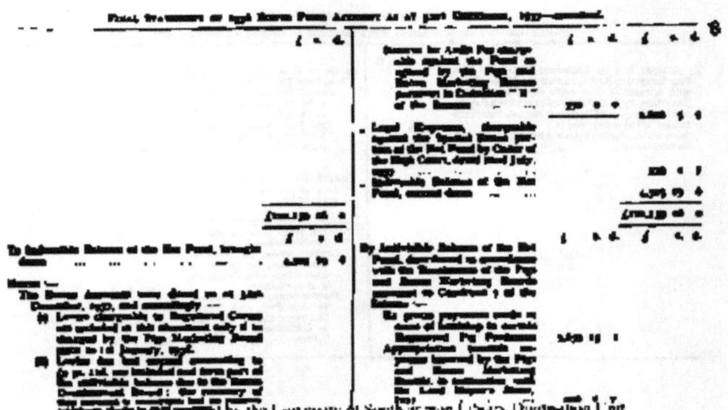

Image digitised by the University of Southampton Library Digitisation Unit

		Balance due to the [illegible] Development [illegible] for the special purpose of [illegible] up [illegible]	[illegible] / [illegible]
		Signed on behalf of the [illegible] Fund [illegible] A. [illegible], [illegible] Fund, A. E. MARSH.	
[illegible]			[illegible]

We have audited the [illegible] Statement of Accounts made up to [illegible] [illegible] [illegible]

[illegible] House,

[illegible], London, E.C.

3rd January, [illegible].

BARTON, MAYHEW & CO.,

Chartered Accountants,

Auditors.

BACON MARKETING BOARD.

INCOME AND EXPENDITURE ACCOUNT FOR THE YEAR ENDED 31ST DECEMBER, 1937,

with comparative figures for the preceding year.

1936 £	Expenditure.	£	s.	d.
[illegible]	Salaries	[illegible]	[illegible]	[illegible]
[illegible]	Expenses of Officials, Inspectors and Members of the Board ...	[illegible]	[illegible]	[illegible]
[illegible]	Printing and Stationery	[illegible]	[illegible]	[illegible]
[illegible]	Rent and Lighting	[illegible]	[illegible]	[illegible]
[illegible]	Postages, Telegrams and Telephones ...	[illegible]	[illegible]	[illegible]
[illegible]	Professional Charges	[illegible]	[illegible]	[illegible]
[illegible]	Accountancy Fees and Expenses ...	[illegible]	[illegible]	[illegible]
[illegible]	Office and General Expenses	[illegible]	[illegible]	[illegible]
[illegible]	Research Office Expenses	[illegible]	[illegible]	[illegible]
[illegible]	Insurance and Bank Charges	[illegible]	[illegible]	[illegible]
[illegible]	Advertising and Exhibition Expenses ...	[illegible]	[illegible]	[illegible]
[illegible]	Remuneration of Members of the Board	[illegible]	[illegible]	[illegible]
[illegible]	Amount written off Furniture, Fittings and Office Equipment ...	[illegible]	[illegible]	[illegible]
[illegible]	Contribution to Bacon Development Board	[illegible]	[illegible]	[illegible]
[illegible]	Income Tax on Interest	[illegible]	[illegible]	[illegible]
[illegible]	Research and Special Expenses ...	[illegible]	[illegible]	[illegible]
[illegible]		[illegible]	[illegible]	[illegible]
[illegible]	Balance, being excess of Income over Expenditure carried to Appropriation Account	[illegible]	[illegible]	[illegible]

1936 £	Income.	£	s.	d.
[illegible]	Bacon Levy Payable by Registered Producers	[illegible]	[illegible]	[illegible]
[illegible]	Fines and Penalties	[illegible]	[illegible]	[illegible]
[illegible]	Sundry Receipts ...	[illegible]	[illegible]	[illegible]
—	Interest on Investments	[illegible]	[illegible]	[illegible]
[illegible]	Interest on Bank Deposits	[illegible]	[illegible]	[illegible]

INCOME AND EXPENDITURE APPROPRIATION ACCOUNT.

£		£ s. d.	£		£ s. d.	£ s. d.
—	Depreciation of Equipment	[illegible]	[illegible]	Balance as at 31st December, 1936		[illegible]
[illegible]	Transfer to General Reserve	[illegible]		Reserve at 31st December, 1936, for Subscriptions maturing in Income under Agreements	[illegible]	
[illegible]	Balance carried to Balance Sheet ...	[illegible]	[illegible]	Less Reserve required at 31st December, 1937 ...	[illegible]	[illegible]
			[illegible]	Excess of Income over Expenditure for year to date		[illegible]
£[illegible]		£[illegible]	£[illegible]			£[illegible]

BALANCE SHEET AS AT 31ST DECEMBER, 1937,

with comparative figures as at 31st December, 1936.

1936. £	Liabilities.	£ s. d.	£ s. d.	1936. £	Assets.	£ s. d.
[illegible]	Sundry Creditors and Accrued Charges ...		[illegible]		Furniture, Fittings and Other Equipment at Cost, less Depreciation—	
	Special Reserves—				As at 31st December, 1936 ...	[illegible]
[illegible]	Contribution to ... Development Board ..	[illegible]			Additions during 1937	[illegible]
	Provision for Liabilities ...					[illegible]
[illegible]	... Agreements ...	[illegible]	[illegible]		Less Amount written off for year to date	[illegible]
[illegible]	General Reserve		[illegible]	[illegible]	... at cost, less Depreciation	
[illegible]	Income and Expenditure Appropriation Account...		[illegible]	[illegible]	Stock of Stationery .	
					Sundry Debtors—	
				[illegible]	On ... Levy Account . .	[illegible]
				[illegible]	Miscellaneous Accounts	[illegible]

			Cash at Bank and in Hand—					
			[illegible]	On Current Account	[illegible]			
			[illegible]	On Deposit Account	[illegible]			
			[illegible]	On Hand	[illegible]			
						[illegible]		
£[illegible]		£[illegible]	£[illegible]			£[illegible]		

[illegible] }
[illegible] } *Members of the Board.*

J. W. H. TAYLOR, C.A.
[illegible] Secretary and Accountant.

REPORT OF THE AUDITORS PURSUANT TO PARAGRAPH 33 OF THE RATINGS AR[illegible] SCHEME, 19[illegible].

We have audited the foregoing Income and Expenditure Account and Balance Sheet of the [illegible] Hon[illegible] Board, made up to 31st December, 1927, and have obtained all the information and explanations we have required. In our opinion the Balance Sheet is properly drawn up so as to exhibit a true and correct view of the state of the Board's affairs as at 31st December, 1927, according to the best of our information and the explanations given to us and as shown by the books of the Board.

London, E.C.

[illegible] *January, 1928.*

BANK, JUDD, [illegible] & CO.,
Chartered Accountants.

MILK MARKETING BOARD.

Accounts for the Year ended 31st March, 193[illegible].

(I) General Pool Account.

	£ s. d.		£ s. d.
To Amount payable to Producers, subject to Transport Deductions per contra ...	[illegible]	By Pool Balance, brought forward as at 1st April, 193[illegible] ...	[illegible]
" Pool charges allocated to Regions in proportion to Wholesale Contract Sales—		" Chargeable to Purchasers for Milk Sales (less Rebates) subject to Transport Deductions per contra ...	[illegible]
[illegible] ... [illegible]		" Realisation of Milk at Board's Creameries ... [illegible]	
Milk-in-Schools Scheme [illegible]		Less Processing and Marketing Expenses ... [illegible]	
[illegible] Reserve ... [illegible]	[illegible]		[illegible]
" General Expenses Levy ...	[illegible]	" Licensed Retailers' Contributions (for Reserve) ...	[illegible]
" Publicity Levy (National Milk Publicity Council) charged to Producers, Producer-Retailers and Purchasers, and allocations from Licensed Retailers' Contributions ...	[illegible]	" Advances receivable under the Milk Acts, 1934 and 1936, credited to the Regional Pools on the basis of the corresponding charge ...	[illegible]
" Amount payable under Special Areas Scheme	[illegible]	" Amount receivable from Commissioner for Special Areas ...	[illegible]
" Appropriation to Contract Contingency Reserve ...	—	" Estimated amount receivable from Aberdeen and District Milk Marketing Board ...	[illegible]
" Transport Deductions chargeable by Purchasers ...	[illegible]	" Transport Deductions, including Special Transport Deductions, chargeable to Producers' Accounts ...	[illegible]
" Pool Balance unallocated ...	[illegible]		

(b) *Inter-Regional Compensation Fund Account.*

	£	s.	d.		£	s.	d.
To Apportionment of Levy to Regional Pool Accounts	[illegible]	[illegible]	[illegible]	By Levy charged to Regional Pool Accounts ...	[illegible]	[illegible]	[illegible]
	£[illegible]	[illegible]	[illegible]		£[illegible]	[illegible]	[illegible]

(c) *Accredited Producers Account.*

	£	s.	d.		£	s.	d.
To Bonus payable to Accredited Producers ...	[illegible]	[illegible]	[illegible]	By Balance brought forward as at 1st April, [illegible]	[illegible]	[illegible]	[illegible]
" Balance, carried forward	[illegible]	[illegible]	[illegible]	" Levy charged to Producers	[illegible]	[illegible]	[illegible]
	£[illegible]	[illegible]	[illegible]		£[illegible]	[illegible]	[illegible]

(d) *Publicity and Research Fund Account.*

	£	s.	d.		£	s.	d.
To Press and Poster Campaign	[illegible]	[illegible]	[illegible]	By Balance brought forward as at 1st April, [illegible]	[illegible]	[illegible]	[illegible]
" Grants to Research Institutions	[illegible]	[illegible]	[illegible]	" Publicity Levy for year: Amounts charged to General Pool Accounts ...	[illegible]	[illegible]	[illegible]
" Payments to National Milk Publicity Council	[illegible]	[illegible]	[illegible]	" Contributions receivable under the Milk Acts, [illegible]	[illegible]	[illegible]	[illegible]
" Balance, carried forward	[illegible]	[illegible]	[illegible]				
	£[illegible]	[illegible]	[illegible]		£[illegible]	[illegible]	[illegible]

(c) Income and Expenditure (General Expenses) Account.

Expenditure.	£	s.	d.	£	s.	d.
To Head Office Expenses—						
Office Rent and Maintenance	[illegible]	2	9			
Insurance	[illegible]	6	7			
Lighting and Power ...	[illegible]	4	11			
Equipment Hire and Maintenance	[illegible]	8	4			
Printing and Stationery	[illegible]	7	11			
Postage and Telephones ...	17,769	6	7			
Salaries and Wages ...	[illegible]	[illegible]	4			
Travelling Expenses ...	[illegible]	[illegible]	1			
[illegible] Stamps and Cheque Books	[illegible]	1	0			
Certification of Claims under [illegible] Acts, [illegible] and 1936 ..	676	[illegible]	0			
Office Expenses	[illegible]	9	10			
				[illegible]	13	6
" Regional Commission Expenses and [illegible]				[illegible]	8	0
" Regional Offices—						
Salaries and Wages	[illegible]	18	7			
Office Expenses	[illegible]	9	9			
Travelling	[illegible]	[illegible]	6			

Income.	£	s.	d.
By General Expenses Levy—Amounts Charged to (Owners) Pool Account	[illegible]	9	9
" Common Registration Fees, Sales of Schedules, and Sundry Revenue ...	[illegible]	7	3
" Expenses of Committees of Investigation Recovered ...	[illegible]	[illegible]	[illegible]
" Penalties Received	[illegible]	[illegible]	6
" Reserve for Cost of Collection and Distribution of Proceeds of [illegible] sold to the month of March, 1936, brought forward	[illegible]	0	0

Publicity and Research Expenses—		
General Publicity and Survey Work ...	[illegible]	
Costing of [illegible] Purchases ...	[illegible]	
[illegible] Campaign ...	[illegible]	
		[illegible]
Expenses of Polls, Hearings, Enquiry, Enquiries and other Legal Expenses—		
Agricultural [illegible] Commission, [illegible]	—	
Poll of [illegible] Producers on [illegible] of Scheme ...	—	
Committee of Investigation for [illegible] ...	—	
Annual General Meeting ...	[illegible]	
Amendments — Expenses of Poll and Enquiry ...	[illegible]	
Other Legal Expenses ...	[illegible]	
		[illegible]
Staff Pension Scheme ...		[illegible]
Reserve for Cost of Collecting and Distribution of the Proceeds of [illegible] to the month of March, [illegible] ...		[illegible]
		[illegible]
Balance carried to Balance Sheet ...		[illegible]
		[illegible]

[illegible]

	£ s. d.	£ s. d.
To Sundry Creditors—		
[illegible]	[illegible]	
[illegible]	[illegible]	
[illegible]	[illegible]	
[illegible]	[illegible]	
[illegible]	[illegible]	[illegible]
[illegible]		[illegible]
[illegible]		[illegible]
[illegible]		[illegible]
[illegible]	[illegible]	

	£ s. d.	£ s. d.	£ s. d.
By Fixed Assets—			
[illegible]			
Leasehold Land and Buildings ...	[illegible]		
Plant and Equipment ...	[illegible]		
Vans and Lorries	[illegible]		
		[illegible]	
[illegible] ...		[illegible]	
Office Furnishings and Machinery—			
Head Office	[illegible]		
Regional Offices	[illegible]		
		[illegible]	
			[illegible]
[illegible]			[illegible]
[illegible]			[illegible]
[illegible]			[illegible]

Notes:—

1. [illegible]
2. [illegible]

Balance of Revenue and Expenditure Account for the year ended 31st March, [illegible] per Account No. [illegible] above [illegible]

Less Transfer to Capital Reserve Account [illegible]

[illegible]

[illegible]

(b) Contracts for the purchase of and sale of such [illegible] for the year to [illegible].

(c) Liability under [illegible] to pay [illegible] money to the [illegible] agreement.

POTATO MARKETING BOARD.

Income and Expenditure Account for the Year ended 31st August, 1937.

Dr.	£ s. d.	£ s. d.
To General Administration Charges—		
Head Office—		
Salaries and Wages ...	[illegible]	
Rent, Lighting and Insurance	[illegible]	
Repairs and Alterations to Premises	497 [illegible]	
Telephone	[illegible]	
Postage	[illegible]	
Stationery and Office Sundries	[illegible]	
Travelling Expenses ...	[illegible]	
Hire of Machinery ...	[illegible]	
General Expenses ...	[illegible]	
	[illegible]	
Less Contributions received from Authorised Merchants	[illegible]	
		[illegible]
Regional Offices—		
Salaries and Wages ...	[illegible]	
Car and Travelling Expenses	[illegible]	
Rent, Rates, Lighting and Insurance	[illegible]	
Repairs and Alterations to Premises	[illegible]	

Cr.	£ s. d.	£ s. d.
By Annual Acreage Levy collectable—		
Levy made on September, 1936	[illegible]	
Less in respect of preceding years	[illegible]	
		[illegible]
" Excess Acreage Levy collectable—		
Levy made on September, 1936	[illegible]	
Less in respect of preceding years	[illegible]	
		[illegible]
" Penalties Recovered, less Costs		[illegible]
" Interest Receivable on Investments		[illegible]
" Bank Interest Receivable ...		[illegible]
" Sundry Receipts		[illegible]

	£	s.	d.	£	s.	d.
Telephone	[illegible]	[illegible]	[illegible]			
Postage and Stationery .	[illegible]	[illegible]	[illegible]			
General Expenses	[illegible]	[illegible]	[illegible]			
				[illegible]	[illegible]	[illegible]
Publicity and Research Expenses—						
Publicity	[illegible]	[illegible]	[illegible]			
Research and Experimental Expenses ..	[illegible]	[illegible]	[illegible]			
				[illegible]	[illegible]	[illegible]
Expenses of Elections, Meetings of Producers and Merchants				[illegible]	[illegible]	[illegible]
Remuneration of Members of the Board .				[illegible]	[illegible]	[illegible]
Expenses of Members of the Board . ..				[illegible]	[illegible]	[illegible]
Legal and Professional Fees and Expenses .				[illegible]	[illegible]	[illegible]
Amount written off Furniture, Fittings and Office Machinery				[illegible]	[illegible]	[illegible]
Balance carried down				[illegible]	[illegible]	[illegible]

BALANCE SHEET AS AT 31ST AUGUST, 1937.

LIABILITIES.	£ s. d.	£ s. d.	ASSETS.	£ s. d.	£ s. d.
Sundry Creditors and Accrued Charges		[illegible]	Land and Buildings at Cost		[illegible]
Reserve for Cost of Checking Accounts—			Furniture, Fittings and Office Machinery—		
As at 31st August, 1936	[illegible]		At Cost, less amounts written off—		
Less Expenditure incurred during year	[illegible]		As at 31st August, 1936	[illegible]	
	[illegible]		Additions during year	[illegible]	
Add Appropriation per annexed Account	[illegible]	[illegible]		[illegible]	
General Reserve Account—			Less Amount written off	[illegible]	[illegible]
As at 31st August, 1936	[illegible]		Debtors, less Reserve, Deposits and Prepayments		[illegible]
Add Appropriation per annexed Account	[illegible]	[illegible]	Investments in British Government Securities, At Cost		[illegible]
Income and Expenditure Account— Balance per annexed Account		[illegible]	NOTE.—The market value of these Investments at 31st August, 1937, was [illegible]		
			Cash at Bankers and in Hand		[illegible]

REPORT OF THE AUDITORS PURSUANT TO SECTION [illegible] OF THE POTATO MARKETING SCHEME, 1933.

We report that we have audited the foregoing Income and Expenditure Account and Balance Sheet of the Potato Marketing Board made up to 31st August, 1937, and have obtained all the information and explanations we have required. In our opinion such Balance Sheet is properly drawn up so as to give a true and correct view of the state of the Board's affairs, according to the best of our information and the explanations given to us and as shown by the books of the Board.

Aldermary House,
[illegible], London, E.C.4
[illegible] September, 1937.

BARTON, MAYHEW & CO.,
Chartered Accountants,
Auditors.

THE ABERDEEN AND DISTRICT MILK MARKETING BOARD.

Profit and Loss Account for the Year ended 31st December, 1937.

	£	s.	d.
To Salaries and Wages	[illegible]	[illegible]	[illegible]
" General Administrative Expenses (including Remuneration to the Members of the Board)	[illegible]	[illegible]	[illegible]
" Rent, Rates, Insurance, etc.	[illegible]	[illegible]	[illegible]
" Repairs and Renewals	[illegible]	[illegible]	[illegible]
" Railway Carriage and Haulage	[illegible]	[illegible]	[illegible]
" Heating, Power, Lighting and Water ...	[illegible]	17	[illegible]
" Advertising	[illegible]	[illegible]	[illegible]
" Interest on Loans	[illegible]	[illegible]	[illegible]
" Donation to Royal Infirmary	[illegible]	[illegible]	[illegible]
" Bad Debts written off, less recovered ...	[illegible]	7	7
" Transfers to Reserves — Capital Expenditure	[illegible]	[illegible]	10
	[illegible]	[illegible]	[illegible]

	£	s.	d.	£	s.	d.
By Ordinary Registered Producers' Contributions	[illegible]	[illegible]	[illegible]			
" Producer-Retailers and Graded Milk Producers' Contributions	[illegible]	[illegible]	[illegible]			
	[illegible]	5	5			
Less Losses on handling milk surplus to Area's liquid requirements, including difference between Standard Price of milk sold for manufacturing purposes [illegible]						
Contributions to English Milk Marketing Board ... [illegible]	[illegible]	[illegible]	[illegible]	[illegible]	[illegible]	[illegible]
" Claims under the Milk Act, 1934 — Advertising during the year	[illegible]	[illegible]	[illegible]			
Milk manufactured and sold by depots during the year	[illegible]	[illegible]	[illegible]	[illegible]	[illegible]	[illegible]
" Fines imposed on Registered Producers ...				[illegible]	[illegible]	[illegible]
" Sale of Cans				[illegible]	[illegible]	[illegible]
" Ledger				[illegible]	[illegible]	[illegible]
" Rents and Rates recovered				[illegible]	[illegible]	[illegible]
" Interest on Investments				[illegible]	[illegible]	[illegible]
" Loss for year				[illegible]	[illegible]	[illegible]
				[illegible]	[illegible]	[illegible]

Printed image digitised by the University of Southampton Library Digitisation Unit

Balance Sheet as at 31st December, 1937.

Liabilities.	£ s. d.	£ s. d.	Assets.	£ s. d.	£ s. d.
Bank ...		[illegible]	Plant and Heritable Property—		
Loans—			Value said at 31/12/36 ...	[illegible]	
Aberdeen & District Milk Agency, Limited ...	[illegible]		Added during the year at cost (Including the cost of [illegible] and Alterations [illegible]) ...	[illegible]	
Bond over Heritable Property ...	[illegible]				
		[illegible]		[illegible]	
Sundry Creditors ...		[illegible]	Less written off—		
Reserve for Bad Debts ...		[illegible]	To 31/12/36 ... [illegible]		
Profit and Loss Account—			At 31/12/37 ... [illegible]		
Amount at Credit 31/12/36 ...	[illegible]			[illegible]	
Less Loss for year ...	[illegible]		Trade Investments at cost ...		[illegible]
		[illegible]	Sundry Debtors ...		[illegible]
			Cash in Hand ...		[illegible]
		[illegible]			[illegible]

Aberdeen, 14th March, 1938.—[illegible]

J. PATRICK JEFFREY, C.A., Auditor.

THE NORTH OF SCOTLAND MILK MARKETING BOARD.

Profit and Loss Account for Year ended 31st May, 1937.

		£	s.	d.
To Stock at 1st June, 1936		[illegible]	[illegible]	[illegible]
" Amounts Paid and Payable to Ordinary Producers		[illegible]	[illegible]	[illegible]
" Haulage and General Charges		[illegible]	[illegible]	[illegible]
" Bottling, Railage and 'Bus Carriage		[illegible]	[illegible]	[illegible]
" Office, &c., Expenses—	£ s. d.			
Legal Expenses	[illegible]			
Salaries and National Insurance	[illegible]			
Stationery, Advertising and Printing	[illegible]			
Postages, Telephones and Telegrams	[illegible]			
Bank Charges and Stamp Duty on Cheques	[illegible]			
Expenses of Board and other Meetings	[illegible]			
Salary of Secretary and Law Agent and Allowance for Clerical Assistance and Office Rent, Auditor's Fee, etc.	[illegible]			
Interest on Bank Overdraft	[illegible]			
Bad Debts written off	[illegible]			
Directors	[illegible]			
Miscellaneous Expenses, including Fee for Recovery of Milk Vessels in London; Fire and other Insurance, etc.	[illegible]			
Chairman's Salary and Expenses for Board's Representatives	[illegible]	[illegible]	[illegible]	[illegible]

		£	s.	d.
By Sales to Distributors (including Accommodation Orders and Milk for Manufacture)		[illegible]	[illegible]	[illegible]
" Stocks on hand—Milk		[illegible]	[illegible]	[illegible]
" Government Subsidy on School Milk and Milk for Manufacture		[illegible]	[illegible]	[illegible]
" Interest on Deposit with Building Society		[illegible]	[illegible]	[illegible]
" Contributions from Producers and Producer Retailers		[illegible]	[illegible]	[illegible]
" Net Revenue from Property in Diamond Street		[illegible]	[illegible]	[illegible]
" Interest on Capital supplied to Distribution Centres—				
[illegible]	[illegible]			
[illegible]	[illegible]			
		[illegible]	[illegible]	[illegible]

		£ s. d.	£ s. d.	
" Inverness Depot Expenses—				
	[illegible], including [illegible]	[illegible]		
	Fire, Light and Power	[illegible]		
	Cleaning	[illegible]		
	[illegible]	[illegible]		
	Miscellaneous	[illegible]		
			[illegible]	
" Depreciation written off—				
	Preliminary Expenses written off	[illegible]		
	[illegible] Expenses and [illegible] written off	[illegible]		
	Depreciation on Equipment	[illegible]		
	[illegible] written off Cost of [illegible]	[illegible]		
	Expenses incurred in connection with [illegible] of New Depot written off	[illegible]		
			[illegible]	
" Profit for year			[illegible]	
			£[illegible]	£[illegible]

PROFIT AND LOSS APPROPRIATION ACCOUNT.

	£ s. d.		£ s. d.
To Cost of [illegible]	[illegible]	By Balance at Credit at [illegible]	[illegible]
" Balance to be carried forward	[illegible]	" Profit for year [illegible]	[illegible]
		" Transfer from [illegible] Reserve Fund	[illegible]
	£[illegible]		£[illegible]

Balance Sheet as at 31st May, 1917.

Liabilities				£	s.	d.
Sundry Creditors and Credit Balances				[illegible]	[illegible]	[illegible]
Share Capital				[illegible]	[illegible]	[illegible]
General Reserve Fund—						
As per last Balance Sheet	£[illegible]	0	0			
Less Transferred to Appropriation Account	[illegible]	0	0			
				[illegible]	0	0
Bad Debts Reserve				[illegible]	0	0
Profit and Loss Account—						
Balance at Credit				[illegible]	[illegible]	[illegible]

Assets	£	s.	d.	£	s.	d.
Office Furniture—						
As per last Balance Sheet	[illegible]	[illegible]	[illegible]			
Additions during year	[illegible]	[illegible]	[illegible]			
				[illegible]	[illegible]	[illegible]
Equipment—						
As per last Balance Sheet	[illegible]	[illegible]	[illegible]			
Additions during year	[illegible]	[illegible]	[illegible]			
	[illegible]	[illegible]	[illegible]			
Less Dep. written off to date	[illegible]	[illegible]	[illegible]			
				[illegible]	[illegible]	[illegible]
Stores on hand—[illegible]				[illegible]	[illegible]	[illegible]
Sundry Debtors and Debit Balances				[illegible]	[illegible]	[illegible]
[illegible] Dairy—						
Compensation Paid to Dairymen, etc.	[illegible]	[illegible]	[illegible]			
Plant of Dairy Utensils, including Lorries, etc., as written down	[illegible]	[illegible]	[illegible]			
Improvements to Premises	[illegible]	[illegible]	[illegible]			
Furniture and Fittings as written down	[illegible]	[illegible]	[illegible]			
Stable Property	[illegible]	[illegible]	[illegible]			
Horses and Harness	[illegible]	[illegible]	[illegible]			
Butter, Cream, Dairy, etc.	[illegible]	[illegible]	[illegible]			
Sundry Debtors and Prepaid Charges	[illegible]	[illegible]	[illegible]			
Supplies on hand	[illegible]	[illegible]	[illegible]			
Cash at bank	[illegible]	[illegible]	[illegible]			
				[illegible]	[illegible]	[illegible]

[illegible]

JAS. C. STEWART, [illegible]

ALEXANDER MUNRO, [illegible]
D. F. MACKENZIE, [illegible]

[illegible]

DONALD [illegible], C.A., [illegible]

Printed image digitised by the University of Southampton Library Digitisation Unit

www.ingramcontent.com/pod-product-compliance
Lightning Source LLC
Chambersburg PA
CBHW021451210326
41599CB00012B/1024

* 9 7 8 3 7 4 2 8 0 2 4 4 6 *